VINTAGE
THE JANNAYAK KARPOORI THAKUR

Santosh Singh has been a Patna-based senior assistant editor with *Indian Express* since June 2008, covering the entire state of Bihar with a focus on politics, society, governance, and investigative and explanatory stories. He has over twenty-five years of experience in print journalism in Bihar, Delhi, Madhya Pradesh and Karnataka. His past works include *Ruled or Misruled: Story and Destiny of Bihar* (Bloomsbury, 2015), *JP to BJP: Bihar after Lalu and Nitish* (Vitasta Sage Select, 2021) and *Kitna Raaj Kitna Kaaj* (Vani Prakashan, 2023).

Aditya Anmol studied at the University of Chicago. He completed his master's in public policy with honours in June 2023, with specializations in finance and policy. He has a bachelor of arts in quantitative economics with honours from New York University.

ADVANCE PRAISE FOR THE BOOK

'Karpoori Thakur was a legend in my childhood, the fulcrum of social transformation in Bihar and beyond, and this detailed book gives substance and depth to what were only memories'—Amitava Kumar, author and journalist

'An essential work on a most essential leader; [this book] can't be bypassed by those who seek to know Bihar'—Sankarshan Thakur, editor, *The Telegraph*

'Santosh Singh, with Aditya Anmol, blends his formidable journalistic acumen with academic rigour to explain a founding father of affirmative action in post-Independence India. In its brilliant and incisive study of Karpoori Thakur, this book is a must-read for all who want to understand the post-Mandal politics around caste and reservation—an enduring story of change, empowerment and competition. With this book, Singh establishes himself as one of the foremost chroniclers of politics and society in contemporary Bihar'—Raj Kamal Jha, chief editor, *Indian Express*

'This book could not have been more timely—with renewed interest in socialist icon Karpoori Thakur, a "Ratna" of "Bharat". A fascinating story of what makes a leader, the book gives new insights into the phenomenal rise of the OBCs in Indian politics'—Neerja Chowdhury, contributing editor, *Indian Express* and author of *How Prime Ministers Decide*

the JANNAYAK

KARPOORI THAKUR
Voice of the Voiceless

SANTOSH SINGH
ADITYA ANMOL

VINTAGE
An imprint of Penguin Random House

VINTAGE

Vintage is an imprint of the Penguin Random House group of companies
whose addresses can be found at global.penguinrandomhouse.com

Published by Penguin Random House India Pvt. Ltd
4th Floor, Capital Tower 1, MG Road,
Gurugram 122 002, Haryana, India

First published in Vintage by Penguin Random House India 2024

10 9 8 7 6 5 4 3 2 1

ISBN 9780143467335

Typeset in Adobe Garamond Pro by Manipal Technologies Limited, Manipal

www.penguin.co.in

To all those who believe in people's power

Ek aadmi
Roti belta hai
Ek aadmi roti khata hai
Ek teesra aadmi bhi hai
Jo na roti belta hai, na roti khata hai
Wah sirf roti se khelta hai
Main poochta hoon—
Yah teesra aadmi koun hai?
Mere desh ki sansad moun hai

(A man rolls out dough for bread,
another man eats the bread,
and there is a third man
who neither rolls out dough nor eats bread.
He only plays with bread.
I ask—
'Who is this third man?'
My country's Parliament is silent.)

—Dhoomil, 'Roti aur Sansad'

Contents

List of Abbreviations

AAP	Aam Aadmi Party
ABVP	Akhil Bharatiya Vidyarthi Parishad
BJP	Bharatiya Janata Party
BJS	Bharatiya Jana Sangh
BLD	Bharatiya Lok Dal
CSP	Congress Socialist Party
DMK	Dravida Munnetra Kazhagam
DMKP	Dalit Mazdoor Kisan Party
EBC	Extremely Backward Classes
ECI	Election Commission of India
HAM (S)	Hindustani Awam Morcha (Secular)
INC	Indian National Congress
INDIA	Indian National Developmental Inclusive Alliance
INLD	Indian National Lok Dal
JD (S)	Janata Dal (Secular)
JD (U)	Janata Dal (United)
JMM	Jharkhand Mukti Morcha

MBC	Most Backward Classes
MGB	Mahagathbandhan
MISA	Maintenance of Internal Security Act
MLA	Member of the Legislative Assembly
MLC	Member of the Legislative Council
NC	National Conference
NCP	Nationalist Congress Party
NDA	National Democratic Alliance
OBC	Other Backward Classes
PDP	People's Democratic Party
PSP	Praja Socialist Party
RJD	Rashtriya Janata Dal
RLD	Rashtriya Lok Dal
RLJD	Rashtriya Lok Janata Dal
RSS	Rashtriya Swayamsevak Sangh
SC	Scheduled Castes
SP	Samajwadi Party; the abbreviation is also used for Socialist Party
SSP	Sanyukt Socialist Party
SVD	Sanyukt Vidhayak Dal
TMC	Trinamool Congress
UPA	United Progressive Alliance

Timeline

1924   Karpoori Thakur is born on 24 January at Pitaunjhia (now Karpoori Gram), Samastipur (then Darbhanga), Bihar.

1938   Formed the Navyuvak Sangh in Pitaunjhia, took part in the farmers' movement led by Swami Sahajanand Saraswati.

1940   Passed Class 10 board examination.

1942   Passed Class 12 board examination, got enrolled in CM College, Darbhanga (Patna University).

1942   Took part in the Quit India Movement, dropped out of college, participated in the Bhoodan Movement.

1943   Arrested for taking part in the freedom movement.

1945   Released from Bhagalpur Central Jail.

1947   Appointed principal secretary of the Bihar Pradeshik Kisan Sabha.

1948   Elected provincial minister of the Socialist Party, formed under the leadership of Acharya Narendra Dev and Jayaprakash Narayan.

1949   Became member of the Central Committee of Hind Kisan
        Panchayat.

1952   Won his first election in Independent India as a Socialist
        Party nominee from Tajpur (Samastipur), defeating
        Congress candidate Ramsukumari Devi, travelled across
        West Asian countries and Europe.

1953   Joined Praja Socialist Party after Socialist Party split, came
        under the influence of Jayaprakash Narayan.

1957   Won his second Assembly election from Tajpur as PSP
        candidate, defeating Congress's Nandlal Sharma.

1962   Won from Tajpur Assembly seat as PSP nominee,
        defeating Ramswaroop Prasad Rai of Congress.

1964   Dr Rammanohar Lohia started merger bid of SP and PSP.

1966   Joined Sanyukt Socialist Party (SSP) after the formal
        merger of PSP and SP.

1967   Won again from Tajpur as SSP candidate, defeating
        Bhubaneshwar Singh of Congress.

1967   On 5 March, became deputy chief minister and education
        minister in the cabinet of Mahamaya Prasad Sinha, who
        led the first anti-Congress government.

1968   On 28 January, resigned as deputy chief minister.

1969   Won fifth consecutive time from Tajpur in mid-term
        elections as SSP candidate, defeating Rajendra Mahato of
        Congress.

1969   Elected national president of SSP.

1970   On 22 December, sworn in as chief minister (CM).

1971   On 2 June, demitted office of CM.

1972   Won as SSP candidate from Samastipur, defeating
        Independent Kamlesh Rai.

1974   Resigned as MLA to express solidarity with the JP
        Movement.

1975   Remained underground after declaration of Emergency
        on 25 June.

1977   On 30 January, appeared on public stage at Patna's
        Gandhi Maidan, arrested.

1977   Won his first and only Lok Sabha election from Samastipur
        as Janata Party candidate by defeating Yamuna Prasad
        Mandal of Indira Congress.

1977   On 24 June, became chief minister of Bihar for the second
        time.

1977   On 11 October, announced free education up to Class 10.

1977   Elected to Bihar Legislative Assembly for the seventh time
        in December from Phulparas (Madhubani), defeating
        Ram Jaipal Singh Yadav of Congress (I).

1978   On 10 November, made the historic decision to give
        26 per cent reservation for other backward classes,
        extremely backward classes, women and poor among
        general category; pioneered quota within quota.

1979   On 21 April, resigned as CM.

1980   Won from Samastipur Assembly seat in mid-term polls
        as Janata (S) candidate, defeating Congress's Chandra
        Shekhar Verma.

1982   Formed Lok Dal (Karpoori), became its national president.

1984   Contested from Samastipur Lok Sabha seat as DMKP
        nominee, faced his first and only electoral loss to Congress's
        Ramdev Rai.

1985   Won his ninth consecutive Assembly polls from Sonbarsa
        (Sitamarhi) as Lok Dal nominee, defeating Independent
        Anwarul Haque.

1987   On 11 August, removed as leader of the Opposition.

1988   Died on 17 February.

Foreword

This timely book by veteran journalist and astute political analyst Santosh Singh and young researcher Aditya Anmol provides an outstanding biography and breakdown of the importance and contemporary relevance of the socialist leader Karpoori Thakur. Karpoori Thakur in many ways embodied the political vision of the great Indian socialist Dr Rammanohar Lohia. In the same way that V.P. Singh later saw Lalu Yadav as being at the forefront of the 'silent revolution' set in motion by his decision to implement the recommendations of the Mandal commission, Lohia saw Karpoori Thakur as representing his vision of socialism adapted to Indian conditions. Furthermore— as the authors analyse in great depth—the legacy of Karpoori Thakur continues to influence politics in Bihar through chief minister Nitish Kumar, who has adopted many of the political ideas and strategies of the socialist luminary. For these reasons, we all have a great deal to learn from the life and politics of Karpoori Thakur.

The most important and obvious contribution of Karpoori Thakur that continues to influence politics in Bihar is his championing of Extremely Backward Classes (EBCs), listed as Annexure One within Bihar's distinctive system of reservation introduced during his short tenure as chief minister from 1977 to 1979. Dividing the OBCs into two groups and privileging the 'backward amongst the backward' was more than just a solution to the so-called 'creamy layer' problem—although it is arguably the best solution to this problem to have emerged in India. Lohia cautioned against replacing the dominance of the forward castes with a new OBC dominance. His aim was not to alter, or even invert, caste hierarchies, but to completely annihilate them. Lohia saw a politics of caste empowerment as necessary because of the central role of caste in maintaining and reproducing India's ruling class, not as an end in itself—a crucial distinction.

One can appreciate the importance of empowering non-dominant castes from the village experience of Karpoori Thakur's own life, which the authors describe in rich detail. Karpoori Thakur came from the Nai (barber) caste, with a few households in most villages but without enjoying dominance anywhere. While collectively making up around 33 per cent of the population, only a few EBCs could be said to be a dominant caste in select regions (Sahanis in Muzaffarpur being a rare example). This means that EBCs generally cannot exert significant muscle and money power during elections, capture voting booths or strong-arm the bureaucracy or police in the ways that Bhumihars, Rajputs or Yadavs often do. In this sense, empowering EBCs reflects a deepening of democratization beyond the empowerment of the handful of numerically large castes that have dominated post-Independence politics.

From Karpoori Thakur's village experience illuminated in this book we can also see the logic of his 'alliance of extremes' between EBCs and forward castes. The Nai caste and other small service castes were traditionally employed through the *yajmani* system, which provided them a share of the harvest in exchange for providing service to their patrons. Unlike larger OBCs, EBCs often could not afford wholesale opposition to the forward castes. Furthermore, as democratization gradually eroded the feudal order, EBCs lost the benefits they had enjoyed in the older system while now facing oppression from newly dominant OBCs.

During Karpoori Thakur's brief tenure as chief minister, the seeds of EBC empowerment were sown, but they took decades to bear fruit during the tenure of Nitish Kumar. I have argued that Nitish Kumar's political alliance was only possible in the wake of fifteen years of Lalu Yadav and Rabri Devi at the helm. Forward castes only accepted this 'alliance of extremes' as a reaction against years of a militant 'backward-caste' government. EBCs, on the other hand, only broke with Lalu's backward-caste alliance in the wake of a 'Yadav Raj', which increasingly oppressed non-dominant castes. Widespread destabilization—negatively termed 'jungle Raj' (a term that obscures the historical transformations that occurred)—in the name of caste empowerment resulted in a demand for *sushasan* (good governance). This became possible because the alliance of extremes included forward-caste bureaucrats, police and journalists. But the fact that Nitish is from the powerful Kurmi caste, especially in terms of education and representation in the civil service, provided a base that enabled his agenda of good governance. Karpoori Thakur, from the non-dominant Nai caste, did not enjoy such a base and likely would have found it hard to control a hostile, forward-dominated bureaucracy had his tenure lasted longer. In short, this book reveals the ways in which Nitish Kumar's political alliance already existed in embryonic form during Karpoori Thakur's brief tenure, but that a consolidation of this 'alliance of extremes' was only possible after a 'backward' versus 'forward' caste politics had exhausted its transformative potential, resulting in a backlash.

In conclusion, it is important to emphasize that Karpoori Thakur, following Lohia, saw a politics of caste empowerment as only one prong of a comprehensive struggle against the ruling classes. For instance, this book describes in great detail Karpoori Thakur's championing of Hindi and the anti-English movement as a means of decolonialization. Another, even more important, example is land reform. Unlike his successors, Karpoori Thakur succeeded in abolishing land tax on small holdings. In sharp contrast, both Lalu Yadav and Nitish Kumar attempted and failed to implement significant land reforms, specifically related to *bataidari* (sharecropping). Clearly, if Lohia's spirit is to remain potent, there is a need to update his formula to account for contemporary conditions and the central characteristics of the ruling classes today. While backward-caste politics have enjoyed stunning success, land reforms and the labour movement have stalled. This book provides an excellent opportunity to reflect on the legacy of Karpoori Thakur and to consider how his brand of socialism can be revitalized beyond caste.

Jeffrey Witsoe
Author of *Democracy against Development: Lower-Caste
Politics and Political Modernity in Postcolonial India,*
and associate professor of anthropology
at Union College in Schenectady, New York

Why Karpoori Thakur?

Eklavya is still wandering. He is still asking questions. Some of his questions are still unanswered.

It was 14 February 1988. Former Bihar chief minister (CM) Karpoori Thakur was attending a function at the MLA Club of Patna to commemorate the assumed birth anniversary of Mahabharata character and famous archer Eklavya. Thakur had cancelled a programme in Gorakhpur to attend this function. Overwhelmed with the very idea of remembering Eklavya, Karpoori Thakur said:

'Eklavya is a symbol of injustice, atrocity, disparity, neglect, and deprivation of one's rights in our social system. What was meted out to Eklavya is a living example of injustice and atrocity, happening for 5000 years in Indian society. Do people, deprived of power, property, education and dignity, lack talent? Eklavya proves that an emphatic "no" is the answer. There is no question of him having less talent. Rather, he was more talented than others because no teacher had taught Eklavya archery. Dronacharya had refused to coach him on account of [his] being [the] son of

Hiranya Dhanu, telling him, "You are son of Nishad. You have no right to learn archery." Eklavya had challenged Dronacharya by arguing that lessons of archery had been hence restricted to palaces and that it should be extended to those living in huts. So far, this art was limited to princes and now it should go to Bheel, Nishad, Vanchar (wanderers in [the] forest) and others. But you know Dronacharya did not accept what Eklavya said. His challenge went in vain, so did his prayers.

'The Drona Parv of Mahabharata, in its 181st chapter and shlokas 10 to 21, deals with the dialogue between Lord Sri Krishna and Arjuna. Sri Krishna tells Arjuna that it was for Arjuna's favour that Drona killed the teacher in Eklavya by telling Eklavya that he was [a] disciple and Drona was his guru. Eklavya's thumb was taken with deceit and by killing Eklavya's teacherhood. Yet, the highly self-respecting and valorous Eklavya used to practise archery in [the] jungles wearing gloves. He used to look like another Parshuram [in] those times. Lord Krishna said: "Hey son of Kunti, Arjuna! Had Eklavya's thumb not been chopped off, gods, demons, and cobras together would not have been able to defeat him. No human could have dared to stand up to him. His fist was as strong as a rock." This is God telling Arjuna.

'The same Mahabharata shows Vaishampayan saying that Arjuna had approached Dronacharya. Everyone left for the jungle after taking permission from Dronacharya. What happened in the jungle is known to everyone, how Eklavya had shut a dog's mouth with seven arrows. He shot seven arrows but without shedding any drop of blood from the dog's mouth . . . You have heard stories about Eklavya making a statue of Drona and seeking his blessing. But I hold it was a statue of Eklavya himself, one of his wisdom. There was no such thing as the blessing of Drona . . . This tells us that talent is not dependent on the support of the crown, nor of wealth. Talent is not servile to palaces . . . Both Dr B.R. Ambedkar and Babu Jagjivan Ram proved this . . . The poor who try to excel in any art form are discouraged, humiliated and even destroyed. The story of Eklavya tells us what to do. What happened to Eklavya has been happening to many even today. We must not stop with celebrating the anniversary of Eklavya . . . Our society has many people who feel the pangs of injustice even today; they are being victimized, their rights are being snatched.'[1]

This was Karpoori Thakur's last public speech; he died three days later, on 17 February 1988. Eklavya had perhaps called out to Karpoori one last time to do his bit to change the 'thumb' rule.

* * *

The legendary Bihar leader and former CM 'Jannayak' Karpoori Thakur would have turned 100 on 24 January 2024 if he were alive. It is also the year the country sees the Lok Sabha elections with incumbent Prime Minister (PM) Narendra Modi seeking his third consecutive term and the Congress and regional parties looking for ways to stem the rise of another saffron tide.

It is also a period when the socialist ideology finds itself at a crossroads like never before. Socialist veterans Mulayam Singh Yadav, Sharad Yadav and Ram Vilas Paswan are no more. An ailing RJD chief, Lalu Prasad, has been trying to put up some resistance to the BJP despite his debilitated frame, frequent raids by the Central Bureau of Investigation (CBI), Enforcement Directorate (ED) and Income Tax department and lingering court cases. Bihar CM Nitish Kumar, who keeps shuffling between the BJP and the RJD, may still have the solace of being called the last socialist. But he has frittered away the chance of being the nucleus of socialist and, for that matter, anti-Modi politics with his politics of convenience under the camouflage of what the JD (U) calls 'pragmatic socialism'. He has been trying hard to play a key role in national politics by frequently invoking Jayaprakash Narayan (JP) and Karpoori Thakur.

Karpoori Thakur is still used as the primary reference for socialism after Dr Rammanohar Lohia and Jayaprakash Narayan. When PM Modi came to Bihar in July 2022, he recalled the contributions of only two former CMs of Bihar—Dr Sri Krishna Singh and Karpoori Thakur. He called Nitish 'an important ally' and praised him for his socialist credentials. But the tottering Nitish perhaps counted himself out of the league of someone like Karpoori Thakur, who never compromised on his socialist ideology and principles.

However, the very first question one may still ask is why we are discussing Karpoori Thakur thirty-six years after his death. After all, what is so important about the man who served as Bihar CM for just about two-and-a-half years in his two stints and deputy CM for less than ten months? One can also argue that Karpoori Thakur does not stand anywhere close to the length of the tenure of the first CM Dr Sri Krishna Singh and socialist CMs, Lalu Prasad and Nitish Kumar. For that matter, Rabri Devi also ruled the state for close to eight years.

But then, Karpoori Thakur is the only Bihar leader who cannot be remembered just for the duration of his tenure as the CM. He is rather remembered for the huge impact he made during this brief tenure. He is often compared with former Tamil Nadu CM K. Kamaraj for his broad political vision and the impact on the masses. Karpoori's mass appeal comes from his close associations with the freedom struggle, socialist and farmers' movements and the JP Movement. In a sense, his leadership contains the essence of many revolutions.

Karpoori Thakur is perhaps the germinator of the game-changing ideas of 'free education' and 'equity within equity'. He is the foundation stone that is not visible but still holds the entire edifice. He has earned several sobriquets—'Lohia in action', 'socialist of the soil' and 'the original subaltern hero'. He is the one who changed the social context and contour of not only Bihar but also of the entire country. The Government of India conferred him with the highest civilian honour, Bharat Ratna, for 2024. He is the only Bihar CM to receive the honour. Prime Minister Narendra Modi posted on the social media platform, X, on 23 January 2024, in Hindi: 'I am very happy that the Government of India has decided to honour the great leader of social justice, Karpoori Thakur Ji, Bharat Ratna. On the occasion of his birth centenary, this decision will make the countrymen proud. Karpoori Ji's unwavering commitment and visionary leadership for the upliftment for the backward and the deprived has left an indelible mark on socio-political scenario of India. This Bharat Ratna is not only a humble recognition of his incomparable contribution but will also further promote harmony in the society.'[2] He also wrote an article published in all major newspapers highlighting how his government is implementing Thakur's vision and priorities.

Karpoori was not interested in national politics but his actions as Bihar deputy CM and CM did have national resonance. Though there had been socialist CMs, such as Choudhary Devi Lal in Haryana; S.R. Bommai, Ramakrishna Hegde and H.D. Deve Gowda in Karnataka; Mulayam Singh Yadav in Uttar Pradesh (UP) and, of course, Lalu Prasad and Nitish Kumar in Bihar, all of them emulated Karpoori Thakur's model of governance in one way or the other.

But what is the enduring legacy of Karpoori and why should it be turned into a book? The one popular and predictable answer could be his decision to give 26 per cent reservation to OBCs, EBCs, women and the poor among the general category. He was the first politician in the country who thought of social classification by insisting that lower OBCs, also called MBCs and EBCs, have to be empowered as well. During his second stint as the CM, he announced the allotment of 12 per cent reservation to EBCs, 8 per cent to OBCs, and 3 per cent each to women and the educationally and economically disadvantaged general category of people. This effort was more to do with making an attempt towards an egalitarian society than appeasing a group of socially, economically and educationally backward castes to create a constituency.

While the Modi government often boasts of having given 10 per cent quota to the EBCs, it was Karpoori who first gave 3 per cent reservation to the economically and educationally disadvantaged among the general category. He was also the first person to recognize women of all sections of society as disadvantaged and thus backward and give them 3 per cent reservation as part of affirmative action. Karpoori was the social assimilator who abhorred the very idea of being a caste leader. Former Janata Party president and later PM Chandra Shekhar gave him the sobriquet, 'Jannayak (leader of the people)', because of his egalitarian politics and unwavering commitment to socialist ideology.

In an article, 'Karpoori Thakur: A socialist leader in the Hindi belt', senior journalist Jagpal Singh writes: 'His (Karpoori's) politics can be analyzed in two parts: as a legislator and minister on one hand and an activist outside legislator on the other. He brought about a reservation policy for the backward classes, which had a provision for a sub-quota for the most backward classes (MBCs). This was all the more important considering the fact that some leaders including Charan Singh were against a sub-quota for the MBCs. Today, there is a regular allusion to Karpoori Thakur's reservation policy of sub-quota generally known as "Karpoori Thakur formula" in debates on reservation.'[3]

Jeffrey Witsoe, the author of *Democracy against Development*, discusses how Dr Rammanohar Lohia 'rejected the claim commonly espoused by many Indian socialists—including Nehru—that caste inequality would automatically wither away once socialism was established'. Witsoe reasons that 'since Lohia held that caste status along with English education and wealth were three primary characteristics of India's ruling classes, he believed that purely class-based socialism would not unseat the ruling classes, even with full public ownership over what Nehru referred to as the "commanding heights" of the economy.'[4]

Francine R. Frankel and M.S.A. Rao write: 'By the 1960s, two new caste formations began to change the contours of Bihar's political life. One was that of the Forward Castes, representing an alignment of twice-born caste groups, whose leaders, although divided by faction, nevertheless cooperated within the Congress parties on issues affecting the dominance of upper castes as a whole. The other was the Backward Classes, whose leadership claimed to represent the interests of all of the downtrodden, but in practice articulated the demands of the advanced upper shudras and consulted across party lines. The emergence of caste-based political categories was led by the state by the late 1970s towards a politics of polarization.'[5]

This is where the role of Karpoori Thakur was so important. He was one of the key harbingers of social transformation from 1952 till his death in 1988. CM Nitish Kumar endorses Karpoori's ideas, saying: 'Just like Karpoori Thakur worked towards reservation for the MBCs within the quota meant for the backward classes xxviii　　　　　　　　Why Karpoori Thakur?

in the (government) jobs, the MBCs among the backward classes should get reservation in the Panchayati Raj institutions. They should get separate reservation. Besides, the Constitution should be amended in order to give them political reservation just like the scheduled castes and scheduled tribes have it. We demand this. The reservation should be given in proportion to population.'[6]

Karpoori had announced reservations for lower OBCs and OBCs because he firmly believed in these words of Dr Lohia: 'Caste restricts the opportunity. Restricted opportunity constricts ability. Constricted ability restricts opportunity. Where caste prevails, opportunity and ability are restricted to ever narrowing circles of two people.'[7]

Former Bihar director general of police and author D.N. Gautam, who worked closely with Thakur, holds that 'since Karpoori had experienced the pain of being disadvantaged himself, he aimed at lifting up the less privileged and hence, calling it just quota could be myopic and inappropriate.'[8]

Thakur's eldest son and Rajya Sabha MP Ramnath Thakur narrates that his father, who could not afford private tuition as a student, would hide close to a place where one Raja Guruji would teach upper-caste children. There was an unsaid arrangement between the teacher (who was not allowed to teach non-upper-caste children) and the child Karpoori—the teacher would speak a bit louder so that Karpoori could take down notes from a distance. Karpoori is important because he worked towards achieving equality in society. It does not matter how far he succeeded in his efforts.

His other lasting legacy is his attempt towards the democratization of education by removing English as a mandatory subject for passing matriculation (Class 10 board examinations) during his tenure as the education minister-cum-deputy CM in 1967. Those against it derided it by calling it 'Karpoori Division' or 'PWE (Pass without English)'. But it did not matter. Passing matriculation in the 1960s and 1970s used to be no mean feat. It was directly related to social prestige and the good fortune of getting good marriage proposals and a government job. If there was a surge in passing matriculation after 1967 among OBCs and Dalits, a lot of the credit goes to Karpoori Thakur's idea. Karpoori Thakur himself was proficient in English and had scored 156 out of 300 marks in Class 12 examinations. And when someone attending his public meeting took a dig at Karpoori removing English, saying perhaps he was 'weak' in English, Karpoori delivered his entire speech, at a function in 1967 in Bhagalpur, in English to prove his point that 'English is just a language and not a certificate of being knowledgeable.'

Practising probity in public life, a quality of Thakur, is now extinct. An ensemble of coarse khadi kurta and dhoti was all that he needed as an outfit, unlike modern-day politicians, who worry about the creases in their starched white kurtas. When former UP CM Hemvati Nandan Bahuguna visited Thakur's paternal village, Pitaunjhia, now called Karpoori Gram, after his death, he cried when he saw the thatched mud house of the two-time Bihar CM. Bahuguna wrote after Thakur's demise: 'He had such decency that he bowed down to his knees in salutation, but when he stuck to his word, he stood upright.'[9]

In another instance, a researcher who had visited the same house during his lifetime, cried when he saw that a serving CM had such a humble house. He smeared the soil outside Karpoori's house on his forehead and carried some in his bag as a 'souvenir'. One may find such behaviour eulogistic, but it speaks of the respect that Karpoori Thakur commanded.

Karpoori Thakur is relevant and important not only for his deft social engineering in his attempt to ensure equality in society but also for his assimilative politics. There was just one Nai family in his village, which was largely dominated by upper-caste Rajputs. But he always tried to reach out to the dominant upper castes to keep the peace. Even when he became the CM, he did not think of reprisals and revenge. He was one victim who was averse to playing the victim card. It was because his brand of politics was not divisive but inclusive and cohesive. He enjoyed the support of all sections of society for a large part of his political career.

At a time when the country's politics has become almost unidimensional, Bihar is the only state that has been offering some resistance to the BJP's aggressive brand of politics that is a mix of welfare schemes, nationalism and Hindutva. Between them, two socialist leaders, Lalu Prasad (with his wife Rabri Devi) and Nitish Kumar, have now ruled the state for over three decades. Nitish had been a part of the National Democratic Alliance (NDA) government in Bihar for thirteen years but reigned supreme. These two Bihar leaders have reaped the harvest of Karpoori's political legacies. While Lalu Prasad chose to practise aggressive backward versus forward politics for most of his tenure, he did end up voicing the concerns of the poor and the subaltern. If people from so-called backward castes and Dalit communities are offered a seat today, it is because of Lalu Prasad. Nitish Kumar adopted the governance model of Karpoori Thakur and also tried to practise assimilative politics by stitching together an alliance which, according to political scientist and Asian Development Research Institute founder the late Shaibal Gupta, was a 'coalition of social extremes'. Former Union minister Arun Jaitley used to call it a 'rainbow coalition', which had upper castes at one end and scheduled castes at the other.

If Nitish Kumar has been talking about cultivating a constituency of EBCs and about dedicated welfare programmes for them, he has imported it from the EBC empowerment idea of Karpoori Thakur. The idea of separate reservations for EBCs for their upliftment has its resonance not just in the politics of socialists but also that of the BJP.

Whether it is strengthening the Panchayati Raj system, waiving school fees or the land rent of farmers tilling up to five acres of land, the whole idea of Karpoori Thakur was to make an attempt towards uplifting the deprived. Lalu Prasad interpreted these ideas in his own way when he bathed the children of the Scheduled Castes on the roads of Patna in front of government officials. His idea of Charwaha and Pahalwan schools was not wrong, but the model lacked the right preparation and wherewithal for implementation. He adopted a more practical approach to expand Karpoori's ideas of social empowerment by giving 50 per cent reservation to women and 20 per cent to EBCs in panchayats and local bodies.

Aligarh Muslim University professor Mohammed Sajjad, in his article 'Karpoori Thakur and the Power of Street Politics', writes: 'Thakur's consistent anti-Congressism, empowerment of the backward castes and removal of English as a compulsory language in high school examinations (thereby, enabling Hindi-speaking rural students for mobility towards higher education) are some of the most significant steps for which he must be remembered. This enabling exercise was condescendingly referred to as "Karpoori Division". Despite being a leader of Socialist conviction, his pragmatism in striking alliances with ideological rivals such as the Bharatiya Jana Sangh, while empowering the religio-linguistic minorities is another equally significant step.'[10] Sajjad added that Karpoori Thakur challenged the upper-caste hegemony in politics and education, even though he did not belong to a caste of numerical preponderance.

Authors Rajiv Malhotra and Vijaya Viswanathan bring new theories, asking, 'Is caste a necessary condition for Hinduism? Can a Hindu avoid caste? Is caste a sufficient condition for Hinduism? . . . In the present age of globalisation, things are taking a different turn. Today, when food or any product gets delivered, who knows, or bothers to know, what the person's caste or sexual orientation is? The free exchange of goods and services is driven by old social classifications. Regardless of one's birth-based factors, one can work, get paid, advance in one's career, and move socially with freedom. Efficiency and optimization are the key success factors overriding everything else.'[11] The authors further reason that: 'The result of modern democracy and social mobility is a new kind of system which is primarily one of vote banks and lobbying for resource allocation. Public education and job mobility have reduced the interests of younger generations to follow in the footsteps of their parents. Technologies and modern trends have rendered old models obsolete.'[12] However, against all expectations of a vanishing caste system, its spread has become global. The United Nations General Assembly, in its Human Rights Council report dated 28 January 2016, calls it a global problem affecting communities in Asia, Africa, the Middle East, the Pacific Region and various diaspora communities.[13] The division along caste lines among Hindus was clearly visible in California during the debate on banning caste discrimination in 2023.[14] The debate also brought to light the existence of a large number of caste groups, both so-called upper castes and those other than upper castes, operating in the USA.[15] Nonetheless, California Governor Gavin Newsom vetoed a landmark anti-caste discrimination bill recently passed by the state assembly, terming it 'unnecessary' as laws to ban caste-based discrimination already exist in the US state.[16]

The life of Karpoori Thakur also shows us that it is possible to be a politician who is uncorrupted by power. He remained unchanged through various life stages, as a boy struggling to pay his school fees to depending on the mercy of the upper castes to support his education, to becoming an MLA and then a deputy CM and then the CM. Born into a traditional barber's family, he continued to walk on the razor's edge throughout his life. Even after becoming an MLA, he would face insults and caste slurs. But he would always pocket the insults and say that the wheel of social transformation would address it all. He did not need to feign greatness unlike several of his peers and successors. In 1971, when he was CM, an upper-caste Rajput landlord sent his musclemen to forcibly get his ailing father to shave his beard. The Samastipur administration got to know about the incident, following which the landlord was taken away by the police. When CM Karpoori learnt about it, he ordered the district magistrate (DM) not to take any action against his fellow villager. He asked the DM: 'You got to know about my father being roughed up because he is the father of the CM. But how about many such fathers who are being beaten and insulted without any police knowledge? Leave it to time to address it.'[17]

The life of Karpoori Thakur should also be read because of his fearlessness and his habit of speaking truth to power—and also for conceding his failings when in power. Senior journalist Hemant recalled how Karpoori visited the office of a Patna-based newspaper after reading that some poor people had died because of a house cave-in during a flood in a Vaishali village and could not be cremated. 'As there was water all around, the aggrieved family left the bodies in the holes of a brick kiln. Karpoori Thakur was deeply moved at the report and ensured that the poor were cremated properly. The CM reasoned that the poor who died might well have lived a life of penury but they did deserve dignity in death.'[18]

This book is an attempt to tell the full story of Karpoori Thakur and deal with landmark social and political happenings which impacted society. The book, through its fourteen chapters, tries to address Karpoori, the family man, the politician, the administrator, the leader of the Opposition, the socialist of the soil, the human and the statesman, who got little time to make the changes he wanted to make. Since Dr Rammanohar Lohia and Jayaprakash Narayan were never in power politics, Karpoori Thakur comes across as a frontline socialist chief minister in the country. Dr Lohia would often talk about the burden of the English language on Indians. But it was very much in theory till someone like Karpoori Thakur took the bold decision of removing English from the list of mandatory subjects required to pass Class 10 board or matriculation. He received flak for it, but in the long run, it was a great attempt in the direction of democratization of education. Karpoori always worked towards popularizing and promoting Hindi in governance.

In his book, *Why Socialism?*, Jayaprakash Narayan writes, 'Socialism is not a code of personal conduct but a system of social reconstruction. When we speak of applying socialism to India, the first thing that strikes us is the strange and painful fact of inequalities—of rank, of culture, of opportunity: a most disconcertingly unequal distribution of the good things of life . . .'[19] Karpoori Thakur tried his best to live up to each word of his idol, JP. Studying Karpoori Thakur is also necessary to understand and appreciate social changes and their new dimensions.

It was important to understand, Manish Kumar Jha writes, 'What was his (Karpoori's) articulation of socialism and its implication for the backward castes and communities that helped him occupy the centre-stage of competitive socialist politics in Bihar and how could one understand his ideological alignment and points of contention with Rammanohar Lohia, Jayaprakash Narayan and Vinoba Bhave?'[20] There was also a need to understand how 'dominant social structures dealt with his "controversial" decisions' and how one could 'understand Karpoori's politics vis-à-vis coalition of extremes and politics of pragmatism'.

Renowned author Paul R. Brass said that Karpoori was one among the leaders whom he loved and admired 'because they see politics as their vocation, pursue clearly stated goals, and do not enrich themselves in the process'.[21] Brass mapped the life and journey of Karpoori Thakur in four phases—his exposure to socialist ideology, his acceptance as a mass leader, his contribution to the politics of Bihar and his contribution in appealing to the conscience of the MBCs.

Whatever new theories may assert, caste remains a reality despite exponential changes in the last two decades. But the crux of socialist politics is never caste but equality. Karpoori Thakur is a great case study to understand the rigorous process of achieving equality. It is debatable if socialist politics can still stand up to nationalistic and Hindutva politics, but one thing is for certain: The spirit of socialism, be it Karl Marx, Mahatma Gandhi, Jawaharlal Nehru, Rammanohar Lohia or the B.R. Ambedkar model, is here to stay. It has the power to bring about a semblance of sanity to any form of governance or any ideology for that matter. Democracy in India will have no meaning and no purpose if the idea of socialism given by Gandhi, Lohia and Ambedkar is removed from it.

The story of the original subaltern hero of the Hindi heartland, Karpoori Thakur, is an untold story. Santosh Singh writes, 'He was the bridge between Congress hegemony and the advent of Lalu Prasad. He was also the first real non-Congress alternative, even though he was deputy chief minister in the Mahamaya Prasad Sinha government. It is a rare incident in history that the 1967 Sanyukt Vidhayak Dal government is discussed more for its deputy CM than its CM. He was not the challenger of upper castes like Lalu.'[22]

Political scientist and Indologist Christophe Jaffrelot wrote: 'An important outcome of the Janata government however was the appointment of the Mandal Commission which had fewer inhibitions than previous, similar commissions regarding the use of caste as a relevant criterion for identifying the Other Backward Classes. Its approach was bound to relaunch quota politics. The Lok Dal—which gathered together opponents of quota politics and kisan politics once again under the aegis of Charan Singh—epitomized the growing synthesis of these two currents. Gradually, quota politics was taking over.'[23]

This book is undoubtedly a biography, touching every aspect of the man. It also deals with how Karpoori Thakur did not change his core ideology during his career. We are also attempting to tell a less frequently told story of why top socialist leader Ramanand Tiwari could not become the chief minister in 1969 because of Karpoori. Karpoori's flip-flop on taking support from the BJS is well covered in the book. Karpoori, who did not let his friend Tiwari take the support of the BJS to become the CM, himself took the BJS's support to do so in December 1970. He had been the deputy CM in 1967 in the Sanyukt Vidhayak Dal government that had the BJS's support. Later, he also became the CM with BJS support in the Janata Party government in 1977 with leading BJS leader Kailashpati Mishra as his deputy. We have also tried to explain how, post-1980, when caste caught up with the Jannayak, all of a sudden, he was branded an OBC leader. The tug of war between the emerging Yadav leaders and him tells a lot about the changing social dynamics of Bihar politics. Karpoori had famously said in the 1980s that dealing with Yadav leaders was like 'riding a tiger'.

On an institutional level, the book traces the entire journey of socialist politics with its highs and lows, from its making and unmaking from the Socialist Party to the Praja Socialist Party to the Sanyukt Socialist Party to the Bharatiya Lok Dal to Janata Party, to the Janata Dal and its diversified offspring. There is also an attempt to retell some stories of the journey of social transformation from caste Sabha to caste Sena and in-between interventions of social groups like the Triveni Sangh and social and farmers' movements led by Swami Sahajanand Saraswati. Of course, they all move around our central character, but all these events too are central to the making of Karpoori Thakur.

The book also covers the story of Karpoori Thakur's death. What was the story of the 'salty solution' and who advised him to take it when he was a heart patient with erratic blood pressure? He had been reportedly made to consume 13 litres of a salty solution before his death. Was it a political conspiracy?

Finally, we also tell the story of Karpoori Thakur's sons, Ramnath Thakur and Dr Birendra K. Thakur. Ramnath Thakur helps tell this story in an authentic manner, which should also strike a note of caution as Ramnath has been a practising politician.

Our objective is to invite readers, old and young, to revisit the stories of Karpoori with the idea that they should be free to draw their own conclusions. Though we have tried to weave in significant theories and historical and academic references for researchers, we have also kept the book open-ended. We have tried to blend facts with a lot of personal details and anecdotes.

We have storified all theories to make the book easy-going. We have tried to tell a complex story in simple words through a sound narrative. We have depended on a lot of primary and secondary sources, including interviews with all those who saw, knew or read about Karpoori Thakur and his times.

1

Petrograd to Pitaunjhia

A Child of Many Revolutions

. . . Remember this - this morning, after that black night -

this sun, this polished brass.
Remember what you never dreamt would come to pass
but what had always burnt within your heart!
. . . Remember the first dispatches from the Soviets,
the dizzying, "For all, for all, for all!"
It's like telling a starving man, "Eat!"
And him replying, "I'm eating!" with a smile
                    —'Russian Revolution', a poem by Mikhail Kuzmin

* * *

On 8 March 1917, riots erupted in various parts of Petrograd, now St Petersburg, in protest against the autocratic rule of Czar Nicholas II. Around 30,000 men and women took to the

1

streets, demanding bread, when clashes with the police ensued. Undeterred, the workers remained defiant, setting fire to police stations and looting vital installations. They had lost faith in the system and held all its symbols in disdain.

History.com writes: 'The imperial government was forced to resign, and the Duma formed a provisional government that peacefully vied with the Petrograd Soviet for control of the revolution. On March 14, the Petrograd Soviet issued "Order No. 1," which instructed Russian soldiers and sailors to obey only those orders that did not conflict with the directives of the Soviet. The next day, on March 15, Czar Nicholas II abdicated the throne in favor of his brother Michael, whose refusal of the crown brought an end to the czarist autocracy.'[1]

The Russian Revolution echoed the spirit of the French Revolution of 1789. In France, the people held such disdain for the Bastille, a symbol of monarchy and tyranny, that broken bricks and stones from its dismantled walls were sold as souvenirs. Similarly, in Russia, there was profound hatred for the Winter Palace, which represented autocracy and opulent aristocracy. While the people were longing for basic sustenance, the Czar's family was feasting on diamonds for dessert.

Lillian Osborne writes: 'As legend has it, when the Bolshevik soldiers raided the Winter Palace, belonging to Nicholas II and his family, they were said to have uncovered vast amounts of fine wine. Some soldiers even reported that Faberge eggs aside, the selection of wine was the most impressive part of their findings. It is said that for weeks following the initial coup, thousands of bottles of the world's rarest and most expensive wines and ports were stolen, sold on, or even drunk by the revolutionaries themselves.'[2]

The Romanov regime, which had ruled Russia for over 300 years, came to an end. Vladimir Lenin assumed power and formed a socialist government, with an influence as powerful as that of the French Revolution. Now, the winds of change were blowing towards India, as the ideals of the Russian Revolution inspired Indians to seek a similar path in their quest to overthrow British colonial rule.

It was a remarkable coincidence that in the same year, 1917, Mohandas Karamchand Gandhi, later known as Mahatma Gandhi, travelled to Bihar in response to a call from Rajkumar Shukla to launch the Champaran Satyagrah, a movement aimed at protecting the rights of Indian farmers. These farmers were being forced by British landlords to grow indigo on a portion of their land. The British had imposed a system known as '*tinkathia*' on the farmers. This system required them to grow indigo on 3/20th of their land, even though it was not a profitable crop. The farmers were not allowed to grow any other crop on that land and were forced to sell the indigo to the British landlords at a fixed price, which was much lower than the market price. Gandhi stayed in Bihar for several months, leading the movement successfully to ensure the abolition of the tinkathia system. The Champaran Satyagrah became the first national movement in India and a significant milestone for the young lawyer who had recently returned from South Africa after bravely resisting apartheid in his own unique way. Pushya Mitra says, 'The most important part of the movement was that farmers and rural India became part of the Indian national movement for the first time and Gandhi returned as Mahatma Gandhi, called so by Gurudev Rabindra Nath Tagore.'[3]

Approximately 150 km from Champaran (now divided into the districts of East Champaran and West Champaran), where Gandhi had launched his satyagrah, lies the village of Pitaunjhia in Samastipur (then part of Darbhanga district). The village was home to just one EBC barber (Nai) and his family, but there were around 100 houses belonging to upper-caste Rajputs, besides about fifty houses belonging to other caste groups.

A Child of Many Revolutions

On 24 January 1924, a child was born to Gokul Thakur and Ramdulari Devi in a thatched house in Pitaunjhia village, located in the shadow of a mansion known as Durbar, which belonged to a zamindar (landlord). Due to their impoverished circumstances, the parents could only provide a haystack for a bed for their winter-born child, whom they named Kapoori. The name was chosen randomly and without any particular reason. Kapoori was just another name added to the village's list of proper nouns. Gokul was not aware of the meaning or significance of the name he had given to his son, and did not pay much attention to it either.

However, Gokul Thakur and Ramdulari could hardly fathom that Kapoori was born into a world of revolutions. He was cradled amidst a plethora of ideologies, nurtured by messages from the Russian Revolution, the Indian freedom movement, the socialist movement and the *Kisan Andolan* (farmers' movement). Though the hands that rocked his cradle were weak, Kapoori, the boy in that ideological cradle, was perhaps chosen by the very revolutions that shaped his surroundings.

One day, a sage visited Gokul's humble thatched hut. He observed Kapoori's forehead and predicted that the child would be famous someday. However, Gokul dismissed the claim, taking it as the customary prediction of a visiting sage who had been fed and treated well. Gokul sharpened his razor against a piece of flint and left for his work. Meanwhile, Ramdulari placed infant

Kapoori under the warm sun on a small haystack, where the sun's bright rays shone upon the boy's face.

Gokul Thakur's grandfather, Sitaram Thakur, had migrated from Rajasthan to settle in Pitaunjhia about 150 years ago at the request of an upper caste Rajput family. Like many other villages in India, Pitaunjhia had a social structure where a few families of blacksmiths and washermen served the rest of the village. Such a social set-up was prevalent in most Indian villages until the 1980s. Being dependent on an agrarian economy, where a system of *begaar* (unpaid labour) was traditionally acceptable even after its abolition through law post-Independence, Pitaunjhia was no exception to this pattern.

Gokul Thakur, a simple and unschooled man, earned his livelihood through yajmani or patronage. He would visit the homes of upper-caste Rajputs in Pitaunjhia and neighbouring villages on a regular basis to shave off beards and cut hair and, in return, he would receive grains, such as wheat or rice, after the harvest. The razor that Gokul used had been passed down to him by his father, Pyare Thakur, and he hoped that his sons, Kapoori and Ramsogarath, would continue the same profession, under the yajmani system, when they grew up. Under the yajmani system, a person of a higher social status, such as a Brahmin or Kshatriya, would be assigned a lower-caste family or community and they would act as their *yajman* (patron). The yajman would provide material support and protection to the lower-caste family or community, while the latter would perform various services and rituals for the yajman, such as farming, cattle-rearing, cooking and serving during religious ceremonies.

Kapoori and his seven siblings grew up in Pitaunjhia and life went on as usual. Gokul Thakur continued with his work as a barber, serving the upper-caste Rajputs in the village and neighbouring areas through his yajmani. His genial nature and friendly interactions with the landlords had helped him develop some good contacts in the community. As barbers often praised their masters during haircuts, Gokul had established a level of comfort with them, which made his work easier, compared to that of others serving their landlords. Kapoori, his younger brother Ramsogarath, and their six sisters—Galho, Siya, Rajo, Sita, Parvati and Shail—had remained unschooled. None of them showed any courage to break the societal status quo except for Kapoori. One day, Kapoori mustered up the courage to ask his father for a slate. Though surprised and unimpressed with his child's request to study, Gokul Thakur still got him a stone slate and some chalks, known as *khalli*.

Gokul Thakur told Ramdulari that he had got Kapoori a slate, but it did not mean that he should go to school. Gokul wanted Kapoori to continue with their traditional profession. Ramdulari, an illiterate woman, said nothing. But she would look admiringly at Kapoori when he used to write alphabets on the slate. Ramdulari, who mostly remained half veiled, used to raise goats and cows to earn some extra money. She would also carry out her duties as a female barber. During weddings and other auspicious events, she would trim the nails of the womenfolk and paint them with a *alta* (a red dye used to paint hands and feet on auspicious occasions).

Kapoori didn't like seeing his mother work so hard and receive very few 'tips' in return. However, he was too young to do anything about it. But the boy somehow knew that he had to study hard to escape the fate of becoming a barber. He learned to write his name and would practise it several times on his slate. One day, he showed it to his father with pride. Gokul Thakur's eyes also reflected that pride.

In 1930, Gokul Thakur got Kapoori enrolled in the village primary school. The school was heavily dominated by children of upper-caste Rajputs. However, Kapoori proved his brilliance to the teachers from his very first day at school. He convinced them that he was just as worthy of receiving an education as the children of the upper castes.

There were many occasions when Gokul Thakur was unable to afford Kapoori's school fees. At one point, he even considered asking his son to discontinue his studies. However, Kapoori's passion for learning and the praise he received from his teachers made Gokul think otherwise. He would often borrow money from Rajput landlords to ensure that his elder son could continue attending school.

Back home, the Thakur family lived a hand-to-mouth existence. They had only two or three aluminium plates, two *lotas* (small steel water pots), and a few aluminium utensils in their kitchen. An earthen pitcher served as their spice box. Their staple diet consisted of rice and lentils or *khichdi* (savoury porridge) with mashed potato. Rice, pulses and vegetables were considered a luxury and were only cooked on special occasions. Survival itself was a cause for celebration.

* * *

The words 'socialism' and 'communism' were first used in India by Bankim Chandra Chatterjee, Rabindra Nath Thakur and Swami Vivekananda in their various writings in the nineteenth century. However, the institutional development of socialist thought in this country began from the beginning of the second or third decades of the twentieth century. The Russian Revolution in 1917 also played an important role in gradually spreading the message of socialism to the people. Santosh Kumar writes, 'The Bolshevik Revolution had a deep impact on the minds and hearts of the people of India. Many people started thinking that by adopting this method one can get freedom from sufferings and exploitation. S.A. Dange's book "Gandhi vs Lenin" related to this revolution was published in 1921 and intellectuals got detailed information about the Russian Revolution and Lenin and Communism.'[4]

Dange writes: 'So we have to think of two things. How to throw off the foreign yoke? With what methods? And then how to destroy evil of capitalism amongst us, which is making fast progress, and will double its speed when we are politically free. Mahatma Gandhi has put forth his methods of working out the destruction of these two monster diseases. Gandhism aims to cure society of modern industrialization and modern civilization. At the same time, Bolshevism is working with the same view in Russia and in European society. Since both the systems are working with a view to find a solution for a common evil, common to all nations and since both, fortunately or unfortunately, are born practically in the same era, we propose to compare and contrast these two systems of philosophy and action and try to see their efficiency to arrive at the desired results.'[5]

The Bolshevik Revolution in Russia in 1917 had already stirred the youth of India, including Bihar. The people of Bihar were actively involved in the freedom movement and concurrent farmers' agitation led by Swami Sahajanand Saraswati. Farmers and labourers were facing oppression from landlords. Whenever the INC launched a movement against British imperialism, these peasant youths participated in it with unwavering devotion. The Russian Revolution had instilled in them the belief that the mighty and powerful could be overthrown, sooner or later.

The Congress party dominated the first General Elections held in 1952 with little resistance. The only formidable challenge to the Congress came from the Socialist Party. Despite the Congress's stronghold in Bihar under the dynamic leadership of Dr Sri Krishna Singh, Karpoori Thakur, the leader of the Socialist Party, emerged victorious from the Tajpur Assembly segment of Darbhanga, one of over a dozen seats won by the Opposition.

The Hut and the Durbar

Karpoori Thakur, then only twenty-eight years old, visited his paternal village, Pitaunjhia, to express his gratitude to the villagers and participate in a modest celebration of his first electoral victory. He had defeated Ramsukumari Devi, an established Congress candidate, by a margin of approximately 2500 votes.

Karpoori had to walk by a mansion known as Durbar or *Laat Saheb Ki Kothi* to reach his thatched house. He had always been in awe of this building throughout his childhood, as he grew up with the stark contrast between the grand mansion and his humble hut.

The Durbar stood as a living and prominent symbol of feudalism in the village. The two-storey coral building boasted of twenty six rooms and sprawling verandas, staring down Karpoori's humble hut. It was a stark contrast of opulence juxtaposed with poverty, a constant reminder of the socio-economic divide in the village.

Ramji Choudhary, the landlord who presided over the reign of terror in the village, was aware of Karpoori Thakur's recent electoral victory and new-found political power as an MLA. He knew that Karpoori was in a position to challenge his archaic and feudalistic rules, including the unwritten rule of removing footwear and dismounting from bicycles when passing by his house, which was enforced through fear and intimidation. However, Ramji Choudhary decided to wait and see how Karpoori would react to his rules.

Karpoori Thakur, despite being an elected MLA, still adhered to the social norms and customs of the village. He removed his slippers before entering the palace and touched Ramji Choudhary's feet, as a mark of respect for the elder. Choudhary muttered his blessings, but Karpoori avoided direct eye contact and looked away, signifying a subtle shift in the power dynamics.

Karpoori then proceeded to the inner chambers of the palace to seek blessings from the womenfolk, showing his humility and respect towards the traditional customs of the village. He maintained his polite demeanour, but he also kept in mind his new role as a representative of the people and the need to bring about change in the social structure that perpetuated inequality and feudalism.

As he left the palace and returned to his humble thatched hut, Karpoori's mind was filled with a determination to fulfill the aspirations of the people who had elected him, and to work towards a more just and equitable society where the divide between the palace and the hut would no longer exist.

The Choudharys' possession of over 1700 bighas of land in and around the village was a testament to their immense wealth, power and authority. The Durbar had sprawling verandas, and evoked feelings of power, authority, awe and arrogance. It remained a symbol of their dominance and superiority in the village, and was viewed with reverence by some and with a sense of entitlement by others.

The new MLA stepped out of the palace and slipped his feet back into his footwear. He made his way to his house where his father, Gokul Thakur, and mother, Ramdulari Devi, were eagerly waiting for their son. Ramdulari Devi offered Karpoori a piece of jaggery to celebrate his victory, a simple yet heartfelt gesture of joy. Karpoori had rejected the idea of beating drums, as suggested by some villagers. He didn't want to do anything that could be seen as jarring or confrontational to the ears of many in the village. He believed in letting democratic processes change the archaic rules set by the Durbar, the symbol of feudalism in the village.

The Humbling of the Durbar

In January 2023, the once majestic Durbar, now weathered, worn out and dilapidated, was demolished brick by brick, as if erasing the last traces of its feudal arrogance. Some of the bricks bore imprints of 1857 and 1906, hinting at the building's age, over 125 years. Om Prakash Singh, a descendant of the Choudhary family and contractor residing in Patna, supervised the demolition. He says, 'The contractor had offered the family a sum of Rs 3.20 lakh as the full and final price for the fallen bricks, wooden gates, windows, and iron beams, a meagre compensation for the lost grandeur of the once-mighty Durbar.'[6]

Singh, a scion of the landlord's family, says, with a sigh: '*Sab samay ka pher hai* (it is all a cycle of time)'. He says, 'They used to have 100 bighas of land till the 1970s but after it was divided among some sixteen descendants, not much land remained, with several of them selling it over the years.'[7]

The Durbar, which had once been the epitome of feudalism in Pitaunjhia, was now reduced to rubble, marking the end of an era. In 1988, the village was renamed Karpoori Gram in honour of its famous resident and two-time CM of Bihar, Karpoori Thakur. Where there once stood a cluster of thatched houses, now stood a modest double-storey house known as Karpoori Thakur Smriti

Bhavan, a tribute to the revered leader. The Durbar, once a symbol of power and privilege, had been humbled to the plains, blending in with the natural colour of the soil, signifying the changing times and the dismantling of feudalistic practices.

One Village, Two Journeys

A journey from Pitaunjhia to the state capital of Patna used to be a day-long affair till the Mahatma Gandhi *setu* (bridge) connected North Bihar to Patna in 1982. Arvind Singh, one of the descendants of the landlord Ramji Choudhary, recalled how they would have to walk down six km from the village to either Samastipur or Pusa to take a local train for Sonepur in Vaishali. 'From Sonepur, we would take a *ghatahi* (one that leads to ghat or bank) vehicle to reach Pahleja Ghat from where a boat or a ship would take us to Mahendru Ghat in Patna. Karpoori Thakur would often start very early for his journey from Pitaunjhia to Patna or vice versa,'[8] says Singh, adding that the village had nothing except a primary school. Karpoori Thakur could add only a high school to the village in his lifetime. 'He never threw his political weight to do any extra favours to his village in the same way that Jayaprakash Narayan did nothing for his Sitab Diara village in Saran'.[9] In the case of Karpoori Gram, several development works were undertaken during the regime of two Bihar CMs, Lalu Prasad and Nitish Kumar, by Thakur's eldest son and JD (U) Rajya Sabha MP Ramnath Thakur, who nurtured it as a constituency.

'Even though my father had become an MLA, he seldom tried to convert our thatched house into a pucca one. We used to complain about it but he would always say he had no money to build a new house,'[10] says Ramnath Thakur.

Socialist leaders, Lalu Prasad and Nitish Kumar, have used Pitaunjhia as a political symbol to further their politics. During their tenures as CMs of Bihar, Lalu Prasad and Rabri Devi did not do much for the village, except for road connectivity. However, during Nitish Kumar's tenure, Ramnath Thakur pursued and brought maximum possible amenities and infrastructure of a modern Indian village, before other villages could get similar ones even though it meant a deviation from his father's approach of not using his clout to accord priority to his constituency.

Ramnath Thakur once referred to Nitish Kumar as the '*manas putra* (ideological child)' of Karpoori Thakur, which is a fitting sobriquet for Nitish Kumar. Ramnath Thakur's endorsement of Nitish Kumar is more symbolic, as it gave him an edge in competition to claim the strong legacy of Karpoori Thakur.

Another journey from Patna to Karpoori Gram in 2023 provides a deeper insight into the making of the village, which is agog with activities in January, the month of Karpoori Thakur's birth. A sub-divisional officer who belongs to Karpoori Gram reflects on how he used to wonder as a child why the entire village celebrated his birthday. It was only when he grew up that he realized the truth that he shared his birthday with Karpoori Thakur.

The journey from Patna to Karpoori Gram has become significantly shorter now, taking just a little over two hours. One can choose to take either the Mahatma Gandhi Setu or JP Setu over the Ganges River to reach Hajipur, which is the district headquarters of Vaishali. Both bridge routes offer an enjoyable ride, and it is a happy coincidence that these two Ganga bridges are named after two legends, who had a profound influence on Karpoori Thakur's political ideology—Mahatma Gandhi and Jayaprakash Narayan.

The once bustling ferry route between Mahendru Ghat and Pahleja Ghat has now become more of a river safari and fishing sight. While some boats still operate on this route, they are primarily used for recreational activities. The significance of the ferry route as a means of transportation has diminished over the years, and it has transformed into a more leisurely activity for tourists and locals alike, providing an opportunity to enjoy the natural beauty of the river.

The road takes one through the picturesque countryside of Vaishali, with its lush green fields and quaint villages. As one travels on the shiny concrete road from Hajipur to Tajpur through Mahua in Vaishali, Karpoori Gram becomes the cusp between these two landmark places in the life of Karpoori Thakur. Karpoori Thakur had studied at both places and represented them in the Assembly and Parliament during his long political career.

The journey from Hajipur to Karpoori Gram is not just a physical one; it is also a symbolic one, as it traces the footsteps of a legendary leader who made a significant impact on Bihar's political landscape. About seven-and-a-half kilometers from Tajpur, along the road to Samastipur, a simple signboard reads 'Karpoori Gram' on the left. While the signboard may not be particularly noteworthy, it carries the name of the person who has left an indelible mark on the village. As one approaches Karpoori Gram, one can see the signs of development and progress, with well-maintained roads and modern amenities.

A short distance of about 400 meters from the main road, a PCC (Precast Cement Concrete) road turns right towards 'Smriti Bhavan (memorial building)'—dedicated to Karpoori Thakur. As per the state government's declaration, Smriti Bhavan is now a memorial and not used for residential purposes. The rear gate of the memorial opens to a one-room Indira Awas house that was allotted to Karpoori Thakur's brother Ramsogarath Thakur. Ramsogarath Thakur's son Nityanand Thakur and daughter-in-law Nisha Thakur take care of the memorial.

At the entrance of the two-storey memorial, a bust of Karpoori Thakur, the former Bihar CM and socialist icon, is prominently placed. However, the shiny bust lacks the ruggedness that was characteristic of Thakur's face, as well as the struggles he faced in his life.

The village primary school, where Karpoori Thakur began his schooling and later taught as a teacher and principal, has now been extended till Class 8. It is known as Lakshminarayan Rajkiya Madhya Vidyalaya and has about 500 students, with almost 50 per cent of them being girls. The school has three new buildings, one of which has replaced the school building of Karpoori's childhood. Ashutosh Bhushan Narayan Singh, a Hindi and Sanskrit teacher at the village since 2005, says: 'I feel fortunate to teach at the school associated with Karpoori Thakur and am very happy to have a job in his backyard.'[11]

The village also has a higher secondary school, established through the efforts of Karpoori Thakur in 1973 as a high school. It is called Prabhavati Ramdulari Inter Vidyalaya and currently has over 1400 students. As Prabhavati Devi, wife of Jayaprakash Narayan, and Ramdulari, Karpoori's mother, had been key influences in the former CM's life, the school is named in their memory.

Shambhu Nath Jha, a teacher at an adjoining village school, says: 'Karpoori Thakur got donations for the school not just from people from this locality but also from his political opponents. Former CM Jagannath Mishra is one of the leading donors to this school.'[12]

Villager Arvind Singh says: 'The school land belonged to our extended family. It was unused land. Karpoori Thakur trusted me so much that he called only me to represent the family to sign land transfer papers for the school. Since Karpoori Thakur had to walk down 8 kilometres to Tajpur for his education after primary school, he knew value of education and ensured that village got at least a high school.'[13]

On 24 January 2023, Bihar CM Nitish Kumar inaugurated Karpoori Gram police station, carved out from the jurisdiction of Muffasil police station. It covered ten panchayats. Ramnath Thakur now dreams of getting Karpoori Gram the status of a block.

While the Bihar government celebrates Thakur's legacy as part of its official functions, prominent political parties, including JD (U), RJD and BJP, organize separate events to commemorate his legacy.

Though there are still some brick and tile houses in Karpoori Gram, almost 90 per cent of the houses have turned into pucca ones over the last two decades. The village has 1664 people on the electoral roll, with about 200 houses belonging to upper-caste Rajputs, eight houses of EBC Nai, and all extended families of Karpoori Thakur. The village is also home to some EBC Dhanuk and scheduled caste Ravidas, Paswan and Pasi families.

To the east of the village, lie OBC Bania-dominated Chandopatti and Rajput-dominated Shambhupatti. Former union minister Satyanarayan Singh, whose family had played a mixed role in Karpoori's life, belonged to Shambhupatti. To the west of the village is Rajput-dominated Shrikrishna Nagar. In the north of Karpoori Gram, there is Muslim-dominated Mokandpur village. To the south of the village is an expanse of agricultural land called *chour* in local parlance.

The village also acquired a railway station in the early 1970s during the tenure of Lalit Narayan Mishra as union railway minister. Originally opened as Pitaunjhia railway station, it is now known as Karpoori Gram railway station, located adjacent to the inter school. Ramnath Thakur, a key figure in the village, also added a degree college to the village. The village has a hospital, a library and an overhead water tank. The village gets almost 24-hour electricity supply. The villagers of Karpoori Gram typically have small landholdings, ranging from 2 bighas (1.2 acre) to 12 bighas (7.5 acres), used for two-crop agricultural practices, such as rice and wheat, as well as vegetable cultivation. There are not many people in government jobs in the village, and like many other villages in Bihar, several individuals from Karpoori Gram work in private firms outside the state. However, what sets Karpoori Gram apart is its role as a hub for stone chips. Stone chips are collected from Jharkhand and brought to Karpoori Gram for wholesale and retail purposes. Local markets in the area purchase stone chips from Karpoori Gram to supply to the entire district and adjoining areas of Darbhanga and Vaishali. Arvind Singh says, 'There are over seventy stone chips traders in the village, employing over 300 labourers. Most villagers say almost in unison that whatever the village has today is all because of its association with Karpoori Thakur.'[14]

During the tenure of Bhagwat Jha Azad as the CM of Bihar (from 14 February 1988 to 10 March 1989), he expressed his gratitude to Karpoori Thakur by naming Pitaunjhia village after him in 1988. This was a rare instance in Bihar's political history where any chief minister's village is named after him, especially considering that Thakur was from a rival political camp and responsible for demystifying Congress and demonstrating a people friendly non-Congress government run by non-traditional upper-caste chief ministers. Notably, even the first CM of Bihar and a prominent Congress leader, Dr Sri Krishna Singh, did not receive such an honour.

In a sense, Karpoori Thakur was *Ajatshatru* (whose enemy is not born), a term often used for former PM Atal Behari Vajpayee for his acceptability across party lines. RJD state president Jagdanand Singh, who had started his political innings under Karpoori's guidance, says: 'Naming his village after Karpoori Thakur is not a big deal for a man who inspired a generation of socialist leaders and was the fulcrum of socialist movement in Bihar. But a Congress CM giving this honour does show how Karpoori Thakur was in the hearts of his opponents as well.'[15]

Any political yatra in Bihar these days usually begins from one of three significant places—Bhithiharwa Ashram of Mahatma Gandhi in West Champaran, Jayaprakash Narayan's Sitab Diara village in Saran, or Karpoori Thakur's hometown in Samastipur. These places hold significant historical and political significance in Bihar and are often chosen as starting points for political campaigns and yatras. The election strategist Prashant Kishore also followed this tradition while entering politics.

Karpoori Gram, however, has its share of woes—some upper-caste families are in denial and refuse to give Karpoori his due; they still use Pitaunjhia in their postal address.

2

Saraswati, Triveni and the Freedom Struggle

On the Edge of a Social Razor

An azure river flows silently,
Saraswati she is, unseen but ever dolorous,
In remembrance, as if the past has slipped away,
No knowledge, no concern for any, it seems.
Pressed to fade away, to retreat and fold,
From all sides, now she gathers herself,
She keeps flowing silently.
. . . Kissed every hand that moistened itself in her stream,
Deceived, she watched as the traveller departed,
Having sipped the water, the pilgrim rose,
When will they pause, by the riverside?
Preoccupied they are with the concern of the journey and the search
*   for destinations,*
Rivers merely quench thirst; they absorb the weariness of the voyage,
*   rejuvenating by drawing upon it,*

And for those departing, they cling with affection, knowing that they
will return, to embark once again . . . (translated from Hindi)
                    —Aparna Anekvarna, *Nadi Chupchap Bahti Hai*

Nothing can describe the life journey of Swami Sahajanand
Saraswati better than this poem. But more about his journey a
bit later.

                              * * *

Hardly had the boy Kapoori taken to writing sentences on his slate,
than his parents, Gokul Thakur and Ramdulari Devi, decided to
get him married to a Muzaffarpur girl. Though his official age at
that time was six, Thakur had himself admitted in an interview
after becoming CM that he was originally born in 1919. So, he was
11 at the time of his wedding, His bride was a nine-year-old girl,
Phuleshwari, from Chandanpatti village of Sakra, Muzaffarpur.

Kapoori hardly remembered any details of his wedding in
1932, except the fact that his bride was draped in a red saree and
he had worn a yellow dhoti and kurta. A few bullock carts had
taken the wedding party to Chandanpatti. He had enjoyed the
ride, sitting in front of one of the bullock carts. The bullocks
pulling his cart were adorned with bells, which kept chiming
through the bumpy ride to Sakra. Child marriage was prevalent
in those days—more so among the children of the poor.

Phuleshwari was brought to Pitaunjhia just for a few days
after the wedding. She would be veiled during the post-wedding
rituals. She returned to her parents' home where she lived for
three years. It was a normal practice to delay the cohabitation
of the bride and bridegroom in case of child marriage until both
attained puberty. *Gouna* or the post-wedding function is a social

ritual during which a bride is brought from her village to finally live with her husband. Phuleshwari started living in her marital home from 1935 onwards.

Kapoori was highly displeased with the idea of getting married at such a young age but there was no way he could have rebelled against his parents as it meant challenging the social order prevalent in the village.

Kapoori had been studying in the village primary school. But he had been trying to persuade his father to find a better school. It was January 1934, the beginning of the new academic year. Gokul asked his son to wait till 14 January—Makar Sankranti, to begin something auspicious. On 15 January, Kapoori, holding his father's hand, excitedly walked a distance of 8 km to Tajpur, a sleepy town that would play an important role in his political destiny.

After being interviewed by the school principal, he was admitted to Class 6 at BME (Boys Middle English) School, Tajpur. His daily routine would now include a 16-km walk. The child would start at 6 a.m. for school after a quick breakfast of mostly stale bread with salt and green chilli, and the occasional raw mango pickle. No one carried a tiffin to school in those days. Kapoori would at times keep some puffed rice and roasted gram in his school bag to sustain himself throughout the day.

He had moved on from slate to paper and pencil and had started enjoying his studies. His other siblings had no interest in studies, even though he had interesting stories to tell them every day about his day at school.

Gokul Thakur was both happy and sad, happy because his son was enjoying his studies, sad because the lad had to walk 16 km every day, barefoot. Back from school, he would assist his family in grazing the cows. At times, he would help his father by carrying bags during *bartuhari* (match-making), *tilak* (a pre-wedding function) or the wedding function. In moments of leisure, he would go swimming in the village pond with his friends. His uncle, Dhrupad Thakur (cousin of Gokul Thakur), used to assist Kapoori financially to pursue his education. Dhrupad was very fond of the talented boy in the family.

It was January 1935. Vishnudev Rajak writes, 'A puny boy in a simple half dhoti-kurta came with his rustic guardian to enter the seventh class. Round face, fair complexion, full body and small size, there was happiness on his face and curiosity in his eyes,'[1] He had come to seek admission in Class 7 at Tirhut Academy, Samastipur, 7.3 km from Pitaunjhia.

This new school had a great reputation in the area. It had been opened with the help of public cooperation to offer quality education, unlike sundry government schools. Harinandan Prasad, a teacher at the school, observed Kapoori, who looked focused. Rajak writes: 'A new change began to become apparent. A newness started coming in Kapoori's practice, activity, music, society, talk, thought, reading and thinking.'[2]

Harinandan Prasad was deeply impressed with Kapoori's dedication and intelligence. He came to know of the long distance the boy had to trudge every day. Moved by his circumstances, the teacher requested the headmaster to allot Kapoori a seat in the school hostel. Prasad volunteered to pay the hostel fees on behalf of the boy.

Soon, Kapoori became the talk of the hostel. Instead of playing on the school grounds like other boys, Kapoori began holding meetings with like-minded boys. His teacher sensed that a leader was taking his baby steps. He would often tell Kapoori to focus on his studies and get a government job. But Kapoori wasn't interested. The feeling of patriotism was rising in his mind.

He started reading the works of famous Hindi writers, Ramdhari Singh Dinkar, Shivpujan Sahay, Gopal Singh Nepali, Dehati Sahridaya and Collector Singh Keshari. He had already started composing poems filled with nationalistic fervour, besides the pain of the common man and the struggle of the farmer.

Kapoori was caught between the social churn and the freedom movement. His tender mind was absorbing it all, shaping his thought process.

The Unquiet Flow of the Saraswati

Jeffrey Witsoe writes: 'By the 1920s, a rival faction emerged within the Bhumihar Brahmin Sabha led by Swami Sahajanand Saraswati, presented the interest of tenants. Sahajanand came to believe that the rich (caste associations) used to strengthen their hold on the community in order to mobilize numerical support to realize their own ends.'[3]

One of the key movements that gave some momentum and direction to the Indian freedom movement and galvanized farmers was the Kisan Sabha Movement. A young man from Ghajipur, UP, Naurang Rai, who later became famous as Swami Sahajanand Saraswati, had formed the Bihar Provincial Kisan Sabha in 1929 to address the grievances of farmers against the landlords who attacked their tenants to get them to vacate the land they tilled. The seed of the Bakasht (self-cultivated) movement was already sown.

Noted author Sho Kuwajima writes about how the leading freedom fighter and farmers' leader Pandit Jadunandan Sharma spoke about the Bakasht movement getting its inspiration from the awakening that gripped farmers across villages. 'This village consciousness worked effectively in the Bakasht struggle against the zamindars in the 1930s, but led him (Jadunandan Sharma) to observe the rural situation as the matter of the government versus the kisans, rather than attending to how the contradiction between the social and economic strata changed after the zamindari abolition.'[4] Sharma also wrote that the fact that Adolf Hitler made peasants a part of his forces also gave some idea about the power of farmers.

In 1935, Sahajanand formally launched the Bakasht Movement to get ownership of self-cultivated land, capturing the imagination of farmers and youth. The movement was launched in Bihar in 1937–38. Sahajanand's farmers' movement owed its genesis to three incidents. He was deeply moved by the death of a seventy-year-old ploughman employed by a Ghazipur landlord. The dead man 'had only a loincloth around his waist!' Another incident that shook him to the core took place in Chakai (Jamui). Sahajanand learnt that 'Tribal Santhals would have to mortgage their land and finally lose it to Banias' and 'this way they were reduced to the position of ploughmen for the Banias'. The third incident, which perhaps forced Saraswati to do something for the cause of the farmers, occurred in Begusarai where he saw 'a dead body on a broken cot, covered only in rags, being taken to Ganga. But there was no wood for burning the body, only a handful of rotten wood . . .'[5]

It is true that Mahatma Gandhi's historic Champaran movement took place in North Bihar. But Gandhi's movement could not inspire peasants elsewhere in Bihar. Ashwani Kumar writes, 'In contrast, the Kisan Sabha led by radical Hindu monk Swami Sahajanand was strongest in the region of Central Bihar. One of the factors in the rise of Kisan Sabha in Central Bihar was the extreme exploitation by zamindars of their tenants. In Bhojpur, the peasant movement has a long history from spontaneous outbursts to organized agrarian struggles.'[6] Saraswati made the small town of Bihta the nerve centre of his movement in Bihar.

Author Arvind Narayan Das says: 'Peasant movements in Bhojpur have gone from the leadership of the zamindars to that of Junker to that of kulaks and finally that of poor peasants, all within one century.'[7]

By the end of 1927, Sahajanand became fully aware of the extent of zamindari atrocities. Witsoe writes, 'By 1929, Saraswati's increasingly radical promotion of tenants' interests inspired him to form the Kisan Sabha. The Kisan Sabha spearheaded one of the most direct peasant movements in late colonial India and represented the most direct threat to the zamindari system.'[8]

The Kisan Movement led to the introduction of the Tenancy Bill in the provincial assembly in the coming years. By the end of 1933, a number of protests by farmers made both landlords and the government jittery. Several Congress leaders, who had been opposing Sahajanand, however, had been unable to organize meetings and get support from farmers.

It was emerging Congress leader Sri Krishna Singh, who first lent support to Sahajanand's movement after coming out of jail in 1933. He said: 'This movement shows that the province is alive and can achieve anything.'

But Sahajanand was utterly dismayed by and disappointed with Mahatma Gandhi's understanding of his movement. 'His (Gandhiji's) suggestions that, "seminars would redress the grievances of farmers; the (Darbhanga) Maharaja's manager is a Congressman and would therefore certainly ease their miseries", amazed me. Gandhiji's ignorance of the way in which the machinery of the zamindars worked was appalling! He had no knowledge of the manner in which they crushed the kisans;

he did not know at all! How can anyone, simply because he is a Congressman, change the whole zamindar apparatus of oppression? He will rather become a part of apparatus. Even this fact Gandhiji did not understand. I have watched thousands of Congressmen contributing to ruin of kisans. But Gandhiji was not aware of this . . .'[9]

Francine R. Frankel and M.S.A. Rao wrote about the social churn and explained how the Congress Socialist Party (CSP) betrayed Swami Sahajanand Saraswati: 'The CSP put the nationalist movement above left unity, deserted Sahajanand as a faction leader and set up its own Kisan Sabha in 1941.'[10]

As a result, the Communist Party of India (CPI) became the dominant group in the Bihar Pradesh Kisan Sangathan (BPKS) organisation. Sahajanand agreed to suspend the agrarian agitation so that the government 'would not have to divert its energies from prosecuting the war to contend with local strife.'[11] Sahajanand isolated himself from the nationalist movement at this point and the socialists took over.

Jeffrey Witsoe explains why the Kisan Movement of Sahajanand did not get the desired success: '. . . despite legacy of Kisan Sabha, an assertive peasant politics never emerged as a powerful force in Bihar politics after Independence. Kisan Sabha, however, was instrumental in eventual abolition of the zamindari system, with the legislation passed under SK Sinha, a Bhumihar chief minister who had also been the leader within the Bhumihar Brahmin Sabha, becoming the general secretary of the Kisan Sabha and then joining the Congress party. In the process, the structure of the post colonial state was transformed.'[12]

Witsoe believed that it 'created new mytho history, new pattern of behavior'. 'But such movements', he reasoned, 'did not pose a broad-based challenge to either the zamindari system or to the dominance of the twice born'.[13] Another reason for the failure of colonial caste movements was the funding of some caste associations by landlords, who had been close to the ruling establishment.

Arvind N. Das gives a vivid description of the presentation of the Zamindari Abolition Bill in the Provincial Assembly. 'Despite heavy resistance from landlords, including the raja of Ramgarh, the final act of introduction of the zamindari abolition bill in the provincial assembly provided the climax. Days before the big event (revenue minister) KB Sahay was run over by a truck, allegedly hired by the Raja of Ramgarh who was not only ideologically opposed to the abolition of zamindari for obvious reasons but also nursed a long-term feud with Sahay. The revenue minister having been incapacitated, there was a problem about who would introduce the bill. The finance minister, AN Sinha, himself a zamindar, was reluctant to do so and even the premier (prime minister) Sri Krishna Sinha, who represented both petty zamindari and Bhumihar junker-kulak interests, was not very enthusiastic despite having been one of the founders of the Kisan Sabha. The Assembly met in Ranchi which was Bihar's summer capital in those days and in the visitors' gallery sat the doughty Sanyasi Swami Sahajanand Saraswati himself. After much filibustering by articulate landlords, the moment came for the introduction of the bill. Even as ministers rose to deputies for their injured colleague, KB Sahay, swathed in blood-stained bandages, made a dramatic entry.'[14]

In sharp contrast to how modern writers like Jeffrey Witsoe interpreted the farmers' movement, Arvind N. Das calls the history of the nationalist struggle in Bihar as 'the history of the peasants' movement on whose back constitutionalist politicians rode to power and began their loaves and fishes of governance'.[15]

He reasoned: 'The character of Champaran Satyagrah and the apparent dominance of Bihar Pradesh Congress Committee during the pre-Independence period by "Gandhians" who were opposed to agrarian reform may also contribute to the impression that the destiny of Bihar was shaped by babus and zamindars and that the peasants had little to do with it. The truth, however, is that the peasants of Bihar were not passive; they organised the strongest Kisan Sabha in any province of India and struggled to dismantle the Permanent Settlement. But peasants in Bihar, as elsewhere, are not a homogenous and undifferentiated class: one section of the peasantry struggled up to the time of zamindari abolition and quite another section is in revolt today.'[16]

Social scientist Ashwani Kumar argues that 'in the 1980s and 1990s that agrarianism has moved deeper yet, in social terms, in those very districts of Central Bihar which where most active and most successful in the 1930s, namely old Patna, Gaya, Shahabad and Munger districts. In an interview with Smitha Kothari in 1986, Dr Vinayan, the founder of the Mazdoor Kisan Sangram Samiti (MKKS) and then underground, attributed the origins of the MKKS and the success of peasant activism in the Central Bihar districts to the force of earlier movements.'[17]

Besides, the report from the 'flaming fields' of Bihar, the most complete CPI (ML) treatment of peasant activism in the 1980s begins its story with a consideration of Sahajanand and the Kisan Sabha in the 1930s.

A large number of farmers took part in the Civil Disobedience Movement of 1930. In 1931, the Congress passed some resolutions. Jawaharlal Nehru wanted to turn the Congress in favour of the farmers and workers. But the failure of the Civil Disobedience Movement greatly discouraged the youth of India.

Some youths of Bihar took the initiative in this direction and founded the Bihar Socialist Party in 1931 under the leadership of Ganga Sharan Singh, on the lines of the Samajwadi Party of Punjab and the Labour Party of Bengal. It was founded in Patna's Anjuman Islamia Hall. Professor Abdul Bari was made its chairman. Ganga Sharan Singh, Phoolan Prasad Verma and Rahul Sankrityayan became its secretaries. Apart from these leaders, Baldev Sahai, Ambika Kant Singh, Jamuna Karji, Dhanraj Sharma, Ramvriksha Benipuri, Ramdin Sharma, Avadheshwar Prasad Sinha, Basavan Singh (he also used Sinha) and Kishori Prasanna Sinha were also instrumental in the establishment of this party.

The socialist movement first started in Bihar and spread through the Bakasht movement. It was only after Bihar that the socialist movement spread to other parts of the country. Not only could Acharya Narendra Dev, Jayaprakash Narayan and Ramanandan Mishra produce the desired impact, Bihar was at the centre of Dr Lohia's political activism. In Bihar, only politics can be effective in creating mass mobilization by launching an ideological movement against the disparity of ideas among the masses.

Om Prakash Deepak wrote in *Dinman* in 1972: 'In the socialist movement, Lohia tried to create new power centres of the socialist movement by formulating the principle of special opportunity for backward groups. But its effect was mainly in Bihar itself. The character of the party did not change in other states. Perhaps this is the reason why the impact of the socialist movement in Bihar is most widespread and deep.'[18]

The present Scheduled Caste community, emboldened by the 'Poona Pact' of 1932, saw a leader like Jagjivan Ram from Bihar while Dr B.R. Ambedkar had already emerged as a national leader of Dalits. Ram formed the 'Khet-Mazdoor Sabha'.

Sahajanand regretted in his autobiography that his 'efforts to bring about an amicable and peaceful settlement between the zamindars and the kisans and to reform the zamindari system' confirmed his belief that it was a futile endeavour.

Two groups had become prominent in the Congress—one Bhumihar group whose leader was CM Dr Sri Krishna Singh and the other group operated by Dr Rajendra Prasad and Anugrah Narayan Singh. The caste equation of individual and personal leadership was present in the Congress of Bihar at that time. In both these groups, Anugrah Narayan Singh was a supporter of the interests of the landlords. They could not accept the Kisan Sabha Movement.

Walter Hauser and Kailash Chandra Jha write, 'Jayaprakash Narayan was a founding member of the Congress Socialist Party in 1934, and worked closely with Sahajanand at the organizational level in the Bihar Provincial Kisan Sabha until issues of war and national politics drove a wedge between them in 1940. And finally, Karpoori Thakur, (was) the only one of this group of informants who was explicitly of a post-1947 generation. As the Janata Party Chief Minister of Bihar in 1978-79, among other issues, his focus was heavily on the social, but also on the agrarian.'[19]

But Sahajanand's struggle continued unabated. Famous Hindi litterateur Fanishwar Nath Renu in his reportage '*Naya Savere Ki Aasha* (Hope of a new morning)' in January 1950, wrote about a farmers' delegation he had led from his Purnia village to Patna, 261 km away, on 25 November 1949, which was addressed by Jayaprakash Narayan. Renu had set out on foot with 550 farmers from Purnia on 13 November and arrived in Patna on the morning of the rally. Renu quotes Gandhian activist Chunni Das in his reportage: 'The landlord neither brings rain nor increases the crop yield. Then what kind of taxation, what kind of treasure?

The land cultivators have no rights, the poor have no food in their bellies, and there are no clothes on their bodies. People have spread rumours that the sun has risen.'[20]

Shri Sitaram Ashram, Bihta

Shri Sitaram Ashram at Bihta near Patna continues to bring back memories of Swami Sahajanand Saraswati, lest we forget.

Shri Sitaram Ashram at Bihta, a small town barely 30 km from the state capital of Bihar, is situated at the cusp of Patna and Shahabad regions, which was a hotbed of conflict between farmers and landlords. A young Swami from Ghazipur set up the ashram on a plot of donated land in 1927 to galvanize farmers against exploitation by landlords. The ashram provided a base for the West Patna Kisan Sabha (1927), Bihar Provincial Kisan Sabha (1929) and the All India Kisan Sabha (1936). Apart from influencing leaders like Dr Sri Krishna Singh and Krishna Ballabh (K.B.) Sahay, he also left a deep impact on socialist leaders like Karpoori Thakur, Ramanand Tiwari and Kapildeo Singh. Though Karpoori Thakur had not passed his Class 10 board examination, he had started influencing farmers and mobilizing them against local landlords in Darbhanga, Begusarai and, in later years, in Barahiya Taal of Patna, along with Kapildeo Singh.

A two-storey building, measuring 10 feet by 8 feet on each floor was all that Saraswati needed for himself. A pair of *khadaun* (wooden slippers), a pen, a watch, a pair of spectacles and over half-a-dozen brass utensils were all that he left behind as his physical legacy. A memorial to him has been created very close to what was once his work area. He was buried as per the customs of his sect. A statue of the Swami has been placed just above the mounted cement structure marking his burial place.

The entire ashram has been decorated with the Swami's quotes and what some of his leading compatriots had said about him and the farmers' movement. Over two dozen photographs on display show Saraswati with some of the leading personalities from his time—Kishori Prasanna Singh, Subhas Chandra Bose, etc. The Swami's condolence message on the assassination of Mahatma Gandhi, written on 31 January 1948, reads: 'Let us take this assassination as the signal of the ascendant hydra-headed monster of religious fanaticism and religio-cultural hysteria determined to triumph at whatever cost, and resolve not to lose our balance . . .'

Another letter written by Subhas Chandra Bose on 10 May 1939, says: 'The Forward Bloc must be a mass party and it should be the rallying centre of the Leftist elements in the Congress. If Forward Bloc grows according to my idea, it should ultimately become the political expression of the Indian peasantry. I count upon the Kisan organisations' support.' Jayaprakash Narayan, on 16 November 1947, wrote to Saraswati in Hindi: 'I hold that clubbing smaller Left parties would not pave the way for Left consolidation. With whatever experience I have, I can conclude that Left parties cannot unite. It is possible only if one among such parties takes the lead and assimilates others into it . . .' Some other rare letters on display are from Dr Rajendra Prasad, Pandit Jawaharlal Nehru, Dr Sri Krishna Singh and renowned Hindi poet Nagarjun.

One quote from Swami Sahajanand Saraswati refers to his conversation with Prime Minister Jawaharlal Nehru: 'When Patna had a couple of demonstrations which were attended by lakhs of farmers, the PM asked me to be cautious of this mob. I kept mum but thought to myself that once they used to address a group of farmers as "mass" but the same mass has become "a mob". Farmers were mob earlier too. In between, they became "mass" for some (political) reasons and they are back to being a mob again. It is because they (the government) do not need farmers anymore . . .'

In another quote, the Swami reacts to a common allegation that he galvanized only Bhumihars. 'I do not organize Bhumihars but want people to revolt against shackles of *purohiti paakhand* (Brahminical pretensions).'

The man behind the metamorphosis of the Shri Sitaram Ashram is Dr Satyajeet Kumar Singh, a renowned medical practitioner from Bihar. Dr Singh, who hails from Amhara village near the ashram, says: 'My father Chintaharan Singh was a disciple of Swamiji. I have grown up listening to Swami's stories. When I took over the management of the ashram trust as its secretary in 2014, the building was in a dilapidated condition. I got the entire structure refurbished while retaining the original architecture.'[21]

The ashram now runs a part-time school, Khel Kendra, for personality development through extracurricular activities. Dr Singh says, 'About 150-175 girls and boys from age of 6-14 years have been attending the Khel Kendra (play centre) after school from 3 pm and 6 pm since May 2023. They are given lessons in language, social and environment science, basic mathematics, computers and fine arts in groups to enhance their mental ability. They have shown tremendous improvement in their persona and abilities in expressions and performances in various aspects. Most important these children growing in huts on embankments and slums are looking happy.'[22] The way in which some of the local girls, Muskan, Priti and Nafisa, tried to speak English and organized their team to sing the national anthem showed a marked change in their personality. All of them were happy to sit on plastic mats in their class as a recall to the *gurukul* system (a type of education in ancient India in which disciples lives near or with the teacher in the same house).

Kailash Chandra Jha, who co-authored the English translation of Swami Sahajanand Saraswati's autobiography with Walter Hauser, has been in charge of research materials on the life and times of Sahajanand (1889–1950). The ashram now plans to open a physical and digital library to help researchers and academicians. Rare manuscripts and his correspondence with contemporary leaders, showing his agreement or disagreement with them, can also be accessed at the library. Walter Hauser returned all manuscripts and other documents in July 2018.

Jha recounts two anecdotes about Karpoori Thakur narrated to him by Hauser: 'Walter Hauser and Karpoori Thakur were close friends and Hauser would often meet Thakur during his Bihta stay. Once, Hauser said how Karpoori Thakur loved to eat boiled eggs. During a breakfast meeting, Karpoori was gulping eggs down; Hauser later imitated Karpoori's style of eating. In the second anecdote, Hauser had told me how Thakur would stay at the home of his close friend and Patna University's Sociology professor Gopi Krishna Prasad to take a break from his busy schedule as CM between 1977 and 1979 without informing anyone.'[23]

Anish Ankur, cultural activist and one of the trustees of the Bihta Ashram Trust, gives a rare insight into the connection between Sahajanand Saraswati and Karpoori Thakur. 'Unlike several socialists who were opposed to Saraswati's farmers' movement, Karpoori Thakur directly came from the stream of the Bakasht Movement led by Saraswati. Karpoori Thakur became a mass leader by leading the farmers' movement.'[24]

Though the ashram does not take active part in the farmers' agitation now, it provides a forum to the farmers where they can voice their concerns and facilitates training for farmers in new agricultural techniques. One thing that saddens the ashram trustees is some people's attempts to attach caste to the Swami in an effort to further their politics. The ashram has a common refrain: 'Just as farmers have no caste, Swami Sahajanand Saraswati is casteless.' Unfortunately, all efforts of Sahajanand to remain casteless were overshadowed by putting the tag of his caste 'Bhumihar' on him.

Triveni Goes with the Flow

Paapin ke paap nashay, traash yamdutan ke,
Bhav-ruj-parivar nashay dhar Triveni ke,
Tihi bhanti traash naashay dusht anyayiyon ke,
Gire ko uthawe nit Sangh Triveni ke

(The sharp edge of Triveni Sangh's swords will destroy the sin of sinners and perpetrators and their families and kill those who do injustice. Triveni Sangh helps in making the fallen rise every day.)[25]

This was the theme song of Triveni Sangh, the first major association of castes in Bihar.

Just as the mythological river Saraswati loses its existence at the confluence of the Ganga and Jamuna at Prayagraj, Sahajanand Saraswati's movement loses its steam to the social churn that was dominated by caste associations and their group formations. There are farmers in every caste but farmers have no caste. Yet, the message of Swami Sahajanand Saraswati continued to have its undercurrent like the mythological river in some form or the other. The fact that farmers are still not united is reflective of caste dominating everything else.

One such dominant group of castes was Triveni Sangh, which was an association of three prominent OBCs—Yadav, Koeri and Kurmi. It came up at Karahgar in Shahabad district on 30 May 1933. Its founder members were Choudhary J.N.P. Mehta, Sardar Jagdeo Singh Yadav and Shivpujan Singh. The whole idea was to make a composite group that would work towards resisting the oppression of farmers and workers from the lower castes by the upper castes and also work for social recognition and the political share of OBCs, lower OBCs and Dalits. Triveni Sangh's tagline was: '*Sanghe Shakti Kaliyuge* (Being united is the only strength in times of Kaliyug).'

In its first bid for assertion, Triveni Sangh submitted a list of OBC leaders to recommend them as Congress nominees for the 1937 Assembly polls. Dr Rajendra Prasad was in charge of ticket distribution. The Congress party did not concede the demand, which strengthened the impression of Congress being a party of upper-caste elites. Finally, Triveni Sangh decided to contest the polls with whatever means they had. Triveni Sangh could not win any seat against the mighty Congress but they got some measure of support even in the face of loss. Caste tensions were also reported at some places in a clear suggestion of Triveni Sangh starting to play the role of a social catalyst.

In 1939, Triveni Sangh contested the Shahabad district board polls by fielding twenty-one candidates. It tasted its first electoral success as four of its candidates, three Kurmis and a Yadav, won.

Triveni Sangh lost its steam by 1942–43 after the Congress co-opted several of its leaders. Finally, the Sangh merged with M.N. Roy's Radical Democratic Party (RDP) in 1945. Prasanna Kumar Choudhary and Shrikant write, 'Seldom did Triveni Sangh launch any campaign against the Congress, nor did it take part in the freedom movement. It only showed great respect for top Congress leaders. Its many workers were associated with Congress and would take part in its activities with great enthusiasm.'[26]

As Sahajanand's Kisan Sabha was dominated by upper-caste leaders, Triveni Sangh never gelled with it. Had Sahajanand and Triveni Sangh come together, the farmers' movement would have got greater backing from farmers and tillers from OBCs and lower OBCs.

Some of the top leaders of the Triveni Sangh were Dasu Singh, who won on a Congress ticket from the Naubatpur Assembly in the 1962 polls; Navdeep Chandra Ghosh, who became the founder chairman of the Bihar Rajya Pichhda Varg Sangh; Ganpati Mandal, Yadunandan Mahto, Devgan Prasad Singh and Nand Kishore Singh. Yet, Triveni Sangh contributed directly or indirectly to the socialist movement, led by the trio of Acharya Narendra Dev, Jayaprakash Narayan and Dr Rammanohar Lohia.

The first precursor of caste assertion and the formation of a group of castes like Triveni Sangh and also the beginning of an organized farmers' movement was the Lakhochak incident on 26 May 1925, in Munger. During the Lakhochak incident, a group of OBCs and Dalit labourers protested against the oppressive practices of the upper-caste landlords. The protestors were demanding fair wages and an end to caste-based discrimination. To suppress such demands, the landlords, who belonged to the upper caste, unleashed a violent attack on the gathering and massacred a large number of OBC and Dalit protestors. Earlier, the Hathitola incident in Maner (Patna) in 1899 was the first recorded incident of mass killings of OBCs and Dalits by the upper castes to prevent the wearing of the sacred thread by OBCs and Dalits.

Caste Considerations

In 1894, after the British government dubbed Kurmis as a criminal caste and barred them from police jobs, Kurmis claimed to belong to the Kshatriya (warrior-noble) caste. They formed the All India Kurmi Mahasabha (Sadar Kurmi Kshatriya Sabha) and held its first session in 1894 to raise their social and political status. The Kurmi Sabha decided to challenge the order of the colonial government, which debarred Kurmis from being recruited into the colonial police service.

The politicization of Kurmis led to the gradual expansion of the Kurmi caste. Soon, the Awadhiyas of Patna, the Dhanuks of North Bihar and the Mahtos of Chotanagpur started calling themselves Kurmis, disregarding social and ritual restrictions.

The Yadavs also attempted to raise their social status in the caste hierarchy in the 1890s. Their attachment to Lord Krishna took them to Vaishnava ideas. Gradually, they claimed to be placed in the Kshatriya varna and adopted the surname 'Yadav,' leading them to drop their current surnames such as Ahir, Gope, Rai, Bhagat and Choudhary.

The biggest blow to caste unity came in 1901, when British colonial administrator H.H. Risley tried to make a list on the basis of caste social stratification, in which Scheduled Castes and Scheduled Tribes were shown separately. While the feeling of high and low became the subject of mockery or attacks in society, in the other community, it created awareness and consciousness of dignity.

Neha Ranjan writes, 'Risley also felt that the fight for caste supremacy would leave a legacy that would form the basis of political and social agitation in the future. As a result, in all subsequent censuses, on the basis of various historical grounds and hypothesized facts, their respective castes would be classified as higher classes. There was a flood in the attempts to get them enumerated and not to be enumerated by the opponents.'[27]

The Koeris or Kushwahas, who were horticulturists, also attempted to attain higher social status by claiming to be the descendants of Lord Ram's son, Kush. They formed the Kushwaha Kshatriya Mahasabha as their nodal caste association and held the first session of the association in March 1922. Several historians, however, call it a trend of appropriating icons from higher castes in a bid to raise one's social or caste status.

The formation of the Akhil Bhartiya Kurmi Sabha led to the formation of many such caste assemblies in subsequent years, until the 1920s. While all such caste assemblies as Gope Sabha and Hitkarini Sabha were primarily against landlords, they also started wearing sacred threads like the upper caste and started bowing to them as before. Both OBCs and lower OBCs started using upper-caste surnames such as Singh, Sinha, Sharma and Pandit. This phase was called the era of 'Sanskritisation' in the social context.

The Yadavs pioneered the formation of caste associations, giving a fillip to the horizontal mobilization of caste. Rasbihari Lal Mandal (father of B.P. Mandal) of Murho, Madhepura, founded Gope Jatiya Sabha in 1910. The All India Yadav Mahasabha came into existence in 1922 to advance the social and political interests of Yadavs. The association made an appeal to Yadavs to refrain from drinking liquor or practising child marriage, dowry, casteism and untouchability. The attempt to seek a higher status in Hindu society led the Yadavs to participate in the prevention of cow-slaughter movement and forge a tenuous agrarian unity with the upper-caste landowning castes in the late nineteenth century. Slowly, the Yadavs came to challenge the dominance of the upper castes, resulting in caste riots against upper-caste zamindars in many parts of Bihar in the early twentieth century.

Prasanna Kumar Choudhary and Shrikant write, '*Janeu* (sacred thread) movement (the phase of Sanskritization when non-upper-caste people had also started wearing the sacred thread to seek parity with the twice-born (Dvija) since the first decade of the twentieth century till the 1930s) was a social movement with definite economic dimensions. Caste-*Lagaan* vs Janeu movement was the distinctive feature of Bihar in those days.'[28]

Even though Bhumihars and Kayasthas enjoyed equal economic and social status as Rajputs and Brahmins, they were clubbed with Vaishyas in earlier censuses. As a result, Bhumihars and Kayasthas started protesting and their protests were not limited just to submitting memorandums to the government; the likes of Sir Ganesh Dutt and Sachchidanand Sinha encouraged their fellow caste people to study English.

The bifurcation of Bihar and Bengal also provided opportunities for social efforts. Naurang Rai, later known as Swami Sahajanand Saraswati, also tried to prove, on the basis of ancient Sanskrit texts, that the Bhumihars actually belonged to the Brahmin class.

First, the Kayasthas in Bihar accepted English education to counter Bengalis who had monopolized government jobs. Among prominent Kayastha leaders, Sachchidanand Sinha, also called the architect of modern Bihar, and Rajendra Prasad (the first president of India), who formed the first student organization in Bihar in 1908, played a key role in getting Kayasthas a place of prominence in government and politics.

The Kayasthas were also frontrunners in the activities of the Congress in Bihar. In the Champaran Satyagrah of 1917, many Kayastha leaders such as Braj Kishore Prasad, Rajendra Prasad, Ram Naumi Prasad and Shambhu Sharan joined hands with

Gandhi. The Kayasthas went on to control the leadership of the Bihar Congress in the pre-Independence era.

However, the influence of Kayasthas in politics came to be increasingly challenged by the Bhumihars and Rajputs, especially after the elections for the local government bodies in the 1920s. The Kayasthas, in a bid to prevent the monopoly of power by the Bhumihars, entered into an informal alliance with the Rajputs. This also laid the foundation for protracted factional struggles in the politics of Bihar.

Social scientist Ashwani Kumar writes, 'Although the political elite came from a narrow social base, they were deeply fragmented leading to vicious intra-elite power conflicts. The effect of caste domination on governmental policy has also been pervasive.'[29]

Unlike the caste associations of the upper castes, the caste associations of the backward castes increasingly raised the demand for socio-economic justice. The formation of the Triveni Sangh, comprising Yadavs, Kurmis and Koeris, in the 1930s was a pointer in this direction whose implication was far-reaching in later years.

Neha Ranjan writes, 'The concept of "class" evolved with capitalism. Only the 1789 French Revolution can be called class conflict. Since Bihar had no big industrialists, it had no capitalists. The basis of class conflict here was clashes between the land owners and labourers.'[30] An easy way to distinguish between the landowner and the landless was through publicly known caste identities.

And herein lies the crux of all human problems, according to writer Kingsley Davis: 'It is the most thorough going attempt known in human history to introduce inequality as the guiding principle in social relationships.'[31]

Dr Rammanohar Lohia also said that Karl Marx tried to eliminate economic classes, without understanding that these classes transform themselves into castes. He said, 'These castes are not as clear and strong as the Indian castes, but they make the classes motionless. Perhaps for the first time in history, an attempt can now be made to break both class and caste together.'[32]

Indian social reformer and journalist Kaka Kalelkar has written that 'Casteism is blind devotion to one's caste which leads to contempt for justice, healthy social values, morality, conscience and feelings of public fraternity.'[33]

Professor of History William R. Pinch says, 'After Independence caste associations change dramatically since Kshatriya identity only had meaning in the context of a colonial political system crafted around visions of martial grandeur.'[34]

Jeffrey Witsoe gives an insight into how the British used the caste divide to the hilt: 'The Raj utilized caste to categorize, rank, criminalize, recruit and divide—in short to govern— colonial subjects. Caste was, therefore, central to colonial "governmentality" and to the government's endeavours to survey, manage and regulate the population under its control.'[35]

Witsoe argued that the 'Raj utilized caste as the glue to connect two spheres of agrarian relations and governmental institutions— the members of dominant castes were given not only effective control over their villages but also privileged access to and support from government institutions.'[36]

When caste crept deep inside the concept of socialism, according to Sachchidanand Sinha, it 'took the form of a sect or a separate sect at the same time when consumerism was engulfing the whole world in the web of economic activities and thus creating new conflicts.'[37]

Indian sociologist and social anthropologist M.N. Srinivas writes, 'The struggle for higher status between structurally neighbouring castes also produced conflict. And in recent years the lower castes have shown an increasing desire to free themselves from the control of the locally dominant caste.'[38]

This is where Dr Rammanohar Lohia's prescription of 'removal of poverty and the politics of caste and religion, open democratic government and dignity and honour for every citizen'[39] seemed difficult.

Author Indumati Kelkar writes, 'The major hurdle in establishing equality is the division of high and low castes; on account of the thousand year old caste system our society is divided and both power and prosperity are concentrated in the hands of a few crore people of high caste. Society should attack it not only socially but also in religious, political and economic spheres so that it is completely shattered. In political assault we should provide opportunity for development through 60 per cent reservation in administrative and public sector not only to Scheduled Castes and Scheduled Tribes but also to women, poor Muslims, backward classes.'[40]

Both the Congress and the British were facing the heat of social upsurge. The Congress leadership also co-opted many prominent backward caste leaders like Devsharan Singh, Bir Chand Patel and Shivnandan Mandal. The alliance of the intermediate castes became a part of Congress politics by 1946.

Bihar has been the playground of the socialist movement. Since the time of Gautam Buddha and Mahavir, Bihar has made every effort to establish an egalitarian society in India. Author Neha Ranjan writes, 'Even in the modern period, socialist ideology gained a lot of emphasis during the national freedom movement. From the very beginning, the goal of the Samajwadi Party was democratic socialism.'[41]

'Navyuvak' in the Freedom Struggle

Kapoori, in high school, composed these lines:

> *"Hum soye watan ko jagane chale hain,*
> *Hum murda dilon ko jalane chale hain.*
> *Garibon ko roti na deti hukumat,*
> *Jalimon se loha bajane chale hain,*
> *Hame aur jyada na chhedo, aye zalim,*
> *Mita denge zulm ke saare nazaare,*
> *Ya mitne ko khud hum diwane chale hain,*
> *Hum soye watan ko jagaane chale hain*

(We have set out to wake up our country from slumber. We have set out to reinvigorate moribund people. We are taking on the establishment that has been denying us bread. Hey perpetrator! Do not provoke us anymore; we will erase scenes of all your terror. Either we will end up fighting or we will wake up our country from slumber.)[42]

Caste feelings baffled Kapoori. It was not easy for Gokul Thakur to forget how a village landlord 'Bachcha Singh had made his son Kapoori fetch 27 buckets of water from a deep well to bathe him when the senior Thakur had taken his boy to the landlord to demand Rs 2 to pay his matriculation examination fee.'[43] But Kapoori perhaps left it to time to settle these things. Vengeance was never his way.

The Quit India Movement was uppermost in his mind. It was one overriding movement over concurrent socialist movements and the farmers' agitation. Kapoori's Navyuvak Sangh was ready. Over fifty youth from Pitaunjhia and adjoining villages were raring to take part in the movement. The winds of change were sweeping across the sleepy village of Pitaunjhia. Gokul Thakur had heard many tales of the Bakasht Movement and the freedom struggle. He would tell his children about how farmers were standing up to landlords for the first time. There were umpteen stories of Mahatma Gandhi. He would also tell his children about the brutal killing of thirty-two people by the British in 1934 at Tarapur, Munger. Later, Pandit Jawaharlal Nehru visited the site at Tarapur, which is now a memorial.

Kapoori grew up listening to these stories. Although he lived in the Tirhut Academy hostel, he continued visiting his paternal village. In 1938, Kapoori was in Class 8. He was doing well in his studies, but even as a student, he wanted to do something for his country. Later, he set up Navyuvak Sangh, an association of village youth, in his village. He also set up a library, where young people could gather to read and discuss relevant topics. The country's freedom struggle was the only topic of discussion. Kapoori loved to deliver speeches as a student leader between 1938 and 1940. His student life coincided with the beginning of the Second World War. Rome had annexed Abyssinia. Germany had usurped Austria. Japan had imposed an unwanted war on China. There was a good collection of literature related to these events in the library of Laheriasarai, Darbhanga. Kapoori used to go there regularly to keep himself abreast of contemporary political events in the country and the world.

The year 1940 was a landmark year for the boy and his family. Kapoori passed the matriculation (Class 10) examination in the second division. But the percentage of marks did not matter as passing matriculation itself was a big feat in those days. Kapoori was the first person in his family, and among a few village youth, to have achieved the feat. Quite excitedly, Gokul Thakur took him to the influential village landlord Bachcha Singh to share the great news. '*Hamro Kapoori matric pass hoy gelay, malik* (Master, my son has passed Class 10).' Nonchalant, the landlord just said, 'Good' and went on to tell Kapoori, '*Pair dabao* (Massage my legs)'. And Kapoori obliged.[44]

Though this anecdote has taken the aspect of folklore, there are many socialist leaders who do not appreciate Kapoori for being so submissive. Senior socialist leader and former MP Shivanand Tiwari says: 'Why did not Karpoori Ji object to massaging the legs of the landlord that day? The message could have gone to the landlord loud and clear that day itself.'[45]

But the social structure of Pitaunjhia village—which had just one Nai family, that too depending on landlords for its livelihood—perhaps did not allow Kapoori to do so. Kapoori believed in assimilation and gradual change rather than relying on aggressive resistance. This is why his version of socialism was more assimilative than divisive.

Kapoori put the 'massage my legs' incident out of his mind and sought admission in the Intermediate at CM College, Darbhanga. He would walk over sixteen kilometres every day (to and fro) to attend his college. He would walk seven kilometres from his village to Muktapur railway station for Darbhanga. He would return the same way after college, reinstating faith in his legs every single day.

Kapoori loved organizing meetings where he would often get a chance to showcase his oratorical skills. In 1938, he established a youth union called Navyuvak Sangh in his village. The upsurge of his patriotism and social service earned him the respect of the community. In 1939, the Indian Club of Samastipur held an essay writing competition for inter-school students. Kapoori won the competition and garnered the attention of his peers and seniors. In March 1940, he volunteered at the Congress convention held at Ramgarh in Hazaribagh. At his college, he was the favourite student of the head of the Hindi department, Pandit Jagannath Prasad Mishra.

Senior journalist Hemant, who covered Karpoori Thakur's tenure as CM, recalls: 'Karpoori Thakur was once told by a friend to travel without tickets. He rebuked his friend for trying to teach him dishonesty and got a monthly travel pass.'[46]

Karpoori passed his Class 12 in the second division. He scored 156 out of 300 marks in two English papers. His son Ramnath Thakur proudly displays his mark sheet, showing the student's name—'Karpoori Thakur' and his marks.

Karpoori got admission in Bachelor of Arts in the same college in 1942. The call of the Quit India Movement beckoned him. He dropped out of his degree course to become a full-time freedom fighter. Gokul Thakur was not too pleased. But he knew that his son could take his own decisions now.

Young Karpoori's idol Rammanohar Lohia had also been catching his imagination as a Congress Socialist Party leader. Jeffrey Witsoe explains in 'Lower Caste Politics as Radical Democracy': 'Rammanohar Lohia, perhaps more than anyone else, influenced the ideology of what came to be known as the "backward caste movement" in north India. Lohia most forcibly articulated the relationship between the socialist political tradition and lower caste movements, recognizing the political potential of the horizontal mobilization of lower castes on issues of social justice and against ritual discrimination.'[47] Lohia rejected Pandit Jawaharlal Nehru's claim that caste inequality would automatically wither away once socialism was established.

But Karpoori was already thinking of the freedom movement. Pitaunjhia's Navyuvak Sangh was ready to throw a challenge to the British.

The upper-caste people of the village watched in disbelief as the boy who had grown up in their backyard slowly grew out of their control. Living on the edge of the social razor, he managed to escape the limits imposed by the razor of his father's profession but adopted its sharpness to use for his future vocation.

3

Krishna Talkies

Making of a Leader

Arre bhagao Is baalak ko,
Hoga ye bhaari utpaati,
Julum mitayenge dharti se,
Iske saathi aur sangaati,
Yah un sabka leader hoga,
Naam chhapega akhbaron mein,
Bade bade milne aayenge,
Bhar-bharkar motorkaron mein
. . . Sabke dukh me dukhi rahega,
Sabke sukh me sukh maanega
Samajhbujh kar hi samta ka,
Asli mudda pahchanega

(Drive away this boy; he will be a big trouble-maker. His friends and associates will erase atrocities from this earth. He will be their leader and his name will appear in newspapers. Big people

49

will come in packed cars to meet him. He will share everyone's pain and happiness. He will identify the real issues with a sense of equality among the people.)[1]

The great Hindi poet Nagarjun might not have written these lines for Karpoori Thakur but his words sound prophetic and close to the life trajectory of Thakur.

'You Are Karpoori, Not Kapoori'

It was sometime in the late 1930s. Renowned socialist leader Pandit Ramnandan Mishra had been invited to speak at a function being held in the auditorium of Krishna Talkies at Samastipur. The students from the BME school in the town had also gone to listen to Mishra. Kapoori was also in the audience. As the boy was already well know to teachers and students for his oratory, the students wanted Kapoori to represent them onstage and say something. Kapoori spoke extempore, leaving the audience spellbound. Pandit Ramnandan Mishra was so impressed with his speech that he called the boy and asked him his name. 'Kapoori,' he said politely. Mishra patted his back and said: 'You are not Kapoori, you are Karpoori. You are the camphor that fills the atmosphere with its overpowering aroma.'[2] Getting a new name based on a Sanskrit word was a rare and unexpected reward to him as Sanskrit-based names were often reserved for upper-caste persons only.

From that day onwards, he was addressed as Karpoori. Kapoori was *passé*. Becoming Karpoori was the first sign of the arrival of a new leader. Mishra, the renowned socialist leader, was his first political mentor.

Karpoori had now been getting direct lessons from school and indirect lessons in politics at a very young age. But then, he remembered having accompanied local leader Satyanarayan Singh (later union minister and governor of Madhya Pradesh) to a salt satyagrah march in 1930. He soon became a member of the INC and took active part in its students' wing activities. 'He started wearing Khadi from student life itself. Despite political activism, Karpoori's studiousness remained uninterrupted. As a result, he often kept getting good marks and scholarships. The amount received from the scholarship was an inexhaustible source for poor Karpoori to continue his studies.'[3]

In 1935, Karpoori became a 14th member (primary member) of the Congress. 'After Jayaprakash Narayan fled from Hazaribagh Jail (in 1942) and also having read his letters to several freedom fighters, Karpoori became a committed soldier of the Congress Socialist Party.'[4]

The Congress won the 1937 provincial elections, thanks to overwhelming support from farmers. Rich landlords were defeated in the polls. Nervous landlords held a meeting in Patna and the infamous Congress–zamindar pact was signed. In response, the Samajwadi Party organized a huge rally of farmers in Patna. The Dalmiyanagar factory saw a workers' strike. The Bakasht movement started across the state to secure the farmers' right to the land they had cultivated for years.

As farm labourers were being persecuted in the villages, farmers were bound to retaliate. Raghuvir Sahay writes, 'Armed with deadly weapons–lances, spears and guns, farm labourers of Jagdishpur village of Darbhanga carried out an organized attack on landlords. A 40-year-old woman and a ten -year-old child were also among the injured.'[5]

Karpoori, now in Class 8, had a rare opportunity to meet all the senior socialist leaders on 3–4 December 1938 during a Provincial Farmers' Conference at Ohni, a village near Pitaunjhia.

Prominent socialist leaders like Acharya Narendra Dev, Mohan Lal Gautam, Rahul Sankrityayan, Pandit Jadunandan Sharma and Ramvriksha Benipuri had come to participate in the conference that resolved that Socialists should take active part in the Bakasht Movement. Karpoori was greatly influenced by the fiery speeches of veteran socialist leaders. On the very first day of the conference, the atmosphere became enthusiastic with the announcement of the Second World War by Britain.

The British rulers of India declared India's participation in the World War as their supporter, but the Congress and the Congress Socialist Party were against India's participation in the war. Yet, India participated in the World War on the advice of Mahatma Gandhi, who looked for a bigger bargain in lieu of their support to Britain in the War. But the British did not concede anything to Indians in return.

1942: The Karpoori Story

In August 1942, Mahatma Gandhi announced the 1942 Quit India Movement. Socialist leaders supported the Movement. But with the arrest of Congress leaders, the movement became leaderless. Author Dr Santosh Kumar writes, 'The socialist leaders, evading arrest, took over the leadership of the movement. Bullets were going on everywhere in Bombay (Mumbai). Socialists began to hold secret meetings. A central governing board was created. The organization work was given to Achyut Patwardhan. Dr Rammanohar Lohia was entrusted with the responsibility of policy making. Jayaprakash Narayan was arrested in Hazaribagh Jail. He, along with his comrades, Ramnandan Mishra, Yogendra Shukla, Suraj Narayan Singh, Gulali and Shaligram escaped from the jail on 10 August. They reached Gaya the next day. It was decided that Jayaprakash, Ramnandan Mishra and Shaligram Dubey would move towards Benares and Yogendra Shukla, Suraj Narayan Singh towards North Bihar.'[6]

A provincial convention of students took place in Darbhanga. Preparations were going on for 9 August. A meeting of the students of CM College (Darbhanga) was also organized. Kamta Prasad Gupta, a freedom fighter and local leader, proposed the name of Karpoori for the chairmanship of the meet. Karpoori gave a call for Satyagrah but the students disagreed as Gandhi had given the slogan of 'Do or Die' for which a peaceful protest might not suffice.

The students might well have disagreed with Karpoori's idea of peaceful protest in a Gandhian manner; they were still deeply impressed with the way Karpoori put across his idea of launching a protest against the British.

Karpoori soon became the undisputed student and youth leader of Darbhanga. He led a huge procession of students in Darbhanga from 10–11 August 1942. The British government took serious note of it and carried out a ruthless lathicharge on a peaceful and unarmed procession of students and youth at Kachahari Chowk in the town. Karpoori escaped the charge of the English brigade but several teenage boys lost their lives, and several others were critically injured. Dr Kumar writes, 'This heart-wrenching and painful incident made the people of the entire Darbhanga district rebel. Railway stations, post offices and all other means of communication were destroyed from the border of Nepal in the north to the banks of the Ganges in the south. The British rule almost came to a standstill in this entire state, but the British oppression started two weeks in an even more frightening manner than before.'[7]

On 14 August, the communication system was disturbed in the Sindhwara area under the leadership of Kulanand Vaidik and Karpoori Thakur. Dr Kumar writes, 'Oil was sprinkled on the Ladha Bridge near Muhammadpur and it was set on fire. The bridge burned for two days and was completely destroyed. Another bridge was also demolished on Rahika Road . . .'[8]

After Jayaprakash Narayan ordered that Azad Dasta would be formed to fight the British, secret offices of the squad were established in every town and district. Suraj Narayan Singh, a resident of Narpat Nagar village of Darbhanga district, was made the head of Bihar State Azad Dasta, a radical and underground organization that sought to carry out operations against the British.

As British operations against protestors intensified, Karpoori had to abscond with other socialists for thirteen months. Professor Pralayankar Bhattacharyya gives a heart-wrenching account of what Karpoori went through while escaping to Nepal. He describes how Karpoori and his friends, after having walked miles without food and water, see hope for life after seeing maize crops. 'Suddenly a river was seen. It was still raining. Some corn plants were seen by the side of a bountiful stream. Life battling with death woke up in hope. Karpoori returned with some corns and peeled them off. But most pearls of corn were rotten and it was not possible to eat them without roasting. . . . The coincidence was favourable. At some distance, a pyre was blazing. The unbearable hunger did not see what was right or wrong. He roasted corn on the funeral pyre and ate them (roughly translated from Hindi description).'[9]

During the chilling Azad Dasta days, Karpoori had vowed that he would not have a child in enslaved India. He kept his word and his first child, Ramnath, was born after Independence.

When the British repression calmed down, Karpoori Thakur returned to Pitaunjhia and became a teacher in the village middle school. It was a pleasant coincidence that he started teaching in the same school in which he had studied.

But the school became a cover for freedom movement activities. Clandestine meetings with leaders like Bashisht Narayan Singh, Ram Bujhawan Singh and Satya Narayan Azad would take place there. They would go from village to village to distribute pamphlets with the message of freedom.

Bhagalpur Jail: A Leader Is Born

It was 23 October 1943. Karpoori and his three friends had slept at the school at night after their daily routine. The police had been tracking them for a few days. A villager from Pitaunjhia, Muneshwar Singh, says, 'At 2 a.m. on the intervening night of 23 and 24 October, the police surrounded the school, woke up the four men and arrested them. They were first kept in Darbhanga jail. As Bashishth Narayan Singh had earlier escaped from Darbhanga jail, they were all shifted to Bhagalpur Camp Jail.'[10]

Karpoori's daily routine in jail included reading the Gita and the Ramayana besides engaging in the worship of Lord Hanuman and taking part in *bhajan–kirtan*, which would take place in the jail almost every day. Karpoori would wear a thick khadi dhoti and half-sleeved kurta.

But mismanagement at the jail, poor quality food, non-allotment of jail uniform and complaints about uncleanliness, gave Karpoori an opportunity to stage a protest. After twenty days of protest with Karpoori hardly eating anything and his condition deteriorating, the jail administration eventually conceded his demands on the twenty-eighth day of the protest. Karpoori became a leader of the prisoners and rose in the estimation of his socialist peers and seniors.

But his father Gokul Thakur was deeply concerned as he had not been getting any news about Karpoori. Ramnath Thakur says, 'In October 1944, when Karyanand Mishra, another leader who was arrested and brought to the gate of Bhagalpur Central Jail, a middle-aged villager came in front of him and said—'Babu, are you also a Swaraji (freedom fighter)? My son is also Swaraji . . . He went on hunger strike for 28 days but survived. I have come to meet him. He is not at all worried about us, but we are worried about him. His name is Karpoori.'[11]

The first thing Karyanand Mishra did in jail was to look for Karpoori Thakur. Prominent socialist leader Basavan Singh helped him meet Karpoori Thakur. 'The form of the first meeting is etched in the mind till date—fair face, stout body, black eyebrows, shiny forehead, broad chest, budding youth. It looked as if Dr Rammanohar Lohia has come in front of me,'[12] Karyanand Mishra later described the meeting.

Karpoori's sacrifice earned him the reverence of not only the political prisoners but also of the criminals in the jail. As everyone got very worried about his health, frail Karpoori was advised to eat meat, fish and eggs to recover fast. The vegetarian man became a non-vegetarian for life.

Karpoori would speak on the Russian Revolution, the French Revolution, India's freedom struggle and the biographies of Lenin, Trotsky and Mao Zedong. He would engage in serious discussions on socialism, communism, capitalism, Dialectical Materialism, Hegel, Marx, Indian philosophy, bourgeois-policy and the origin of family–society–property.

Basavan Singh and Karpoori used to be the foremost speakers in the jail which housed over fifty prisoners, all arrested for taking part in the 1942 movement. In a sense, the Bihar unit of the Socialist Party was largely moulded inside the bars of the Bhagalpur jail by Karpoori Thakur and Basavan Singh.

In November 1945, when Karpoori came out after serving twenty-five months of imprisonment, all the veteran socialist leaders, Jayaprakash Narayan, Ramnandan Mishra, Basavan Singh, Suraj Narayan Singh, Ganga Sharan Singh and Ramvriksha Benipuri started treating Karpoori with parity and respect.

Karpoori was back at the village school, this time as its headmaster. After teaching at the school, he would go home to have food and return to the school. After the school closed for the day, he used to go to Samastipur on foot to teach some students in the evening and return on foot at night. Despite this busy and laborious routine, Karpoori continued to give his active support to the underground activities of the Azad Squad. On the way to Samastipur, he used to meet revolutionaries like Chandrabhanu Mehta and distribute handwritten or cyclostyled bulletins, news and poems on the revolution among the youth of the area.

The Land and the Leader

From 1945 to 1947, he served as minister of the Darbhanga district unit of the Congress Socialist Party. In 1947, he was elevated to the position of prime minister of the Bihar Pradeshik Kisan Sabha. 'Meanwhile, in the interest of poor farmers, he started a movement against Hanuman Bhagat, the landlord of Ilyas Nagar (Samastipur). Hundreds of farmers were put behind bars, but in the end the farmers got thirty-five bighas of land from the landlord. Another thirty-five bighas of land was obtained from the zamindar of Vikrampatti. A total of sixty bighas of land was obtained from the zamindars and distributed among the poor farmers.'[13]

From January 1947 to 1951, the Socialist Party started the organizational movement of the Kisan Sabha and then the Hind Kisan Panchayat. The Bihar incharge of these movements, Pandit Ramnandan Mishra, made Karpoori its provincial secretary and later principal secretary. Karpoori also got an opportunity to travel outside Bihar. He came to know Mishra even more closely and was deeply influenced by his thoughts.

Wherever Karpoori would go, his eloquence, deep knowledge of socialist principles, simplicity, soft-spokenness and sociability impressed intellectuals and illiterate, poor people. He had devised eighteen mantras for an effective speech, which he would call 'Mohini mantras (mantras that would enchant audiences).' People would get inspired to become members of the Socialist Party in the hundreds, filled with enthusiasm. 'Once when a meeting of the party was called at Suryapura village, Karpoori gave a speech on socialism and the objectives of the Socialist Party. Such was the impact that five teachers of Suryapura High School and forty-five people of Suryapura village joined the Socialist Party on the same day.'[14]

After his release from jail, he was made a minister of the Darbhanga district unit of the Congress Socialist Party. Narendra Pathak writes, 'The Kisan Sammelan of Pusa in 1946 further helped to give Karpoori Thakur the image of a leader. Acharya Narendra Dev and JP also participated in this. At that time, most of the peasant leaders of Darbhanga district, who were mostly of the upper castes, had considered Karpoori Thakur as their leader.'[15] Among them were Bashisht Narayan Singh, Rajendra Narayan Sharma, Ramakant Jha, Jagdish Poddar and Ramavatar Sharma.

In 1947, when Dr Lohia established the All India Hind Kisan Panchayat under the leadership of Pandit Ramnandan Mishra, he brought Karpoori Thakur from district politics to provincial politics. Since the central office of the Hind Kisan Panchayat was in Patna itself, Karpoori Thakur participated in it with keen interest. He shone through his outstanding work in the Hind Kisan Panchayat, which later helped him travel to Yugoslavia and Israel to learn new lessons in farming and agro-based industries. After his return, he raised an organization of workers to farm in the same way by going from village to village in Bihar.

It is important to note that by the 1940s, the peasant movement in Bihar had slipped out of the hands of the Congress to socialists and communists. Dr Lohia got a detailed report of the situation of Champaran farmers and got it distributed in every area of Bihar through Karpoori Thakur. This way, Karpoori travelled from village to village and got a chance to see the true picture of the backwardness of Bihar. He wanted to make the peasant movement the basis of his politics so that an egalitarian society could be built on the ruins of the old zamindari system.

The big landowners had started a campaign to evict the poor from their land. Karpoori, along with other socialists, stood up against it. On the one hand, the freedom movement was at its peak; there was a war in the rural areas of Bihar over Bakasht land on the other. The zamindars now feared that steps would be taken towards the abolition of zamindari after Independence. They started grabbing more and more cultivable land. Poor ryots, who had been ploughing the fields for years, were being evicted on flimsy grounds. Karpoori Thakur intensified the Bakasht movement in Darbhanga and Muzaffarpur.

Author Narendra Pathak quotes Naxalite leader Dr Vinayan: 'I think that the social and historical vision of the non-Left socialist stream that developed in India was developed in the Bakasht movement from 1936–37 to 1946–47. It is the result of the political conditions of that period that a person of weak social base like Karpoori Thakur got an opportunity to develop his historical vision. He united the poor castes and made them realize their own strength. He wanted to convert socialism into ground reality. To begin with, everyone must have their own homes.'[16]

From 1948 to 1952, Karpoori Thakur, as the minister of the Bihar Provincial Socialist Party, visited almost every area of Bihar to build members of the Socialist Party. On 17 March 1948, Karpoori led a hunger march organized by the Samajwadi Party at Sakra (Muzaffarpur). His friends, Shiv Nandan Paswan and Raghunath Thakur, had joined the Socialist Party by then. Manjay Lal and Ram Trisha Pandey also joined later. Manjay Lal remained a close confidante of Thakur throughout his life. Shivnandan Paswan even became the deputy speaker of the Bihar Legislative Assembly in 1985. He was also the acting speaker of the Bihar Legislative Assembly in February–March 1989.

Karpoori had established himself as a strong provincial socialist leader by then. At the national level too, his identity began to emerge. He was being noticed by top Socialist leaders, Jayaprakash Narayan and Dr Lohia.

Karpoori was made the first minister of the Samajwadi Party of Darbhanga district of Bihar and then the general secretary. From 1948 to 1953, he also worked as the provincial general secretary of the Samajwadi Party.

Bihar: The Harbinger of the Socialist Movement

In 1934, the meeting of the All India Congress Committee was held in Patna, in which the Chauri-Chaura incident of the Civil Disobedience Movement was discussed. Congress was in a dilemma regarding its future course of action. The Mahatma was also silent. Congress, short on ideas, had grown indifferent.

Under these circumstances, Jayaprakash Narayan organized the All India Socialist Conference on behalf of the Bihar Samajwadi Party in the Anjuman Islamia Hall of Patna on 19 May 1934. Acharya Narendra Dev presided over the meeting with the main objective of presenting new possibilities of Independence. The conference also decided to form an organization of left-oriented youth of all the provinces of India to infuse new energy into the Congress.

Congress Socialist Party, a radical group within the INC, was born with Jayaprakash Narayan, Dr Rammanohar Lohia, Ashok Mehta, Acharya Narendra Dev, Achyut Patwardhan, M.R. Masani, Kamala Devi, Purushottam Vikram Das, Yusuf Mehar Ali and Ganga Sharan Singh as its key leaders. Dr Lohia called the leaders of this phase the 'mirch (chilli) group' and this period the 'ginger era' because of the revolutionary nature of CSP. According to the CSP, the meaning of socialism was not only to change the laws related to the right to property but also to eliminate all the inequalities created against humanity. The party adopted this idea of social and political change from Marx's ideology.

The Bombay (Mumbai) Conference of 21–22 October 1934, after the Patna Conference of Socialists, is of great importance in Indian history. It was at this event that a systematic structure of the party was prepared considering the organizational aspects. In this All India Conference convened under the chairmanship of Dr Sampoornanand, 137 representatives of provincial organizations attended. Before the Patna and Bombay conferences, there were thirteen provincial socialist organizations working all over India, which were tied in a garland to form the Congress Socialist Party in 1934. These thirteen provinces were Bihar, Uttar Pradesh, Gujarat, Bengal, Bombay, Maharashtra, Andhra Pradesh, Kerala, Delhi, Berar, Central Provinces, Utkal and Ajmer.

The ideology of CSP was put forward by JP for its approval in the Ramgarh Congress session of 1940. JP was the secretary of the CSP. Due to some reasons, the draft of CSP presented by JP could not be accepted in the session but Mahatma Gandhi accepted it with conscience and also wrote about it in *Harijan* magazine. Karpoori Thakur had joined the Ramgarh Congress in 1940 as a student leader.

Indian socialism can be divided into two periods—ancient and modern. Dr Lohia called the second period, which started in 1934, the 'real socialist stream'. It can also be divided into four eras—from 1934 to 1946, from 1947 to 1951, from 1952 to 1955 and from 1956 onwards.

But the socialists were disillusioned with the Congress by 1947. At the Kanpur session of 1947, Acharya Narendra Dev's proposal to drop the Congress from the CSP and call it Samajwadi Party was passed unanimously. The annual meeting of the party, held in Nasik in March 1948, decided to completely break away from the Congress because Mahatma Gandhi had also expressed his desire to dissolve the Congress after Independence. By this time, the Congress had become the centre of mutual discord and factionalism.

Immediately after the death of Mahatma Gandhi, the CSP severed its ties with the Congress. The most far-reaching effect of this split was the party being divided into two parts, the right wing and the left wing. CSP established its independent existence as the Socialist Party.

Pandit Jawaharlal Nehru's take on socialism is worth noting. Often taken as the biggest socialist face of the Congress, Nehru did endorse socialism.

The Communist Party of India was formed in December 1925. In 1927, Jawaharlal Nehru participated in the International Congress, organized against colonial repression and imperialism in Brussels, and came in contact with communists and warriors fighting against colonialism all over the world. In the same year, he also visited Russia and was greatly influenced by the new Soviet society. Returning from there, he published a book on the Soviet Union. Sarvepalli Gopal has written that he had returned from Russia as a 'self-conscious revolutionary'.

In the Lahore session of the Congress in 1929, Jawaharlal Nehru declared, 'I am a socialist and a democrat and I do not believe in kings and princes. I also do not believe in the system which gives birth to modern kings in industries. If India is to end its poverty and inequality, it will have to adopt a holistic socialist programme.'[17] He said: 'I have understood that the solution to India's poverty, unemployment and inequality is possible only in the socialist system.'[18]

There is no evidence to suggest what the role of Jawaharlal Nehru was in the formation of the CSP due to the change in his political thinking after his visit and return and his announcement made at the historic conference of Lahore Congress. But it is certain that at the ideological level, it had a deep impact on the young revolutionaries and workers of the Congress, who were between the ages of twenty-five and twenty-eight, and their thoughts were shaped significantly by the socialist ideology.

Pitaunjhia Files

After getting a name change from Kapoori to Karpoori, he was busy bringing a social and political change along the lines of modern ideology of democracy and equality, but there was no sign of change in difficulty either in his personal life or in the thatched house, housing his parents, uncles, and his wife Phuleshwari Devi. Karpoori would walk till Samastipur and catch a train to reach Darbhanga to attend classes at CM College there. His earnings from tuition would sustain his train travel, food and other expenses including expenses relating to political activities.[19]

Phuleshwari had no complaints with ever life she had but Karpoori's sudden arrest on 28 September 1943 brought her untold emotional misery. She went to live with her parents. Worried by the uncertain future of Karpoori, Phuleshwari's father started looking for another man to marry off his daughter as release from jail of the British Raj was not anticipated in foreseeable future. However, she put her foot down and conveyed in clear terms that she would not desert even if it meant living in penury all her life.[20]

4

The Tajpur Tower

The Invincible MLA

I pace upon the battlements and stare
On the foundations of a house, or where
Tree, like a sooty finger, starts from the earth;
And send imagination forth
Under the day's declining beam, and call
Images and memories
From ruin or from ancient trees,
For I would ask a question of them all

—*The Tower*, W.B. Yeats

The results of the first General Elections were announced. It had been Congress all the way, both in the Lok Sabha and Assembly polls. Congress had won forty-seven out of fifty-five Lok Sabha seats. The Socialist Party had won three seats. In the Assembly polls, Congress won 285 out of 330 Assembly seats. The Socialist Party won seventeen seats.

Young socialist leader Karpoori Thakur had won from the Tajpur Assembly segment of Darbhanga, defeating Congress candidate Ramsukumari Devi.

Karpoori Thakur had already been discussed among his rivals for his eloquence. Wearing his usual khadi kurta and dhoti, he made his maiden entry into the Vidhan Sabha. Dr Sri Krishna Singh had taken over as the first chief minister of Bihar. When the young MLA got his chance to speak, he welcomed the CM, addressing him as 'Bihar Keshari (lion of Bihar)' and said: 'Today we are fortunate that freedom fighters fought and got independence from the British. We are also fortunate that the foremost leader of the freedom movement Babu Sri Krishna Singh is today sitting on the throne of Bihar province in independent India. We hope that the leader of this state Shri Babu will run the state in the same way as King Naseeruddin used to run the state and loved all the subjects equally like a son.'[1] The CM was greatly impressed with the young MLA, more so with his humility, knowledge and oratory. From this day onwards, the CM would listen with intent whenever Karpoori would speak and, at times, would also answer his questions.

At a personal level, the acknowledgement from the CM was very touching and rewarding. It was also a kind of poetic justice for Karpoori to represent Tajpur, the place where he studied. Tajpur was dominated by OBCs, Yadavs and Kushwahas. There was hardly any presence of EBC Nai castes in the area. But then, Karpoori had mass appeal from his very first election.

The Tajpur of today is a block-cum-sub-division town of Samastipur. It has sixteen panchayats with sixty-one villages as per the 2011 census. Samastipur is named after a landowner called Samsuddin, a kind-hearted man. Samastipur is also known for a rare example of Hindu–Muslim unity as *Khubni Bibi ka*

Makbara (tomb of Khubni Biwi) is housed in the temple of Lord Shiva near the Morba national highway. It is also a coincidence that BJP leader L.K. Advani was also arrested here by the Lalu Prasad government in 1990 when the BJP leader's rath yatra was stopped. The event changed the political alignments of people and was somehow responsible for socialists having their strong roots in Bihar. Since 1990, Bihar has been ruled by socialist leaders.

When Yogendra Shukla Threatened to Throw Karpoori in the Ganga

Karpoori was almost the unanimous choice for contesting from Tajpur, given his rising popularity. The Socialist Party workers of the Tajpur Assembly constituency under the then Darbhanga district wanted Karpoori Thakur to be their candidate, because they knew that the other potential contenders, Mahendra Narayan Rai, Shatrughan Sharan Singh and Dr Harivansh 'Tarun', could not ensure victory from the seat. Socialist Party's district minister Siyaram Sharma proposed to make Karpoori Thakur the Tajpur candidate.

When Karpoori Thakur came to know about this, he flatly refused the offer, leaving the party workers disappointed. But the state-level meeting of party representatives, held in Jhajha, also unanimously decided to make Karpoori their candidate.

Karpoori Thakur still refused, but the pressure of Yogendra Shukla, a strong freedom fighter and revolutionary leader of the socialist movement, and the soulful instructions of Ramnandan Mishra and Jayaprakash Narayan compelled him to contest the elections. Yogendra Shukla, known for his brashness and use of expletives to show displeasure, told Karpoori Thakur: '(an expletive), I will throw you in the Ganga if you refuse to contest. If you are not interested in contesting polls, why are you in electoral politics?'[2]

Thakur was now convinced. The 'Tajpur train' had left the station.

But Karpoori put a rider that he would not go seeking money from anyone to meet his election expenses. He went only to Prabhavati Devi (wife of JP) who donated five rupees as a blessing. He banked on public support and a bicycle he used during the poll campaign. He filed his nomination with financial support from his friend Shivnandan Agarwal and Bhola Sah of Tajpur. He had some unknown supporters—Bihar workers in the tea gardens of Assam and Tinsukia, leather and iron factories of Calcutta, miners of Jharia and Giridih, petty workers in Katihar, Delhi and Bombay, hotel workers and farm workers from Punjab–Haryana.

On the one hand, there were taxis, motorcycles and cars moving in support of Congress candidate Ramsukumari Devi, wife of Raja Kamakhya Narain Singh, the last ruler of the princely state of Banaili in Samastipur. On the other hand, there was a spontaneous platoon of wobbly cyclists. On the streets, in the villages where Karpoori Thakur went, children, the old, young and women surrounded him and showered their love and blessings upon him.

During the election campaign one day, Rajendra Rai (a Madhopur–Digharua resident), Karpoori Thakur and three or four other workers went campaigning on their cycles. At Sarsauna village, they saw some women pasting *goitha* (dung cake) by the side of the road. Seeing them, Karpoori got off the cycle and urged the women, with folded hands, to vote for him. 'On hearing this, a strong woman brandished her dung-smeared hand towards Thakur in anger and said in her language—"*(an expletive), ihe gobar se tora sabke muh rang debau. Hum apna vote Kapoori ke debay* (Expletive, go away or else I will plaster your face with dung cake. We will vote for Karpoori)" . . . Hearing the woman's words, Thakur smiled and said—"*Maayi, humhi na Karpoori Thakur hatiyau* (Mother, I am Karpoori Thakur). Awestruck and stunned, the village woman grabbed Thakur with her dung-soaked hands and blessed him profusely, assuring him of their support . . .'[3]

Thakurji

Karpoori Thakur, the Socialist Party nominee, defeated Congress stalwart Ramsukumari Devi by 2431 votes. Madhu Limaye compared him with the eminent Marxist leader A.K. Gopalan because at a time when the socialists had been defeated in the elections all over the country, Karpoori Thakur was one of the few socialists who had managed to win.

But there were no wild celebrations at Pitaunjhia. Gokul Thakur was now the father of an MLA. But there was no change in the family's lifestyle. Gokul Thakur continued with his traditional profession. Karpoori's wife Phuleshwari Devi had given birth to a son, who had been named Ramnath by his grandfather. Karpoori was also very happy as his son had been born in independent India—as he had once promised himself during the tumultuous escape from Nepal. Karpoori's mud and thatched house remained the same. Phuleshwari Devi still tended her cows and took her goats out to graze in the village field. People would address their MLA as 'Thakurji', elders and peers would call him 'Karpooriji' or 'Kapooriji'.

In the Vidhan Sabha, Karpoori Thakur emerged as one of the key speakers from the Opposition, along with Suraj Narayan Singh and Basavan Singh. Young Karpoori spoke on subjects ranging from unemployment, corruption, the Damodar Valley

Corporation proposal, the price of sugarcane to the Bhoodan Yagna Bill, unavailability of school textbooks to the Bihar Official Language Bill during his first term as an MLA.

Taking part in the debate on the Bihar Maintenance of Public Order (Amendment) Bill, 1953, on 4 January in the same year, Karpoori Thakur said in Hindi: 'If you want to stop communalism, the government will have to distribute land. If you want to drive away communalism, you will have to target capitalists, remove unemployment . . . So long as you do not bring equality and economic changes, you cannot stop poverty, unemployment, inequality by using guns and bullets . . .'[4]

In 1952, Karpoori Thakur went with the Indian delegation to Vienna and Yugoslavia for the International Youth Convention. There he met Marshal Tito. At that time, Karpoori was on a foreign tour for three months. He also visited Lebanon, Egypt, Yugoslavia, Italy, France, Switzerland, England, West Germany and Australia, where he met diplomats and was involved in matters related to international politics.

In 1959, he once again visited Israel, Greece, Italy, Holland, Belgium, Denmark, Sweden, Germany, Yugoslavia and Egypt. During his second foreign trip, he studied the agricultural system and tried to understand the social, economic and political conditions of the countries he visited. He also visited Yugoslavia and the newly independent nation of Israel. He believed that the bravery and valour with which the displaced and exiled communities established itself economically and politically was an example of social assertion. Karpoori Thakur was greatly influenced by the Israeli agrarian system. Since the Israeli system of irrigation amid scarcity of water was the most advanced in the world then and had the potential of being adaptable to Indian conditions, he had come back with the idea of implementing the system in India. He was also greatly impressed with the kind of houses constructed for poor people and the management of public toilets. 'He had come up with a plan for farming and building a house at a low cost and submitted its outline to the then Planning Commission. He also visited Lebanon, Egypt and Austria. The most important aspect of this visit was that he became very close to Marshal Tito and after that whenever Tito came to India, he used to meet Karpoori Thakur exclusively. Tito, having gifted him a black overcoat during his 1959 trip to Yugoslavia, has become a part of Bihar's political folklore.'[5]

Karpoori was fast emerging as a strong leader from the Opposition. Even top leaders like CM Sri Krishna Singh and his cabinet colleague K.B. Sahay waited for his interventions in the Assembly. Speaking on 10 March 1953, on the government's administration, Karpoori said: '. . . If you call yourself the maker of the country and want to remain so, you have to throw out the old structure of the British rule and devise your own structure. Lucknow University's head of department of economics Dhurjari Prasad Mukherjee has written a book—*Economic Civil Service*. He has written that the old structure of civil service cannot do the economic restructuring of India . . .'[6] When minister K.B. Sahay, who later became the CM, asked Thakur to explain the difference between economic civil service and rural civil service, Thakur said: '. . . We need to engage such people to work for villages who have knowledge of villages and cultivation and ways to increase produce . . .'[7]

As he had taken an active part in the Bakasht Movement to uphold the rights of land-tillers, Karpoori Thakur raised his concern on the Bataidari on 30 April 1953: '. . . Bataidars or land-tillers are being prevented from cultivating land across the state . . . The state should not make any further delay in bringing in a law to protect rights of bataidars.'[8]

On 16 September 1953, Karpoori delivered perhaps the most powerful speech of his first tenure when he laced his speech with references from the Ramayana and *The Discovery of India*. Reading out a text on the French Revolution, he said: 'Ideas and economic conditions make revolution. Foolish people in authority, blind to everything that does not fit in with their ideas, imagine that revolutions are caused by agitators.'[9]

In an Assembly debate on 24 November 1955, he surprised the treasury benches by saying that it is the establishment that often raises slogans of peace. He quoted English economist Harold Laski: 'Every state contains innumerable stupid men who see in unconventional thought the imminent description of social peace. They become ministers; and they are quite capable of thinking that a society of Tolstoy, an anarchist is about to attempt a new gun powder plot . . .'[10]

On 1 March 1956, demanding minimum wages, Karpoori said: 'This government that claims to be socialist should realize that the salary of a top-level government servant is 66 times [that] of a bottom-level public servant. With this kind of disparity, how can one imagine to realize socialism?'[11]

He had as much concern for those who earned their living by plying bullock carts. On 31 March 1956, he opposed the Bihar Registration of Carts Bill, saying: 'I wonder when the British establishment did not impose tax on bullock carts, why has our own government been doing this injustice? This is why farmers are asking if the government intended to harass them.'[12]

In the second Vidhan Sabha (legislative assembly) of Bihar polls held in February 1957, he defeated Nandlal Sharma of the Congress by 10,826 votes, as a candidate of the Praja Socialist Party (PSP). In 1962, once again as a PSP candidate, he defeated Ramroop Prasad Rai of the Congress by 18,157 votes from Tajpur to retain his legislative assembly seat.

He was an ardent supporter of Hindi from the beginning. He targeted the government for favouring only English-speaking people for government jobs. Taking part in the debate on the Bihar Official Language Bill, 1957, on 11 November 1957, he said: 'Those who know Hindi are waiting to get employed but they are not getting jobs because they do not know English. Let the government make provision to give similar kind of education to Hindi-knowing people as is being given to English-knowing people.'[13]

Karpoori's interventions in the Vidhan Sabha ranged from atrocities on common people by the police to socialism, communism and capitalism and national and international topics. He would write his speeches with meticulous care.

On 2 January 1962, he expressed his concern about deep-rooted casteism in every sphere of life, right from society to jobs to politics. 'When we think of dealing with social evils, casteism has led to political evils . . . When a child is born in a Hindu family, we mention caste in the police report, panchayat register; we have to seriously think over it if it is necessary to do so. When we apply for jobs, we mention caste. We also have to think if it is necessary . . . Caste is like an insurance company and the basis of this bigger insurance company is casteism.'[14] Then he questioned why the Constitution cannot demand that those who get jobs have to opt for inter-caste marriages. Karpoori would attend inter-caste weddings and would, at times, do the *kanyadaan* ritual for poor girls.

Karpoori continued to put pressure on the Sri Krishna government by taking up the cause of land tillers. Narendra Pathak writes, 'Karpoori Thakur had to make a lot of effort in irrigation and in connecting the farmers of high and medium holdings with the PSU (Public Sector Unit). This was the first political rally under his leadership in which the peasant problem was the nodal issue. It was through the meeting of medium and some big farmers apart from Bakasht, that the socialists had expanded the PSP base and showed a mirror to their government in front of CM Sri Krishna Singh.'[15] During the Bakasht Movement, about 700 people and their leader Karpoori were arrested from Shahabad (present Buxar, Bhojpur, Rohtas and Kaimur).

In December 1953, after the first national conference of the PSU, Dr Lohia started seriously looking into farmers' problems in Bihar and Uttar Pradesh; he also led the ongoing anti-government movements in this direction. In the midst of these movements, the stature of Karpoori Thakur in socialist politics was increasing. Dr Lohia, at the national level, and Karpoori Thakur, at the provincial level, were looking for solutions to social and economic problems through political movements.

Chandapuri Joins the Social Churn

Dr Rammanohar Lohia, who greatly influenced the 'backward caste movement' in North India, forcefully articulated the relationship between the socialist political tradition and lower caste movements. He recognized the political potential of the horizontal mobilization of lower castes on issues of social justice and ritual discrimination.

He rejected the claim commonly espoused by many Indian socialists—including Nehru—that caste inequality would automatically wither away once socialism was established. Lohia held that caste status, along with English education and wealth, were three primary characteristics of India's ruling classes. He believed that purely class-based socialism would not unseat the ruling classes, even with full public ownership over what Nehru referred to as the 'commanding heights' of the economy. He asserted, 'A vested interest socialism talks of political and economic revolution alone.'[16]

In September 1947, a group of veteran freedom fighters from the backward caste communities came together to form the Bihar State Backward Caste Federation. The federation, constructed on the model of Triveni Sangh, was established as a political party to contest the upcoming parliamentary elections. Almost immediately, the new organization was 'infiltrated' by backward caste Congressmen hoping for ministerial positions after the 1952 elections. At a meeting in December 1947, a 'loyal' Congressman was elected president of the Federation, and those present voted to convert the federation into a social organization.

R.L. Chandapuri launched a magazine called *Pichhra Varg* in 1948 to publish articles and speeches to awaken the backward classes. Chandapuri wrote in 1949: 'Whenever any revolution is to take place in India, it has to be spearheaded only by the backward classes and downtrodden people. The landed aristocrats and forward class leaders who are in league with capitalism are blackmailers. They are only slogan mongers and their aim is to maintain status quo in Indian society.'[17]

Prof. Keshav Rao Jadhav writes, 'At the peak of movement in 1950, Chandapuri claimed to have members from 127 castes, exclusive of some forward castes, and to enroll about 4 lakh members. The circulation of *Pichhra Varg* reached 10,000.'[18] In 1950, Chandapuri was also influential in the formation, in Delhi, of the All India Backward Classes Federation, which adopted the same mass base orientation. Yet, Chandapuri was outmanoeuvred in Patna and Delhi by power brokers.

Prof. Jadhav writes quoting Chandapuri, 'They picked up our men and said I will give you scholarships, money, jobs and power.

In the end, I was always opposed by my own men who were given jobs and power. They were people long neglected and they did not have the moral character to resist temptation.'[19]

After 1950, the momentum of the backward classes' movement declined. Congress leaders offered Chandapuri's supporters government contracts, business licenses and, the most alluring of all, Congress tickets in the upcoming 1952 elections. Chandapuri was asked to suspend the publication of *Pichhra Varg*. When Chandapuri started another newsletter, *Pichhra Varg Sandesh*, the government continued to harass him.

When Chandapuri became president of the Bihar Backward Caste Federation in 1952, the Congress set up a parallel organization, Backward Classes Federation, under the leadership of Jagjivan Ram. In 1957, a faction of the All India Backward Classes Federation, led by Chandapuri, formed a short-lived political party, and then merged with the Socialist Party after the latter supported a 60 per cent reservation for backward classes in political and government positions.

The correspondence between Chandrapuri and Dr Lohia is worth reading to understand the social context.

*Patna, 30-8-1957

My Dear Dr. Lohia,

I was very glad to meet you at Simultala and to have a talk with you beginning from August 15 to August 19 on the varied problems facing the country and [the] merger of the Indian National Backward Classes Federation with the Socialist Party of India. I shared the view of my colleagues when I told you at Simultala that the need of a separate political party of the Indian backward classes was there so long as 'caste-varna' complexion played a dominant role in moulding [the] social and political life of an individual. I have no mental reservation when I say that other political parties of the country though they look outwardly to be possessing very attractive and progressive ideals and programmes but they are virtually paralysed in carrying out their programmes into action. I think that [the] caste system is at the root of [the] paralysis of Indian political parties which gives special meaning to political theories in India. Caste system is and had been in the past the real cause of disunity and disintegration of our national life and downfall of the country. Vivisection of our Motherland into Pakistan and [the] Indian Union, demand for Achhutistan by Dr. BR Ambedkar and murder of Mahatma Gandhi were the results of vicious circle created by counter revolutionary forces led by upper castes Hindu imperialism. Now Congress rule under Pt. Nehru's leadership is on its highest phase of development of Hindu imperialism. I say on my personal experience that barring Socialist Party every other political party specially in Bihar is under direct clutches of Congress rulers whose modus operandi is to use their respective caste. The Indian backward classes who form overwhelming majority of the population of India can never expect establishment of socialism by such political parties. Amidst confusion and turmoil of ideologies of various political parties, the Socialist Party of India by its policy and programmes from its very inception attracted the attention of every right thinking person in the country.

In the light of the talk which I had with you at Simultala and the opportunity which I got there to study camp life of the Socialist Party, I am convinced that the implementation of the policy and programmes of Socialist Party, in the present shape and form will surely land India in a new era of socialism and democracy.

I had agreed with you on the constitution, policy and programmes of Socialist Party and also on the proposal of the merger. I liked some minor adjustment here and there in Executives of the Socialist Party about which you had no objection.

The final decision on the question of the merger of our party will be taken by a convention of the party which will be held sometime in the month of October next. I assure you that I shall exercise my full influence in favour of the merger proposal. In the meantime, I shall like to have still more clarification on the policy and programmes of the Socialist Party by you with special reference to the problems of backward classes.

Yours Sincerely,
R.L. Chandapuri[20]

*Hyderabad, 4th September 1957.

Dear Chandapuri,

I received your letter today and I am replying it today itself. I was happy to meet you both the times and likewise I am happy on reading your letter. Your opinion in regard to the Socialist Party is correct. To mend it wholly it is necessary that the backward classes join the Socialist Party in large numbers and not only make socialism as an ideal but as a voice of the oppressed soul too. I am also fed up with Bania-Brahmin politics. It appears that this politics has resolved to finish every one who wants to raise all the 40 crores of India. I have no enmity with the (sacred) thread.

I want to raise them too. But I know that they can rise only when Sudra, Harijan, Women and Muslims also rise. This the thread-wearers do not understand. They think that if the backward class rises, they will degrade. This ignorance is the root of evil. I would want that your men too strengthen the Socialist Party with this idea. It is possible that some of them may be working with the idea of vengeance against thread-wearers. This is neither proper nor possible. With this mentality only those amongst the Sudras will go ahead who are double faced, or can flatter, or who are possessed with the special ability of making use of hatred. We have to produce such men who are actually capable. Only then a politics will blossom through which nomenclatures such as Dvija and Sudra will be destroyed forever.

What you have in regard to clarifications, much more than that is included in the principles and election manifesto of the Socialist Party. I am having them sent separately. You will observe in these that by the abolition of tax on profitless agriculture backward classes stand to gain more. Similarly, all the people will benefit if the price policy is fixed in accordance with the principles laid down by the Socialist Party. To a certain extent there must be reservation in the services. But, for education scholarships should be given in larger number to backward classes. But there should be no such protection by which Dvija boys and girls are prevented from education. I think that the Dvijas, in special conditions, should not get government services. But in education full and equal opportunity should be given. Many Dvijas ask me in panic what is the use of educating them when they are asked to seek ways other than the government service. Likewise, when primary schools, where children of 5 to 10 years are educated, are made of one type, as required by the Socialist Party, then every child of Bhangi, Kurmi, Brahmin, Kisan and prime minister will get the same education. I believe that this is the first necessary reform for India without which nothing can be done. Limitation on land ownership, nationalization and the ratio of 1:10 of minimum and

maximum income and expenditure, all these aims in a way he
Socialist Party a party of backward classes.

There will be an all India camp of the Socialist Party near
Hyderabad. It will be nice if you could attend it as a special
invitee. At the same time the national committee will also meet. As
you are not yet a member, therefore you yourself would not like to
attend the meeting, but I hope that on an important occasion you
will participate in a formal or informal meeting of the committee.

You have observed that I want such leaders from among the
backward classes who are neither flatterers nor hatred mongers and
who by taking a straight and self respecting course, become leaders
of all India and all people of the country. Therefore, it is necessary
that you do this work very early. Firstly do not be seated in Patna
and, as far as possible, move about in Bihar,. Uttar Pradesh and
Bengal in this month of September and clarify the ideas among
the backward classes on a large scale and prepare their mind in
accordance with your letter.

Yours sincerely,
Rammanohar Lohia[21]

Chandapuri held the All India End Caste Conference in Patna
from 31 March to 2 April 1961. It came out with resolutions
of mixed dinners, inter-caste marriage and distribution of land.
Chandapuri also later suggested that titles should be abolished
and more importantly, 'preferential opportunities for backward
castes' as he held that the 'caste system reduces and diminishes
strength and ability in the country. The caste system creates deep-
seated traditional habits.'

But things did not happen the way Chandapuri expected
them to. But like Swami Sahajanand Saraswati, he did leave some

questions for the Congress and society. Some of those questions were answered and some still remain unanswered.

Sri Krishna Singh and the Zamindari Movement

Sri Krishna Singh and K.B. Sahay finally reconciled to the demands of zamindari abolition. They now believed that zamindari abolition would not only benefit the farmers, but also increase the power of their group, with several OBC leaders. Sahay first destabilized the Permanent Settlement. They knew that unless they eliminated the dominance of the middlemen and removed their domination in society and politics, their welfare schemes would not be implemented. The zamindari abolition law was passed in Bihar, long before it was passed in any other province of India, despite being opposed by many senior Congress leaders.

Umesh Prasad Singh says, 'With Dr. Rajendra Prasad becoming the President of India in 1952, Dr. Sri Krishna Singh established himself at the top of Congress politics in Bihar. As he inducted his relative Mahesh Prasad Singh into his cabinet, the infighting between the two factions of the Bihar Congress—Sri Krishna Singh faction and Anugrah Narayan Singh faction, took a serious form. Caste polarization was now getting pronounced in Bihar. K.B. Sahay, who did have influence in the party, however, did not see realising his dream of becoming CM too soon. As a matter of pragmatism, Anugrah Narayan Singh (he would also use Sinha surname) took Singh's side. To strike a balance, Dr. Sri Krishna Singh stopped his reformist bid and joined hands with landlords and re-inducted many big landlords into his cabinet. He took into confidence Darbhanga Maharaj, Kumar Ganganand Singh and Ranjandhari Singh of Dharhara Estate and Shyamanand Singh of Baaghi Estate. By 1960, Sri Krishna Singh and Mahesh Prasad

Singh started giving shelter to the Bhumihars in power. This increased caste animosity and created tension between Bhumihars and non-Bhumihars.'[22]

Slamming Congress but Praising Nehru

Karpoori Thakur kept shining in the Legislative Assembly. Even though the Socialists had been going through a process of breaking, bending and mending, he had been taking on Binodanand Jha and later the K.B. Sahay government with the voice of reason. On 26 September 1962, he countered the Congress claim of bringing about zamindari abolition: 'I want to ask how many Congressmen are responsible for zamindari abolition. Those who ran the movement to abolish zamindari are Swami Sahajanand Saraswati, Jayaprakash Narayan, Ramnandan Mishra and Basavan Singh who created the atmosphere for zamindari abolition.'[23]

Karpoori's knowledge of international affairs was as sound as his knowledge of domestic affairs. Speaking on the threat from China on 8 February 1963, he quotes Mao Zedong: '"India's faith in the past and her faith in the future are similar to those of China" . . . Whatever form of communism is there in China is not communism but extremist imperialism. It is the same thing which MN Roy had said 10 years ago about China's communism being a pure nationalism . . .'[24] Thakur then elaborates on why China is afraid of India: 'China holds that India is its biggest enemy in Asia. India is an island where peace reigns and every citizen has full freedom to achieve social and economic development and stability.'[25]

He was effusive in his praise for the contribution of the first PM Pandit Jawaharlal Nehru. He said in the Assembly on 20 July 1964: 'If there is anyone who has contributed to the renaissance of India, rather development of Asia after Mahatma Gandhi, it was Pandit Jawaharlal Nehru. Not just India but the entire world is a witness to the fact that when democracy and progressiveness were trampled upon during the Civil War in Spain by General Franco, when Abyssinia was at the receiving end of Italy's communism and a conspiracy was being hatched to take away its freedom and when foreign imperialism had been trying to subjugate several countries in Asia, Africa and the Arab world, it was Nehru who had raised his voice against them . . . Had he not been in politics, he could have been a litterateur of high order.'[26]

Senior Bihar minister Bijendra Prasad Yadav, who had trained under Karpoori Thakur, recalls: 'Karpoori Thakur would often say that there are three kinds of pains—an upper caste can be poor but still has his honour intact, an OBC may be monetarily well-off but does not get respect and the scheduled caste suffers from both kinds of pains.'[27]

Karpoori Thakur was a rare leader, who knew how to use his platform to effectively communicate a political agenda. Manish Kumar Jha writes, 'His initial mobilization endeavour was directed against the zamindars that led to the release of land which was subsequently distributed among poor Dalits.'[28]

Participating in the Assembly debate in support of a proposal for a referendum on the Bill by fellow Socialist leader, Ramesh Jha, on 16 September 1953, Karpoori Thakur brought out the importance of minority opposition voices for protecting the liberty and freedom of the people. Challenging the arrogance of the ruling regime that considered that 'democracy is the rule of the majority', he cited political thinker, Harold Laski, who said, 'Friends of liberty are always in the minority in human society.' Emphasizing the need to use the Bill to ascertain public opinion through a referendum, he stressed upon the greater engagement of people in the running of the state and the government.[29]

Karpoori would support teachers against unscrupulous elements. Recalling one such instance, Ramlal Mahato, the former principal of LKVD (Lohia Karpoori Visheshwar Das) College, Patauri (Samastipur), recalled: 'Sometime in 1963, a teacher at a Shahpur–Patouri school had complained against a local MLA who would twirl his moustache to bully the teacher. Karpoori suggested that the teacher drop his (Karpoori's) name. It worked because Karpoori had become an important Opposition leader by then and his voice mattered to the government.'[30]

This was a time when dynastic elements had not yet fully crept into Congress's scheme of things, whether at the Centre or in the states. Senior Congress leader and author Shashi Tharoor quotes the then PM Pandit Jawaharlal Nehru: '. . . the offspring of Cabinet ministers, for instance, benefiting from reservations and lower entry thresholds into university and government that were designed to compensate for disadvantages these scions of privilege have never personally experienced. This has been augmented by the increasing importance of caste as a factor in the mobilization of votes. Nehru scorned the practice, though some of his aides were not above exploiting caste-based vote-banks, but today candidates are picked by their parties principally with an eye to the caste loyalties they can call upon; often their appeal is overtly to voters of their own caste or sub-caste, urging them to elect one of their own. The result has been a phenomenon Nehru would never have imagined, and which yet seems inevitable: the growth of caste-consciousness and casteism throughout Indian society.'[31]

A letter from the then PM Pandit Jawaharlal Nehru to Bihar CM Dr Sri Krishna tells us a lot about the high standards of politics. This letter also tells us how the Centre would greatly respect state leadership and would not overreach its power.

Confidential

No. 3817-P.M.
New Delhi
May 6, 1952
My Dear Sri Babu,

I have just had a visit from the Maharaja of Darbhanga. He talked to me about the land legislation in Bihar and reminded me that I had agreed to go into this matter and give my advice. I told him that this happened about eight months ago and since then we had a great deal of trouble on account of litigation and references to courts. I did not blame the Maharaja for this, but some of his brother-zamindars had proved exceedingly troublesome and deserved no sympathy.

The Maharaja was rather excited and shed tears and said that he placed himself in my hands completely and would do what I told him. He had realized long ago that these changes were coming and he had not opposed them. But now something must be finalized so as to prevent chaos.

I told him that I was only out of touch with this matter now and did not know what the exact position was except that I had seen that the Supreme Court had given its decision. The Maharaja told me that I had all kinds of papers which the Bihar Government had sent me long ago. I do not remember this. Probably the papers had been sent to me many months ago and I put aside till they were wanted. I shall try to find them.

I should like you to tell me what the position is now and what you expect me to do. Naturally, we cannot go into basic questions

now or challenge the whole structure of your legislation. All one can
do is to remove anomalies and hardships, wherever possible.
Anyhow, please let me know how matters stand.

Yours sincerely,
Jawaharlal Nehru[32]

Pitaunjhia Files

As Karpoori would be away from his home, he got little time to focus
on the education of his sons, Ramnath and Birendra, and daughter
Renu. Ramlal Mahato, then LKVD College principal, recalls a 1965
incident: 'When Karpoori Thakur came out of a meeting, he told
me that his son Ramnath had no interest in studies and I should take
care of him. Ramnath started living with me and got serious about
his studies. He passed his matriculation with first division in 1967.
This one example showed how he valued education.'[33]

Karpoori Thakur's younger son Dr Birendra K. Thakur,
who retired in March 2023, recalled a no less interesting story of
how he studied. 'It was sometime in the mid-1960s that a local
resident Sahdeo Mahato gave my father the idea of bringing us to
Patna for better education. Though I was in Class 6 in my village
school, I got admission in Class 4 in Bal Vikas Public School,
Bank Road, Patna. My sister Renu got admission in Class 2 in
the same school. Renu and I would walk down 3 kilometres from
our MLA Flats to the school. My father said he had no money to
engage a rickshaw for us.'[34]

Birendra recalled that he later got admission in Class 6 in Sir
Ganesh Dutt Pataliputra School. The same year, he was taken
ill after catching a cold during a trip to see his maternal family
in Chandanpatti, Muzaffarpur. Birendra says: 'It was the rainy

season. My father had got us to cross the Ganga on a steamer to reach Hajipur and later reach the home of our maternal family. On reaching the village, I ran a high temperature and later developed rheumatoid arthritis. Doctor suggested that I should study somewhere in a rural area to avoid the pollution in Patna. I was admitted to Tirhut Academy at Samastipur and started living in the school campus residence of the principal, Collector Singh Keshri. I did my Class 12 in 1971. I later sought admission in the pre-science undergraduate course in Samastipur College, Samastipur.'[35]

While Karpoori Thakur lived in Patna, his father Gokul Thakur and mother Ramdulari Devi used to take care of his family at Pitaunjhia. Karpoori would visit the family during Holi and Chhath puja without fail. He would join his father in singing Holi songs, *phaag* (Holi song), along with his friends, including several friends from upper caste Rajput families. Though Karpoori's family had been slowly getting social acceptance, most upper caste villagers would still maintain a distance from their MLA. Karpoori would get political workers to send his family rations. There was a fixed khadi shop at Pusa from where his family members would buy clothes. Ramdulari Devi and Phuleshwari Devi would buy cotton sarees and the male members would buy khadi kurtas, dhotis and pyjamas.

Birendra's earliest memory of his father goes back to the 1962 polls. He says: 'I was barely six years old. I have a faint memory of going to Tajpur along with my brother and others to celebrate the victory of my father in the elections.'[36] Ramnath Thakur adds: 'I remember Ramnarayan Singh, a supporter of my father, having lifted me on his shoulders after the victory of my father from Tajpur. I enjoyed every bit of attention given to me as the son of Karpoori Thakur. That perhaps was the beginning of my interest in politics.'[37]

5

SP to SSP

When Karpoori Almost Joined the Congress

Samajwad babua, dhire dhire aayi
Samajwad unke dhire dhire aayi,
Haathi se aayi,
Ghoda se aayi,
Angrezi baaja bajai samajwad,
Votewa se aayi,
Birla ke ghar mei samai, samajwad,
Gandhi se aayi,
Aaandhi se aayi . . .

(Son, socialism will come slowly, it will come riding an elephant, it will come on the back of a horse, socialism will blow the trumpet, it will come through votes, socialism will enter the house of Birla, it will come with Gandhi, it will come like a tempest . . .)[1]

* * *

Imagine what could have been the course of Indian history if two legends, Dr Rammanohar Lohia and Dr B.R. Ambedkar had come together. Dr Ambedkar's premature death in 1957 prevented that from happening.

Sample their conversation.

Hyderabad, 10th December 1955

Dear Dr. Ambedkar,

The enclosed folders are self-explanatory. 'Mankind' would try earnestly to reveal the caste problem in its entirety. It would therefore be very happy to have an article from you. It expects its articles to range between 2,500 and 4,000 words. You are of course free to select your own subject. Should you select one or the other aspect of the caste system prevalent in our country, I would want you to write something which makes the people of India sit up, not alone in anger, but also in wonder. I do not know whether the speeches I made about you during the parliamentary campaign in Madhya Pradesh were communicated to you by your Lieutenant who also travelled with me. Even now I very much wish that sympathy should be joined to anger and that you became a leader not alone of the scheduled castes, but also of the Indian people . . .

I do not know whether the foundation conference of the Socialist Party would have any interest for you. Although you are not a member of the Party, the conference would want to have you as a special invitee. The conference will take up among other subjects, problems relating to agricultural labour, artisans, women and parliamentary work, on any one of which you have something significant to say. If you feel like participating in the proceedings of the conference in order to bring out one or another point, I trust that the conference will extend you special permission to do so.

With warm greetings,
Yours sincerely,
Rammanohar Lohia[2]

And here is Dr Ambedkar's reply:

24th September 1956.

Dear Dr. Lohia,

Your two friends had come to see me and I had quite a long talk with them although we did not enter into any discussion about your election programme.

The working committee of the All-India Scheduled Castes Federation is meeting on 30th September 1956 and I shall put to the committee the proposal which your friends have left with me. After the working committee meeting is over I should like to have a discussion with the important members of your Party so that we can finally settle as to what we can do in coming together. I would therefore be glad if you can be in Delhi on Tuesday, the 2nd October 1956 at my place. If you are coming, please let me I know by wire so that I can retain some people of the working committee also to meet you.

With kind regards,
Yours sincerely,
BR Ambedkar[3]

But history willed it otherwise and socialists have to traverse a long course, struggling, uniting, disintegrating, reuniting and diversifying. But Karpoori remained a diehard socialist. A 1962 Lok Sabha elections incident will confirm this. Congress had fielded Satyanarayan Singh from Samastipur. Praja Socialist Party (PSP) had fielded Rajendra Mahato, an OBC Kushwaha leader.

Vishnudev Rajak writes, 'As the constituency was Kushwaha-dominated, Singh approached a local socialist leader Chandrabhanu Mehta to speak to Karpoori Thakur and consider withdrawing the candidature of Rajendra Mahato. Singh promised that if Karpoori Thakur agreed to do so, he would be made a cabinet minister in the Bihar government and Chandrabhanu Mehta an MLC. But Karpoori Thakur refused the offer flatly.'[4]

This was the first time that Karpoori Thakur had got a direct offer to join the Congress. The committed socialist stood his ground. He knew very well that Satyanarayan Singh had often helped him pay his school fees. Singh, a towering Congress leader and a member of Pandit Jawaharlal Nehru's cabinet, was like a father-figure to Karpoori. But Karpoori chose not to mix his personal life with his political ideology.

Satyanarayan Singh managed to win the elections. But it was Karpoori Thakur who had scored a moral victory over him.

Yet, not everything had been smooth for Karpoori Thakur in his party. With the fast emergence of the trio of Karpoori Thakur, Ramanand Tiwari and Kapildeo Singh, there had been discomfort among the veterans and stalwart politicians and freedom fighters, Basavan Singh and Suraj Narayan Singh.

Since Karpoori was influenced by Jayaprakash Narayan, he had stayed with the Praja Socialist Party (PSP) when Lohia was suspended in 1955 from the Socialist party. In PSP, Karpoori had to face Basavan Singh and Suraj Narayan Singh. When it came to the selection of candidates for the 1957 Assembly polls, attempts were made to deny Karpoori Thakur a ticket from Tajpur, even though he was the sitting MLA. There was a precedent of generally recommending one candidate from the regional unit of the party. The state and central units would endorse it. Rajak writes, 'But in 1957, the Samastipur unit of PSP recommended two more candidates besides Karpoori and the two candidates had been under pressure from a PSP lobby not to withdraw their candidature. But given the immense popularity of Karpoori Thakur, the two had to eventually withdraw their candidature. Karpoori contested and retained his seat.'[5]

Karpoori's political stock in PSP continued to rise. While Karpoori and Kapildeo completely dominated the Vidhan Sabha with their well-prepared speeches, Ramanand Tiwari and Karpoori Thakur were taken as the rising stars from the Opposition camp. Kapildeo, however, seldom showed his ambition. He remained an intellectual companion of Karpoori Thakur. The Vidhan Sabha speeches of these leaders testify to the high quality of their debates.

In 1963, Karpoori became the chairperson of Parisiman Ayog (delimitation commission). He was the party's state secretary from 1957 to 1962 and also a member of its national executive. Umesh Prasad Singh, a close aide of Dr Rammanohar Lohia in Bihar, says: 'Suraj–Basavan held supreme in the organisation; Karpoori Thakur and Ramanand Tiwari were new stars. By 1960, they had openly started taking on the two respected elders if they tried to prevail over them.'[6]

The Socialist Royal Rumble

After Independence, the Congress party had appeared to tower like a monolith over the Opposition. The rivals in the Left were weakened by splits among their ranks. The Communists, who formed the Bihar unit in 1939, could not consolidate a base because of confusing shifts of strategy, dictated by their ties to Moscow. The context in which socialist thought developed in India was different from that in which it developed in Europe. Socialism in India developed not only as a scheme of social and economic reconstruction but also as an ideology of political liberation from the shackles of cruel foreign imperialism. Between 1900 and 1947, India focused solely on the political independence of the country. It was necessary for Indian socialist thought to present the theory and plan of the agricultural labour industry to do something distinct.

In 1951, Acharya J.B. Kriplani, along with his supporters, broke away from the Congress and formed the Kisan Mazdoor Praja Party. Acharya Narendra Dev was then the president of the Samajwadi Party. The two parties became one in October 1952. On 20 December 1954, the Congress General Convention was held in Avadi (Tamil Nadu) to give a socialist form to society. The outline of five-year plans started as its first initiative. Two conflicting factions started forming inside PSP, reacting to the changed socialist trend of the Congress. Dr Lohia was in favour of opposing the Congress. As differences increased, it culminated in a split in the PSP on 31 December 1955. Dr Lohia formed the Socialist Party with Madhu Limaye and Raj Narain. Dr Santosh Kumar writes, 'According to Kapildeo Singh, the period from 1967 to 1977 can only be called the era of greed and sabotage for the formation of the Janata Party and according to him, the period from 1977 to 1992 has been the disorientation era of the socialists.'[7] The era between 1992 and 2005 indicates the power era of socialists in which Lalu Prasad came to power. From November 2005 till today, Nitish Kumar carries forward the socialist ideology.

The era from 1956 to 1967 can be called the era of revolutionary or socialist unity. Ganga Sharan Singh was the national president of PSP during 1964–65. Raj Narain was the national president of the Socialist Party. By that time, Jayaprakash Narayan had taken up the cause of the Bhoodan movement. Pandit Ramnandan Mishra had also retired from politics. Acharya Narendra Dev and Meher Yusuf Ali had died. Dr Lohia was left as the seniormost socialist leader.

When Karpoori Almost Joined the Congress

With Jayaprakash now being part of the Bhoodan and Sarvodaya movement for some years, Karpoori Thakur too had his moments of disillusionment. Surendra Kishore writes, 'Suraj Narayan Singh and Basavan Singh did not appreciate the rise of Karpoori and Tiwari. But JP liked Karpoori because of his humility and eloquence, though much to the discomfort of Suraj and Basavan.'[8]

It was 1964. Dr Lohia had been trying to unite the Socialist Party and the Praja Socialist Party. Both parties had fared badly in the past three elections. But there was a group of socialists, led by Ashok Mehta, who wanted to join the Congress for they saw no future within a socialist fold.

Karpoori had great admiration for Ashok Mehta as a leader. Karpoori's cabinet colleague and friend for years Kapildeo Singh writes in his diary on 24 February 1964: 'Ashok Mehta delivered a powerful speech. Full of facts, Karpooriji was also with me, he took some notes. Of late, Karpooriji has shown bigger interest in reading, People say it is because of my company. But I hold that he has this habit from the beginning. He is a self-made man. One day I gave him a book titled *Nehru Ke Baad*. He jumped in joy to get it. This gave me a lot of happiness.'[9]

About 1000 members of the PSP from all over the country, decided in the All India Labour Convention on 12 June 1964 to join the Congress. There were also twenty-five prominent leaders of the party in that session. PSP was upset with Mehta's anti-party activities. PSP passed a resolution by fifteen votes against three and expelled Ashok Mehta from the party. This proved to be a trigger point for socialists influenced by Mehta to join the Congress. Karpoori also had a proposal from the Ashok Mehta camp to join the Congress.

Socialist leader Shivanand Tiwari says: 'It was a time when Karpoori Thakur had been very low in confidence. Genda Singh, a sugarcane farmer and UP leader close to Ashok Mehta, had approached Karpoori Thakur, who had almost made up his mind to join the Congress. When my father came to know about it, he went to Karpoori Thakur and took him in a warm embrace. The two friends cried and Karpoori Thakur decided never to quit the socialist party. He kept his word all his life.'[10]

A convention of the united socialists was called in Varanasi in 1965. It was mainly a session for the dissolution of the party. The overwhelming majority PSP faction called for a separate session by rejecting the merger proposal of both the parties.

Dr Lohia succeeded in bringing about the merger of the Praja Socialist Party and the Socialist Party on 29 January 1965 at the Sarnath session. It was named Sanyukta Socialist Party (SSP). But a section of the PSP did not agree with the merger and PSP continued to stay afloat as a party. Karpoori became part of SSP while his arch-rivals Suraj Narayan Singh and Basavan Singh remained with PSP.

The merger started a new innings in Karpoori's life. He got his mentor in Dr Lohia, who was also greatly influenced by Karpoori's work. In Lohia's own words, 'If I had a leader like

Karpoori Thakur in every province, I would change form of the socialist party in the country.'[11]

'Socialist' Sahay Falters, Lohia Leads

In the ruling Congress, there were few signs of backward leaders getting their due. Upper castes were still able to prevent the rise of a low caste leader to the position of CM. After the death of Dr Sri Krishna Singh in 1961, non-Bhumihars diminished the importance of Mahesh Prasad Singh and made Binodanand Jha, a Brahmin, the CM K.B. Sahay changed his camp to support Jha. In 1963, Jha had to step down under the Kamaraj Plan. He supported the OBC Kurmi leader Bir Chand Patel as his supporter. Prasanna Kumar Choudhary and Shrikant write, 'Since it was deemed unpalatable amongst so-called predominant castes to accept a member of a Backward caste as their leader, Bhumihars, Rajputs and Kayasthas suddenly combined to support the candidacy of K.B. Sahay, a Kayastha, who formed the government.'[12]

Sahay, however, was the first Congress CM who started giving importance to non-upper caste leaders. Prem Kumar Mani says, 'He started assimilating backward caste people. OBC Yadav leader Ram Lakhan Singh was among some prominent OBC leaders who were made ministers in the Sahay cabinet.'[13]

Francine R. Frankel and M.S.A. Rao write, 'Such a kaleidoscopic pattern of caste, ethnic and class conflict revealed the critical awakening in the moral authority of the upper castes. The ability of Brahminism to continue to justify hereditary inequalities of caste, ethnicity, class and power heralded the breakdown of the traditional social order.'[14]

But by 1965, the K.B. Sahay government in Bihar had started getting unpopular owing to rising prices and complaints of corruption and general slackness in governance. Santosh Kumar writes, 'As open market prices soared, pushing hundreds of thousands of low-paid government employees, the opposition on 9 August 1965, called for a bandh in Patna. Rioting, led by students and government workers, spread to all important towns and spilled over to the villages.'[15]

Socialist leader Shivanand Tiwari, who had attended the protest march at Gandhi Maidan, recalls the August 1965 incident: 'I was sitting with my father Ramanand Tiwari, Karpoori Thakur and CPI leaders, Ramavatar Shastri and Chandra Shekhar Singh. As the function was going on smoothly, the police started lathicharge without any provocation, injuring many of us. This episode further made K.B. Sahay government unpopular.'[16]

Kapildeo Singh writes in his diary on 13 August 1965: 'I was arrested for taking part in the protest march against the misgovernance of Congress and put inside Bankipore jail. Ramanand Tiwari, Karpoori Thakur, Ramavatar Shastri and Ramcharan Babu were already there. We all were injured during the brutal lathicharge by police.'[17]

A few months later, fresh protest demonstrations resulted in more police firings. On the eve of the 1967 elections, K.B. Sahay and his administration were very unpopular.

In a lethal attack on the K.B. Sahay government, Karpoori Thakur said in the Assembly on 12 March 1965: 'I had written a letter to the CM in January 1964 regarding local people not getting employment in the electricity department work despite the government order to employ them. I got a reply from the CM office in February 1965 after a year. This alone shows the worthlessness of this government.'[18] Further on 14 September 1966, Karpoori said: 'I would like to tell a story. A sage used to live by the sea. The sage told the sea that its roars and waves are worthless and so is its expanse and greatness because big fish eat the smaller ones right in its heart. Similarly, this government is useless because there is injustice, corruption, hoarding and price rise. This is not socialism but capitalism . . .'[19]

The Patna Bandh of 1965 was an unprecedented success. Lathis and bullets were used at many places. A curfew had been imposed in the city. Despite the curfew, Dr Lohia addressed the Ramavatar group of about one lakh people at Gandhi Maidan. On his way back, he was arrested the same night at Patna Junction. On the same night, *Searchlight* editor K.M. George was also caught. Karpoori Thakur, Ramanand Tiwari, Chandra Shekhar Singh and some others reached Gandhi Maidan in Patna to protest against this oppression. Karpoori Thakur fractured his left hand in the incident. He had not left the venue after the lathi charge. A police vehicle took him to Patna Central Jail. Karpoori's non-cooperation struggle and fearlessness indicated that he was a great leader in the making.

The leadership of the Backward Classes always 'claimed to represent the interest of all of the downtrodden, but in practice they used to articulate the demands of the advanced upper shudras and were consulting across party lines.' [20]

Witsoe argued: '. . . the centrality of caste in Indian political life results from interest-oriented politicians or voters seeking control over an expansive state . . . In stark contrast with many liberal democracies, in which the poor and the marginalized are less likely to vote, popular participation in the electoral process surged in North India during the late 1980s, especially among people from lower-caste backgrounds as well as among those in rural areas—a phenomenon that Yogendra Yadav has termed the "second democratic upsurge".'[21]

Pitaunjhia Files

Ramnath Thakur, still studying in a Samastipur school, would hardly get a chance to meet his father. Whenever they would meet, Karpoori Thakur would try to motivate his son to do well in his studies. 'My father would often say that Satyendra Narayan Singh was a politician but his son Nikhil Kumar had become an IPS officer. I was average at studies. In 1966, when I was in Class 9, my father wrote me a letter saying that he had broken his left hand during protests. He advised me to study well and serve my grandparents as he would be away from home most of the time.'[22]

Karpoori Thakur's father Gokul Thakur had continued to follow his traditional profession. His son rising in political influence hardly brought in any change in his life, other than a slow social acceptability.

Chief Minister K.B. Sahay was sitting at his Chhajju Bagh, Patna, residence. The 1967 Assembly campaign had started. Suddenly he heard his grandson shouting slogans of '*Gali, gali me shor hai, K.B. Sahay chor hai* (every street echoes with slogans of K.B. Sahay being dishonest).'

The grandfather was stunned but not the chief minister. He knew that the monolithic Congress had developed wide cracks.

Karpoori 'Mahamaya' Thakur was arriving.

6

1967: Socialists' Tryst with Power

A Deputy More Famous than the CM

'After the 1967 Assembly poll results, Dr Rammanohar Lohia visited Vivekananda Rocks with Raj Narain. They saw a saint there. Dr Lohia asked Raj Narain to approach the saint and ask if Swami Vivekananda faced the Himalayas or the Hind Mahasagar when he had meditated here. The saint smiled and said, 'Is Dr Lohia around? Only someone like him would ask such a question. Please tell him that Vivekananda faced the Himalayas while meditating.'[1]

The year 1967 was a turning point for Indian politics, as it marked the arrival of the socialists and also heralded an era of coalitions at the state level. For the past three elections, the Congress had remained unchallenged, but in 1967, it suffered a major defeat in nine states, including Bihar, UP and Gujarat. For Dr Rammanohar Lohia, it was an emotional moment, as he had witnessed the struggles, divisions and reunions of the socialist party under different names since his Congress Socialist Party days. With clear intent and a lot of determination, Dr Lohia had proved that the Congress could be defeated.

Here are some of the slogans used by the Sanyukt Socialist Party (SSP) during the 1967 poll campaign:

'Congressi raj mitana hai, Socialist raj banana hai' (We have to end Congress rule and bring in Socialist rule)

'Karpoori Thakur ki lalkaar, badlo badlo yah sarkar' (Karpoori Thakur's call for change, let's change this government)

'Angrezi me kaam na hoga, phir se desh gulam na hoga' (We won't work in English, the country won't be a slave again)

'Rashtrapati ka beta ya chaprasi ki santaan, Bhangi ya Brahman ho, sabki shiksha ek saman' (Whether it's the son of the President or a lowly peon, whether it's a sweeper or a Brahmin, let everyone have equal access to education)

'Sansopa ne baandhi gaanth, pichhda pawe sau me saath' (SSP has pledged to provide 60 per cent reservation to OBCs)

Nakamizo Kazuya writes, 'Voting (in the 1967 polls) took place while the political–economic regime built by Nehru was badly shaken by India's loss in the Indo-China Border Conflict in 1962, the passing of Nehru in 1964, the Second Indo-Pakistani War in 1965, the sudden death of Prime Minister Shastri in 1966, the food crisis caused by severe droughts in 1965 and 1966 and the worst post-Independence inflation rate that approached 14 percent. This election heralded the end of the Congress system and a shift to the Congress–Opposition system. In Bihar, the 1967 state election saw the undermining of Congress's landlord mobilization model . . .'²The desertion of the Congress by powerful landlords and new voters, who were disinterested in taking part in the election in contrast to the massive support to the caste mobilization strategy of the socialists turned the tables on the Congress.

There was a lot of political turmoil and controversy surrounding the Congress party and its leadership at the time. Shivanand Tiwari says, '(Karpoori) Thakur had been a popular figure among the people of Bihar, particularly for his ability to connect with all sections including Muslims and energize his supporters through his powerful oratory.'³

Sho Kuwajima writes, 'It is well-known in Bihar that in 1966–67 the Bharat Coffee House at the Dak Bangalow Chauraha (Crossroad), Patna, was the place where the opposition leaders such as Ram Manohar Lohia, Ramanand Tiwary and Karpoori Thakur, novelists like Faneshwarnath Renu, and many journalists came together. A journalist Jitendra Sinha alias Arun Sinha writes that the idea of the Non-Congress United Front was formed through the heated discussion there.'⁴

PM Indira Gandhi felt the need to hold a public rally in the Tajpur Assembly constituency to challenge Karpoori Thakur. This was a complex phase of Indian politics during the mid-twentieth century, and highlighted the important role that individual leaders and their personal connections with voters can play in shaping election outcomes.

Ramnath Thakur says, 'Indira Gandhi delivered a speech near Karbala Pokhar of Tajpur. However, as she saw red flags of the SSP all around, she refrained from saying much and simply urged the audience to vote for the better candidate. It seems Gandhi had received the message.'⁵

The SSP emerged as the biggest non-Congress party with sixty-eight seats. 'Despite the Congress winning the most seats with 128 out of 319 in the House, it became apparent that the first non-Congress government would be formed as the Congress failed to secure any allies. The Congress lacked support and moral courage.'[6]

Although the Opposition had contested separately, they sensed a great opportunity to form the government. The Praja Socialist Party (PSP) had won fourteen seats, while the Bharatiya Jana Sangh and the CPI had secured twenty-two seats each. In terms of percentage votes, the Congress received 33.08 per cent of the votes (44,79,460), followed by 17.62 per cent (23,85,961) for the Opposition.

This defeat was one of the major setbacks for the Congress party at the state level. 'The party's popular vote declined from over 41 per cent in 1962 to 33 per cent five years later, and the number of seats dropped from 185 to 128. In contrast, the socialists achieved the biggest gain of any group, increasing their votes from just over 5 per cent in 1962 to over 17 per cent in 1967, and their seats from seven to 68.'[7]

Prior to the 1967 election, Yadav representation lagged behind each of the twice-born castes. However, in 1967, the Yadavs emerged as the single largest caste group after the Rajputs, representing a remarkable change in the political and social order.

Although the differences between the forward and backward castes regarding reservation had not become a significant political issue, this was the first election in which a popular leader from the backward classes emerged, one who did not have a significant caste base. This leader was Karpoori Thakur, a socialist and member of the small, lower Shudra nai or barber caste. As the undisputed leader of his party, Karpoori Thakur was the most likely candidate to become chief minister, and all eyes were on him.

Karpoori Thakur won the Tajpur seat for the fourth consecutive time, defeating Congress's Bhubaneshwar Singh by a margin of 16,452 votes.

Vishnudev Rajak writes, 'When Karpoori Thakur was being felicitated in Pusa, a senior party colleague, Ambika Sharan Singh, tracked him down and urged him to return to Patna to form the government.'[8] Dr Lohia had also arrived in Patna and strongly advocated for Karpoori to become the Chief Minister due to the SSP being the largest party in the Opposition and Karpoori being the most popular leader.

It was agreed that the SSP, PSP, Jan Kranti Dal, Swantantra, CPI and the Bharatiya Jana Sangh would form the government, which would be called the Sanyukt Vidhayak Dal (SVD) government. Since the SSP was the largest component of the SVD, all that remained was for the SSP to declare Karpoori as their CM candidate.

A Raja Delays Arrival of Karpoori as CM

But Raja Kamakhya Narayan Singh whose party, Jan Kranti Dal, had won thirty seats, had something else in mind. Before the formal SVD meeting at Vidhayak Club, it was agreed that the top Opposition leaders would meet at the residence of senior SSP leader and Barahiya MLA Kapildeo Singh. Arjun Singh, son of former minster Kapildeo Singh, recalled, 'A meeting of Sanyukta Vidhayak Dal was called at the R Block (Patna) residence of my father. As the leaders of Jan Kranti Dal, Maharaja Kamakhya Narayan Singh and his brother Kumar Basant Narayan Singh were coming, blankets were laid on the ground. As SSP was the biggest party among the non-Congress parties, everyone was guessing that Karpoori Thakur was going to be the next chief minister. As leaders from Jan Sangh, CPI and SSP spoke, Maharaja kept listening. Karpoori had not said a word. He kept looking at the ground as others spoke and some of them suggested that Karpoori should lead the first non-Congress government in the state. The Maharaja and his Oxford-educated brother had to speak last. The Maharaja said he could not accept Karpoori as their leader. He suggested the name of his party MLA and senior Mahamaya Prasad Sinha for the CM post. As others did not want to miss the historic opportunity of forming the non-Congress government, they agreed on Sinha's name . . . Basant Narayan Singh would speak in-between and if somebody interrupted him, he would silence them with his line "Do you follow my English?" Karpoori still kept looking at the ground, He still did not say a word during the entire meeting. My father supported Raja's idea, Ramanand Tiwari also gave his nod saying, *thik ba, thik ba* (it is ok, it is ok).'[9]

This proves that the decision to choose Mahamaya Prasad Sinha as the CM was largely based on his credentials as a veteran freedom fighter and his recent victory over the incumbent CM K.B. Sahay in the Patna (West) constituency. The slogan 'one who has defeated the CM should be CM' was used to support his candidacy, and this may have helped to ease any potential resentment towards him among the other parties in the SVD coalition. Prem Kumar Mani says, 'It is interesting to note that Raghunandan Prasad, another Jan Kranti Dal candidate who had also defeated Sahay in the Hazaribagh constituency, was not considered for the post. The same slogan did not apply to him.'[10]

With the selection of Mahamaya Prasad Sinha as the chief ministerial candidate, the SVD government was formed. Vishnudev Rajak writes, 'It was the first non-Congress government

in Bihar, which was formed on April 1, 1967. The formation
of the SVD government was a significant milestone in Bihar's
political history.'[11]

Former Bihar minister Gajendra Prasad Himanshu recalls:
'I had won my first elections from Hasanpur from SSP and was
excited to be part of the government. It seems like Karpoori
Thakur had to compromise and accept Mahamaya Prasad Sinha
as the Chief Minister candidate to form the non-Congress
government in Bihar. Despite being the leader of the largest party
in the Opposition, he had to settle for the position of Deputy
Chief Minister. However, it appears that he still retained his status
as the unchallenged leader within his party, the SSP. This way, he
also succeeded in scuttling an outside chance of a senior leader like
Bhupendra Narayan Mandal becoming CM.'[12]

But it was a shock for Dr Lohia, who was not in Patna
and had left it to the Bihar unit to make a decision. The high
command culture had not yet taken hold in any party until
then. Karpoori Thakur became the deputy CM and kept two
important portfolios of education and finance. Prem Kumar
Mani says, 'Bihar entered a half-socialist era. In a sense, it was
the age of Karpoori "Mahamaya" Thakur. Dr Lohia expressed
his displeasure with Maharaja for his high-handedness. Dr. Lohia
also pointed out that another candidate who had also defeated
Sahay was not made even a minister. At the same meeting,
Dr. Lohia also reprimanded BP Mandal, a Lok Sabha MP, for
becoming a minister in the Bihar government. Mandal had to
resign soon after.'[13]

Upset with the political manoeuvrings of Kamakhya Narayan
Singh, the Raja of Ramgarh, 'Dr. Lohia summoned Kamakhya
and his brother Basant Narayan Singh at Patna's Circuit House.
The two brothers stood in front of Dr. Lohia as he addressed

Kamakhya: "Ramgarh, do you remember that I had taken a special flight to Patna when the Congress government had got you arrested? Now, decide whether you want to do business or politics. I want your reply in 15 minutes". The brothers left the scene and later confirmed that they wanted to pursue politics.'[14]

Dr Lohia also expressed his displeasure with the fact that an upper caste leader was chosen as the CM instead of someone from an OBC or a Dalit background due to pressure from the Maharaja. However, the matter was put to rest in order to avoid spoiling the success of forming a non-Congress government. Dr Lohia had previously established three principles: not sending a losing Lok Sabha or Vidhan Sabha leader to the Upper House, an MP not resigning to become a minister in a state government, and not giving any important position to any person who has joined the party from outside.

In the Mahamaya Prasad Sinha government, several ministers from different parties were appointed. Ramanand Tiwari from SSP, Chandra Shekhar Singh and Indradeep Sinha from CPI, Vijay Kumar Mitra, Ramdev Mahto and Rudra Pratap Sarangi from BJS were among them. Kamakhya Narayan Singh and his brother Basant Narayan Singh from Jan Kranti Dal also became ministers.

Two things became clear at this point: first, Maharaja Kamakhya Narayan Singh wanted to claim his share of political power. Previously, he had been on the losing end of the Zamindari Abolition law, in which K.B. Sahay had played a significant role.

Under the belief that Kapildeo Singh and Ramanand Tiwari had indirectly supported Sinha's nomination for CM, Karpoori Thakur delegated a less significant portfolio to Tiwari and excluded Singh from the cabinet.

Umesh Prasad Singh says, 'Tiwari visited Kapildeo at his residence and then called Karpoori, who was now the deputy CM. The conversation between Tiwari and Karpoori ended on a bitter note, with Tiwari slamming the phone down on him. A few minutes later, Kapildeo Singh called Thakur and asked, "If you have become the deputy CM, does that mean you have become a *laat sahib* or dictator?"'[15]

Madhu Limaye intervened to clear the air between the two friends. Dr Arjun Singh says, 'Limaye stayed in Patna until Kapildeo Singh was sworn in as the food minister, responsible for tackling the severe food crisis at the time. Tiwari was later appointed as the police minister, the second-in-command in SSP after Karpoori Thakur.'[16]

One leader who was unhappy with the ministerial appointments was Jagdeo Prasad. He was not made a minister and his junior, Upendra Nath Verma, from the same Kushwaha caste, was made a minister of state instead. This 'miscalculation' in political ambition sowed the first seed of disgruntlement against Karpoori Thakur even before he started his work as the deputy CM.

When Lohia Met Golwalkar

With the SVD experiment, Bihar entered the phase of alliance politics, with a rainbow coalition consisting of the Left, Bharatiya Jana Sangh and Socialists. The RSS Sarsanghchalak M.S. Golwalkar and Dr Rammanohar Lohia can be credited as the harbingers of coalition politics. This was an era of Congress versus the rest, much like the post-2014 era is the era of BJP versus the rest. It is ironic yet poetic justice that the Jana Sangh, which had been labelled untouchable due to allegations against its mother organization RSS as being responsible for the assassination of Mahatma Gandhi, gained its first political acceptance in 1967.

One can easily recall the image of the then RSS Sarsanghchalak M.S. Golwalkar shaking hands with Dr Rammanohar Lohia with a broad smile, while Dr Lohia's expressions in the picture remain difficult to decipher.

In an article titled '*Main Kahta Rah Gaya Ki RSS Ke Saath Hamara Taalmel Nahi Baithta* (I kept saying that we cannot get along with the RSS)', Madhu Limaye expressed the dilemma of Dr Rammanohar Lohia, who had talked about giving a coalition with the BJS a 'trial' in pursuit of strong anti-Congressism. Limaye wrote, 'When we were fighting Congress, our leader Dr. Rammanohar Lohia used to say that the Congress that got India insulted by China, he would do everything to defeat Congress and save the country and for that we would get together with other opposition parties. We used to discuss it a lot and the discussion went on for two years, and I kept saying that we cannot get along well with RSS and Jan Sangh . . . Dr. Saheb used to tell me that he could disagree with me on some issues and would argue that he wanted such an alliance to defeat a bigger enemy. Give it a try. It is quite clear that eventually, a clash is bound to happen between the ideologies of RSS and Dr. Rammanohar Lohia.'[17]

Limaye went on to argue in the same article that they had disagreements with the RSS on the concept of nationalism, particularly with the 'RSS calling democracy a Western concept' and 'praising Hitler'. While they were against the varna system, the RSS was in favour of it.

Fast forward to 2023, BJP, which is a revamped version of the Bharatiya Jana Sangh, is almost unbeatable now. From being untouchable to almost unbeatable—is perhaps why politics is called a great leveller.

A Deputy More Famous than the CM

Karpoori Thakur made his presence felt, despite being the second in command in the government, garnering more attention than Chief Minister Mahamaya Prasad Sinha during this period.

Karpoori Thakur wasted no time in imparting some lessons on socialism to the bureaucrats. 'During one incident at the Old Secretariat, an official took him to the lift, which had a sign reading "only for officers". Karpoori Thakur was angered by this elitist practice and, despite opposition from government officials, he succeeded in changing the rules to allow everyone to use the lift.'[18]

During his presentation of the budget in the Assembly, Finance Minister Karpoori Thakur not only outlined his priorities but also highlighted the significance of the historic opportunity that the Opposition had against the monolithic Congress. Karpoori Thakur remarked that there were many apprehensions regarding the fourth General Elections. However, with courage and loyalty, the country had successfully executed the election, which was a matter of pride for us. The true seed of democracy, which was sown in our Constitution, blossomed in the fourth election. 'People showed a serious interest in the democratic process and freely exercised their right to vote. This was the first time non-Congress governments were formed in many states, and non-Congress parties fairly competed with the Congress in the Lok Sabha. This has opened up new possibilities for the constitution and strengthened democracy towards development-oriented goals. This house and the new government are the fruits of the fourth election, and the people of Bihar have been given the chance to run administrative arrangements in a new way.'[19]

The finance minister also noted that the Congress government 'persisted in running the expenditure of the state despite the deficit and did not recognize the necessity for financial management reform'.

According to V.S. Dubey, former food department secretary and later the chief secretary of both Bihar and Jharkhand, the Mahamaya–Karpoori government's most significant accomplishment was managing the food crisis. 'Their first priority was to prevent anyone from dying of hunger. The credit for this achievement goes entirely to the then food minister Kapildeo Singh and Deputy CM Karpoori Thakur, who collaborated on methods to address the crisis.'[20]

Dubey also recounted a situation where there was a clash between the bureaucracy and politicians. 'Palamau did not qualify as a famine-stricken district under the prevailing rules, but Kapildeo Singh presented enough reading material to Karpoori Thakur, who argued the case with facts and figures, impressing upon the bureaucracy to treat the matter humanely instead of relying on outdated English codes. The chief secretary eventually agreed, shook hands, and requested for more such debates. What made this episode noteworthy was that Kapildeo Singh, as the minister, could have overruled the bureaucracy, but he and Karpoori chose to debate.'[21]

During his tenure as finance minister, Karpoori Thakur made a decision to halt the collection of revenue (*malgujari*) from farmers who owned 3.5 acres of irrigated land or 7 acres of unirrigated land. This policy announcement was consistent with Lohia's slogan '*jis kheti se laabh nahi, us par lage lagan nahi*' (No tax on farms that do not yield profit). The decision provided significant relief to small and marginal farmers and exemplified the government's dynamic socialist character.

Manish Kumar Jha writes, 'These progressive pronouncements attenuated the apprehension that the right-wing Bharatiya Jana Sangh-supported coalition government would compromise on pro-poor socialist ideologies and agenda.'[22]

As finance minister, Narendra Pathak writes, 'Karpoori Thakur abolished the tax on ghats, having witnessed first hand how contractors would arbitrarily collect taxes from people, even stopping bridal processions to demand payment. This decision provided great relief to the common people who were burdened by the arbitrary collection of ghat tax by officials.'[23]

Ramnath Thakur highlighted several accomplishments of the SVD government, including the 'introduction of a scheme to provide grains as remuneration for manual labour to ensure availability of food grains to the vulnerable section even during food crises under the Antyodaya scheme, the establishment of student scholarships, and the removal of English as a mandatory subject for Class 10. The government also waived school fees up to Class 7, benefiting many families in Bihar.'[24]

While it was technically the Mahamaya Prasad Sinha government, Karpoori Thakur, Indradeep Sinha and Chandra Shekhar Singh were the most influential ministers, with Deputy CM Karpoori Thakur often leading the charge.

The Aiyer Commission

The Mahamaya Prasad Sinha government, which fought the entire election on a corruption plank against the K.B. Sahay government, set up the Justice Aiyer Commission to investigate corruption allegations against former CM K.B. Sahay and his ex-cabinet colleagues, Satyendra Narayan Sinha and Mahesh Prasad Singh. Later, the commission indicted six Congress leaders.

The T.L. Venkatrama Aiyer Commission, constituted on 5 January 1970, indicted all of them in its report.

Aryavrata, a Hindi daily, writes: 'During this time, the SVD government established the Aiyer Commission to investigate corruption allegations against K.B. Sahay, Mahesh Prasad Singh, Satyendra Narayan Sinha, Ram Lakhan Singh Yadav, Ambika Sharan Singh, and Raghvendra Prasad Singh.'[25]

The Fall of SVD

The SVD government lost majority after the Ranchi–Hatia language riots, which took place between 22 August and 29 August 1967 over the government's decision to make Urdu the second official language, which was not palatable to some dominant sections and Hindu-centric ideologues. S.K. Jain, author of *Caste and Politics in Bihar* writes: '. . . Karpoori Thakur was keen to buy the political support of the Muslims by promising to make Urdu the second official language in Bihar.'[26]

Bindeshwari Prasad Mandal, an influential OBC Yadav leader from Madhepura, had been sulking after being forced to resign as a minister in the Bihar government. Mandal, who later became the chairman of the landmark Mandal Commission, had been nursing big ambitions in state politics. He found company in Jagdeo Prasad. Congress's top leaders, K.B. Sahay and Satyendra Narayan Sinha, had already been embarrassed by the findings of the Aiyer Commission. They had been looking for an opportunity to bring down the Mahamaya–Karpoori government. Sahay and Sinha assured Prasad and Mandal of Congress's support if they broke away from the SSP.

The SVD government eventually fell in January 1968. Jagdeo Prasad and Mandal, with the help of some leaders, broke away from the SSP and formed the Shoshit Dal, which had forty MLAs coming from SSP and other parties. Senior Congress leader and former minister L.P. Shahi writes: 'The leaders who faced a probe under the Aiyer Commission, Mahesh Prasad Singh, Satyendra Narayan Singh, K.B. Sahay, Ram Lakhan Singh Yadav and Ambika Sharan Singh, joined hands to topple the SVD government.'[27]

R.L. Chandapuri gave an account of why he had backed Mandal in an interview on 8 March 1980: 'At that time in 1968, the top Congress leaders of Bihar were involved in corruption, and they were chargesheeted by the Aiyer Commission. They wanted the united front government to be toppled so that they could be saved from conviction. So I joined hands with these Congress leaders. I told them it would be better if you make B.P. Mandal chief minister, and he would be prepared to topple the SVD government if he were to be chief minister himself. I did it because I wanted to have a Backward Class chief minister and break the Forward caste tradition.'[28]

Satish Prasad Singh (28 January 1968 to 1 February 1968) was CM only for five days. B.P. Mandal continued as CM from 1 February 1968 to 22 March 1968. As B.P. Mandal was not a member of either House, he had to be nominated to the Upper House to become CM. Satish Prasad Singh was made the CM so that B.P, Mandal could be nominated to the Upper House. Once Mandal became a member of Bihar Legislative Council, Singh resigned as the CM to make way for Mandal as per mutual agreement between them.

Congress leader L.P. Shahi writes why Mandal could not hold on to his chair: 'Senior Congress leaders Deepnarayan Singh, Binodanand Jha, Krishnanandan Singh and Pratibha Singh had also played a role in destabilizing the Mandal government.'[29]

Speaking in the Assembly during the no-confidence motion against his government on 18 March 1968, CM B.P. Mandal said:

'Let me assure that I will remain CM only till I enjoy majority in the House. The moment I get in minority, I will resign as CM within a minute without any sorrow or happiness.'[30] Mandal also responded to the allegation that he had left the Lok Sabha membership to become a minister in the Mahamaya Prasad Sinha government. '. . . That time Karpoori had requested me to join the (SVD) government. Why did you (Karpoori) forget the principle of an MP not becoming a minister in state? When I had gone with you, people had started humiliating me. I revolted as a common man as I hold that no one becomes big or small because of one's birth . . .'[31]

B.P. Mandal's grandson and JD (U) leader Nikhil Mandal says: 'One of the key contributions of B.P. Mandal during his brief tenure as CM was the clearing of the Dumri bridge project connecting Saharsa and Khagaria. In a way, he connected Madhepura, Saharsa and Supaul to Khagaria, Begusarai and adjoining districts.'[32]

Fifteen MLAs broke away from the Congress to form the Loktantrik Congress. L.P. Shahi writes, 'All non-Shoshit Samaj Dal parties came together to form the next government under Bhola Paswan Shastri (12 March 1968 to 29 June 1968).'[33]

It was the first time that a group of OBC leaders formed a political party. The reason was purely political ambition and political vengeance. The formation of Shoshit Dal by a group of OBC leaders was a significant milestone in the political history of Bihar, as it marked the emergence of backward castes as a formidable political force in the state. It also showed that the OBCs were no longer willing to be relegated to the sidelines of politics and were ready to assert their identity and aspirations.

Francine R. Frankel and M.S.A. Rao write, 'The conflict between the contending upper caste and upper shudra groups was nothing less than which political formation would become dominant in Bihar. In this context, the state itself became the prize over which the rival caste groups were fighting. Each side came to believe that its control over senior ministerial and administrative offices was essential for its claims. Political power could be used to protect either the entrenched social and economic power of the Forward Classes or to substitute it for the dominance of the backward classes.'[34]

Jeffrey Witsoe writes, 'Caste became increasingly imagined as trans local communities that could be democratically mobilized into "vote blocks", represented by caste-leader politicians, but most Indians also continued to experience caste as inseparable from the realities of local dominance by caste lineages.'[35]

In the mid-term elections of 1969, the SSP's tally in the Vidhan Sabha decreased to fifty-three seats, while the Congress won 118 seats. Karpoori Thakur won his fifth consecutive election from his home-turf, Tajpur, defeating Congress candidate Rajendra Mahto by 13,485 votes.

Pitaunjhia Files

The once-sleepy village of Pitaunjhia experienced a rollercoaster of emotions within the span of just one year, with Karpoori Thakur rising to the position of deputy CM only to be forced to resign within ten months. However, despite these ups and downs, Pitaunjhia had come alive on the political map of Bihar. It didn't matter that Karpoori had lost the CM race to Mahamaya, as the villagers were pleased that during the brief SVD rule, the entire state was talking more about the deputy CM than the CM himself.

Gokul Thakur was overjoyed, but he kept his emotions in check. Many of the upper-caste villagers were still staunch

Congress supporters, so he was cautious. However, he did notice that some upper-caste individuals began visiting his home more frequently now.

The only furniture in Gokul Thakur's house was a simple wooden cot or chowki. The front courtyard of the house would often be given a fresh coat of dung-water wash, a common practice in the villages to spruce up the appearance of the home.

In 1967, Ramnath got admission in Patna Science College in Intermediate of Science (10 plus two classes). He says, 'I was the only student who was attending classes in dhoti-kurta. I used to stay at Dariyapur training school. But I never liked studying mathematics and science. Anyhow, I passed my intermediate science examinations,'[36] recalled Ramnath.

Ramnath's mind often wandered away from his studies, as he was always close to the centre of power and fascinated by the stories he heard about his father and other politicians. He yearned to be a part of the political world. By 1970, he had become a full-time politician, devoting himself entirely to the profession. He became a constant companion and attendant to his father, immersing himself in the world of politics.

Thakur's unique connect with people was a frequent topic of discussion. Ramnath would now accompany his father everywhere, including his visits to Pitaunjhia. Rambriksh Singh, a neighbour of Karpoori, says: 'Karpoori had a special way of addressing women, such as Lal Chachi, and would even go straight to their kitchens to ask for food. This helped him cultivate a strong women's constituency through food communication.'[37]

7

No English, Please

Democratization of Education

On 31 July 1967, renowned American journalist and author Paul R. Brass interviewed Dr Rammanohar Lohia:

'Brass: What do you have to say on your insistence on Hindi?

Lohia: Forget Hindi. The point is that there must be people's language.

Brass: Why not a system of translation in the states, the states will themselves adopt a common language?

Lohia: We have had several councils of national integration. They have talked about religion. They have talked about incomes; I mean personal income or about caste. And these are the true issues which cause disintegration the most.

Brass: How do you get rid of the fear of Hindi?

Lohia: Well, I have not been able to get rid of it in my own Hindi states. You have been thinking of the fear of Hindi in Tamilland or in Bengal. I am thinking of the fear of Hindi in

*the Hindi states of UP and Bihar. These blasted scoundrels of the
upper middle classes, whatever they are Bengali. Bengali or Bihari,
they just do not want to get rid of English . . . Why doesn't Vijaya
Laxmi Pandit talk in Hindi in Parliament? Why doesn't Indira
Gandhi do so?'*[1]

With exactitude, this reveals to us the perception of Dr Lohia
regarding the language of one's nation's origin. Moreover, this
explains the cause of his vexation towards the Bihar Deputy Chief
Minister and Education Minister Karpoori Thakur.

Within three months of his appointment as Bihar's deputy
chief minister, Thakur visited Delhi to meet his party's supreme
leader, Dr Rammanohar Lohia. 'After being made to wait for half
an hour, he was told that "Dr Saheb" was indisposed. As a matter
of fact, Dr Lohia's personal assistant, Urmilesh Jha, had been
persuading him to grant an audience to Bihar's visiting deputy
CM. Dr. Lohia, displeased with Karpoori over an undisclosed
matter, did not give Karpoori an audience.'[2]

The astute Karpoori Thakur had also perceived the reason
behind the discontent of his leader, Dr Lohia.

The Bihar education minister had also attended a meeting
called by the then Union education minister Trigun Sen on the
education policy during the same trip. Several ministers, including
Trigun Sen, were astonished by the speech delivered by Karpoori
Thakur on a progressive education policy. The originality and
eloquence of his words were widely praised in newspapers and
magazines.

Returning to Bihar, Karpoori sought an audience with CM
Mahamaya Prasad Sinha and took two important decisions. The
first was to remove the obligation of English as a mandatory
subject in the tenth board examinations. The second was to

exempt farmers cultivating less than 7 acres from paying rent for their land.

The bold move of eliminating English as a compulsory subject for passing matriculation startled both the government and the Opposition, sparking controversy. It was an incredibly courageous decision by any measure, with significant social implications. The ruling class and feudalists vehemently criticized the decision, branding it an assault on the education system.

Nonetheless, Karpoori staunchly defended his decision as the democratization of education. He contended that it was unnecessary to mandate the passing of a non-Indian language for matriculation, even if it was included in the curriculum. He also discovered that the requirement for English proficiency was a major obstacle for students from the Scheduled Castes, Extremely Backward Castes and Other Backward Classes and poor upper caste people in achieving success in the Class 10 board exams, colloquially known as matriculation.

Being labeled as a 'non-matric' was considered an insult and a stain on one's reputation. Karpoori vehemently rejected the notion that he was a product of the Macaulay system. He believed that while learning English was valuable, it was not the sole priority. Instead, he supported Dr Lohia's perspective of elevating the importance of one's native language, be it Hindi or any other language spoken and written in the country.

During that era, individuals who had earned degrees or mastered the English language were held in high esteem, and people would go to great lengths to meet them. Speaking English was associated with prestige and supremacy, and it often elicited feelings of conceit and superiority. It mattered little what one actually spoke in English; the mere ability to speak the language was sufficient to be considered part of the elite. It was akin to holding a certificate of superiority.

I have also been regaled with tales by my father, Sanjay Prasad Singh, and my uncle, Mrityunjay Prasad Singh, who were both teachers from the 1970s until early 2000. They would often be hired to attend wedding parties to engage the wedding party in debates in English and were paid with a pair of dhoti-kurtas and Rs 51 each for outperforming the guests. My father used to recount how the visitors would ask a question in English, and if no one in the wedding party could answer it, it would be considered a triumph for the hosts.

The burden of English weighed heavy on many shoulders, regardless of their caste or creed. Upper-caste students too faced the same fate, as prospects of marriage and jobs seemed to abate for those who were 'non-matric'. A job as a police constable or any modest opportunity for employment seemed unattainable for many just because they had faltered in their English examination.

Karpoori Thakur, the leader who dared to change the norm, took a brave decision, weathering many a storm because he believed in democratizing education by giving all students a fair chance, without discrimination.

With this bold move, Karpoori Thakur broke away from the colonial mindset that had placed too much emphasis on the English language at the expense of the native languages. Even today, the convent education system continues to prioritize English-medium schooling as its core, perpetuating a culture that glorifies English and demeans other Indian languages.

Karpoori Thakur's decision challenged this dominant narrative and paved the way for a more inclusive and equitable education system that valued all languages and dialects spoken in the country. It was a decision that not only helped OBC and

Dalit students, who were struggling to pass matriculation because of their lack of proficiency in English, but also benefited a large section of upper-caste students, especially girls who faced similar challenges. The bold step taken by Karpoori Thakur continues to inspire generations of students and educators to rethink the role of language in education and to work towards a more diverse and inclusive learning environment.

Jeffrey Witsoe writes, 'Since Lohia held that caste status along with English education and wealth were three primary characteristics of India's ruling classes, he believed that purely class-based socialism would not unseat the ruling classes, even with full public ownership over what Nehru referred to as the "commanding heights" of the economy.'[3]

Dr Lohia believed that a true socialist movement in India needed to go beyond just political and economic revolution, and actively combat the deeply entrenched caste inequality in the country. He advocated inter-caste marriages and even proposed making them a prerequisite for public employment. According to him, socialism with a vested interest only focused on political and economic aspects and failed to address the social and cultural inequalities in India. He believed that the socialist movement needed to adapt to the unique conditions of India and take a comprehensive approach to achieve true equality and justice.

The decision to end the compulsion of passing in English in the Bihar board Class 10 examinations during the era (1967–1972) of the 'unstable governments' was a significant achievement, given the prevailing English and elite mindset. Even though some parties supported it, they also suffered from this mentality. Dr Lohia had great faith in Karpoori and would often say, 'If circumstances arise for Karpoori to leave Bihar, then within 10 years the Samajwadi Party's organization should be established throughout the country, and it should form the government.'[4]

Dr Lohia also wanted Bihar to be the laboratory of socialism, with Karpoori at its epicentre. Therefore, the main tool for social change and development was the focus on languages spoken and written in Bihar.

The authors of *Bihar Me Samajik Parivartan Ke Kuchh Aayam*, Prasanna Kumar Choudhary and Shrikant, note that Karpoori Thakur's 'English-not-mandatory' policy and other socialist initiatives began to yield positive results. They speculate that 'if Dr. Lohia had lived longer, he would have expanded its scope nationally. As time passed, the social composition of students in universities, including the elite Patna University, began to change. The number of rural students from backward castes also started to increase.'[5]

Narendra Pathak, in his book, *Karpoori Aur Samajwad*, referred to it as an experiment in 'indigenous socialism that created a strong attraction among the backward castes'. He argued that the 'language policy of removing English as a mandatory subject helped student-youth and intellectuals of backward agricultural communities to connect emotionally with the socialists. Consequently, the social structure of students began to change in universities, even in the prestigious Patna University. The number of rural students from backward castes has increased in these universities over the years.'[6]

The move started impacting the social fabric, as it created ladders of power for the backward castes. The ground was being prepared for the four upper castes to challenge the growing influence of the top four backward castes—Yadav, Kurmi, Koeri and Bania.

The move also led to a proactive participation of backward students from universities in the 1974 JP Movement. Backward community students, who came in large numbers from the villages, gained the support of their urban counterparts and started becoming a social block, opposed to Bhumihar–Rajput groups commonly referred to as 'Rifle-bullets' because of their muscle power and dominating nature. This movement led to the emergence of an independent generation of leadership from among the backward castes. By the early 1970s, there was an increase in the number of OBC students enrolling in undergraduate courses in universities.

Despite not being the main focus, this movement gave impetus to the process of change in the balance of power within society and acted as a school for the new generation of leadership. Dr Lohia frequently asked the Congress ruling party what should be the language of national identity post-Independence, but could not find an easy answer due to the plurality of Indian society. This is why Dr Lohia talked about 'own language' rather than advocating only Hindi.

Narendra Pathak provided a historical perspective on the language debate in India, pointing out that the spread of English and Persian in the past led to divisions in society and a difference between the elite and the common man. 'During the British period, the language barrier between the rulers and the people worsened, and those who knew English became facilitators between the government and the rest of the population, leading to an inferiority complex among the masses. Mahatma Gandhi and other leaders advocated for a new composite language called "Hindustani" to be the official language of India, while some wanted to retain English due to its importance in science and technology and as a window to the world.'[7]

Socialist leaders like Dr Lohia strongly opposed English and advocated for Hindi to be the official language. Jawaharlal

Nehru maintained the importance of English as the language of government alongside Hindi, while countries like Japan, Germany, France, Russia and China established themselves without relying on English.

Lohia strongly advocated the use of vernacular languages in governance and democracy. During a debate in the Lok Sabha, Dr Lohia emphasized that democracy cannot function if the work of the country is not carried out in the language of the people. He believed that without the use of vernacular languages, Lok Rajya (people's rule) is impossible. Lohia suggested that instead of using English, which only a small percentage of people can understand, speeches and debates should be conducted in various Indian languages. He also criticized the emphasis on English education, saying that it only benefits the top percentage of students and creates a divide between the elite and the common people.

Dr Lohia's belief in the importance of social equality and the empowerment of marginalized sections of society led him to view language as a crucial tool for achieving these goals. He saw language as a way to promote equal participation of all sections of society in the nation's development, and argued that the dominance of English was an obstacle to this goal.

In his view, the use of Hindi as a national language would create a level playing field, where individuals from all backgrounds could contribute equally to the nation's progress. He believed that English was a symbol of colonial domination and that its continued use perpetuated a sense of inferiority among non-English-speaking Indians. Therefore, he advocated for the adoption of Hindi as the official language of India.

Dr Lohia's vision of social and economic justice was also closely linked to his views on language. He believed that true democracy and egalitarianism could only be achieved if all citizens had equal access to education, opportunity and political power. In his view, language was a critical component of this larger project and had to be addressed as part of a broader effort to transform Indian society.

Overall, Dr Lohia saw language as a means to promote social equality and empower marginalized sections of society. He believed that language could be a tool for achieving a more just and egalitarian society, and advocated the adoption of Hindi as the national language of India to further this goal.

Karpoori Thakur aimed to minimize the dropout rate in Bihar and Uttar Pradesh by replacing English with a simple vocabulary for the study of mathematics. According to government reports, children from villages in these states were dropping out of school due to the difficulties of learning English and Mathematics.

After evaluating the situation ten years later in 1977, Karpoori Thakur realized that a significant number of Dalit, backward and poor children had not studied English but were still qualified for jobs. Therefore, he issued a government decree to reserve government jobs for them. Even though it led to the fall of his government, he had achieved a complete cycle of social change through his actions. He justified his choice of becoming a political worker and gaining power. His language policy, education, reservation, land reforms and social change programmes should be viewed as a whole, as they are interconnected. He carefully and silently used his policy intervention to blow off well entrenched state support to the feudal structure, but invited the wrath of elites and privileged classes, which often coincide with privileged castes in India.

Those who grew up in privileged societies could never understand the struggles faced by the marginalized. They attempted to paint Karpoori Thakur, who was a known progressive socialist leader and a believer in casteless society, as a propagator of caste. They also criticized Karpoori Thakur for creating a rift amongst castes by disturbing the equilibrium. Karpoori did shake the centuries-old caste equilibrium based on exploitation of lower castes by the higher castes as it was antithetical to the idea of equality and democracy.

There might have been circumstances that led to the assigning of birth based social hierarchy and different levels of purity to different works but Karpoori knew that independent India in the twentieth century could not afford any system that allowed exploitation and did not afford equal opportunity to all. The privileged section might ignore prevalent discriminatory practices or try to justify them on one pretext or another, but the discriminatory practices did deny the provision of equal opportunity to all. This was why the constituent assembly had decided to extend reservations to other backward classes after conducting a survey for the identification of other backward classes. The grant of reservations to backward castes, women and the poor was a fulfilment of constitutional obligations that others had failed to fulfil.

There is also no denying that Karpoori disturbed the unwritten monopoly of the elite over education as the state was using language as a means to perpetuate the deprivation of education to the masses in order to support a handful of elites. English, being a foreign language, had been difficult to adapt to in the absence of good teachers. Only a select few could afford English teachers. It simply meant that only a few could get education beyond the school level, effectively reserving higher education and all higher jobs for a few elites. Karpoori opened the gates of education for all at one go, destroying the age-old monopoly of a few over access to education.

These two changes continue to invite debates. Nevertheless, Karpoori Thakur's fight for language and equality remains an unforgettable episode in post-independence Indian history.

The 'Karpoori Division' continues to generate controversy and interest, with intriguing stories being told about its legacy. Despite the criticism he faced from Congress and some members of his own SVD alliance, Deputy CM Karpoori Thakur's decision to remove English as a mandatory subject for passing matriculation has not been reversed by any successive government. According to socialist writer Prem Kumar Mani, Chief Minister Lalu Prasad Yadav attempted to restore English as a mandatory subject for Class 10 state board exams, but faced significant resistance from both the opposition and members of his own party. Even his party MP and undeclared number two in the party, Ranjan Prasad Yadav, had proposed the idea of improving education quality by reinstating English, but Lalu ultimately chose not to tamper with Karpoori Thakur's legacy of democratizing education.

Jagdanand Singh says, 'What Lohia had advocated about using one's own language, Karpoori Thakur implemented it on ground. There was no logic in failing a student just because he did not know English. It is talent that matters. He used to say if there is lack of content; it does not matter if a person can express himself in tenlanguages.'[8]

In his book *Sach Yahi Nahi hai*, Mani notes that 'the dispute over English in Bihar has been ongoing, and that even leaders like Shivanand Tiwari and Raghuvansh Prasad Singh opposed the reversal of the Karpoori formula'. Ultimately, Mani argues that Karpoori Thakur's formula was well-considered and democratic, and should not be changed.[9]

It is interesting to note that 'even today, in Bihar School Examination Board's examinations, it is not mandatory to pass in English, while several state boards have made it mandatory. In Bihar, one only has to appear for the English paper examination in order to qualify for the overall examination.'[10]

Several other state boards have kept English mandatory. 'According to Ramnath Thakur, there was a misconception among many people that his father's decision was influenced by his own issues with the English language. However, Ramnath Thakur clarifies that his father was proficient in speaking and writing English, having scored 156 out of 300 marks in his Class 12 board exams, which was an impressive achievement in those days.'[11]

Bihar's energy minister and veteran socialist leader Bijendra Prasad Yadav recalls a 1967 incident. There was a seminar at TNB College, Bhagalpur, and Education Minister Karpoori Thakur was the chief guest. 'A professor named Dr C.P. Singh remarked that since Karpoori Thakur was a barber who would not know English, he removed English as a mandatory subject for Class 10 examinations. Somehow, Karpoori heard it. Though he had prepared his speech in Hindi, he spoke in English throughout and used some difficult words. He also reasoned that Dr Lohia was very good at English and spoke it where necessary. His logic was that English was just another language. After the programme, the organiser asked the red-faced professor in local dialect, Angika, "*Ki re CP, bujhlay angrezi* (So, Mr. CP, could you follow Karpoori Thakur's English?)"'[12]

Muneshwar Singh, a Samastipur resident who knew Karpoori Thakur closely, recalled an incident: 'After his decision on giving 26 per cent reservation, there was a jamboree of national and international journalists in Patna. He addressed the Press Conference with great aplomb and spoke in English during most of his interaction with the Press.'[13]

What Dr Rammanohar Lohia and Karpoori Thakur meant by democratization of education had its resonance in formulations of national policies, such as Sarva Siksha Abhiyan (SSA). Senior bureaucrat Amarjeet Sinha, who played a key role in the formulation of SSA, writes: 'The SSA has indeed made more children come to school. Children from households afflicted by poverty and ignorance have also trudged their way into the school system . . . Communities construct and maintain school infrastructure. More and more locally accountable teachers join the schools even if at less than formal pay scales . . .'[14] Sinha was principal secretary, education, in the Bihar government before he took up key assignments at the Centre.

Love for Hindi

For someone who grew up reading Acharya Hazari Prasad Dwivedi, Ramdhari Singh Dinkar, Jaishanker Prasad, Mahadevi Verma and Rahul Sankrityayan, and had friends like Acharya Janaki Vallabh Shastri, it is not difficult to imagine the foundation of Karpoori Thakur's language: Hindi. One can gauge his hold over Hindi, his erudition and eloquence from his Vidhan Sabha speeches. If one has not read anything on Karpoori yet, one must spare some time to read his speeches from 1952 to 1987.

Karpoori Thakur was a trailblazer in many ways. He was the first chief minister in India to set a precedent by speaking in Hindi at a National Development Council (NDC) meeting. He also made it mandatory for official work in Bihar to be conducted in Hindi, becoming the first CM of the state to do so. Thakur's commitment to the Hindi language was evident in his speeches, which were not only erudite and eloquent but also reflected his deep understanding of the language.

Authors Naresh Vikal and Harinandan Sah write:'During his second term as Chief Minister, Karpoori Thakur ensured that all administrative work in Bihar was conducted in Hindi. He also mandated that all IAS and IPS officers enforce the use of Hindi in their sub-ordinate offices.'[15]

Karpoori Thakur actively participated in various meetings and committees related to promoting the Hindi language in Bihar. Despite his busy schedule, he made sure to attend meetings of the Bihar Rashtrabhasha Parishad, Hindi Pragati Samiti and Hindi Legislative Committee. He also played a key role in establishing the 'Bhojpuri Academy'. In addition, he was the president of a literary organization called 'Sangmani', which earned him the title 'Hindi-Bandhu' among Hindi speakers.

One instance that demonstrates Karpoori Thakur's deep respect for litterateurs was when Acharya Janaki Vallabh Shastri suffered a hip injury and was unable to receive proper medical treatment for several days in Patna. Upon hearing the news, Karpoori immediately went to Patna Medical College and Hospital (PMCH) and met the chief minister and health minister to ensure that Shastri could receive the necessary surgery. On the day of the operation, Karpoori and his son sat outside the operating room to comfort Shastri's wife. They waited until Shastri emerged from the successful surgery before leaving. The same day, Karpoori sent a sealed envelope with Rs 1000 to Shastri's wife to assist with medical expenses.

During his tenure as CM, Karpoori had ensured the nomination of poet Poddar Ramavatar 'Arun' and famous singer Siyaram Tiwari as members of the Bihar Legislative Council. A chief minister can recommend the names of individuals to the governor of the state for appointment as members of the Legislative Council.

During his tenure as chief minister, there was an unprecedented expansion of the activities of the Bihar Rashtrabhasha Parishad. Karpoori Thakur's efforts to form a legal vocabulary in Hindi at the state level will always be remembered. He also gave an impetus to the formation of the Department of Official Language of the State Government. He actively promoted the modern Marathi Dalit literature movement and carefully read the works of writers such as Bhalchandra Phadke, Shankar Rao Sarat, Daya Pawar and Kamalakar Gawane. He greatly admired Dr B.R. Ambedkar's autobiography *Kasa Jhalo*.[16]

Ram Khelavan Rai, former head of the Hindi Department at Patna University, wrote that when Karpoori Thakur took charge as chief minister, he formed the Hindi Pragati Samiti at the state level with the aim of promoting the use of Hindi language in official work. 'The committee's sole purpose was to ensure that Hindi was used in all government offices and private establishments, and to check whether the Official Language Act was being properly complied with. As a result of Karpoori's efforts, the promotion and annual increment of those who violated the Official Language Act was stopped, and even District Magistrates were afraid to violate the Act.' Rai remembered that when he inspected the use of Hindi in government offices as a member of the Hindi Pragati Samiti in 1971–72, there was a sensation throughout the office from top to bottom. All the employees started working in Hindi indiscriminately, fearing that their promotion would be interrupted.'[17]

This practice continues to this day. If Karpoori had not been in power and had not implemented the Official Language Act so ruthlessly, the use of Hindi in official work would not have progressed at the current pace.

Karpoori Thakur firmly believed in the dominance of Hindi, regardless of the stage. He demonstrated his conviction during a meeting of the NDC, where all activities were typically conducted in English. When Karpoori began speaking in Hindi, the other members of the council were reportedly amazed and looked at him in awe. It is worth noting that the NDC approves plans for all states in the country, and Hindi had never been used in its meetings prior to Karpoori's statement.

During Karpoori Thakur's tenure as chief minister, he broke tradition and established the supremacy of Hindi on the platform of the 'National Development Council'. He instructed all government officials to submit files in Hindi only, and no officer dared to violate this rule. Those who did met with swift consequences.

Ramjivan Singh says, 'He further made it mandatory for Christian missionary schools to teach Hindi. Making education more accessible, he did away with the fee for children from a weaker economic background. The movement for making Urdu a second official language got a great boost and encouragement from Karpoori Thakur.'[18]

It was not just a matter of Hindi-service at the government level; Karpoori Thakur was also a great lover and scholar of Hindi literature at a personal level. His personal room was adorned with the complete works of his favourite poets and writers. If even a single volume was missing from his library, Karpoori would immediately notice and become restless until it was found. Collecting the works of his favourite writers and poets brought him immense satisfaction. Some of his favourite literary figures included Dinkar, Benipuri, Nagarjuna, Janaki Vallabh Shastri, Premchand and Renu.

Karpoori's philosophy of life was inspired by the divine mantra of Atharvaveda—'*Kritam me dakshine haste jayo mein savy ahitah*,' which means, 'I hold duty in my right hand and victory in my left hand'. Guided by this philosophy, Karpoori continues to be revered in the public mind of Bihar as an unwavering Hindi devotee, a politician, a freedom fighter, a successful chief minister, an efficient administrator, a social worker, a fierce socialist and a strong opposition leader.

Acharya Janaki Ballabh Shastri recalled that a Kavi Sammelan (a poetry session) was scheduled to be inaugurated by Jayaprakash Narayan. However, he was unable to attend the function due to his illness. The organizers had mostly invited poets from the same caste. 'When I arrived at the function, I was subjected to a great deal of humiliation.' The organizers did not even know Shastri. Despite this, he decided to stay and watch. As the poet was sitting in the audience feeling anxious, Karpoori Thakur suddenly appeared. Karpoori's unexpected arrival held some significance. Some people speculated that since Jayaprakash Narayan had just undergone dialysis, only Karpoori would be able to inaugurate the function.

Karpoori Thakur's electrifying voice echoed through the microphone as he spoke. Quoting Karpoori, Janaki Vallabh Shastri wrote: 'If I were to say anything about poetry and literature in the presence of Acharya Janaki Vallabh Shastri, it would be audacious of me. I request him to do us the honour of carrying on with the proceedings.' The assembly fell silent, struck by the profound appreciation expressed by Karpoori Thakur for Acharya Janaki Vallabh Shastri's literary prowess.'[19]

On a previous occasion at Patori College in Samastipur, many poets and artists from all over the country had gathered. As the president of the event, the final poetry reading was given by Shastri. During his recital, he took notes on Shastri's poems and later asked him to fill in the gaps Karpoori had missed.

Shastri recalled an incident when he and Karpoori Thakur were both admitted to Patna Medical College and Hospital. Shastri had broken his legs and Karpoori Thakur had suffered a mild heart attack.'I too was resting in a corner of the hospital cot with two broken legs. Other patients who shared the hall with me were surprised to see how frequently Karpoori visited me at least twice during my one-month stay. This was particularly notable because Karpoori himself was recovering from a heart attack at the time,'[20] wrote Shastri. As Karpoori Thakur was not allowed to climb the stairs and Shastri was not able to walk, Karpoori would see his poet friend from downstairs.

Karpoori was well known for his love for art and music. While he greatly admired the works of Ramdhari Singh Dinkar and Sachchidanand Hiranand Vatsyayan Agyeya, he was also a great aficionado of Pandit Ravi Shankar's sitar and Ustad Bismillah Khan's shehnai.

In Love with Maithili and Bhojpuri Too

Karpoori Thakur's passion for language extended beyond Hindi; he also took several strong steps to promote the Maithili language and was an avid fan of the work of Vidyapati and Nagarjuna, just as he was of Hindi writers and poets.

According to Satyanarayan Prasad Yadav, a researcher at Lalit Narayan Mithila University (LNMU), Karpoori Thakur raised questions regarding the spread of the Maithili language in nearly every Assembly session between 1952 and 1967. 'He frequently criticized the Congress for neglecting Maithili and advocated for primary education to be conducted in one's own language.'[21]

Naresh Vikal and Harinandan Sah wrote: 'On 22 December 1977, Karpoori Thakur wrote a letter to the then Union law minister Shanti Bhushan, requesting that Maithili be included in the Eighth Schedule of the Constitution. He emphasized that Maithili was a widely spoken language in Bihar and was even being studied at universities in Kolkata and Nepal. Despite the Bihar government's efforts to promote and recognize Maithili, it was not afforded the same facilities as other languages, such as being used as a medium for primary education and receiving translation services from various languages.'[22]

Karpoori Thakur believed that Maithili was a vibrant language with immense potential for growth. He argued that Maithili deserved its own independent form and identity due to its unique script and independent grammar. He maintained that Maithili met all linguistic criteria for a fully developed language, including sound, terms, sentence structure and meaning. Indeed, universities had been granting masters, PhD and DLitt degrees in Maithili for over fifty years.

Ramnath Thakur says, 'Karpoori Thakur once spoke to Dr Lohia about Bhojpuri, which is spoken in a large part of Bihar and Uttar Pradesh. He said, "It is the language of men. Manhood drips from every word and phrase . . . If Jagjivan Babu had shown a sign of manhood in Delhi, then I would have considered him a true man . . . " These words were spoken in the presence of former Union Minister Jagjivan Ram.'[23]

The state government waived off the school fees of students till Class 7. In the thirty-three-point programme announced on 5 June 1967, the government also decided to give dearness allowance (DA) to state government employees on parity with the DA hike given by the Central government. The government also passed an order saying that teachers in non-government secondary schools would get the same salary as teachers in government schools and college teachers would now be paid, as per the recommendations of the University Grants Commission.

* * *

What Karpoori Thakur meant by empowerment through education can be exemplified through the instance of Manisha Priyam, who hailed from a village in Bihar and is now a professor at the Department of Education Policy, National Institute for Educational Planning and Administration, New Delhi. She grew up seeing Karpoori Thakur often visit her Patna home and hold intense political discussions with her MLA father, Baidyanath Pandey.

She recalled: 'Karpoori Thakur was to play an important role in my higher education, even fighting with my father to let me study in a reputed college in Delhi. I had topped Patna University in the Intermediate, and wanted to join Lady Shri Ram College. My father knew it was good for me to study, but was hesitant to send me to Delhi. Economist and Patna University Vice Chancellor Ganesh Prasad Singh was staying in Bihar Bhavan. So were Karpoori Thakur and my father. Thakur discussed the matter with the VC, and the next morning I saw Karpoori Thakur roaring at my father in the Bihar Bhavan lawns "*Baidnath, padhne do usko. Woh America bhi jaayegi* (Let her study. One day, she would go to US too)". Thus, I came to Delhi and Thakur's words for me proved prophetic.'[24]

NEP–2020: The Full Circle

What Lohia and Karpoori strove for with reference to the importance of one's own language is the very core of the National Education Policy 2020. Speaking at the inauguration of the Akhil Bhartiya Shiksha Samagam at the Bharat Mandapam in New Delhi on 29 July 2023, Prime Minister Narendra Modi emphasized that many developed nations, including European countries, had an edge owing to their local languages. 'But in India, despite an array of distinguished languages, they were presented as a sign of backwardness, and those who could not speak English were neglected and their talents were not recognized . . . As a result, the children of the rural areas remained most affected,'[25] said the PM, adding that this belief was being shed now as he would often speak in Hindi even at the United Nations. What Lohia and Karpoori had said in the 1960s has come a full circle now.

8

Yes, Chief Minister

When Karpoori Checkmated Ramanand Tiwari

You may remember that as the elected President of the Sanyukt Socialist Party (SSP) in Bihar (in 1969), I was given the right to nominate members of the state committee. However, every time the committee was nominated, your opinion was sought. After the Sonpur conference of the SSP, where the question of forming a joint legislature party and joining the government came up, I was chosen as the leader of the SSP Legislature Party and could have become Chief Minister. But you believed that the SSP should not join hands with reactionary and communal parties like Congress (O), Bharatiya Jana Sangh, and Swatantra Party. At the SSP's national committee meeting in Varanasi, there was pressure on me to become Chief Minister. However, I opposed the proposal to form the government in alignment with your wishes.

. . . After the fall of Daroga Prasad Rai's government in December 1970, when the question of forming a coalition

government again came up, you took me to the audience gallery of the Assembly and said that since now a piece of SSP has been included in this coalition, its character has changed and you have asked me to accept the post of chief minister. You will remember that I had said that with the arrival of only three persons from Praja Socialist Party (PSP), the organization will be divided into reactionary and communal parties like Congress, Jana Sangh and Swatantra Party. How the character of the coalition changed, then you again insisted on your argument and even against my wish, I accepted to become the coalition leader and chief minister, which I had rejected once. But when I accepted your proposal and got elected as the leader of the coalition, Raj Narain and his colleagues from the Centre came and talked to you and asked you to become the leader of the coalition and Chief Minister, then you agreed. I was asked to give up the post of SVD leader for Karpoori Thakur and let him become the Chief Minister. . . . I rejected the post of Chief Minister twice for you.

Incidentally, I remembered one more thing. After the Sonpur Conference and Varanasi National Committee meeting when I was about to resign from the post of SVD leader, a central leader told me that you were befooling and cheating me and don't want me to be the chief minister . . .[1]

This letter, written by socialist leader and former Bihar minister and ex-MP Ramanand Tiwari to his friend and compatriot Karpoori Thakur sometime in 1972, clearly blames Thakur for preventing Tiwari from becoming the chief minister twice—first in 1969 and then in 1970. This lesser-known fact of Bihar's political history shows that Karpoori Thakur was no less astute than others when it came to the game of power. Ramanand Tiwari was perhaps his biggest rival in the party and Karpoori Thakur manoeuvred his way to get the better of him, and hoodwink him out of the race to be the CM.

Though Karpoori Thakur had replied to Tiwari's letter, he did not touch upon the sensitive subject raised by his colleague. This shows that he refused to give any legitimacy to the serious allegations made against him.

Senior journalist Surendra Kishore, who was the personal assistant of Karpoori Thakur, in the early 1970s, narrates the Tiwari–Karpoori rivalry story: 'Karpoori Thakur's supporters had perhaps advised him not to allow Ramanand Tiwari to become chief minister. Some supporters also argued that only a leader of a backward caste should become CM from the socialist camp. MLC Indra Kumar, a close aide of Karpoori Thakur, had also played a key role by saying that it was not proper for Tiwari to take the help of Bhartiya Jana Sangh to become CM but sometime later, Karpoori took BJS support to become CM in December 1970. It might well be a political victory for Karpoori Thakur over Ramanand Tiwari but it was a moral loss for Karpoori Thakur.'[2]

In his 28 February 1970 letter to the SSP, Tiwari emphasized that BJS intended to push the country towards Hindu fascism. Tiwari wrote, 'the foundational edifice of BJS is communal tension and hatred. It is unacceptable for SSP to form a government with BJS . . . we should always remember that forming a government is only the means and not the end.'[3]

Shivanand Tiwari, Ramanand Tiwari's son and former Rajya Sabha MP, says that although his father never directly spoke to him about his differences with Karpoori Thakur, their friendship was never the same after his father missed the opportunity to become the CM twice. He says, 'I remember Karpoori Thakur visiting my ailing father regularly in the late 1970s but my father would barely talk to him and would answer Karpoori Thakur's queries in one or two words. At times, my father would turn his back in his bed to avoid looking at his old friend.'[4]

Ramnath Thakur, however, played down the episode. He says, 'Ramanand Tiwari and my father were great friends. But some people in the party tried to create differences between them.'[5]

But there are other ways to look at it. Karpoori Thakur, despite being the only MLA from the EBC Nai (barber) caste, took over the leadership of all backward castes. He made his way to get the acceptability of the upper castes and become the unchallenged leader of OBCs despite the presence of Yadav, Koeri and Kurmi leaders. A unique aspect of Bihar's politics was that non-Congress leaders were repelled by the Congress leadership. Neha Ranjan writes, 'Socialist leader Ramanand Tiwari, who was critical of the tallest Congress leader and former CM Sri Krishna Singh, had become silent during the tenure of Binodanand Jha as Bihar CM. PSP leader Basavan Singh was more critical of Jha than Tiwari.'[6] The changed approach gave credence to the belief that he was more loyal to his caste than to his party.

According to Paul R. Brass, 'this only helped Karpoori Thakur establish himself as the leader. In the Socialists' campaign for backward caste empowerment, any Socialist leader from an upper caste background could not have succeeded.'[7]

Call it politics, opportunism, peer rivalry or pure ambition, Karpoori Thakur, the original subaltern hero, finally arrived on the scene.

Main Karpoori Thakur . . .

In the mid-term elections of 1969, the SSP's tally in the Vidhan Sabha decreased to fifty-three seats from sixty-eight, while Congress won 118 seats. Karpoori Thakur won his fifth consecutive election from his home-turf, Tajpur, defeating Congress candidate Rajendra Mahto by 13,485 votes.

On 22 December 1970, Karpoori Thakur became the CM of Bihar. 'SSP, Congress (O), Janata Party, Bharatiya Kranti Dal, Shoshit Samaj Dal (Mandal group), Hul Jharkhand Party, Swatantra Party, PSP, Loktantrik Congress and some Independents joined his government.'[8]

Just before becoming the CM, Karpoori Thakur had taken part in a hunger strike to express solidarity with the demands of workers of several factories in Jamshedpur. The hunger strike gained widespread public support from different parts of the state, ultimately compelling the administrators of the Tata factory to concede to the workers' demands on the twenty-eighth day of the strike.

But the story of how Karpoori Thakur became the CM is very interesting. Socialist leader Umesh Prasad Singh (83), a close aide of Dr Rammanohar Lohia in Bihar, recalled: 'Pranab Chatterjee, a close associate of Karpoori Thakur, instructed me to inform Thakur that Satyendra Narayan Sinha wanted to meet him immediately. I found Thakur at the residence of a party leader near Gandhi Maidan, where I saw Thakur and Ramanand Tiwari arguing over some matter. I mustered the courage to whisper the message to Thakur. Later, Tiwari also agreed to come along, and Sinha's Congress (O) extended support to Karpoori Thakur, along with Jan Sangh and other parties. Thakur staked his claim to form the government on the same day. If this had not happened, the Assembly could have been dissolved.'[9]

Satyendra Narayan Sinha is an interesting case study in Bihar politics due to his role in both forming and destabilizing governments. While Sinha was responsible for the fall of the SVD government in 1968, when Karpoori was the deputy CM, he was instrumental in making Karpoori Thakur the CM in 1970 after the fall of the Daroga Rai government.

Among the first set of people who welcomed Karpoori Thakur to the chair were educationists. Taking forward his decision of democratizing education by removing English as a mandatory subject in the Class 10 board examinations during his tenure as deputy CM-cum-education minister in 1967, he made education free in the state till matriculation (Class 10). The government also started providing free books to primary school children. Teachers and non-teaching staff also started getting dearness allowance (DA). The government also decided to waive off land rent payable by small farmers. He also waived off rent from all unprofitable holdings and abolished the surcharge on land.

The government started old age pensions. The idea came from the CM's own experience with his parents. Ramnath Thakur recalled: 'After becoming the CM in 1970, he visited Pitaunjhia and touched the feet of his parents. My grandmother gave him 25 paise as a blessing. My grandfather had also wanted to give him some money as blessing. As he had no money, he silently went out of the house to escape embarrassment. My father could sense his father's helplessness. This is where he got the idea of starting old age pensions.'[10]

Karpoori Thakur also encouraged the Khadi village industry. He set up a book bank for poor students and took the initiative for providing livelihood to agricultural labourers. He also started strengthening the local administration by resuming Panchayat polls to realize Mahatma Gandhi's dream of political and economic decentralization.

Ravish Chandra Verma, finance minister in the Karpoori Thakur government, said during his budget presentation in 1971: '. . . .The percentage of the number of reserved seats (In the

Assembly) for Harijans was increased from 12 per cent to 14 per cent. Education up to middle school has been made free. Apart from this, the government has decided to provide interim assistance to the government employees . . . Population is our asset, not a liability.'[11]

Responding to a question by MLA Haricharan Roy on the Dhebar Commission in the Assembly on 23 March 1971, Karpoori Thakur said: 'All the commissions for backward castes like Dhebar Commission, Kaka Kalelkar Commission, Niyogi Commission etc., their recommendations and why those recommendations have not been implemented, this commission has given an extensive report on all such issues while also giving its recommendations on how to implement them.'[12]

Then the CM faced tricky questions on the status of the recommendations of the Aiyer Commission that had indicted top Congress leaders.

Replying to Sunil Mukherjee's query, Karpoori Thakur said: 'It has been one-and-a-half years and we have written to the Central Government inquiring about the actions taken against those against whom allegations have been proved. It has been a year and a half since the investigation was started. We are stuck. One and a half years passed but the work of investigation was not completed. I have written to the Prime Minister today itself to complete the investigation and demanded that the guilty should be brought to book . . .'[13]

The day after taking over as the Chief Minister, Thakur's cabinet took the first major decision to strictly implement the Official Language Act and made it mandatory to use Hindi for all official communication. With the caption '*Janta ki bhasha ka aadar, loktantra ka aadar*' (respecting the people's language is respecting democracy), *Aryavarta* newspaper's editorial reported 'Chief Minister Karpoori Thakur has informed the press that adverse comments will be mentioned in the service book of all those who would violate this directive . . . needless to state that the common people of Bihar faced enormous trouble due to the usage in English in official work . . . The gulf between the government and people that is preserved by English is not letting people experience that they live in a democratic society.'[14]

During his tenure as CM for just 163 days, he introduced free elementary education in schools till the eighth standard and made Urdu a second official language of Bihar.

He gave a broad vision of his government in his speech in the Assembly on 26 March 1971:

Speaker Sir, I was requesting that we are going to implement the laws regarding land reform. We are going to do this with great speed and strength. The Revenue Minister has sent circulars to all the districts. A programme has been prepared to implement the laws regarding Bataidar, Basgeet etc. It has been asked to send it by April 15, 1971. We will not leave it to the officer, we will hand it over to the district ministers. We will analyse the work done in every district by each and every minister and minister of state so that we can implement the laws that have been made by us. One more thing that we are going to do is for the poor who have been living in the Notified Area Committee for 50 years but did not have the right over Basgeet land. We are going to amend the law. That the poor who are settled in the Notified Area Committee should be given the right over Basgeet land, we will get them what you did not get them (clap). Not only this. Those who do eviction will be punished with imprisonment of six months and a fine of one thousand rupees. Now the matter of Hindi; we have taken steps for complete Hindiization. Not only have we taken the steps, but we have implemented almost 95 per cent of them. Only 5 per cent have not been implemented because all the existing typewriter machines and teleprinters support only English language. We have ordered that English typewriter machines should be removed, English teleprinters should be removed. Money has to be arranged for this . . .within a month, English machines will be removed from government offices and 100 per cent Hindi work will be completed. You have talked about Harijans and Adivasis. We have told that we have facilitated them. We have set up a commission with the aim of ensuring that the Harijans, the backward people, get the facilities they should get . . . Panchayati Raj Act will remain in force in the entire state till June 30. . . . Apart from the Demarcation Act, all the works related to land reform, whether it is the work of consolidation, the work of distribution of Basgeet land papers, the question of distribution of land among the poor, whether it is the matter of implementing the Emergency Cultivation and Irrigation Act, All these laws will be implemented, they will definitely come . . . We have taken such a decision that not even a single student is left . . . You should know that we are going to give more scholarships to tribal and Harijan students than what we did last year. Similarly, we have approved scholarship for other students who are poor.[15]

One of the reasons for Karpoori Thakur's mass appeal was that he was never afraid of facing a crowd even if it threatened to become a mob. Soon after becoming the CM, when he was at Patna's Circuit House, a group of protestors had been waiting outside. When the CM went to meet the protesting youths, some of them pushed the CM aside. Shiv Kumar says, 'Seeing the security threat to the CM, the police guards rushed. Just when the police was thinking of lathi-charging to drive them away, he stopped the police and took it upon himself to calm down the youth and asked them what their demands were. The students listened to the

CM with great patience and calmness as the CM took note of the students' grievances.'[16]

Karpoori Thakur's commitment towards the socialist ideology remained unwavering. When Prime Minister Indira Gandhi came to Patna, Karpoori Thakur, the Chief Minister, went to the airport to receive the PM. While walking, Indira Gandhi said: 'Can't you come with us? If it happens, I will change the contour of North Indian politics.' Karpoori kept quiet. But when the PM was climbing the stairs of Raj Bhavan, the CM replied: 'I cannot come with you. I had turned down a similar offer from your great father as well.'[17] This was the third instance after 1962 and 1964 when Karpoori Thakur had said no to the Congress.

Karpoori hated doing any undue favours to his relatives and friends after becoming the CM. A Pitaunjhia villager Muneshwar Singh recalled: 'Once when Karpoori was the Chief Minister, his brother-in-law went to him asking for a job. Karpooriji became serious after listening to him and gave him fifty rupees out of his own pocket.'[18]

On 2 June 1971, his government fell, partly because of the protests following the riots in Jamshedpur but mainly because of the inherent contradictions in the coalition experiment and also because of legislators from his alliance crossing over to other parties. He had tried to keep his allies in good humour by expanding his cabinet in February 1971 but his government still could not survive. He was succeeded by Bhola Paswan Shastri, who became CM for the third time in a brief span of three years.

Pitaunjhia Files

Pitaunjhia village was no longer a nondescript village, especially after five-time MLA from Tajpur Karpoori Thakur became CM in December 1970. Even though Karpoori Thakur would hardly visit his paternal village, his Pitaunjhia house caught people's attention. The thatched house in front of Durbar was under the spotlight now.

A few days after Karpoori Thakur became CM, his father Gokul Thakur was surprised to see one morning that someone had unloaded some truckloads of bricks in front of his house. It was assumed that Gokul Thakur would accept the gift from the unidentified contractor and use it to build his house. But Gokul Thakur knew his son very well. The CM came to know about it. He immediately called up the Darbhanga DM and said: 'It is 2 p.m., you must ensure that the bricks are removed from my place by 6 p.m. . . . The CM's order was followed and the bricks were finally used in construction of the village school.'[19]

The fact that Karpoori was the CM did not change Gokul Thakur. He continued to follow his traditional profession as a barber. Once Gokul Thakur, feeling slightly under the weather, had refused to respond to the call of an upper-caste person. The enraged man sent his musclemen to Gokul Thakur's house to thrash the unobliging barber. The entire district administration went into a tizzy. After all, the father of the serving chief minister had been roughed up. The offender was held, beaten up and held in police custody. When Karpoori Thakur got to know about the incident, he asked the Samastipur district magistrate not to file an FIR. The DM could not believe his ears for a while, but recovered to protest mildly: 'Sir, this is a question of the prestige of the entire state. How can we tolerate this?' A calm Karpoori Thakur said: 'DM Saheb, you can save the father of the chief minister. How about thousands of such fathers being beaten up without the knowledge of the administration every day? Time will settle these questions. It is a slow process.'[20]

Anisur Rahman, former associate professor, LKVD College, Tajpur, recalled how Karpoori Thakur ensured that Samastipur area had many colleges. 'It was sometime in 1971. Karpoori Thakur had been finding ways to get land donation to start a college at Tajpur. Someone suggested that Mahant Visheshwar Das of Darbhanga could donate land if approached. Karpoori did so and told Das that the college would have his name too. Das donated the desired 10 acres of land and later gave five more acres of land at Darbhanga. This is how Lohia Karpoori Visheshwar Das College came into being at Tajpur.'[21]

The Socialists' Struggle Continues

'In 1971, at the railway station in Pune, the son was complaining to the father, "When will you get me a warm coat, my coat is torn, there is a patchwork on it". The father was saying, "I will get you a new coat, you are still wearing the old one." . . . the father was Karpoori Thakur, the two-time chief minister of Bihar, and the son, Ramnath Thakur, both were talking at the station in Pune, returning after the end of the National Convention of the United Socialist Party.'[22] This is how Prof. Rajkumar Jain, a socialist academician, recalled an instance of probity Karpoori Thakur practised in real life.

Though Thakur had become the Leader of Opposition after the 1972 Assembly polls, he had no car. Leaders of Opposition (LoP) got the rank of cabinet ministers only after 1977, when the Morarji Desai government gave LoP parity with a cabinet minister and the states also replicated the norm. A rickshaw was the usual mode of travel in Patna for Karpoori Thakur. Once when he had to go to Samastipur to placate a rebel party MLA, he asked former CM and Congress MLA (in 1972) Mahamaya Prasad Sinha for help. Surendra Kishore says, 'Sinha gave Karpoori Thakur Rs 400 to hire a taxi from Patna to Samastipur.'[23]

Surendra Kishore, then Surendra Akela, was a witness to Karpoori's legendary rivalry with Ramanand Tiwari. The two kept attacking each other through letters and articles published against each other in *Dinman*. Karpoori Thakur was allotted a bungalow along Bir Chand Patel Path. Kishore recalled an incident from the early 1970s that tells a lot about the social churn: 'Senior socialist leader Suraj Narayan Singh was the neighbour of Karpoori Thakur. There was a function at Singh's place. Ramanand Tiwari, who was sitting next to Karpoori Thakur, said "*Karpooriji, aap ghabraiye nahi, aapka chhou aana to fix hai*" (you don't need to worry as your share is secured). At this, Karpoori Thakur said gnashing his teeth: "*ab chhou aana se kaam nahi chalne wala*" (we can no longer do with this share).'[24]

Kishore too recalled an instance of Karpoori Thakur's honesty: 'Sometime in 1972, he gave me a bill of Rs 600 to take to the accounts section of the Bihar Vidhan Sabha. The dealing clerk scorned me and asked me to come with an inflated bill of Rs 1300 saying "*Rs 600 se Karpooriji jaise neta ka kaam kaise chalega* (how could a leader like Karpoori Thakur do with Rs 600)?" When I narrated it to Thakur, he called the clerk a swindler and the Congress system corrupt. Karpoori Thakur took the bill back and kept it in his drawer.'[25]

Even after serving once as deputy CM and CM, he had no problem riding any kind of vehicle if he needed to travel somewhere. A.N. Pandey says, 'In 1972, when he was not getting any vehicle to go to Darbhanga from Samastipur, he waved at a truck carrying soil to stop. He sat next to the driver without telling him who he was.'[26]

Given the socialist experiment between 1965 and 1972, the Congress had to prop up a number of backward castes and Dalits as its chief ministers in Bihar. The Socialists in Bihar were divided in two factions during this period too—one led by Bhola Prasad Singh who advocated an alliance with BJS and the other group led by Ramanand Tiwari.

As the Congress got an absolute majority in the 1972 Assembly polls with 167 seats and formed the government under Kedar Pandey, the disintegration of the socialists started again. Meanwhile, Karpoori Thakur won his sixth consecutive Assembly poll from Tajpur as the SSP candidate, defeating the Congress candidate Kamlesh Rai by 10,568 votes. The process of the socialists' merger and demerger started afresh.

On 9 August 1971, PSP, headed by N.G. Gore, and SSP, headed by Karpoori Thakur, merged to become the Socialist Party. Karpoori was unanimously made its president. But in 1972, differences cropped up in the party. Karpoori Thakur and Mama Baleshwar Dayal made every possible effort to address the differences. But when things did not work out, Karpoori resigned from the post of party president. He formed the 'Ektavadi Samajwadi Manch' to work on unity. But most socialists joined to form the United Socialist Party with Mama Baleshwar Dayal as its president. Before the 1972 Assembly polls, he was again part of the Sanyukt Socialist Party.

For meeting election expenses, Karpoori Thakur would never press for large donations. In an incident in 1972, someone from SSP asked a businessman to give adonation to Karpoori Thakur. Senior journalist Surendra Kishore recalled: 'The businessman had arranged Rs 50,000—a big amount in those days, but had been hesitant on giving the sum thinking it a "small sum for the big leader". When he asked Thakur how much "*seva* (donation)" he expected, the leader said: "*Agar aap paanch hajjar de dete hai to hamara kaam chal jayega* (If you can give Rs 5,000, we will manage)". Karpoori's emphasis on *"paanch hajjar"* showed how small a purse SSP had. Later, when his associate learnt about the businessman keeping ready Rs 50,000 cash ready, he revealed it to him during a rickshaw ride. Thakur had said: "If you accept Rs 5,000, it will be considered as a donation but if you take Rs 50,000, it will be conveniently regarded as a bribe."'[27]

Author Narendra Pathak quotes socialist leader Janeshwar Mishra to describe Karpoori Thakur: 'Dr Lohia died at a young age and Karpoori Thakur thought it appropriate to remain active in Bihar, worrying about mobilizing his people in exchange for a national role . . .'[28]

But then, JP was beckoning. The Bihar Movement was going to change it all for socialist and coalition politics.

9

Let's Go to JP

The Movement That Heralded Coalition in India

6 December, 1976

Dear Jayaprakash Babu,

Some say that there is an obstacle in the making of a national alternative. Choudhary Charan Singh is also taken as a reactionary leader opposed to socialism. This must have come to your notice as well. But in reality, Singh is not reactionary but progressive, socialist, Gandhian and believing in Mahatma Gandhi's interpretation of villages, agricultural farmers, village industries, poor, dalits, economic and social equality, decentralization, peaceful means, satyagraha and agitation and civil liberties . . .

I hold that among the leaders of the four Opposition parties today, Charan Singh's party has undeniably the widest mass base and influence among the villages and farmers. Therefore, not only from the point of view of justice, but also from the point of view of

*selfishness and benefit of the new party, Singh should be made the
President (of a proposed party after its merger)* . . .

*So far as satyagrah is concerned, Charan Singh is in favour
of engaging in any big fight to safeguard civil liberties. He wants
to prepare well for it. You may well speak to him. He believes that
any new party should have a better image than Congress* . . .

*Now, let us discuss Total Revolution. If he can be convinced
either with Gandhism or Total Revolution, he should have no
objection. In any case, he is not the kind of person to say yes to
anything without giving it a thought. You know him very well and
just in case, do you think if one does not take an oath in name of
Total Revolution, one cannot be a national alternative* . . . *I still
hold that we should vouch for Gandhism and civil liberty for an
alternative because Total Revolution is not fully defined yet.*'[1]

This letter speaks a lot about the role of Karpoori Thakur in the
Bihar Movement, popularly known as the JP Movement, and
his efforts to stitch together a national alternative against the
Congress. The students' movement that had shaken PM Indira
Gandhi, later forcing her to impose Emergency in the country,
brought about the first fall of the Congress at the national level.

The movement also provided a bridge between the old
and new generations of socialists. It introduced the post-Lohia
generation of socialists, Raj Narain, Madhu Limaye, George
Fernandes, Hemwati Nandan Bahuguna and Karpoori Thakur
to the younger generation of Mulayam Singh Yadav, Ram Vilas
Paswan, Lalu Prasad and Nitish Kumar.

But the important takeaway of the JP Movement was not
the much talked about rivalry between Jayaprakash Narayan and
Indira Gandhi but the fact that it heralded an era of coalition at
the national level, an experience that was replicated by V.P. Singh

in 1989 and Atal Behari Vajpayee in 1998. The JP Movement had also gone on to end the untouchability of the Bharatiya Jana Sangh (BJS) forever with the formation of the Janata Party in which the saffron party was a key player.

Even though Jayaprakash Narayan led the Bihar Movement of 1974, Karpoori Thakur played a very crucial role in mobilizing mass support for the movement. Karpoori used the movement to showcase his leadership skills and connect with the masses even when he had been in hiding, moving from one place to another for nineteen months since the Emergency had been imposed.

As his letter to JP shows, he is not fully convinced with the idea of Total Revolution. Rather, he vouched for the Saptkranti slogan of Dr Lohia on no discrimination on the lines of gender, caste, religion and nationality. He also openly questioned the 'silence' of Acharya Vinoba Bhave against Indira Gandhi's decision to impose Emergency. His letters to Bhave are well-reasoned and show his moral courage against the Bhoodan Movement saint. One often talks more in terms of the JP Movement producing second-generation Bihar leaders like Lalu Prasad, Nitish Kumar, Sushil Kumar Modi, Ashwini Choubey, Raghuvansh Prasad Singh, Narendra Singh, Jagdanand Singh and Ravi Shankar Prasad. It also went on to establish Karpoori Thakur as the most important non-Congress leader. Even though Karpoori had already served as the CM, he further cemented his position as the leader of socialists in Bihar, especially when socialist ideology was at a crossroads.

The biggest problem with socialist parties over the years was the lack of leadership. Acharya Narendra Dev died before the second General Elections. Dr Rammanohar Lohia was leading a faction of it for over a decade. It was only after Dr Lohia came to the centrestage before the 1967 polls, that there was a socialist upsurge again and the Congress faced the toughest resistance. But after the death of Dr Lohia in October 1967, there was a big vacuum until another big leader Jayaprakash Narayan came out of political hibernation to lead the 1974 Movement and the entire Opposition was galvanized.

Karpoori Thakur, who had appeared to be in the doldrums after the 1972 polls, also found a strong reason to reboot his politics and challenge the Congress afresh with new vigour. Vishnudev Rajak writes, 'Before the movement of 1974 started, Karpoori Thakur and Ramanand Tiwari started attending meetings of Jayaprakash Narayan in the Patna University campus. This way, students got an opportunity to listen to the trio.'[2]

It was also because of the glue factor, JP, that Karpoori and Ramanand forgot their personal differences for a larger cause.

Gujarat's Navnirman movement provided a prelude to the Bihar Movement. The students of Gujarat had been demanding the dissolution of the Legislative Assembly following the resignation of Chimanbhai Patel as CM.

The First Bihar State Student Leaders' Conference was held on 8 February 1974 under the leadership of Patna University Student Union President Lalu Prasad. On 17–18 February 1974, a comprehensive state level student leaders' conference was organized in Patna University and a steering committee was formed to prepare for a big conference.

Rajak writes, 'This was the first time in the history of the student movements of Bihar that conferences were organised on the issues of hostel problems, food bills and difficult question papers in the examination.'[3]

The Bihar Students' Chhatra Sangharsh Samiti was formed at the state level. The Bihar State Students' Struggle Committee decided to gherao (surround) the Bihar Assembly on 18 March 1974. Legislators from non-Congress parties were asked to boycott the Governor's address in the Legislative Assembly. By 8 March, BJS, the Communist Party and the Socialist Party announced the boycott of the first day's meeting of the Legislative Assembly. Later, other opposition parties also followed suit. Karpoori played an important role in it. On 15 March, a seven-member delegation of Chhatra Sangharsh Samiti met the governor and requested him not to address the Legislative Assembly but the governor refused to do so.

Just in the midst of the movement, student leader Lalu Prasad said at a Gandhi Maidan function that their movement must not be owned by politicians. The next day, Karpoori Thakur held a press conference and said: '*Andolan kisi ke baap ka nahi hota. Andolan me koi bhi bhaag le sakta hai* (A movement cannot be patronized. Anyone can take part in a movement).'[4]

On 18 March, thousands of students reached the Vidhan Sabha. The Congress government under CM Abdul Ghafoor decided to deal sternly with the agitators. Scores of unarmed students were lathi-charged. Subsequent police firing killed eight people. The offices of two local dailies, *Pradeep* and *Searchlight*, were torched.

Sushil Kumar Modi, the former Bihar deputy CM and BJP Rajya Sabha MP, then a student leader, recalls: 'When we started the march from Patna Science College, there would not be more than fifty-odd students. But as we moved on, people started joining us at every key point and when we reached Vidhan Sabha, it was like a sea of humanity.'[5]

Karpoori Thakur and Dhanik Lal Mandal of SSP and Thakur Prasad of BJS were among the top leaders to face arrest. JP condemned the arrests of these leaders in his first statement on 20 March. Karpoori was released after a few days. Student leaders now got Jayaprakash Narayan to take over the movement that had now taken a pan-Bihar shape with the active involvement of several political leaders.

On 8 April, JP hit the road. A silent procession was taken out from the Congress Ground at Kadam Kuan. The huge turnout at the protest sounded the first big alert to the Congress establishment in Patna and Delhi.

On 9 April, a big meeting was held at Gandhi Maidan in Patna. It was at this event that student leader Lalu Prasad Yadav honoured JP with the title of 'Loknayak'. JP gave a call to all legislators to resign and demanded that the Congress dissolve the Assembly. Among those who promptly responded to JP's call for resignation from the Assembly included Karpoori Thakur, Puran Chand, Hukumdev Narayan Yadav, Ramjivan Singh, Sachidanand Singh and Dhanik Lal Mandal.

By August 1974, it was a complete political movement with all Opposition parties minus Left working towards building mass support for the movement. Under the leadership of Karpoori, socialist workers were now taking to villages. The state government was getting nervous with momentum building in favour of the Bihar Movement. Eminent socialist leader Raj Narain was stopped at Patna Junction by the state government.

Karpoori was not only active in the Bihar movement but also tried for the integration of the opposition parties. On 29 August 1974, eight opposition parties of India came together to form the Bharatiya Lok Dal with Choudhary Charan Singh as its president.

By the end of 1974, the student movement had taken the shape of a mass movement. Delhi had started feeling the heat. On 20 November 1974, Chandra Shekhar invited MPs for tea with JP at his place. Vibhuti Mishra, Dwarka Nath Tiwari, Mama Ray, Santabakhsh, Krishnakant, Sumitra Kulkani (granddaughter of Mahatma Gandhi), Shukdev Verma and Shankar Dayal Singh were among those who attended the meet. Chandra Shekhar had tried to negotiate between JP and Indira Gandhi, although unsuccessfully.

In June 1975, elections to the Gujarat Legislative Assembly were held due to the pressure of students and Morarji Desai's fast. Congress emerged as a minority and a non-Congress government was formed under the leadership of Babu Bhai Patel under the Janata Morcha.

On 12 June 1975, the Allahabad High Court annulled the election of Indira Gandhi from Rae Bareili (Uttar Pradesh) in the 1971 polls. This made JP further intensify his movement. The meeting of the national committees of the Akali Dal, Congress (Organization) and Bharatiya Lok Dal was held in Delhi from 21 to 24 June. They decided to carry out nationwide protests to demand the resignation of PM Indira Gandhi. Non-Congress and non-communist parties held a big public meeting on 23 June 1975 at Ramlila Maidan in Delhi. But Congress ensured that JP did not attend the meet as his flight was diverted.

Ramnath Thakur recalled: 'Information had reached the Prime Minister that Jayaprakash Narayan was to hold a mammoth rally on the Ram Lila grounds in Delhi on 25 June at which he was going to ask the armed forces and the police to revolt and disobey orders which they did not consider lawful.'[6]

Recounting Indira Gandhi's conversation with Siddharth Shankar Ray, Pupul Jayakar, Indira Gandhi's friend and biographer, writes, quoting Indira: 'Siddhartha, we cannot allow this,' said a tense Prime Minister, 'I want something done. I feel that India is like a baby and just as one should sometimes take a child and shake it, I feel we need to shake India.'[7]

At 8 p.m. on 25 June 1975, Prime Minister Indira Gandhi addressed the nation, announcing the Internal Emergency.

Speeches, meetings, gatherings and processions were banned. The government was particularly harsh on news and articles that were critical of the government. Freedom of press was seriously compromised and the voice of the people was strangulated. The top leaders of the country, including JP, Morarji, Raj Narain, Chandra Shekhar, Ramdhan, Piloo Mody, Ashok Mehta and L.K. Advani were sent to jail.

Opposition leaders, civil society and the media were not the only ones to disagree with Indira Gandhi's decision. Even senior Congress leader K. Kamaraj expressed his dismay: 'I am shocked to hear that leaders have been arrested throughout the country. This state of affairs is not good for the nation . . . Such an event has no parallel even under British rule.'[8] A day later Kamaraj told students at Tiruvellore that he felt as though he had been 'left in a jungle blindfolded.'[9]

Jayakar, although known as a close friend of Indira, described Delhi on her return in July post Emergency. 'I found Delhi a city of outrage, seething with rumours of arrests, hunger strikes, deaths in jail.' Jayakar also recalls her meeting with the prime minister in the Parliament House office. 'She embraced me but the easy, relaxed poise of the past was missing. Her body had slimmed down; there was aridity in her eyes which made me aware of her isolation and her conflicts. I could not help reaching out to her. For a moment we sat quiet, hesitating to speak of what was uppermost in both our minds. It was I who broke the silence. I kept my voice very low, allowed for pauses. I knew that to reach her, she should not feel threatened. "I have just returned," I said. "The city is full of fear. How can you, the daughter of Jawaharlal Nehru, permit this?" She was taken aback. I could see my words were of shock, perhaps few people had spoken to her so directly. I could sense the turbulence within her.'[10]

Indira told her friend that Jayaprakash and Morarji Desai had always 'hated her' and were determined to see that she was 'destroyed'. '. . . .Why does he (JP) refuse to accept that he has never ceased to be a politician and desires to be the Prime Minister?' Indira told Jayakar.

But there is always a counterpoint.

Bimal Prasad and Sujata Prasad write, 'Having known Indira intimately since her childhood, it can easily be speculated that Jayaprakash was thinking of dipping his toes into mainstream politics as Indira's adviser or mentor. He imagined that she would establish with him the same sort of relationship that Nehru had with Gandhi.'[11]

JP said, 'Dissent is not just an intellectual luxury but a necessary catalytic agent to which society owes its progress, its revolution, and its technological and scientific advances. Without dissent, society would become stagnant and moribund.'[12]

Corn Roasted on Funeral Pyre and Long Escape to Fame

Ramnath Thakur says: 'It was veteran journalist Kuldeep Nayyar who first informed my father about the imposition of Emergency in the country.'[13]

During the Emergency, the state government forcibly vacated the official residence of Karpoori Thakur at Bir Chand Patel Path. Surendra Kishore says, 'No one was willing to keep the luggage of Karpoori. Ramnath Thakur requested his father's friend and MLC Indra Kumar to keep his luggage but he refused to do so for fear of being arrested. However, another MLA, Virendra Kumar Pandey, kept Karpoori's luggage. Interestingly, Karpoori made Indra Kumar MLC again when he became the CM in 1977.'[14]

Karpoori Thakur also gave his frank assessment of the Bhoodan Movement running concurrently. Rajya Sabha deputy chairperson and senior journalist Harivansh Narayan Singh recalled an incident: 'Jagdish Babu, a close JP aide, told JP about Karpoori Thakur's complaint that 90 per cent of the land being donated under the Bhoodan Movement had been a farce. JP called Karpoori to crosscheck it. Karpoori said it was not a case of 90 but 95 per cent of land donation fraud.'[15]

Singh recalled how Karpoori would often visit Sitab Diara to meet JP even though it used to be a full day's journey with the village being situated between two rivers—Ganga and Ghaghra—with no bridges.

Karpoori's aggression during the JP Movement could be seen during his intervention with the police. Shiv Kumar says, 'After about two dozen students were arrested and put inside Munger jail in 1974, some students were injured in the police lathicharge in the jail. Karpoori told the jail superintendent: "Do not be under the impression that the present establishment would not fall. Is this the way you treat protestors? Our government would come and people like you would be shown their place."'[16]

Karpoori's political journey during the Emergency also tells us a lot about the grit and resilience of the leader. After the promulgation of the Emergency, Karpoori participated in a protest in Purnia. From there, he went in hiding to Nepal's Raj Viraj forests of Birpur; he created a comprehensive programme of the underground movement. Throughout the period of emergency, he led an underground movement in the country.

He went to Nepal on 27 June and wandered along the Indo-Nepal border areas such as Raj Viraj, Hanuman Nagar, Viratnagar and Chatra, operating from a forest base to mobilize support for the movement. The Indian government had been putting pressure on the Nepal government to arrest Karpoori, who argued that if V.P. Koirala could live in India, why could he not stay in Nepal? The Nepal government wanted Koirala in exchange for Karpoori but the proposal did not work out. But the Nepal government started keeping tabs on Karpoori's activities to ensure that its ties with India did not worsen. Ramnath Thakur says, 'Despite a house-arrest-like situation, Karpoori Thakur maintained contact with the British, American, Israeli and Chinese embassies.'[17]

On 5 September 1975, Karpoori disguised himself and came out of Prof S.N. Verma's house at midnight and fled from Nepal to India. Those who had supported him in Nepal had to suffer. Prof. Verma from Kathmandu lost his job for hosting Karpoori. In Chhapra, Bihar, a barber whose shop Karpoori would often visit was beaten to death.

While he was hiding in Nepal during the Emergency, his car broke down once, and he decided to take a bus. It was a decision that backfired. Bijendra Prasad Yadav says, 'When he started walking, a luxury car stopped by him. It belonged to a notorious smuggler from Bihar. The car owner offered him a lift but he refused. Only someone like Karpoori could have done so.'[18]

Ramnath Thakur says, 'After being underground for a while in Bihar, he left for Madras (now Chennai) in Nepali dress to attend a meeting of underground leaders, Snehalatha Reddy, George Fernandes, M.S. Rao, Deoras and Achyut Patwardhan. A cyclostyled news bulletin was brought out and programmes were fixed for its distribution at the all-India level. After ten days in Madras, he went to Bangalore and met K.S. Hegde, Virendra Patil and Ramakrishna Hegde.'[19]

He moved to Bombay in the guise of a maulvi to attend the Lok Sangharsh Samiti meeting attended by S.N. Joshi, N. Gore, Sundar Singh Bhandari, Subrahmanyam Swamy and Digvijay

Narayan Singh. He reached Gorakhpur via Delhi. Ramnath Thakur says, 'He again went to Nepal with help from a Sikh gentleman to cross the border to reach Merwa, this time in kurta, pyjama, karbhi cap and short beard. Finding Prof. Verma's house locked and fearing arrest, he decided to flee by boarding a truck to reach Kathmandu–Birganj Road. He went to Janakpur and narrowly escaped arrest.'[20]

Ramnath Thakur says, 'Karpoori went to Calcutta on 11 October 1975, and stayed in a hotel on Free Street as Noor Ahmad, a local resident. Ahmed arranged his clandestine meeting with Pranav Chatterjee, Shiv Nandan Paswan, Lakshmi Sahu, Munshi Lal Rai and Manjay Lal from Bihar and Anil Bhattacharya, Ama Mayati, Nirmalendu De, Sureshwar Dutt, Ravi Shankar Pandey and Devdas Ghosh from Bengal and discussed new strategies. Karpoori also went to meet Ajit Rai, an advocate of the Calcutta High Court, to discuss the plight of JP in jail. Later, he met leaders such as Prafulla Chandra Sen, Ashok Krishna Dutt, Anil Bhattacharya and Vijay Singh Nahar.'[21]

Ramnath Thakur adds, 'He left for Hyderabad by train in Multani dress and later travelled to Madras to meet the family of K. Kamaraj, who had died. After returning to Calcutta, he met leaders of other opposition parties of Bengal on 21 October 1975.'[22]

He reached Raj Viraj, Nepal, via Cuttack and took part in a meeting on 28 October in a forest. He went there via Bokaro and published leaflets that said, '*Aao Veero Mard Bano, Phir Jail Tumhe Bharna Hoga* (Bravehearts, you have to show guts again and fill the jails).' Noor Ahmed and Ram Vilas Paswan took the leaflets from Calcutta to Patna and distributed them among the people.[23]

Noor Ahmad recalls: 'He would not stay at one place for more than three days because the police needed at least four days to do search for an address despite the best intelligence input . . . I kept rotating around places of at least 100 addresses in Kolkata and around and I started living with Karpoori. On 1 November, a meeting of the All India Lok Sangharsh Samiti was held secretly in Delhi. It was the follow-up meet of the Samiti in Delhi in which Ravindra Verma was made its president and Karpoori was also taken in its executive committee.'[24]

Karpoori Thakur, while hiding in Delhi, needed Rs 500 to replace his tattered clothes with new ones. K.C. Tyagi says, 'He approached Partho Ghosh, a Bihar resident who was teaching at JNU. Ghosh was so impressed with Karpoori Thakur that he insisted on giving Rs 1,000. After arguing for half an hour, Karpoori agreed to take Rs 750.'[25]

Naresh Vikal and Harinandan Sah wrote: 'On 15 January, 1976, Karpoori was going to attend a meeting at Abha Mahato's house, but could not go because he was being hunted by the police. The second day, in the meeting held at Parmanand Das's house, discussions were held on underground leaders going abroad. Karpoori opposed it but later agreed to go because of the argument that going abroad would strengthen the struggle'.[26]

By now Gujarat had also turned hostile as the Janata Morcha government of five parties headed by Babu Bhai Patel was toppled. Naresh Vikal and Harinandan Sah wrote: 'Patel said that his party had got a majority in 1975, but it was toppled by the Congress through the fear of Maintenance of Internal Security Act (MISA). After returning to Calcutta for two days at the end of his 17-day Maharashtra–Gujarat stay, he went to Bombay with the intention of meeting JP at Jaslok, but reached Calcutta on 23 February, fearing arrest under strict police surveillance. Karpoori started living at Parmanand Das's place in Park Circus in the guise of a monk. He started going for a walk in the field every morning with the children. The vigilance of the police also increased at the house of Karpoori's brother-in-law Pradeep Thakur on Kidwai Road. One day the police caught him and took him to the police station.'[27]

While in Kolkata, 'he also stayed at a brick kiln once. He once stayed at a cowshed saying that he was the father of one of the workers there. But people would be surprised to see him read several newspapers'.[28]

Mangani Lal Mandal, Ram Vilas Paswan and Ramnath Thakur stayed with Karpoori for a while during his hiding. Kailashpati Mishra would also visit him to discuss their strategy. Shivnandan Paswan was also a close aide. 'He held that once Emergency was lifted, Indira Gandhi would also be politically finished. There was great terror of Sanjay Gandhi because of forcible vasectomy.'[29]

Karpoori often held talks with the Bengal unit of the Congress (Organization). The members of the Congress (O) were adamant on holding on to their name, but Karpoori Thakur had no prejudice towards the name.

At 9 p.m. on 20 March 1976, Karpoori Thakur left Park Circus and started living in the guise of a Pandit at Shiv Shankar Saav's home in Howrah. There he used to regularly recite the Gita and the Ramayana. In Valur, he lived as a very poor person, wearing patched clothes and walking barefoot. Money was so tight that he was very grateful for any help. There were nights when they slept hungry. Work was affected by the lack of money. By now it had become absolutely impossible for Karpoori to live in Bengal. Therefore, he left for Benares.

He called a meeting of his party workers on the banks of the river near Sarnath. There was some dispute regarding the members of the Vichar Samiti (a forum to discuss strategy during the Emergency). Police vigilance and action in Benares was a bit too swift. So Karpoori returned to Calcutta again.

Muneshwar Singh says, 'Once while on the way to Gaya, a train ticket examiner (TTE) recognized him and whispered to him that the police were conducting a strict check and made him cross through the second gate.'[30]

Later, Karpoori went to Delhi several times. Once while going to Delhi, he contracted high fever in the train itself. He reached Delhi in great distress. Muneshwar Singh says, 'There Gauri Shankar Rai, Ravi Rai, Loknath Joshi, Rama Shankar Singh and many youth leaders met him. Once Karpoori went to meet Piloo Mody along with Noor Ahmad, Mody could not recognize him, because then he was in the guise of a Maulvi. Meanwhile, Satyendra Narayan Singh also reached there. They were also surprised to see him. He said that the failure to arrest Karpoori had caused an uproar in Bihar. A reward of Rs 10,000 was also announced for the arrest of Karpoori.'[31]

Meanwhile, JP, who had been ailing, was released. JP was sent to Patna but the government was sceptical. Security was tightened. Police, army and CRPF personnel were deployed at every step in Patna. Various restrictions were imposed. Despite this, thousands of people came and greeted JP on 20 July.

Letters to Vinoba Bhave

During the Emergency, Karpoori wrote to Vinoba Bhave, asking him to abandon his resolution to fast unto death. Acharya Vinoba Bhave withdrew his decision to fast, announced in favour of banning cow slaughter in the country. The hunger strike was going to start from 11 September. Karpoori urged Baba, as Vinoba Bhave was known, to come forward to fight against Indira's dictatorship.

Karpoori's four letters to Acharya Vinoba showed his thought process as a leader who could ask tough questions of one of the most revered persons of the time. In his first letter to Bhave on 21 December 1975, Karpoori wrote: 'It was a time of war, even the British government did not kill freedom of speech in the manner the Indira government is doing in the name of emergency. Despite the relatively greater freedom of speech than today, Mahatma Gandhi felt the need for a Satyagraha-struggle against the British government for the desired freedom of speech (complete or substantial freedom of speech). As a senior member of the family, do you not feel the need for Satyagraha today? . . .In such a situation (Emergency), do you not think that the first Satyagrahi of freedom of speech, in today's stifling situation, should be made the first commander of the Satyagraha-struggle? Do you analyse the reasons given for the Emergency imposed in the country, do you justify it?'[32]

He wrote the fourth and last letter to Vinoba on 13 November 1976. Vinoba had postponed his conference scheduled in the last week of October so that there should not be any disturbance to Indira's decision to lift the Emergency, hold general elections and restore civil liberties. But Indira postponed the Anti-Defection Bill, pending for four years in the Lok Sabha, till the next session, got the 42nd Constitutional Amendment Bill passed immediately and extended the duration of the Lok Sabha for one year. It was further extended and the impending general elections were again put in jeopardy. 'Parliament has passed the 44th Constitutional Amendment Bill. The fundamental rights of citizens have been imprisoned by giving priority to prescriptive rules. The powers of the courts have been taken away.' Karpoori wrote to Vinoba: 'You are silently watching the end of the freedom achieved by the sacrifice of the people.' In the end, he said that you must take such a step so that people's faith in you gets re-established.'[33]

Heralding the Era of National Coalition

During this time, Choudhary Charan Singh discussed the status of a possible merger of Opposition parties with Karpoori's party in the latter half of 1976. Senior JD (U) leader K.C. Tyagi, who was a close aide of Charan Singh, recalled: 'Charan Singh had the largest mass base and influence among Opposition leaders. Karpoori Thakur played a key role in stitching together Opposition parties . . .'[34]

As there was a bid to unite the Opposition, the Samajwadi Yuvjan Sabha (the student wing of SSP) played a key role in mobilizing the underground movement during the Emergency. Young leaders like K.C. Tyagi, Mahendra Malla, Ravindra Chowdhary, Jawahar Pratap, Mangani Lal Mandal, Rameshwar Thakur and Ram Kumar Jain played an active role in mobilizing the mass movement.

On November 13–14, a meeting of opposition parties keen on the merger took place at JP's Patna residence. Bharatiya Lok Dal (BLD), the BJS and the Samajwadi Party authorized JP to announce a new party. After this meeting, police raids started on Karpoori's hideouts in Calcutta. Attempts were also made to close down the magazine *Hamara Sangharsh*.

Meanwhile, Indira tried to bring about peace with the Opposition. Karpoori and other leaders refused to budge an inch. Some Congress leaders had also been growing restive with Indira's authoritarian attitude. A nervous PM gave a speech at Bhubaneshwar that 'there is no threat to the Congress from the opposition parties, it has been due to internal conflicts only.'[35] The Congress government of Orissa, headed by Nandini Satpathy, was dismissed. West Bengal CM Siddharth Shankar Ray, who had given the idea of imposing the Emergency, was also fed up

Karpoori Thakur inspecting the Patna floods on 19 December 1969.

Young Lok Dal leader Lalu Prasad Yadav by the side
of Karpoori Thakur's mortal remains in Patna.

Karpoori Thakur's funeral procession.

BJP leader L.K. Advani consoling Karpoori Thakur's family members in Patna on 18 February 1988.

Karpoori Thakur's funeral procession in Patna on 18 February 1988.

Karpoori Thakur during his swearing-in ceremony as chief minister of Bihar in 1977.

Senior journalist and former *Jansatta* editor Prabhash Joshi with Karpoori Thakur.

Karpoori Thakur at his swearing-in ceremony in Patna in 1977.

Karpoori Thakur being sworn in as chief minister of Bihar in 1977.

Karpoori Thakur with Choudhary Devi Lal.

Karpoori Thakur with then chief minister Bindeshwari Dubey at an iftar party in Patna.

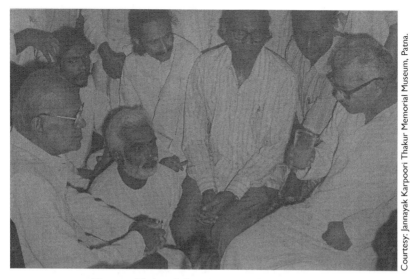

Karpoori Thakur (left) with Jayaprakash Narayan.

अक्तूबर

Karpoori Thakur (right) with Bharatiya Lok Dal leader
and former prime minister Charan Singh.

Karpoori Thakur addressing the public through All India Radio on 23 September 1970.

of the dictatorship of Indira. Noor Ahmad, a close JP associate, recalls: 'Ravi Rai talked to Thakurji about the movement and the attitude of BLD. At that time the people of socialist ideology were firm on the point that the struggle should continue. Therefore, Ravi Rai suggested that Karpooriji write a letter to Chaudhary Charan Singh. He was determined to continue the struggle.'[36]

On 18 January 1977, Indira Gandhi relaxed the Emergency and announced the election. The protesting leaders were released one by one from jail. Due to this, the opposing forces again started to swell. On 21 January, a new party was announced in New Delhi. A huge press conference was held at the residence of Morarji Desai, where many opposition leaders were present. The party was named Janata Party. On 24 January 1977, at the Gandhi Peace Foundation, he joined JP.

On 30 January 1977, Karpoori, who was still in disguise, appeared at a huge meeting in Patna. A sea of humanity was present at Gandhi Maidan. Slogans of Jayaprakash and Janata Party Zindabad were heard all around. A new hope had also awakened among the people. JP was about to deliver his historic speech. 'We knew that Karpoori Thakur would attend this meeting, but would be arrested. However, we always made sure that they reached the meeting place safely. The meeting started at 3 p.m. JP came on stage amidst thunderous applause from all around. Even before the meeting started, JP announced from the stage that their leader Karpoori Thakur, who remained underground for nineteen months and whom the police could not arrest, is present on this stage. There was a stir among the people. He got up and sat down greeting him. This meeting lasted for one and a half hours. JP appealed to the voters of this country to choose between dictatorship and democracy.'[37]Though there is no confirmed record of the turnout, Gandhi Maidan, when packed to capacity, could accommodate over 10 lakh people.

As the meeting ended, the police cars started chasing Karpoori and surrounded him near Apsara Hotel. As the police had no arrest warrant, there was huge resentment and resistance from the public, forcing the police to open lathicharge. Noor Ahmad, who was accompanying Karpoori Thakur, was also badly beaten up. After being arrested, Karpoori Thakur questioned the police lathicharge. The DM calmed Karpoori down and asked, 'Sir, where have you been for so many months?' Karpoori replied: 'I stayed in this country. You people are useless, so you could not catch me. Your government is also useless and when I myself have come to Patna, you are showing bravery.'[38]

There is also one lesser known aspect of how the operations of the Naxals had started increasing during the JP Movement.

There are also reports from non-official sources that Naxalite attacks intensified during the JP movement. Shashidhar Khan writes, 'Naxalite groups tried to strengthen their position against the police. There was a spurt in incidents of police encounters. The police had a free hand to do anything and it was legal during the Emergency.'[39] During the Emergency, the Maintenance of Internal Security Act (MISA), Defence of India Rules (DIR) and Defense of India Act (DIA) were enforced; student agitators and leaders of various non-Left parties, who supported them, were jailed. Shashidhar Khan wrote: 'But most of the people associated with the Naxal agitators were killed in an encounter on the spot itself.'[40]

Karpoori Thakur was not in favour of people getting bail after being arrested during the movement. Shiv Kumar says, 'He perhaps wanted to draw its parallel with the Freedom Movement and reasoned that those arrested should face trial and get convicted or acquitted. Movements, he said, would make leaders.'[41]

Janata Power

For the first time, a non-Congress government was formed at the Centre. Karpoori's voice now echoed in the country's Parliament. Karpoori said: 'There is no dearth of natural resources in Bihar. Bihar alone can fulfill many needs of the whole of India. But the lack of these resources is so much that the people there have been living a life of poverty for centuries. Even after thirty years of independence, the government could not provide means of irrigation; every year thousands of people were killed due to floods, but they could not be saved. There is no electricity in the villages. There are thousands of houses where even earthen lamps do not flicker in poverty. There are no roads in the villages. There are no bridges. There are no school buildings. The condition of unemployment is such that lakhs of educated youth are roaming around. We will take these problems to the centre.'[42]

Karpoori suggested that the Constitution be amended to restore the five-year term for Parliament and Legislative Assemblies.

The central leadership and the cabinet of Janata Party were unanimous in favour of dissolution of the legislative assemblies in those states where the Congress had suffered a humiliating defeat in the Lok Sabha elections. Charan Singh, the home minister wanted to implement this idea strongly. Despite the resistance of the then Congress MPs, leaders and the acting president, the Legislative Assemblies of nine states were dissolved and elections were held in ten states.

Karpoori Thakur contested the 1977 Lok Sabha election from Samastipur on the advice of JP and won the seat by defeating Congress candidate Yamuna Prasad Mandal by 3,27,434 votes. Janata Party took the centrestage by dethroning Indira Gandhi.

On a personal level, JP had settled a score with Indira. JP could have been the unanimous choice for becoming the PM but he had never wanted to become one in the first place. Indira Gandhi perhaps got her answer on her misplaced assumptions of JP nursing the ambition to become PM.

Pitaunjhia Files

Between 1974 and 1977, Bihar and the country saw big political turmoil. The period also marked a phase of personal turmoil in the life of Karpoori Thakur.

His younger son Birendra was diagnosed with serious heart complications. But Karpoori maintained a great balance between his head and heart.

Dr Birendra K. Thakur, who retired in March 2023, after prolonged service as a medical professional, tells the full story. 'I had to write my finals in 1974 but the college boycotted the examination during the JP Movement. I applied to three private medical colleges. Each college demanded a donation fee of Rs 25,675. As I needed my father's signature, I went to meet my father in Hazaribagh jail. He clearly told me that he could not afford heavy donation money. But he wrote two letters, one in the name of the secretary of Sri Krishna Medical College and another in the name of Satyendra Narayan Sinha, whose nephew Vijay Sinha was the secretary of Magadh Medical College. The SKM College secretary Raghunath Pandey assured me admission but added that I would have to pay some money. I explored the second option. Satyendra Babu warmly received me and assured me admission in Magadh Medical College without taking any fee. My father had only written to him that I wanted to study medicine. Though my father and

Sinha had been political adversaries, they had been great friends in personal life.'[43]

In 1974, Birendra got admission in Magadh Medical College, now known as Anugrah Narayan Magadh Medical College, Gaya. But only a few months later, he had to be admitted to Wellington Hospital in New Delhi with heart valve problems. As the JP Movement had already started, Karpoori Thakur was apprehensive of his arrest. But he was very much in Delhi. The first person who came to meet the ailing Birendra was Raj Narain. When he saw that Birendra was admitted to the same room in which Dr Rammanohar Lohia had died in 1967 and that the mother of the then Union Minister Bhagwat Jha Azad had also died a few days ago in the same room, Birendra was shifted to another room.

'Somehow, PM Indira Gandhi came to know about my illness through a Saharsa worker. She came to see me at the hospital and sat on the attendant's stool. She talked to me in whispers and did not let me rise from the bed. She came to see me again after a few days and wanted to send me to Australia for heart valve replacement. But I said no to treatment at the cost of the government.'[44]In a subsequent review at CMC Vellore, doctors suggested heart valve replacement in Australia.

Birendra returned to Patna where other doctors suggested treatment in New Zealand instead. Karpoori decided to send his son to Auckland in 1975.

Karpoori Thakur also took the tough decision of sending Birendra alone to Auckland. 'If you have to survive, you will. If you are not destined to survive, even my accompanying you will not help. Besides, I have no extra money to bear the additional cost of my travel,' Karpoori Thakur told his son.

In Auckland, a Chhapra resident took great care of him and several fellow Indians would come to meet him, because in those days, rarely any Indian could visit New Zealand for treatment. Within a week, his heart valve was successfully replaced. He called on the then Union minister, and later the Bihar CM, Bhagwat Jha Azad's phone about his successful surgery. After one-and-a-half months, he returned to India.

Birendra stayed in Ranchi at his sister's place for a while before joining his medical classes in Gaya. Karpoori Thakur reached a fellow politician Upendra Nath Verma's house in Manpur, Gaya, to meet Birendra. 'He took me in a tight embrace and asked in a choked voice, "*Ab thik ho na?* (Are you alright now?)"'[45]

In his third year of MBBS, he asked his father, who had become CM now, to get him a bike. 'His father's personal assistant Lakshmi Sahu bought the bike after paying half its price—Rs 7,500, and decided to pay the rest in equal instalment of Rs 500 per month. But Sahu never paid it. In the early 1990s, Dr Birendra K. Thakur got a notice from the bank to pay dues of Rs 3.2 lakh, as accrued amount of unpaid bike instalment with compound interest. Dr Thakur was stunned. It was only with the help of Yashwant Sinha, who had become an influential politician, that he settled the dues at Rs 10,500.'[46]

10

Pioneering Quota Politics

The Lasting Legacy of Jannayak

*The people known as the Forwards and the Backwards have been
created by the Shastras. I have not created them. In this country,
millions and millions of people are backward by birth. When we
say we want reservations and job opportunities for those people,
we say our struggle is not caste-based but class-based. But when I
want to do away with these things* [the caste system], *the upper
castes call me casteist. Unfortunately, the underdogs belong to the
Backward Classes, Scheduled Tribes, Scheduled Castes, Muslims,
and so on, and those who fight for the underdog will be labelled
as casteist.*[1]

This is perhaps the most comprehensive and candid explanation
that Karpoori Thakur ever gave regarding his decision to
implement 26 per cent quota in Bihar government jobs. This was
a landmark decision because no state government, or the Centre
for that matter, had previously given a separate quota to Extremely

Backward Classes (EBCs). Out of the 26 per cent reservation, the Janata Party government had allocated 12 per cent to EBCs and eight per cent to OBCs. Karpoori Thakur also pioneered a quota system for women and the poor in the general category, providing them with a 3 per cent quota each. Narendra Modi emulated the Karpoori formula by bringing in a 10 per cent quota for the EWS (Economically Weaker Sections) in January 2019.

* * *

As Indira Gandhi dissolved the Lok Sabha on 18 January 1977, Jayaprakash Narayan (JP) welcomed the announcement of the polls. On 23 January 1977, the Janata Party was formed with Chandra Shekhar as its national president. JP played a pivotal role in bringing together political parties of different ideologies under the banner of one party. The Janata Party comprised Congress (Organization), Bharatiya Jana Sangh (BJS), Bharatiya Lok Dal (BLD), Samajwadi Dal and other smaller parties, creating a unique coalition experiment. Instead of entering into a pre-poll alliance, JP advocated for all parties to merge into one political entity. Despite the leaders of these parties maintaining separate electoral constituencies, they settled with the single party. Through this 'collaborative-coalition' approach, JP potentially put an end to the untouchability of Bharatiya Jana Sangh forever.

On 2 February 1977, heavyweight Congress leader Jagjivan Ram resigned from both the Cabinet and the Congress, and announced his new party, Congress for Democracy (CFD), which also joined Janata Party. This further weakened Indira Gandhi.

As the need to unite against the Congress arose, even fierce adversaries like Karpoori Thakur and Satyendra Narayan Sinha found themselves part of the same political party. This was made possible due to JP's unifying leadership and the shared goal of dethroning Indira Gandhi from power. Shantanu Gupta writes, 'Since there was no time to complete the formalities with the ECI (Election Commission of India), it was agreed that the BLD (Bharatiya Lok Dal) symbol of '*haldhar*' (man carrying a plough) would be adopted.'[2]

But Indira Gandhi was more surprised at the speed with which the Janata Party merger had worked out. Coomi Kapoor writes, 'They (non-Congress parties) quickly succeeded in tying up electoral alliances with the CPI (M), the Akali Dal in Punjab and the DMK in Tamil Nadu. Taken aback by these unexpectedly rapid developments, Indira Gandhi attacked the concept of opposition unity, calling it an opportunistic alliance of disparate elements with nothing in common.'[3]

The widespread anger against the Emergency resulted in the Janata Party facing little resistance and gaining significant support in the elections to oust Indira Gandhi from power. The party's united front and anti-Emergency sentiment worked in its favour. Despite being a unanimous choice for Prime Minister, JP had already decided against taking any position in the government. This proved Indira Gandhi wrong about JP's desire to become Prime Minister and showcased his selflessness and his commitment to restoring democratic values.

Harivansh and Ravi Dutt Bajpai write, 'JP trusted the advice of Acharya J.B. Kriplani, Radhakrishna and Narayan Desai and all of them were in favour of Morarji. Amidst hectic lobbying, Choudhary Charan Singh sent a letter to JP, stating that he favoured Morarji Desai as the prime minister. He mentioned that Jagjivan Ram had not only supported the Emergency, but had also presented the proposal in the parliament to impose the Emergency.'[4]

The results of the Assembly elections, held in Bihar in April 1977, were on expected lines. Janata Party got 224 seats out of 324 seats in the Bihar Legislative Assembly.

Social scientist Ashwani Kumar writes that Harry W. Blair's 'prognosis sounded prophetic as the social ascendancy of the backward castes almost matched their newly found political dominance. And Karpoori Thakur also interpreted his victory as a mandate of numerically preponderant backward castes.'[5]

Blair further explained how a large group of lower backward classes, later known as Annexure I or Extremely Backward Classes (EBC) or Most Backward Classes (MBC), had been heavily under-represented despite their larger population compared to the upper backward classes (Annexure II or OBC). Some prominent Annexure I backward classes include Dhanuks, Hajjams, Kahars, Kewats, Mallahs, Noniyas and Nai (to which Karpoori Thakur belonged).

Harry W. Blair writes, 'Even back in 1962, the four Upper Backward castes had 28.8 per cent of the general MLA seats, as against only 24.3 per cent of their population. By 1977, their percentage of seats had grown to 34.9. The Lower Backwards, on the other hand, constitute over 40 per cent of the population, but have never had more than 3.6 per cent of the general seats.'[6]

Karpoori vs Satyendra Narayan Sinha

Karpoori Thakur was undoubtedly the most prominent leader from Bihar in the Janata Party, with wider acceptability than anyone else. However, upper caste politics had not yet given up. But the results of the 1977 polls proved to be a turning point for the assertion and arrival of OBC politics. Karpoori Thakur knew that he had missed a significant opportunity to become the chief minister in 1967, losing to Mahamaya Prasad Sinha. He served as CM for less than six months in 1970–71, a short tenure that provided him with very little time to prove himself to himself and others.

Now, Karpoori faced resistance from Satyendra Narayan Sinha, an upper-caste Rajput leader. Sinha came from a political legacy as the son of former finance minister Anugrah Narayan Sinha. Satyendra Narayan Sinha had played a crucial role in K.B. Sahay becoming chief minister in 1963, instead of Bir Chand Patel, who could have become the first OBC (Other Backward Classes) chief minister at that time had Sinha supported him.

During the turbulent period between 1967 and 1972, Sinha played a pivotal role in helping Bindeshwari Prasad Mandal to become chief minister. He also played a key role in destabilizing successive governments until the 1972 polls, which gave the Congress an absolute majority. While Sinha did not become chief minister himself (until 1989), his influence as a prominent Rajput leader was evident in the political landscape.

The power struggles within the Janata Party during this period saw a short-lived unity between upper castes and backward castes, which came together in their fight against Indira Gandhi. The 1977 Assembly election results presented a significant opportunity for Satyendra Narayan Sinha to become chief minister. Claiming the support of forty-five Rajput MLAs, Sinha challenged Karpoori Thakur for the CM position.

Francine R. Frankel and M.S.A. Rao write, 'It was in this situation that word suddenly came from Delhi of the BLD–BJS bargain that each party would select the chief minister in three states. According to (Satyendra Narayan) Sinha, once it was decided that Bihar was in the BLD sphere, high-ranking BJS leaders, anxious to preserve their party's power in the national government, came to Patna and forced (BJS) MLAs to vote for Karpoori Thakur. JP had already given his blessings to Karpoori Thakur since he wanted a Backward Classes man.'[7]

Lalit Kumar writes, 'Just before the selection (of the CM candidate), Satyendra Narayan Sinha had gone to seek the advice of Basavan Singh, who had declared before the results that Sinha would not be able to become CM till he defeated Karpoori with a huge margin.'[8]

Yet, the showdown between Karpoori and Sinha took place. Journalist and author Arun Sinha gives an evocative description: 'Located on the western fringes of Patna, in the Braj Kishore memorial, 235 legislators of Janata Party had met to elect their leader . . . Even before the voting was completed, it was clear that Karpoori Thakur was winning. With the solid support of about fifty BLD legislators and about sixty eight belonging to Jan Sangh, he had a head start over the other candidates . . . Despite this foregone conclusion, the air was thick with speculation while the voting was in process. Karpoori Thakur was a barber by caste, wasn't he?'[9]

The result was out: Karpoori Thakur got 144 votes and Sinha got eighty-four votes.

Senior Congress leader Ram Lakhan Singh Yadav had said in an interview (10 October 1979): 'Initially, the Central Parliamentary Board of the Janata Party had directed that the choice of Chief Minister be decided without interference from the top. Based on this directive, Sinha was confident of winning majority support. His Rajput group, with 45 MLAs, was the largest single caste group in the Assembly, and they were receiving a good response to their canvassing efforts. Moreover, the caste issue was raised clearly at the outset. The Yadavs, who were the second largest group with 36 MLAs, did not allow themselves to be divided due to personal ambition. Instead, they knowingly pressed for Karpoori Thakur to become Chief Minister, as he was seen as a symbol of the backward classes.'[10]

The assertion of OBC leaders in Bihar had gained momentum since Bindeshwari Prasad Mandal had become chief minister in 1968. Mandal's rise to power paved the way for other non-upper-caste leaders, like Bhola Paswan Shastri (from the Scheduled Caste Paswan community) and Daroga Prasad Rai (from the OBC Yadav community), to also hold the position of chief minister in the state. This marked a significant shift in Bihar's political landscape, with increased representation and empowerment of OBC leaders in positions of power and governance.

Meeting Nikhil Kumar, former Nagaland governor and son of former CM Satyendra Narayan Sinha, at his residence at Sopan House at Boring Road, Patna, reminds one of all that this legendary address has witnessed in the last five decades. This place tells the story of Bihar Congress's legacies and liabilities. Nikhil Kumar is a 1963-batch IPS officer, who served as a Delhi police officer. His father served as minister between 1961 and 1967 before becoming CM in March 1989.

Anugrah Narayan Sinha was perhaps the only pan-Bihar upper-caste Rajput leader. The legendary friendship and clash between Anugrah Narayan Sinha (also Singh) and Dr Sri Krishna Singh have been a part of Bihar's political folklore. Sinha contested against Dr Singh unsuccessfully for the CM position after the 1957 Assembly polls.

The story continued, as years later Satyendra Narayan Sinha contested against Karpoori Thakur for the CM position. Nikhil Kumar says, 'My father believed that he had enough backing and contested and lost to Karpoori Thakur . . . But they enjoyed great camaraderie too. I remember Karpooriji visiting our place several times as an Opposition MLA between 1961 and 1967 when my father was a minister. My father would often ensure his grievances of public concern are addressed.'[11]

Sopan, which means 'goal or destination', once used to be the hub of political activities until Congress lost the plot in Bihar in 1990. The house now looks serene and calm, with no sentry at the gate. The august 'white house' still sparkles in the sun but has lost its political sheen. The big waiting lounge displays portraits of Anugrah Narayan Sinha and his son Satyendra Narayan Sinha, who poses wearing his trademark Gandhi cap. There are also signs of royalty and majestic elegance. Satyendra Narayan Sinha's portrait holds a special place here.

Cut to the present, as we talk about the decline of the Congress in Bihar since 1990, it seems to remind Nikhil Kumar of old wounds. He appears pained by the present state of the Congress. The once legendary address now looks barren, with no sentry, much like the Bihar Congress which seems to have lacked strong leadership for a long time now.

Gandhi Maidan Cheers

Karpoori took an oath as chief minister in front of a massive crowd at Patna's Gandhi Maidan on 24 June 1977. As the Janata Party had come to power through a people's movement, it was only fitting that Karpoori Thakur took the oath as CM and announced his 'second coming.'

Karpoori's ministry included ten cabinet level ministers. L.P. Shahi writes, 'In the first cabinet expansion on 8 August, 1977, he included seven cabinet level and seven state level ministers. Again in the second cabinet expansion on 16 August 1977, he included six cabinet level and five state level ministers in the government. After this, on 20 August, 1977, 17 parliamentary secretaries were made.'[12]

The government had, for the first time, more OBC (42 per cent) than upper caste (29 per cent) ministers but among the latter, the Lower Backwards, Yadavs got the major share in the Karpoori cabinet in acknowledgement of their dominant presence in the Assembly. Nakamizo Kazuya writes, 'This represented a significant step towards the dissolution of the gap between participation and representation (of non-upper castes), a hangover from the Congress age.'[13]

Empowering the religious and linguistic minorities was a significant step, as important portfolios such as education and health were held by Ghulam Sarwar and Professor Jabir Husain, respectively. Mohammed Sajjad writes, 'Not only this, these ministers were granted enough space to implement their vision and programmes. Urdu was made a vehicle for employment in government offices and schools.'[14]

Out of forty-seven members in the ministry, nineteen belonged to the backward castes, fifteen belonged to the upper castes and five were Scheduled Caste. The forward classes still accounted for over 29 per cent of MLAs, compared to 23.5 per cent of upper backwards.

Francine R. Frankel and M.S.A. Rao write, 'Yet, Karpoori Thakur constituted a cabinet in which Forwards were dramatically cut back to 29 per cent and for the first time, the Backwards gained the pre-eminent position at 38 per cent.'[15]

Narendra Pathak, author of *Karpoori Aur Samajwad*, gives a historical perspective: 'Dr. Lohia had been working to deepen and expand the process of social polarization since the 1950s.

Since 1954, he has been reflecting on the interaction of caste and politics . . . Dr. Lohia always had in mind how the backward and weaker sections of society should obtain their rightful place in the system.'[16]

Phulparas Bypolls

As Karpoori Thakur had to become a member of either the Assembly or the Council within six months to retain his position as CM, he decided to contest the Assembly bypolls. He had resigned as Lok Sabha MP within three months of being elected from Samastipur. Instead of choosing his home turf of Samastipur, he decided to contest from Phulparas in Madhubani. It was a very courageous decision as Phulparas was a Yadav-dominated seat. Devendra Prasad Yadav, a young MLA from the Janata Party, vacated the seat for him. Congress fielded a dominant Yadav leader, Ram Jaipal Singh Yadav, against Karpoori Thakur. Since Phulparas had been a traditional socialist party seat since 1967, the Janata Party appeared assured of Karpoori's victory. However, Congress sensed that most of the Yadav votes might not go to the ruling party, even as Janata Party members had been openly telling Yadavs that none of the previous cabinets had as many Yadavs as they had in the present House. Congress also tried to impress upon Yadav voters that the election of Karpoori could end the dominance of Yadavs in Phulparas. They even went on to say that if Karpoori lost, there was a chance of the Yadav leader and former CM B.P. Mandal becoming CM again.

However, Congress's caste card failed to work against Karpoori's immense popularity and the chilling memories of Emergency that were still fresh in people's minds. Moreover,

Yadavs were more focused on OBC assertion rather than just Yadav assertion, which gained momentum only post-1980.

Karpoori was known for his great crowd-connect. Often he would want the police to refrain from controlling or managing the crowd. Former DGP D.N. Gautam, who was then a young IPS officer, recalls one such instance from the Phulparas bypoll. 'When Karpooriji was speaking, three-four youths stood up and started talking nonsense. When I tried to intervene, the CM said: "Don't let the police come between me and the public . . . " He told the crowd no matter how much they disturbed him, he would speak. Even when hardly twenty-five-thirty people were present, Karpooriji kept speaking. As soon as the speech was over, he said to me laughing, "Haven't you seen, I have done your work by dispersing everyone?"'[17]

Karpoori defeated the Congress candidate Ram Jaipal Singh Yadav by over 69,000 votes. He also proved that he could win convincingly in a Yadav-dominated constituency, purely on account of his popularity.

Political Vendetta or Anti-Corruption

When the Janata Party government was formed in 1977, a twenty-six-point corruption complaint was lodged with the Morarji Desai government with help from MP Karpoori Thakur. Later when Karpoori Thakur formed the government in Bihar, the matter was being investigated. A total of seventeen FIRs had been lodged, including two on Mishra. These were filed for allegations including mortgaging Gandhi Maidan to a bank. Umesh Prasad Singh says, 'The government changed at the Centre and in Bihar and Mishra got relief and became the Bihar CM in 1980. He was later acquitted by the Supreme Court.'[18]

When a Rickshawpuller Got Raghuvir Sahay an Appointment with the CM

Karpoori Thakur's return as the chief minister was welcomed by the people. He would often be accompanied by a minimal police escort and prefer to freely interact with common people. The CM residence along Bailey Road in Bihar would often be crowded with ordinary people.

Ravindra Bharati, a noted litterateur and editor of the six-volume *Kapildeo Singh Samagra*, recounts an incident where a rickshaw puller helped *Dinman* editor Raghuvir Sahay to secure an appointment with CM Karpoori Thakur. When Sahay expressed his desire to interview Thakur but hadn't sought any appointment, rickshaw puller Ajore Paswan assured him that he would be able to meet the CM easily. Sahay was amused by the rickshaw puller's confidence and asked if it was really that simple to meet the chief minister. Paswan affirmed that it was indeed that easy as Karpoori Thakur was known as the people's CM.[19]

The rickshaw puller's confidence was not misplaced. Sahay recalled: 'I had an impromptu meeting with CM Karpoori Thakur. There were minimal security measures at the CM House, and people were freely coming in and out. Thakur's personal assistant, Lakshmi Sahu, whom I knew, helped facilitate the meeting. When Thakur arrived, we greeted each other warmly. Even the rickshaw puller, who was standing at a distance, greeted the CM, and Thakur responded with a radiant look.'[20]

'In 1977, a Gandhian economist visited Patna and stayed at my house in Rajinder Nagar,' recalled the BJP Rajya Sabha MP and former Bihar Deputy CM Sushil Kumar Modi. 'He expressed a desire to meet CM Karpoori Thakur, so I went to the CM house and left a message. The next morning, to my surprise, Karpoori

Thakur himself came to my house without any escort. He pressed the call-bell, and when my sister-in-law opened the gate, he politely introduced himself as "Karpoori Thakur". She was awestruck that the Chief Minister of the state was standing in front of her. This incident revealed the simplicity of the man. He could have asked the economist to come to the CM House, but he chose to personally visit my house out of respect for a learned person.'[21]

Karpoori Thakur had said an interview to *Dinman* after becoming CM that he was 'not at all happy', because he realised his 'responsibility and hundreds of complex problems of Bihar at the same time'. For tackling corruption, he said the institutions of Lokayukta and Lokpal had to be strengthened and 'Prime Minister to the Chief Minister would have to be brought under the purview of the law.'[22]

One of the top priorities of CM Karpoori Thakur was to install 15,000 hand pumps, using non-government resources, in the settlements of the poor. In addition, as the Janata Party came to power on the success of the JP Movement, CM Karpoori Thakur announced compensation to the next of kin of students who were killed during the movement, acknowledging their sacrifices. The state government also introduced welfare schemes for the poor, tribals and the elderly, including an old age pension scheme, Employment Guarantee Scheme and Bhangi Mukti (liberation of scavengers). Another significant initiative was the establishment of a fund to support Bihari writers and artists of Hindi, Urdu, Maithili, Bhojpuri and Magahi languages, promoting local arts and culture.

Dr Jagannath Mishra says, 'It is worth noting that during the Congress regime, a lot of land was allotted on paper, but possession was not given to the rightful beneficiaries.'[23] CM Karpoori Thakur's government aimed to address this issue and ensured that the allocated land was handed over to the intended beneficiaries, reflecting his commitment to social welfare and addressing the needs of the marginalized sections of society.

Under CM Karpoori Thakur's leadership, the government celebrated Harijan Adivasi Month from 1 to 20 September, focusing on the welfare of marginalized communities. 'A cooperative was initiated specifically for tribals, which had an impressive membership of 1,73,558 individuals. Tribals were provided loans amounting to Rs 25,769, and outstanding loan dues of Rs 70,51,597 were waived off, providing much-needed financial relief to the tribal community. Salaries of policemen were increased.'[24]

The government also took measures to protect the interests of employees by reinstating the Wage Revision Committee. Furthermore, when the prices of essential food grains, particularly mustard oil, rose significantly, the government took proactive action by arresting twenty-five individuals and recovering mustard oil worth Rs 40 lakh, demonstrating their commitment to addressing issues related to rising food prices and ensuring fair practices in the market. These initiatives reflected the government's efforts to prioritize the welfare of marginalized communities, address economic challenges faced by the common people and promote social justice during CM Karpoori Thakur's tenure.

Finance Minister Kailashpati Mishra presented the budget of 1978–79, with a focus on education and healthcare. As education for all was a top priority, the government announced the waiver of school fees for students up to Class 10, making education more accessible to all. Free textbooks were provided to students in Class 1, further promoting education at an early stage.

In the field of higher education, Senate, Syndicate and Academic Statistics were formed in five universities across the state, aiming to improve governance and administration in the higher education sector. The government also approved dearness allowance for the teachers and the non-teaching staff of universities and colleges at the same rate as government employees, recognizing their contributions to the education system.

In the healthcare sector, the government took significant steps to improve access to quality healthcare. All private medical colleges were taken over by the state government, and capitation fees were abolished, making medical education more affordable and transparent. The Jan Swasthya Rakshak Yojana, a health protection scheme, was implemented with the support of the Central government in October 1977, aiming to provide healthcare coverage to the people of Bihar.

Jabir Hussain, then a cabinet colleague of Karpoori Thakur, recalled the 1978 incident that led him to construct homes for the homeless and those living on pavements in Bihar. He said, 'Patna Municipal Corporation (PMC) had carried out a demolition drive of slums and footpath shops in an anti-encroachment effort. However, PMC had made it clear that illegal pucca (permanent) buildings should be removed before clearing up slums. During the encroachment drive, the area near Pearl Cinema, which was owned by the then Governor of Uttar Pradesh, C.P.N. Sinha, was being cleared. However, the next day, the district administration stopped providing armed reserve forces to PMC as the demolition of the cinema hall was halted due to the owner's political influence. In response to this, CM Karpoori Thakur ordered the removal of pucca establishments, including the cinema hall, while stopping the removal of slums until alternative arrangements for the slum dwellers and pavement shopkeepers were made.'[25]

Within a few months, small shops were built for the footpath shopkeepers at various locations, including Employment Exchange Complex, New Secretariat Complex, Dhobi Ghat and Officers Flat in front of Patliputra Hotel. Colonies were also built for slum dwellers at multiple places, including Kaushal Nagar and Kamala Nehru Nagar, as part of the government's efforts to provide housing and improve living conditions for the homeless and those living on pavements.

Jabir Hussain says, 'This incident and the subsequent policy implementation under CM Karpoori Thakur's leadership highlights the government's commitment to social welfare and addressing the needs of marginalized communities in Bihar by providing alternative housing arrangements and improving living conditions for those living in slums and on pavements.'[26]

On 11 October 1977, which was JP's birth anniversary, CM Karpoori Thakur announced the waiver of school fees till Class 10 as a tribute to the ailing JP. The decision aimed at providing educational opportunities to children from economically disadvantaged backgrounds.

Unlike the *Janata Ke Durbar Mein Mukhyamantri* programme of the current Bihar CM Nitish Kumar, Karpoori Thakur and, to a great extent Lalu Prasad, believed in meeting people without any fuss and without putting visitors through the unnecessary rigours of security checks.

On 25 July 1977, Karpoori Thakur wrote this note to someone who wanted an appointment to meet him. 'I am available to meet you at my residence from 7 am to 7:30 am. I stay in the secretariat from 8 in the morning until 11 at night, but my work schedule is not fixed. . . . I can claim that I meet more people than most,'[27] wrote Karpoori Thakur in a note.

Recalling an instance of easy accessibility to CM Karpoori in 1978, Barahiya socialist leader Shiv Kumar says: 'Karpoori

Thakur had called me at his residence at 5 a.m. I was surprised if it was the right time to meet the state CM. When I visited the CM's Bailey Road residence, I was let in. A sentry took me to a small room via a big hall in which some 50 people had been sleeping on carpets laid over haystacks. In the room I was taken to, four people had been sleeping on a bedstead. Karpoori Thakur came and shared tea with us and passed necessary instructions to the office concerned. He later left for the hall to address grievances of others.'[28]

His principal secretary Yashwant Sinha found the CM 'a thoroughly disorganised man'. But he calls Karpoori 'a true mass leader, he was almost always surrounded by people and found little time for official work. My main job, therefore, was to catch hold of him and force him to dispose of official files, which was easier said than done. During one of our trips to Delhi, I advised him to organise his time better, in the interest of better governance. Realising that he would not be amenable to any form of discipline, we decided to just whisk him away for a few hours every day instead, during which he could attend to important files. We would usually go to some obscure Dak Bungalow or rest house near Patna, late in the evening. If our location was discovered by those who chased him, we would simply abandon it and move to a new one. Once there, I would present the files to him and he would either record his minutes on them, the draft of which I would have prepared in advance, or simply sign them to approve the proposals they contained. Our preferred hideout was the guest house of the 5th Unit of the Bihar Military Police in Phulwari Sharif near Patna because it was under police security, which could not be easily breached.'[29]

Shiv Kumar further recalled that the students of polytechnic colleges sat on a dharna, demanding three terminal examinations instead of two so that the maximum number of students could clear their examinations on the basis of the best of two terminal results. As the Vidhan Sabha was in session, the Kharagpur MLA Shamsher Jung Bahadur raised the matter of students' arrests. CM Karpoori Thakur did not know about it. He alerted the DM and later met them personally. He later conceded all their demands and rebuked his officers saying that the students who were responsible for making Janata Party government must always be given a patient hearing. He ensured that the government order was passed in front of him. The best of three terminal examinations is still in practice.

In a similar instance, once the CM's private secretary Lakshmi Sahu came looking for an unknown Barahiya political worker, Shiv Kumar. 'I was greatly surprised that the CM wanted me to accompany him to some place. Sahu did not disclose or perhaps did not know where they were going. Sacks of files were loaded in two Ambassador Cars. The CM took along just two of his bodyguards and left behind his escort. On the way to Barbigha, Karpoori Thakur said he was hungry. We finally found a line hotel. The CM ate roti and dal tadka while the line hotel owner could not believe he was serving the state CM. We reached a Dak bungalow of the agriculture department where he stayed for three days to dispose of pending files. When I later shared this with Kapildeo Singh, he laughed his heart out, calling Karpoori an "*ustaad* (master)"[30] Karpoori would often visit Patna zoo and use its tree house to dispose of files as well.'

Karpoori had a most unique style of eating as well. He enjoyed non-vegetarian food and the tiffin carrier, which brought him home-cooked food, would often have fish and chicken as well. Yashwant Sinha writes, 'He never mixed one dish with another, not even rice with dal. He would eat each dish separately, often polishing off the last grain of rice or the very last bite of roti and, after having chicken or fish, would leave the bones neatly on the plate. He often joked that anyone who saw him eating would start feeling hungry all over again, even if fully satiated.'[31]

Panchayat Elections—a Step Towards Choukhamba Raj

As per the principles of Choukhamba Raj (four-tier governance system) propounded by Lohia, empowerment of local self-governance was considered one of the four pillars. In line with this ideology, CM Karpoori Thakur decided to hold panchayat elections in 1978 in Bihar, despite apprehensions of violence due to caste factors that could potentially play out during the polls.

The decision to hold panchayat elections reflected the government's commitment to promoting grassroots democracy and decentralization of power to local self-governing bodies. Despite the challenges and concerns of violence based on caste dynamics, the government, under Karpoori Thakur's leadership, took the bold step of empowering local communities through the process of democratic elections.

This decision was aligned with the vision of Choukhamba Raj, which emphasized the importance of empowering local governance institutions as a means of promoting participatory democracy, inclusive decision-making and effective delivery of public services at the grassroots level.

Mohammed Sajjad, AMU professor, writes that by holding Panchayat elections, Karpoori sought to 'reconfigure the upper caste hegemony in the rural power structure. The next Panchayati Raj elections were held in Bihar only in 2001, that too after a protracted judicial battle against the reluctant Congress and Lalu Yadav–Rabri Devi regimes.'[32] Nitish Kumar has been trying to strengthen the Panchayati Raj system by holding elections since 2006 without fail every five years.

D.N. Gautam says, 'All kinds of dividing lines came to the fore in the panchayat elections. This was opening the way for participation in local governance. Local rivalries intensified. As a result, the Bihar Panchayat elections in 1978 were very violent.'[33]

Urdu as Second Official Language

While working strongly towards the promotion of Hindi, Karpoori had deftly started social engineering to broaden his constituency. Dr Arjun Singh says, 'In a private conversation to his cabinet colleague and longtime friend Kapildeo Singh, Karpoori had said if he got en bloc Muslim votes, he would not have to work so hard to remain in power.'[34]

Karpoori declared Urdu as the second official language. Those who resisted it included renowned Hindi poet Nagarjuna, who wrote very scathing pieces in newspapers. Thakur Prasad, Jan Sangh leader, also sharply reacted by saying, '*it se it baja denge* (we will fight it tooth and nail).'[35]

Despite facing the odds for his pro-poor and somewhat populist polices, Karpoori stuck with his socialist agenda. On 22 March 1978, Finance Minister Kailashpati Mishra said in his budget speech that the Janata Party government was committed to the 'economic development of the weakest section of the society'. The government announced a new campaign of Antyodaya and also decided to provide legal aid to Harijans, tribals and landless labourers. From July 1977 to February 1978, 5944 acres of land had been acquired under the Land Ceiling Act; 16,470 acres of land had been distributed, benefiting 16,336 families.

Shivanand Tiwari says, 'The data from 1977–78 highlights the disparity in poverty levels between the Scheduled Castes and Scheduled Tribes (SC/ST) communities and other caste groups in India. The data shows that among the total rural population of SC/ST communities, which accounted for about 27 per cent at that time, around 70 per cent of the people were victims of poverty. In contrast, among other communities, which accounted for 73 per cent of the population, only 54 per cent of the people were in poverty.'[36]

Similarly, in urban areas, the data indicates that 13 per cent of the population belonging to SC/ST communities experienced 60 per cent poverty, while 87 per cent of the non-scheduled caste population had only 43 per cent poverty-stricken people. These figures highlight the disproportionately higher levels of poverty among SC/ST communities compared to other caste groups.

The data also suggests that there has been little improvement in the ratio of population to poverty among SC/ST communities over the last two decades, indicating persistent economic and social inequalities. These disparities may be attributed to various historical, social and economic factors that have led to systemic discrimination and marginalization of SC/ST communities, resulting in higher poverty levels among them.

Dhirubhai Seth writes, 'The data underscores the need for targeted efforts and policy interventions to address the specific challenges faced by SC/ST communities in order to reduce poverty and promote inclusive and equitable development. This may include measures such as affirmative action, social welfare programs, education and skill development, land reforms, and access to basic services and opportunities, aimed at empowering and uplifting SC/ST communities and addressing the underlying structural inequalities.'[37]

Liquor Ban

Karpoori Thakur, the former chief minister of Bihar, was indeed known for his strong stance against alcohol consumption. In fact, Karpoori Thakur was the first chief minister to implement prohibition in Bihar during his tenure in the late 1970s. Like Nitish Kumar, the current chief minister of Bihar who has enforced a total liquor ban in Bihar since April 2016, Karpoori Thakur also faced challenges, such as pressure from liquor mafia and smugglers, during his time. The issue of alcohol consumption and its associated problems, including social, health and economic issues, has been a persistent challenge in Bihar and other parts of India. Both Karpoori Thakur and Nitish Kumar took strong measures to tackle this issue and enforce prohibition in Bihar, though they faced opposition and challenges in doing so.

Karpoori Thakur's efforts to implement prohibition in Bihar were aimed at addressing the social and economic consequences of alcohol consumption, particularly among vulnerable communities. Similarly, Nitish Kumar's decision to enforce a liquor ban in Bihar in 2016 was based on similar concerns, including the adverse impact of alcohol on the well-being of individuals and families, particularly women from marginalized sections of society.

Yashwant Sinha writes, 'Some political decisions often had a direct impact on the administration itself, like when prohibition was introduced in Bihar in 1977 under the direction of Prime Minister Morarji Desai. The minister for excise, Baidyanath Mehta, instructed the excise commissioner Abhimanyu Singh, to transfer all the excise superintendents posted in Patna out of the city as he was not satisfied with their work. Despite Abhimanyu Singh's reservations, the minister's orders were carried out, leading to a huge protest by the concerned officers.'[38]

The Print draws a parallel between Karpoori Thakur and the current PM Narendra Modi in terms of their social backgrounds. 'The influences of Karpoori Thakur, Bihar's two-time former chief minister and veteran socialist leader, can be felt even today. A supporter of reservations, a politician who banned alcohol and a man known for his simplicity finds echo in contemporary politics. Before Prime Minister Narendra Modi was elected in 2014, then Bharatiya Janata Party president Rajnath Singh claimed Modi was similar to Kapoori Thakur—BJP's Prime Ministerial candidate Narendra Modi also belongs to extremely backward caste and shares a similar poor background.'[39]

Karpoori Thakur vehemently opposed CM Jagannath Mishra when he learnt about the Congress government's plans to lift the liquor ban. Karpoori Thakur told the Assembly as leader of the Opposition on 9 July 1980:

'I claim an emotional connection with Mahatma Gandhi and identify myself as a soldier of the freedom struggle and national movement. Gandhi argues that the ban on liquor is necessary to protect the welfare of the poor, Harijans (Scheduled Castes), and tribals (Scheduled Tribes) in Bihar. I express concern that reversing the liquor ban would be harmful to these marginalized communities, and that any revenue generated from liquor sales would be outweighed by the negative impact on the poor, Harijans and tribals. The reference to Sarvodaya, a social and economic philosophy espoused by Mahatma Gandhi that emphasizes the upliftment of all sections of society, suggests that the speaker sees the continuation of the liquor ban as being aligned with Gandhian principles and values. It is important to note that this statement reflects the perspective of the speaker and their support for maintaining the liquor ban in Bihar at that time. Prohibition policies, including the ban on liquor, can be complex and have both positive and negative consequences, and their effectiveness and impact on different sections of society may vary. It is important to carefully consider various perspectives and conduct a thorough analysis of the social, economic, and public health implications of such policies when making decisions on this issue.'[40]

Appointing 6700 Engineers and Optics

The decision taken by the Karpoori Thakur government in July 1978 to restore jobs to around 6700 engineers and the subsequent appointment letters being given at an open function at Gandhi Maidan was a significant political and administrative move. It sent out the message that employment opportunities would be provided to people and was seen as a positive gesture towards addressing unemployment and creating job opportunities in Bihar.

It appears that the Bihar government, led by Chief Minister Nitish Kumar and his deputy Tejashwi Prasad Yadav, also focused on employment generation as per their respective political agenda. Both leaders had been highlighting their commitment to providing job opportunities to the people of Bihar, with the target of creating ten lakh (one million) jobs, as mentioned on their political platforms.

Emulating Karpoori Thakur can offer a valuable lesson in shaping current policies and initiatives aimed at addressing unemployment. Now, both the present Prime Minister Narendra Modi and the sitting Chief Minister Nitish Kumar publicly distribute appointment letters.

Interestingly, when the Jagannath Mishra government said in the Assembly in 1980 that the Karpoori government had taken the decision to appoint engineers without a nod from the Cabinet, Karpoori tore apart the Congress government with his facts in the Assembly on 19 July 1980: 'On July 20, 1978, there was a debate in the House on the demand of the Irrigation Department. On that day, it was said in the House that 18,000 people would be recruited in the Irrigation Department, in which about 6,700 would be engineers. This House approved the recruitment of 18,000 people, of whom 6,700 were engineers. Mr. Speaker, the decision of our cabinet on 18th (July), then the decision of the House on 20th July, both the decisions are in front and on that day the Chief Minister has said that you appointed the engineers without the approval of the cabinet.'[41]

Karpoori Thakur continued with his prior decision on the waiver of land rent on seven acres of irrigated and three-and-a-half acres of irrigated land, the political moves that had made him popular.

Pioneering Quota within Quota: The Game Changer in Indian Politics

Prime Minister Morarji Desai was delivering a powerful speech at Patna's Gandhi Maidan on 3 November 1978. However, during his speech, the PM made adverse remarks against reservations, which received cheers from a section of the crowd. Bihar CM Karpoori Thakur, who was accompanying the PM, did not appear too amused. He seemed rather embarrassed, as implementing the Mungeri Lal Commission report on creating a quota within a quota was a significant part of the Janata Party's manifesto in Bihar and the Janata Party had also promised to implement the recommendations of the Kaka Kalelkar Commission report at the Centre.

Seema Chisti writes, '. . . he (Ramnath Thakur) vividly remembers that Diwali afternoon . . . in Patna's Gandhi Maidan, where he watched his father, the then Janata Party chief minister in Bihar—Karpoori Thakur, look askance as PM Morarji Desai on the stage railed against reservations . . . Jannayak (as Thakur was to be known later) duly escorted PM Desai back to the airport for Delhi, and drove back straight to Sachivalaya, issued a notification at 8.30 pm for reservation for backwards . . .'[42]

Karpoori Thakur had initially decided to give 20 per cent reservation on 3 November 1978. But his allies, BJS, in particular, opposed it vehemently. Neerja Chowdhury writes, 'The national leadership set up a committee to go into the matter, committees being a tried and tested way to defuse tensions. Finally, a compromise was evolved. Karpoori Thakur agreed to modify his policy. He decided to give 3 per cent reservations to women of all castes and another 3 per cent to the poor of all castes.'[43]

On 10 November 1978, the Personnel and Administrative Reforms Department of the state government passed three separate resolutions, one for 20 per cent quota (12 per cent to EBCs and 8 per cent to OBCs) and 3 per cent quota to women and another 3 per cent to the economically disadvantaged upper caste people, taking the total reservation to 26 per cent.

The resolution on the quota for EBCs and OBCs, signed by Chief Secretary K.A. Ramasubramanian, reads: 'In 1971, the State Government formed the Backward Classes Commission, which was entrusted with the task of giving suggestions for the all-round development of the backward classes. The Commission inquired whether the representation of OBCs in government services is adequate or not and came to the conclusion that their representation is negligible in Category 1 and 2 and inadequate in Category 3 and 4. He has recommended that the state government should take immediate steps to engage the backward class in service. Article 16 (4) of the Constitution of India provides that if in the opinion of the State Government, the representation of backward classes of citizens is not adequate in their services, then Article 16 (4) does not interfere with the reservation of appointments or posts for them. In Article 16 (4) of the Constitution, backward citizens, classes are considered to have the same meaning as in Article 15 (4) of any socially and backward citizen. It is worth mentioning here that Article 15 (4) mentions the socially and educationally backward class of citizens. After examining the report of the Commission, the State Government is satisfied that the representation of OBCs in government services is inadequate, therefore the State Government has decided to reserve 20 per cent seats for OBCs in all categories of state services. Arrangements should be made, but this facility will be available only to those families whose annual salary does not exceed the exemption limit. The state government has decided that in 20 per cent reserved posts, other backward classes will reserve 12 per cent seats for extremely backward classes, and 8 per cent seats will be reserved for other backward classes. Vacancies for backward classes should be done for 3 years. If candidates are not found even after that, then it should be filled from second category backward class. The reservation will not be in promotion, only in first appointment. The arrangement will not be perpetual. As the people of the backward classes will progress, the reservation for those classes will end. This work will be done from time to time after revision and review. All the process related to reservation will be the same as applicable for Scheduled Castes/Tribes. This reservation will also be applicable in the services of the State Government, Zilla Parishad, Municipality, Semi-Government Institutions, Universities and Public Undertakings as has been applied for

Scheduled Castes/Scheduled Tribes, and this order will apply to those vacancies which will be available on, and after, 31 October 1978 . . .'[44]

Karpoori Thakur also pioneered a quota for women by giving them 3 per cent reservation through a separate resolution passed the same day. The resolution read: 'In 1971, the state government formed the Backward Classes Commission, which was entrusted with the task of making recommendations, among other things, on what arrangements should be made to provide education, employment, government jobs and facilities to women. The commission inquired into the condition of women employed in the services. In the second chapter of his sixth report, he said that he had asked for reports regarding the number of female workers working in various government departments and offices and on the basis of those reports, it was found that except the education and health department, there are no women workers in any department and even if there are, their representation in other services is negligible except for these two services. That's why it is necessary that reservation should be arranged for them also so that the number of women employees increases. The provision of special arrangements for women has been made in section 15 (3) of the constitution. Therefore, the state government has decided that three per cent seats in government services should be reserved for women . . .'[45]

The Bihar Government Personnel and Administrative Reforms Department, in the third simultaneous Resolution, also decided to give three per cent quota to 'Non-Scheduled Castes, Non-Scheduled Tribes and Non-Other Backward Classes' saying: 'It is a principle of the State under Article (49) of the Constitution of India that the State Government shall specially promote the educational and economic interests of the weaker sections of the society and protect them from social injustice and other forms of exploitation. In 1971, the State Government constituted the Backward Classes Commission, which was asked to make recommendations for the all-round development of Scheduled Castes, Scheduled Tribes, Other Backward Classes and women. Although the Commission was not entrusted with the task of giving suggestions for the upliftment of the economically backward people of the advanced community, but the commission has also made many recommendations for the upliftment of these people. As far as the employment of economically weaker persons belonging to the advanced community in Government service is concerned, the Commission suggests that the claims of such persons should be given due consideration by the appointing authority and a policy of liberal preference should be adopted for them. He has said that the state government should give necessary instructions in this regard so that the advanced community and economically weak families can be brought to the general level of the country in the least possible time. The State Government holds since most of the appointments are made on the basis of the competition, it would be difficult to liberally adopt a policy of preferential treatment. Apart from this, the members of the economically weaker sections are usually first generation students and due to the unfavourable home environment and the absence of road facilities which are available to the affluent household, they are unable to succeed in the competitive examinations. That's why it seems necessary that reservation should be arranged for their employment in government services. Therefore, the State Government has decided to reserve 3 per cent seats for non-scheduled castes, non-scheduled tribes and economically weaker sections of backward classes in each category of government services. The government has decided that only those families whose annual income does not exceed the exemption limit of income tax, should be considered economically weak . . .'[46]

The Mungeri Lal Classes Commission, set up in 1971 during the tenure of Bhola Paswan Shastri and submitted during the tenure of Jagannath Mishra in 1976 in the midst of the Emergency, had drawn up a list of the seventy-nine most educationally and socially backward classes as Annexure II. The reservations scheme provided that 12 per cent of government posts should be reserved for Annexure II backwards and 8 per cent for Annexure I backwards. The forward classes argued for the establishment of a new backward commission to assess if certain castes, particularly Yadavs, had progressed over the years, or if caste considerations should be replaced with economic criteria. However, the lobby led by the backward classes, with their letter-writing campaigns, memoranda and public meetings, proved to be highly effective. This caused concerns among the national Janata leadership about a potential split along forward–backward lines.

While Morarji's speech had provided the immediate trigger, Karpoori took eighteen months to implement the recommendations of the Mungeri Lal Commission. Karpoori Thakur decided to fulfil the pledge made by the party based on the evidence in the (Mungeri Lal) backward classes commission's report that the percentage of backward class representation in Class I and Class II positions of the government services was 'negligible' and Class III and IV, it was 'low'.

Christophe Jaffrelot writes, 'As noticed by R.K. Hebsur in the second Backward Classes Commission Report, Thakur was only pursuing the Lohia line of further mobilising the backward classes, even if he amended this approach by following the Mungeri Lai Commission and distinguished MBCs from OBCs. According to Blair, the new reservation policy concerned only 1800 jobs per annum (since the administration recruited 9000 new employees each year) and was therefore a "symbolic" measure.'[47]

Madhu Limaye, as convener of the JP Movement Programme Committee in 1975, had drafted a document reading: 'Caste hierarchy based on birth is the biggest obstacle in the path of achieving social equality. In an unequal society, the doctrine of judicial equality and equal opportunity—cannot by itself remove caste disabilities. The doctrine of preferential opportunity, therefore, had to be invoked in order to enable the backward sections to come up to the level of the upper castes. Reservation in the services that we have today has not enabled us to overcome the disabilities from which our suppressed communities suffer.'[48]

Author Christophe Jaffrolet writes: '. . . the Janata Party election manifesto had promised a "policy of special treatment" and even a "New Deal for weaker sections". If voted to power it would "reserve between 25% and 33% of all appointments to government service for the backward classes, as recommended by the Kalelkar Commission". However, most of the manifesto's promises were addressed to the kisans. One of the party's objectives was to narrow down the "rural–urban disparities" by giving "the farmer . . . remunerative prices". The Janata Party did not speak about land reform but about "agrarian reform", which should be covering tenurial relationships, ownerships and consolidation of holdings and abolish landlordism.'[49]

Mohammed Sajjad writes, 'More importantly, it split the backward castes in two blocs, so that the upper Shudras (Yadavas, Koeris, and Kurmis) should not take away the cake of the lower Shudras. This became popular as the "Karpoori Formula".'[50]

Narendra Pathak writes, 'Dr Lohia had also given the idea of special representation to women because of their educational backwardness. Karpoori believed that reservation was only a step in the direction of social change. The landmark decision went on to polarize Backwards and Dalits in Bihar. A political ground for backward class politics was created. It had its resonance in the politics of Lalu Prasad and Nitish Kumar, who worked on their social engineering along the same lines.'[51]

With the announcement of reservations, mobilization of support and opposition started in Bihar. Nitish Kumar, then a budding young leader of Yuva Janata, was asked by Karpoori to study his reservation policy and suggest amendments accordingly. Nitish introduced a formula that suggested that the basis of reservations should be social and educational. Narendra Pathak writes, 'At the same time, it deprives the special class of backward castes (creamy layer) from the privilege of reservations and also provides protection to the family members of the upper caste.'[52]

Nitish's formula stirred the debate on whether there should be reservations on an economic basis or not.

On 2 September 2005, CM Nitish Kumar said, at a public meeting at Patna: 'Just like Karpoori Thakur worked towards reservation for the MBCs within the quota meant for the backward classes in the (government) jobs, the MBCs among the backward classes should get reservation in the Panchayati Raj institutions. They should get separate reservation. Besides, the Constitution should be amended in order to give them political reservation just like the scheduled castes and scheduled tribes have it. We demand this. The reservation should be given in proportion to population . . . We were observing the birth anniversary of Karpoori Thakur in Ravindra Bhavan. It was being discussed that the annexures I and II be merged. We declared then and there itself that no power can snatch away the rights which were given to us by Karpoori Thakur . . .'[53]

Senior journalist Jagpal Singh writes: 'This (sub quota) was all the more important considering the fact that the dominant OBCs like Yadavs, who formed the core group of his support, and Charan Singh were against a sub-quota against the MBCs. He himself belonged to a community (caste) that was in minority and was politically ineffective as a group: the Nai (barber) community. Today, there is a regular allusion to Karpoori Thakur's reservation policy of sub-quota generally known as "Karpoori Thakur formula" in debates on reservation.'[54]

Against the backdrop of the Karpoori Thakur government's implementation of the Mungeri Lal Commission's recommendations, an initial shift in the political landscape could be observed during the 1978 Panchayat elections at the village level, indicating a change in the centre of gravity. It is significant that the All India Backward Classes' Federation marched through the streets of Patna on 14 March demanding, along with reservation of jobs, also the release of all the accused in the Belchhi massacre case, particularly of Inderdeo Chaudhary, MLA, the main accused in the case and a caste hero of the Kurmis. Manish Kumar Jha writes, 'This was a clear indication of caste conflict that reflected a rupture in backward caste and schedule caste relationship.'[55]

The reservation decision triggered a prolonged wave of violent protests by forward caste youth. The refusal of senior members of the Janata Party to accept the reservations policy, and their tacit encouragement to the young men who rioted against it, resulted in polarization between the backwards and forwards in towns and villages throughout the state. The first elections to block panchayat samitis in 1978 sparked a bloody battle between backwards and forwards for the control of local bodies.

Narendra Pathak writes, 'A consensus began to emerge on a political strategy for challenging the dominant position of the

upper castes. Whereas Communists had given greatest emphasis
to an economic revolution but had failed to organise all the poor,
the leadership of backward classes recognised the need for social
and economic revolution because the poor remain divided.'[56]

More than anything else, the reservation issue politicized
caste forever. Noting the true nature of reservation politics, Harry
Blair writes: 'The whole struggle is not really over the 2000 jobs;
rather, the reservation policy is a symbolic issue and has gripped
the imagination of virtually everyone in Bihar who has even the
slightest degree of political awareness. Through the reservation
issue, Karpoori Thakur asserted that the Backwards had displaced
the Forwards as the dominant force in Bihar politics, that the old
days of dominance in public affairs from village to Vidhan Sabha
by the twice-born were gone forever, and that his government
would be the one based on the support of the Backwards. The
forwards interpreted things this way as well, fearing that their days
of dominance might indeed have departed, and responded with a
volatile mixture of fear and rage. Karpoori Thakur succeeded in
his goal partially, ending effectively any nonpartisan compromise
on the reservation issue. The conflict on the reservation issue once
again demonstrated the salience of politics in the increasing no-
holds-barred power struggles in Bihar. Years later commenting
on the reservation stir, Karpoori Thakur himself pointed out,
'the agitation was definitely politically organized. Newspapers
helped them (the agitation leaders) with publicity. There was a
whispering campaign . . . including lies. The crowds were mainly
students. Political trouble was mainly urban . . . Rural masses were
not involved. Most observers noted the role of political parties
and leaders opposed to Karpoori.'[57]

Francine R. Frankel and M.S.A. Rao write, 'Caste feelings were
ignited over the issue of reservations for OBCs. The national Janata

leadership, at a time when they saw no hope of capturing power, had acceded to the Socialists' demand that the party's election manifesto include a promise to implement the recommendations of the 1955 Backward Classes Commission report.'[58]

The announcement immediately provoked large-scale street rioting and destruction of public property by forward caste youth protesting against the reservation policy. A determined Karpoori Thakur took the issue to the Central Parliamentary Board of the Janata Party where reservations were discussed threadbare in a general conference that included upper-caste members of the Bihar cabinet and all Bihar MPs.

The compromise formula, agreed upon by Karpoori Thakur and the Janata Party president, Chandra Shekhar, was a reservation policy that reserved 20 per cent of appointments in the state civil services and professional colleges for OBCs (so long as they did not pay income tax). In addition, 3 per cent appointments were reserved for women and 3 per cent for the economically backward among the upper caste.

Jagpal Singh writes, 'His reservation policy divided the state along caste lines; his suggestions about security divided the state along caste and class lines and his language policy especially divided the state's politics on the class and rural–urban axis. Karpoori Thakur seemed to be in a hurry to introduce these policies. For example, he introduced the reservation policy immediately after having become the chief minister of the Janata Party government. This was in contrast to one of his contemporary counterparts—Devraj Urs of Karnataka. Unlike Karpoori Thakur, Urs introduced the reservation policy for the backward classes during the last two years of his seven years of rule.'[59]

Violent protests took place at several places. Schools and colleges also came under its grip with students getting divided on caste lines. Two young legislators, who led anti-reservation protests, were Vikram Kumar and Ram Jatan Singh, who were rendered politically irrelevant in the coming years. Upper caste leaders in BJS were opposed to reservation. Sushil Kumar Modi says, 'Though the official stand of Jan Sangh was to support it but in practicality, most of its leaders were opposed to it. Leaders like Vikram Kumar, Ramjatan Sinha and Mithilesh Singh had been at the forefront of reservation protests.'[60]

Similar protests took place in Uttar Pradesh and interestingly civil servants themselves took part in the agitation in some areas. As a result, CM Banarsi Das withdrew all the reservation schemes announced by his predecessor Ram Naresh Yadav. Quotas could not be implemented at the national level either.

Ramnath Thakur recalled how abusive slogans were used against Karpoori Thakur. *'Ye aarakshan kahan se aayi, Karpoori ki mai biyayi* (where does this reservation come from, Karpoori's mother has perhaps given birth to it).'[61]

Though I was a primary school student at my paternal village of Ramchua, Banka, I have faint memories of being taken to attend a students' march at the neighbouring village of Kurmadih, where students of over a dozen schools were brought. We were lined up to walk five km to the block town of Shambhuganj to raise anti-Karpoori slogans. One such slogan was *'Karpoori-Karpura, chhod gaddi, pakad ustura* (Down with you, Karpoori, you better quit your throne and take up your razor).'

Socialist litterateur Prem Kumar Mani recalled how CM Karpoori Thakur had to hide in a train bathroom at Darbhanga when protestors learnt about his arrival there. Senior BJP leader Sushil Kumar Modi said those who protested against the quota were mainly upper caste leaders.

Several leaders, who had earlier opposed reservations, slowly realized its political and social significance. Kapildeo Singh, a close aide of Thakur, wrote: 'I was a minister in Karpoori Thakur's government and I am fully aware of what that government has done to make this reservation policy universal. Still some upper caste people created a whirlwind against it and today they are accepting the reservation policy of Karpoori Thakur as right. Those who were agitating against him at that time are today accepting his formula as correct and those who were in support of the reservation policy of Karpoori Thakur, some of them are calling that formula inappropriate today.'[62]

In an interview with *Dinman*, Thakur wrote: 'So much hue and cry is being made on reservation of jobs that the fact has been hidden from the common people that there are many economic programs of the government where backward and non-backward castes, high or low, there is no distinction of any kind.'[63]

Here is what Karpoori Thakur told the Assembly on 24 July 1980 (*Karpoori Ka Sansdiya Jeevan*) and also responded to some questions asked by CM Jagannath Mishra:

'Yes, they are very less represented in the job. That report (Mungeri Lal Commission report) was given to you, not me. When I came (as CM), I was a member of the Janata Party. It was written in the election manifesto of the Janata Party that as there is reservation in jobs for Harijans and tribals, in the same way reservation will be given to the backward classes. This was in the manifesto of the Janata Party and it is recorded in section 15 (4) of the Constitution that Backward people will also get reservation. When we implemented the provision of reservation, we were told that we practise casteism. I was surprised what kind of society and world is this. What is written in the Constitution, we took action as per the provisions of the Constitution. This kind of work is being done in many provinces of India. When we implemented what was applicable, we were told that we do casteism. We did not do any work for any one class. When we waived the land tax, we did it for everyone, when we waived the fees till high school, we did it for everyone. We made arrangements for giving books not only for the boys but also for the girls, we did it for everyone . . . You can see the appointments made by us in our times . . . No *Mai Ka Laal* (son of a mother) is going to say that we acted on the basis of casteism. By giving a speech, Pandit Jagannath Mishra was explaining to us that the casteist people were defeated. Is it casteism to implement reservation? Mr. Mishra, let an impartial person investigate. But Karpoori Thakur cannot become a casteist just because a few people say so. The province knows us too. A nationalist cannot become a casteist just because being told so by others. I want to say that after becoming the Chief Minister, you said that you are not going to interfere in the reservation implemented by Karpoori Thakur. Once reservation is implemented, it will continue . . . Mr. Mishra, you protested from inside, protested from your soul. Now that reservation has come into effect, it cannot be reversed . . .'[64]

Senior journalist and writer Anil Chamaria shares his personal experience on how educational institutions differed on reservation.'The college I had been studying in was dominated by OBCs and Dalits. But these students did not have the courage to join pre-reservation meetings. Though upper caste students were in a minority, they would call the shots because the college management was dominated by upper castes.'[65]

When Karpoori implemented reservations in 1978, 'Dharmyuga was only one of a few magazines or newspapers that supported Karpoori's decision.'[66] In the midst of anti-reservation protests, when some foreign journalists came to Patna, Karpoori Thakur took up their questions in English with aplomb. 'The foreign journalists were stunned and one of them said someone who is so deep-rooted can understand and analyse reservation so well.'[67]

Jagdanand Singh says, 'Lohia wanted special opportunity for those who were not given equal opportunity. Karpoori Thakur would say if five of 10 persons in a family are handicapped, the five could be a burden on the family. Similarly, people without education and equal opportunity can become a burden for society.'[68]

Mantosh Kumar, a Bihar born US citizen who belongs to the upper caste but abhors the caste system, recalls his father, a senior government officer in Bihar, who had a special fondness for Karpoori as he aligned with Thakur's socialist agenda and his great example of probity in public life in an era when using public office for personal profit was becoming increasingly common. His father was not alone in the list of Karpoori's supporters. But suddenly a great commotion arose, not only among the upper caste public but also his cabinet members belonging to the upper castes. Overnight, Karpoori Thakur became a khalnayak (villain) from a Jannayak (people's leader). Mantosh asked his father, 'Babuji, why this sudden change in people's attitude towards Karpoori Thakur, who once was a beloved leader of the people?' Babuji replied thoughtfully, 'Son, this reservation is like snatching food from your plate and giving it to someone else. There is a difference between ideals in theory and a reality that hits you where it hurts.' This was the first time in the history of Bihar that the privileged minority felt wronged and helpless at the same time; something the numerically superior but socially, educationally and economically underprivileged majority had felt for ages. Justice was meted out, but the medicine was too bitter to swallow![69]

Mantosh understood this to be a delivery of justice to the wrongfully denied masses, but still the pain of losing the food off one's plate, enjoyed for generations, didn't seem quite palatable.

The US Supreme Court and the Indian Supreme Court have dealt with this issue at length. The five-judge bench of the Supreme Court headed by the Chief Justice, M.N. Venkatachallah in the Indra Sawhney case writes:

> *52. We have examined the decisions of the U.S. Supreme Court at some length only with a view to notice how another democracy is grappling with a problem similar in certain respects to the problem facing this country. The minorities (including blacks) in the United States are just about 16 to 18% of the total population, whereas the backward classes (including the Scheduled Castes and Scheduled Tribes) in this country - by whichever yardstick they are measured - do certainly constitute a majority of the population . . . Untouchability - and 'unapproachability', as it was being practised in Kerala - is something which no other country in the world had the misfortune to have - nor the blessed caste system. There have been equally old civilisations on earth like ours, if not older, but none had evolved these pernicious practices, much less did they stamp them with scriptural sanction . . . "[70]*

The Indian Supreme Court found reservation constitutional.[71] The Supreme Court of the USA also found giving priority to the disadvantaged races at the cost of others constitutional and held that it does not go against the principle of equality.[72] The nine-judge bench of the American Supreme Court, headed by Chief Justice Warren Burger, found the Public Works Employment

Act of 1977, which mandated that at least 10 per cent of federal funds for local public works projects be allocated to Minority Business Enterprises constitutional to remedy past discrimination and promoting diversity in government contracts.[73] Now, the reservation policy extends to women, EWS of upper caste, OBCs except the creamy layer, Schedule Caste, Scheduled Tribe, physically challenged, etc., showing the social acceptability of the policy of quota.

Anointing 'Jannayak'

Going back to 1978, the Janata Party president Chandra Shekhar, who was fondly called Adhyakshji, however, fully backed Karpoori's decision of reservation. At a party meeting around the end of 1978, Chandra Shekhar bestowed the honorific of 'Jannayak' (leader of the people) on Karpoori Thakur. The sobriquet has now become the first reference for Karpoori Thakur. Ramnath Thakur, who had, since 1970, been accompanying his father to almost all his political meetings, recalled: 'Just when there had been differing views on my father's reservation decision, Chandra Shekhar called it a historic decision and termed Karpoori Thakur Jannayak amidst thunderous applause at a party meeting.'[74]

In an interview with *India Today* (Hindi), December, 1978 issue, Karpoori had spoken about the controversies surrounding reservation: 'This controversy is illogical and unethical. The Constitution (of India) has provided for reservation on grounds of educational and social backwardness. Many states have implemented it. Economically backward people are being added under it. Some states have not done so. But I have said repeatedly, this scheme (reservation) has to be reviewed from time to time.'[75]

Here are some more questions he took up during the interview:

'Are you isolated on your job reservation policy and has your party also distanced itself on it?'

I am happy that they are making allegations against me. But I am firm on this (reservation) and can face anyone. I am implementing what was laid out in the party manifesto. I am not afraid of criticism, nor can I make compromises. I do not believe in caste. Those against me are casteists of the first order.

So you remain firm on your decision . . .

If someone is willing to test my firmness, one may well try.

What are the achievements of your government?

What the Janata Party government has achieved in 20 months, the Congress government had not achieved in 20 years . . . We have waived *lagaan* (land rent) on five acre land in the plains and seven acre land in hilly areas. We have also waived agriculture surcharge on land up to 10 acre and also put an end to the condition of minimum guarantee for electricity connection. Bihar is the only state in North India where education has been made free up to matriculation (Class 10). Books have been made available free of cost to about 23 lakh children . . . Under grains against employment scheme, 4 kg grains are being given to a labourers every day. Under Antyodaya scheme, Rs 75 lakh has been distributed among 12,500 families.[76]

Senior journalist Farzand Ahmed who chronicled the times of Karpoori Thakur, writes that 'Karpoori Thakur made a significant change in his policy on March 21, 1979, conceding the "economic basis for the purpose of reservation". After consulting New Delhi, his Cabinet approved a reservation policy with a significant modification—it barred people from the backward classes whose monthly income exceeds Rs 1,000. Besides, the policy assured a 10 per cent reservation for women.'[77]

This development only added fuel to the fire. The anti-reservationists stepped up their agitation, while the Backward Classes Federation condemned the policy. The hardline Forward League held an *in camera* session on 22 March and pledged to continue fighting against the Government's policy.

Erstwhile BJS leaders in the Janata Party organized a huge rally on 31 March 1979 in Patna against the policy and also decided to carry on an anti-reservation campaign at the block level. Ahmed argued that Karpoori intended to consolidate his position as a leader of the 'have-nots' by keeping up the heat on reservation. As his cabinet was sharply divided, he got the approval of the party's Central Parliamentary Board on the reservation.

Farzand Ahmed writes, 'What provoked the so-called "upper" castes was the fear that only the Yadavs, Kurmis, Koeris and similar communities (often described as the neo-rich class) would be benefited by the reservations. These castes are socially and educationally better off and have been striving to take over the power-politics in the state.'[78]

The young leaders who supported Karpoori Thakur included young MPs Ram Awadhesh Singh and Lalu Prasad, who started a parallel movement. The two MPs invited Shahi Imam Abdullah Bukhari of Jama Masjid to address a rally. 'In a procession in Patna on March 9, (1979), they idolized Karpoori Thakur and condemned JP who had been propagating the idea that reservations should be made on an economic basis.'[79]

As a counter to it, a group of students created a ruckus at JP's function in Patna on 12 March 1979 by throwing stones and slippers at the venue. Senior pro-reservation leaders Acharya J.B. Kriplani, Jagjivan Ram and George Fernandes were targeted by protestors at different places.

Finally, former Union minister Yashwant Sinha, who was the principal secretary to the then CM Karpoori Thakur, shares an interesting anecdote of the period. 'The reservation for the other backward classes (OBCs) was also done with a great deal of finesse, and without it leading to any violence. There were some expected protests, no doubt, but the administration was fully prepared to meet the challenge. The media, however, made much of the small and isolated disturbances. I remember how, one day, an American journalist walked into my office with all kinds of camera equipment and demanded to know where the war zone was. I dismissed him by saying that there was no war zone and that he would not be able to get a story out of Bihar.'[80]

Karpoori in Assembly

Karpoori Thakur's exemplary performance in the Legislative Assembly as an MLA, Opposition leader and CM has become part of the legislative record, serving as a prime example of his meticulous preparation for his speeches and his skilful intertwining of political ideology and vision with it. Often, he employed witticisms, veiled sarcasm and a great sense of humour. Here are some examples of his legislative brilliance during his tenure as CM (1977–79) and also as a leader of the Opposition afterwards.

Speaking on his favourite topic, language, on 15 July 1977, the CM told the Assembly: 'We hail from the Hindi heartland, encompassing states such as Uttar Pradesh, Haryana, Punjab,

Bihar, Madhya Pradesh, Rajasthan, and Himachal Pradesh. In these Hindi-speaking regions, the current practice is to teach three languages: Hindi, compulsory English, and any modern Indian language. We recommend revising the three-language policy for Hindi-speaking provinces, with a specific emphasis on incorporating the language of South India. Such a change could potentially trigger a significant revolution in our provinces and across the nation. As per the central government's order, the priority should be given to teaching Hindi, English, and one modern Indian language, with preference given to the language of South India. Our proposal is to teach Hindi and English until Grade 10, with the option to add a language from South India, though not mandatory. While English cannot be made optional, those who wish to study it should have the choice to do so.'[81]

Karpoori, however, clearly emphasized his viewpoint on English: 'We would like to clarify that our intention is not to be anti-English or against any language in the world. When we say "optional", it means that students should have the freedom to choose any language they wish to study. However, we believe that those who do not wish to study English should not be burdened with it unnecessarily. Our proposal is to make Hindi and one South Indian language mandatory in our language policy. We are aware that Tamil Nadu is often perceived as an anti-Hindi state, but we believe that emotional and national unity require us to follow the direction of the central government in including a language from South India. It is important to consult with teachers and education experts to build consensus and avoid agitations. We are committed to implementing this language policy with love, advice and consultation, and we believe that it will lead to a positive outcome. When the time comes, we are ready to initiate a process of consultation to build consensus.'[82]

In the context of the Karpoori Thakur government's order to conduct official work only in Hindi in Bihar, his principal secretary Yashwant Sinha recalled: 'One day we came across a file in which the deputy secretary of the law department, whose mother tongue was not Hindi, had valiantly tried to write a note in Hindi. He had, however, used a fair amount of English words as well. Karpoori sent the file back with a cryptic note of his own, "*Hindi mein achha Angrezi note likha hai.* (You have written a nice English note in Hindi)". Erring on the side of caution, I did not even write any English words on my notepad that I used to carry with me all the time, fearing that Karpoori might see them. Every communication to the ministers of GoI, including the PM, was in Hindi, accompanied by an unsigned English translation.'[83]

Speaking on 24 July 1978, on the menace of booth capturing, he cited the Report on the Fifth General Election in India, on the 1971 Lok Sabha elections and the 1972 Assembly elections in Bihar. '(The ECI report) reveals various menaces and nefarious practices that occurred in some parts of the country on the day of the poll. One particularly disturbing practice is urchin voting, where boys and young children as young as 10 or 11 years old (sometimes even younger) vote in elections. This practice mainly occurs in Bihar . . . The report apparently did not call for an amendment to the People's Representative Act . . . (Booth capturing) practice, which involves seizing control of polling booths and intimidating or threatening election officials, has been in vogue in Bihar since at least the Second General Elections of 1957. The speaker accuses someone of "creating the booth capturing disease here since 1957," and notes that this problem has only gotten worse over time.'[84]

In the same speech, Karpoori elaborated on the voting pattern in which 'riotous mobs armed with deadly weapons such as revolvers and pipe guns attacked polling stations', would 'overwhelm security forces, and forcibly remove ballot boxes in Bihar, Haryana, and Jammu and Kashmir.'[85]

In his speech in the Assembly on 24 January 1980, Karpoori paid rich tributes to JP following the latter's demise. 'The time when he did the "jumping" of crossing the boundary wall of Hazaribagh Jail, he clearly did it with the preparation of death. At the time when he organized the Azad Dasta in Nepal in order to end the violent measures of British imperialism, he ran away from the jail. Apparently, he was prepared to face death! At the time when he took a pledge to lead the procession in Patna on November 4, 1974, at that time, in Patna, on that day, the army, CRP jawans, BSF, their guns were ready to fire, according to the (Central Reserve Police) CRP's IG (Inspector General), tanks and machine guns were lined up to rain thunderous fire . . . There are few men in the world who are ready to play with coals, who are ready to take risks, who are ready to play with death in disasters and calamities, who are ready to turn the wheel of history. We are proud that we were born in such a state, in such a country, where great men like the revered Jayaprakash were born . . . He was the symbol of the best qualities of not only Indian culture, but of human culture . . .'[86]

Former MP and RJD state president Jagdanand Singh, who had first become an MLA in 1985, recalled: 'What we learnt from Karpoori Thakur was to use the forum of the Assembly to address the grievances of the poor. He also advised us against lodging protests and going into the well of the House. For a large part of our political career, we stuck to his advice. But with Speakers not being neutral and often found working on party lines, the Opposition bench is rising in protest now.'[87]

Belchhi Massacre

In August 1977, less than six months after Indira Gandhi was
voted out of power post-Emergency, Bihar's first caste carnage
'brought Indira Gandhi to Belchhi atop an elephant, an image
that transfixed the nation long before TV, a photo-op which
lifted the hopes of the Congress reeling across the Hindi
heartland.'[88]

Belchhi, where a tragic incident took place when the Janata
Party was riding high on the glory of ousting Indira Gandhi
from power, remains etched in the memory of many. It was the
first caste massacre in which backward Kurmis were accused of
burning eleven landless Dalits. Indira Gandhi had to traverse
slushy roads on an elephant to reach the village, which was
barely 60 km from the state capital of Patna, creating a powerful
visual imagery. However, despite the attention garnered by the
incident, the victims' families received meagre compensation
in the form of three litres of kerosene on their ration cards
every month, one acre of barren gairmajurua land each, and an
open pan toilet. It is safe to say that without the symbolism of
Indira's 'accidental elephant ride,' the incident may have gone
unnoticed.

Since March 1977, major outrages have taken place against
Harijan sharecroppers and labourers in Kargahar, Belchhi,
Pathadda, Chhaundadano, Gopalpur and Dharampura. In most
cases, the accused belonged to backward castes. 'What does this
explain about the coalition of assorted political formations,
the nature of the state and the conduct of government and
limits of popular politics? Thakur's 26 per cent reservation as
a masterstroke, though it attempted to address the political
constituents of the socialist bloc, led to an open confrontation

between the backward castes and the upper castes. There were open armed clashes, arson, inter-community riots; backward castes vs forward castes became the defining moment of the phase. Forward castes league and backward caste federations were formed to mobilise castes/communities against and for the reservation respectively. Karpoori Thakur was opposed both by the upper castes and by the advanced sections of the backwards and turned out to be a misunderstood leader towards the close of his political career . . .'[89]

'The caste wars Belchhi triggered would not stop until 2000, with 700 people killed in 91 attacks. And nearly half those attacks and deaths were in the last six of those 23 years, a period when the Ranbir Sena was at its peak . . .The Ranbir Sena is now defunct but remains the name one associates with the worst of the caste wars. The period between 1994 and early 2000 saw the deaths of 337 SC members and Naxals, 50 of the Naxals by the police and the rest in 44 massacres. Naxals, in turn, killed 93 of the upper castes. The Belchhi massacre paved the way for Indira Gandhi to return to power in 1980. One could see the helplessness of CM Karpoori Thakur in dealing with the challenge. "I have put the best officers in Bihar to look after the welfare of agricultural labourers, within the state structure. What else can I do?" the CM had said.'[90]

Karpoori Thakur could hardly have anticipated that the aftermath of the Belchhi incident would continue to haunt Bihar for years to come. In a similar vein, as the leader of the Opposition, Karpoori Thakur appeared equally helpless when he visited the site of the Dalelchak-Bhagora massacre in Aurangabad in 1986. In that incident, forty-two people, mostly from the upper caste, were brutally killed. The sight of Karpoori Thakur standing apart looking at the village perhaps conveyed his deep anguish and pain.

Pitaunjhia Files

Rajendra Sharma has written in *Karpoori Ji Ka Jeevan Sangram*, in 1979, that when Karpoori was the CM, a journalist went to his house to see the real situation. He saw that the CM's wife Phuleshwari Devi was grooming the cow and cleaning out the cow dung. Her sari was dirty and Karpoori Thakur's father was shaving the beard of a farmer, who was from scavenger caste, at the door itself. The journalist was shocked to see all these scenes and asked Phuleshwari Devi some questions:

> *Your husband is the Chief Minister of Bihar, so why don't you live a comfortable life with him in Patna?*

> If I stay there (Patna), my father-in-law is old, who will serve him? Who will tend to these cows and who will take care of our little farm; all of them will be lost.

The same reporter asked some questions to Karpoori's father, Gokul Thakur:

> *What does Karpoori Thakur do with his salary?*

> His salary goes to help poor students with school–college fees, service expenses and social work.[91]

Ramnath Thakur says, 'Once a government official named G. Krishnan visited Pitaunjhia. It was after Karpoori Thakur had become CM for the second time. Krishnan was stunned to see that the CM's wife Phuleshwari Devi was taking out her goat to graze. She was also carrying a sickle in her hand then.'[92]

Yashwant Sinha writes: 'I had heard several stories of his early life and was keen to visit his village and see for myself the conditions in which his wife lived. One day, along with his private secretary Lakshmi Prasad Sahu, I made the trip to his village in Samastipur district. I was introduced to Mrs. Thakur and she was happy to see me, even though there was no chair for me to sit on. We made ourselves comfortable in whichever way we could. She insisted I have a cup of tea and, as we hung around, she lit a wood fire to heat the water. The house itself was a thatched hut with absolutely no trappings of modernity or comfort. The family lived in the village with a bare minimum of worldly possessions. I can't help but compare this with the palaces of politicians that are built in record time now, as soon as they become an MLA or an MP.'[93]

Prem Kumar Mani, a socialist thinker, recalled a story that shows how deeply Karpoori Thakur felt for the poor. 'Sometime in 1977, a person called Thakaita Dom died in police custody. Thakur, who was then the CM, took the responsibility for the police lapse. And when he learnt that the victim had no son or daughter, the CM took it upon himself to perform the last rites of Thakaita Dom.'[94]

A Controversy

Karpoori was under pressure from his detractors in politics, including those from within his own party, after they raked up a pending rape allegation against the CM. 'A certain lady from Nepal had even accused him of raping her during her visit to Patna. So, Karpoori undertook a five day fast, which was meant as a reply to his detractors, choosing the Gandhi Sangrahalaya, across from the Gandhi Maidan, to do so. It was unusual, to say the least, for an incumbent CM to undertake a fast like this and it created quite a stir in those days. He was inundated with visitors who came to congratulate him on his unique gesture and pledge their unflinching support.'[95]

The lady was a zoology teacher in a school in Nepal. She wanted to become an MLC. 'She made allegations and allowed Opposition to play it up with hope that she could get an MLC berth from some Opposition party. But her ploy did not work.'[96] In 1981, she withdrew her allegations against Karpoori Thakur from a Patna court after she told the court that she had made the allegations under duress and for political motives.

The Fall of a Government, Rise of the Leader

The arguments among Morarji Desai, Choudhary Charan Singh and the leaders of the former Bharatiya Jana Sangh over the appointments of chief ministers in Hindi-speaking states often led to casualties during the Janata Party days. However, Bihar, being distant from the influences of both Desai and Singh, provided Karpoori Thakur with a more assured position in his role as CM, compared to some of his counterparts in Uttar Pradesh and Madhya Pradesh within the Janata Party.

In Karpoori Thakur's final days as chief minister, there was communal violence in Jamshedpur in April 1979. A few hours before quitting office, he instituted a three-member enquiry team under Justice Jitendra Narayan.

However, Karpoori Thakur's differences with PM Desai sharpened after the reservation row. In April 1979, several ministers from the former BJS, Congress (O) and Bharatiya Lok Dal resigned from the Karpoori cabinet, with the former BJS leader and finance minister announcing a split from the Janata

Party. Jagjivan Ram's CFD also decided to quit the Karpoori-led Janata Party. On 19 April 1979, Karpoori had to face a floor test, which he lost by 135 votes against 105. The fall of Karpoori Thakur's government led to eighteen MPs from Bihar resigning from the Janata Party government at the Centre. The toppling of Karpoori Thakur's government proved costly for Morarji Desai's government in July 1979, just three months later. Led by Raj Narain, Karpoori Thakur, Biju Patnaik, Devi Lal, George Fernandes and Madhu Limaye, about one-third of the members left the Janata Party and formed a new party called Janata 'S' (Secular). Choudhary Charan Singh also resigned from Morarji Desai's government and joined Janata (S). A no-confidence motion against the Desai government was passed in Parliament. The president of India invited Y.B. Chavan, the leader of the Opposition, to form the government, but he could not succeed. Then Choudhary Charan Singh was invited to form the government. Under his leadership, the Janata 'S' government was formed, with the support of CPI, CPI (M) and Forward Bloc. The Indira Congress, which had also offered its support to Singh, however, did not support Singh during the floor test. Singh had to resign only twenty-three days after becoming PM. He, however, retained the position of caretaker PM till the Lok Sabha elections were held in January 1980.

Delhi University professor Manisha Priyam, daughter of former MLA Baidyanath Pandey (a close aide of Karpoori Thakur), said the announcement of the reservation policy 'marked the first tremors'. 'I remember how BJS leader and then finance minister Kailashpati Mishra, who was otherwise not known to lose his cool, had been visibly upset with my father. Satyendra Narayan Sinha and Thakur Prasad (senior BJS leader and father of former Union minister Ravishankar Prasad) came to our house late at night in the midst of anti-reservation protests. The next few days saw tremors in the Assembly and the support for Karpoori was gone. Gone also was the bonhomie I had seen in the verandah of our residence at 25, Hardinge Road of Patna where the three famous Ks—Karpoori Thakur, Kailashpati Mishra and Kishori Prasanna Singh (CPI), would often gather for hours for healthy political discussions over cups of tea. Karpoori Thakur was lonely. My father, an upper caste Bhumihar leader, was amongst the first to embrace Karpoori and his reservation formula. The costs were very high. Upper caste elite drawing rooms started avoiding us. In my English medium school, I was unable to open my mouth for years, not able to tell anyone that my father was a Karpoori follower because of upper castes' resentment against his reservation policy.'[97]

Reservations became such a combustible issue that Prime Minister Morarji Desai decided to set up a new commission to look into the matter. The Second Backward Class Commission, as it was called, was set up on 1 January 1979, and notified on 1 February 1979. Desai appointed a former chief minister of Bihar, Bindeshwari Prasad Mandal, to head it; soon enough, it came to be known as the Mandal Commission. Desai wanted to retain the support of the OBC MPs, who were becoming increasingly restive, buy time for his beleaguered government, and keep his challenger, Charan Singh, in check.[98]

And for Karpoori Thakur, the Janata Party experiment started failing soon after the death of the biggest binding factor, JP.

The successor Janata Party government, headed by Ramsunder Das, restored to the upper castes their strongest position in the state government since 1967. They received 50 per cent of the ministerial posts, while the Backwards were pushed back to 20 per cent. A letter from the chief secretary to all department heads and commissioners, dated 10 July 1979, said: 'Total percentage of persons recruited on the basis of merit in general category would be deducted from the reserved quota. For example, if 5 per cent of candidates are selected according to merit, in that case, reservations stand at 15 per cent.' This principle was also to be applied to reservations for the Scheduled Castes and Scheduled Tribes so that reservations would be reduced to 9 per cent (from 14 per cent) and to 5 per cent (from 10 per cent) assuming that 5 per cent of candidates were selected according to merit.'[99] The Das government amended Thakur's reservation policy 'in such a way as any recruitment of SC/ST, OBC and MBC candidate on a "merit" basis would be deducted from the quotas. For instance, if 2 per cent of MBC people joined the Bihar administration by passing the competitive examination for posts, which were not covered by the quota, this quota would be reduced in the same proportions. The same rule was to be applied for the other quotas.'[100]

This attempt to whittle away reservations for the most socially disadvantaged was not only gratuitous but also betrayed the deep social hostility towards all efforts at raising the position of low-caste groups.

But what made Karpoori Thakur stand out as a leader was the all round appreciation from his peers, colleagues and even detractors. His cabinet colleague Kapildeo Singh talked about an instance of his moral authority against PM Desai after he did not allow Singh to resign from the government after the 1978 Barahiya firing. 'The CM put his foot down and said that it was a law and order problem. If Singh, who represented Barahiya in the Assembly, should resign, then the CM should also resign.'[101]

Kapildeo Singh wrote a candid entry in his diary: 'Thakur was needed more today. If Thakur had not been ousted from Bihar, then perhaps the Janata government at the Centre would not have broken. I had told this to the central leaders and also told it in front of Thakur that with the chair, Thakur becomes an easy and accessible person, but when he moves away from the chair, he becomes equally dangerous. Keep Thakur engaged in work, he will surely avenge the insult if he is useless. . . . Thakur told me whosoever will throw a stone at him, he will launch a mountain on him. His calm mind was disturbed after personal insults and abusive words were hurled at him by the upper castes. Today, Bihar and the country needed him. There is a rare man like him who is balanced, humble, intelligent, tactful and sociable.'[102]

Kapildeo Singh was also an ardent fan of Karpoori Thakur's oratory. 'Saraswati also sits on his tongue. When he used to speak, the listeners used to get electrified. His speech in the Legislative Assembly is a heritage of history. His speech was based on factual data.'[103]

Karpoori Thakur, the man himself, who often faced jibes on his quota decision, spoke his heart out at the Bihar Pradesh Kaivart Sammelan, 19 June 1983 in Katihar:

'There are many people who waged a war against the British. I am one of them. If there was no British government, all would not have gotten the right to education in Hindustan. I can say with authority that Rajputs, who were not supposed to get educated but were supposed to learn Yuddh vidya, Vaishyas whose occupation was commerce and business were not supposed to get educated, and Shudras were not supposed to get educated at all. To study was considered a sin for them. Such was our country. That is why a social revolution has to be made . . . If we want to win two types of wars, social and economic revolutions, an organization is needed. Consciousness is needed. I am regularly saying that nothing can be achieved by begging—rights will not be achieved, power will not be achieved . . . If you want to achieve, awaken. If you want to achieve, awaken and move on.'[104]

Christophe Jaffrelot summed it up: 'While quota politics and kisan politics crystallized in the 1960s as two distinctive methods of promoting social transformation, they had many similarities and their social constituencies overlapped to such an extent that the proponents of the former, the Socialists, and of the latter, Charan Singh and his group, began to make common cause in the 1970s. This rapprochement was intended to catapult their coalition to power.'[105]

11

Caste Catches Up

The Leader of Unopposition

The campaign for the 1984 Lok Sabha elections had begun, and the Congress was riding high on a sympathy wave following the assassination of Indira Gandhi. Karpoori Thakur, who had formed the Dalit Mazdoor Kisan Party (DMKP) after becoming disillusioned with the Janata Party and the Lok Dal experiment, decided to contest his second Lok Sabha election from Samastipur. The Congress had fielded a low-profile candidate, Ramdev Rai, against Karpoori. During his campaign, Karpoori was once visiting a Yadav-dominated village. When he saw a person milking his cow, he stopped there and started milking the cow himself. Although the Jannayak succeeded in getting some milk from the cow, he could not secure enough votes to win the election. This was his only electoral defeat in his 36-year political career, during which he won nine consecutive Assembly elections and one Lok Sabha poll.[1]

In 1986, the twin village of Dalelchak-Bhagora in Aurangabad witnessed one of the worst massacres in the state, with 42 people, mostly upper caste Rajputs, being killed. Karpoori Thakur was the first Bihar leader to reach the spot. However, as he came from the EBC community, he faced resentment from some of the villagers. Sensing a potentially embarrassing situation, Karpoori had to leave the spot.[2]

From being forced to milk a cow in 1984 to being dismissed as an EBC leader at a massacre site in 1986, Karpoori was rapidly losing his grip on state politics. The growing dominance of Yadav-driven OBC politics had begun to push him to the brink, first as a leader of the Opposition and then as the very leader of the socialist block. Yet, he managed to hold the fort until he was removed from his position as the leader of the Opposition in 1987.

* * *

After the fall of the Karpoori Thakur government, tensions between the erstwhile Bharatiya Lok Dal (BLD) leaders and the Socialist camp, as well as ex-Congress (O) and formerly Bharatiya Jana Sangh (BJS) members, only intensified. While the Socialist and BLD components had been trying to push through quota politics and farmers politics respectively, the Congress (O) of Morarji Desai and the BJP were not willing to allow Charan Singh to occupy centre stage. The BJP, not quite a supporter of quota politics, wanted to go back to its core constituency of upper, urban and middle-class voters. Charan Singh, the biggest mass leader in the group, wanted to reboot his politics around his pet theme of the farmers' cause.

The Socialists were clueless, while a faction of the Congress in the group wanted to revive its separate identity.

Karpoori Thakur walked out of the Janata Party along with Charan Singh, Devi Lal, Madhu Limaye and George Fernandes and formed Janata (S). While Karpoori's close friend, Kapildeo Singh, had joined Janata (S) with him, his estranged friend Ramanand Tiwari decided to stay back in the Janata Party with Chandra Shekhar and Satyendra Narayan Sinha.

Karpoori started asserting his position in the new party. Shiv Kumar, Barahiya socialist leader and a close aide of Karpoori Thakur and Kapildeo Singh, recounted: 'Legislators of Janata (S) had decided to make Kapildeo Singh the leader of the party in the Assembly. All MLAs signed on a blank paper. But when it came to submitting the application to the Assembly Speaker, Karpoori Thakur gave his name for the party leader's post. When Kapildeo Singh got to know about it, he laughed it away, saying "Karpoori would be our leader in government and in Opposition both".'[3]

Veteran socialist leader Gajendra Prasad Himanshu, a popular Yadav leader from Karpoori Thakur's time, also recalled an incident after the 1980 Assembly polls when Thakur wanted a scheduled caste leader Shivnandan Paswan to become the deputy speaker in the Assembly ahead of the popular Himanshu. Somehow Karpoori Thakur had been trying to check the rising dominance of Yadav leaders in state politics. Himanshu recalled: 'The politics of Yadav versus non-Yadav had now been coming to the fore. Lok Dal was often called Gope Dal. But when Karpoori Thakur saw an overwhelming support for me, he had to support me. It was quite unlike a leader of his stature and calibre to resort to political gimmicks.'[4]

Charan Singh had made the first move in the break-up from this confused alliance by forming Janata (Secular) in June 1979 and later receiving Indira Gandhi's support to become the PM. 'It was the first time that a non-upper caste and a rural leader occupied the post and in his speech on Independence Day, on

15 August 1979, he accordingly focused on rural issues, even if he tried to correct the anti-city portrait that the media was assiduously painting of him at that time. The appointment of Charan Singh generated a great deal of excitement among farmers and the OBCs. The OBC leader Ram Lakhan Singh Yadav, commenting upon this event, considered that "a great enlightenment came to the Backward classes" and that it combined all Backward Classes together.'[5]

After serving as PM for only twenty-three days with Indira Gandhi not keeping her promise to lend support on the floor of the House, Charan Singh was livid. While keeping his chair as the caretaker PM, he converted Janata (S) formally into the Lok Dal at Talkatora Garden in Delhi on 26 December 1979. Many delegates wanted to call it Indian Lok Dal, while Union Foreign Minister Shyam Nandan Mishra wanted to stick to Janata (S) because it had gained fame in the country and abroad. However, Raj Narain, who was the president of Janata (S), and Charan Singh took the final call, naming it Lok Dal. Narain and Singh were made working presidents of the new party.

Dual membership became an issue in 1980 when the socialists in the Janata Party sought to distance themselves from the Bharatiya Jana Sangh group of leaders. 'Even though there was no official RSS membership, the socialists made it clear that those with affiliations to the RSS could not remain in the Janata Party. We finally formed the Bharatiya Janata Party under the leadership of Atal Behari Vajpayee on 5 April, 1980,' says Sushil Kumar Modi.[6] The dual membership was simply an excuse to part ways. The disintegration of the Janata Party was now complete. However, Chandra Shekhar, Morarji Desai, and Satyendra Narayan Sinha continued to stay with the Janata Party, or rather with its name, JP.

Ramsunder Das, who had become the CM in April 1979 with the support of the Congress, soon fell out with Indira Gandhi. She returned to the Centre as PM in January 1980 with her party winning 351 seats in the 542-member Lok Sabha. The Lok Dal emerged as the second-largest party with forty-one seats, while the Janata Party was relegated to the fourth position with thirty-one seats.

In April 1980, Bihar held its Assembly polls, and Karpoori Thakur contested his eighth Assembly election as the Janata (S) nominee, defeating the INC (I) candidate Chandra Shekhar Verma by 27,159 votes. This victory once again confirmed that his individual appeal and popularity had not diminished.

During the first three years of their alliance, Karpoori and Charan Singh seemed to have great camaraderie. Once during a Samastipur trip in 1980, Singh asked Karpoori if he could contribute some funds to the depleted Lok Dal treasury. Karpoori promised to collect Rs 1 lakh donation, a significant amount in those days. Karpoori's mass appeal was demonstrated in the way he went about collecting the donation. He carried a receipt book in his hand and first set a target of collecting Rs 1000 from Ujiyarpur. Former RJD MLA Durga Prasad Sah recalled that he was amazed at how Karpoori came to his house at 6 a.m. and started the collection. When Sah managed to collect Rs 1500 from Ujiyarpur, Karpoori was overjoyed. 'One contributor had given him Rs 2.50, and as Karpoori had run out of printed receipts, he had to send him a receipt from Patna. When someone said that the registered post cost was close to the donation money, Karpoori said that it was not about registry cost but about the trust a common man reposed in his leader. Karpoori believed that the contributor should know where his money was being used.'[7]

Karpoori Thakur was always known for his great empathy for the poor. Upon learning about the death of a man in the police firing in Samastipur, he immediately prepared to visit the site. However, a party worker urged him to have his meal before leaving. 'Karpoori, bewildered, shot back at the attendant, "Would you feel like eating if your brother had been killed in the firing?"'[8]

Sah, who worked very closely with Karpoori in those days, recalled the former CM's ingenious way of addressing people's grievances. 'Sometime in 1980, he was traveling to Samastipur and had stopped at a tea shop. An old woman suddenly came and grabbed his feet. Karpoori Thakur lifted her up and asked why she was doing so. She said the local *daroga* (inspector) had arrested her husband for trying to protect his land. The police took a bribe from the trespasser who had raised a shop on her land. Karpoori went to the police station and politely told the in-charge that he could face suspension if he raised the matter in the Assembly and could take it up with the CM. The police in-charge got the message and dropped the case against her husband and drove out the trespasser.'[9]

Prem Kumar Mani says, 'New challenges emerged after 1980 with the fall of the Janata Party. The socialist movement's values became diluted when it aligned with Charan Singh, and Yadavs began deserting Karpoori Thakur. As a result, Ambedkar's ideology became more relevant as the politics of change became more important than the politics of power.'[10]

The Congress government in Bihar faced tough administrative challenges due to a spurt in communal violence throughout the 1980s. Congress rule witnessed even worse communal violence in Bihar Sharif in May 1981.

Karpoori Thakur told the Assembly: '. . . I want to say something regarding the riots that took place in Bihar Sharif in Nalanda district. The Chief Minister (Dr Jagannath Mishra) stated that communal riots occurred during the Janata government in 1977–78 and 1979, but since the Congress government came into power, there has been no communal riot. But riots have taken place in many areas. I want to present the report of the Ministry of Home Affairs of the Government of India, which highlights some statistics . . . The Jamshedpur riots had been contained within a smaller area and were brought under control within three days. In contrast, the Bihar Sharif riots lasted twice as long and had spread to surrounding regions.'[11]

Karpoori Thakur, however, began to fall out with Charan Singh by early 1982 due to Singh's 'autocratic leadership'. Singh was getting wary of Karpoori's growing stature and was apprehensive about Thakur and other socialists moving the party too rapidly in a radical direction or, worse still, taking over his Lok Dal.

In August 1982, Lok Dal was bifurcated into Lok Dal (Charan) and Lok Dal (Karpoori). Devi Lal, Karpoori Thakur, George Fernandes, Sharad Yadav, H.N. Bahuguna and Ram Vilas Paswan became part of Lok Dal (Karpoori). Interestingly, Lalu Prasad, who later called himself the successor of Karpoori's legacy, preferred to remain part of Lok Dal (Charan). Devi Lal, Sharad Yadav and Bahuguna rejoined Charan Singh before the 1984 elections.

There was an attempt to unite the Janata Party and Lok Dal (Karpoori) in 1983. K.C. Tyagi, veteran socialist leader and former JD (U) MP, recalled his journey with Karpoori Thakur from Delhi to Bangalore. 'In January 1983, Janata (S) merged with Janata Party. During the journey, Karpoori Thakur spilled coffee on his dhoti, but he did not change it and took part in the national meet of the unified Janata Party, still led by Chandra Shekhar. However, the meeting was a big flop since there were also leaders who had been responsible for the fall of the Karpoori government in Bihar and the Devi Lal government in Haryana. Later, Chandra Shekhar expelled Satyendra Narayan Sinha (who joined the Congress) to keep Karpoori in good humor, but Karpoori left the Janata Party again.'[12]

As the Leader of the Opposition, Karpoori Thakur was known for keeping the state government on its toes and using innovative methods to intervene in matters concerning people's interests. 'Dr. Jagannath Mishra was the Chief Minister at the time when the Bihar Public Service Commission (BPSC) chairman Kumar Vimal was under pressure from the Chief Minister's office to reserve half of the sub-inspector posts for political appointees. Karpoori Thakur could have accused the Chief Minister's office directly and made it a political issue, but instead, he chose a different approach. He called up CM Mishra and said, "I have heard that some people under your nose are trying to sell half of the Daroga posts. You must find out who is trying to defame your office." After Karpoori's call, there was no interference from the Chief Minister's office in the BPSC's functioning,'[13] recalled Durga Sah, who was privy to Karpoori's telephone conversation with CM Mishra.

In another instance, Karpoori's intervention with the system saved the academic year of a girl studying at Pusa Training College. 'The girl was about to be rusticated because her marks did not match her original marks certificate, which was due to the fault of the Patauri school headmaster who had interchanged her Class 10 marks with those of another girl by the same name. Karpoori Thakur intervened by calling the Pusa Training School principal, who then contacted the Patauri school to rectify the mistake and allow the girl to complete her course.'[14]

Karpoori Thakur, who had revived Panchayat Raj elections during his tenure as CM, was lethal in his criticism of the Congress government for not boosting Panchayat Raj institutions:

> 'This government does not believe in Panchayati Raj. As we know, since the time of Mahatma Gandhi, decentralization of administration, political governance, administrative system, and economic system have been crucially important. It is being realized that there should be decentralization in both fields, but the dignity of decentralization is being taken away by the current Chief Minister. During the Congress era, the election of Gram Panchayats was not held for 15 years, then 12 years, and then 11 years. However, in the recent election, we reduced the age of adult franchise from 21 years to 18 years for both boys and girls, and on that basis, elections for village panchayats, panchayat committees, and chiefs were held. Nevertheless, the election of district councilors was about to be held, and our rule has come to an end.'[15]

In contrast to the popular perception that emerging leader Lalu Prasad was a protégé of Karpoori Thakur, there are some instances showing obvious differences in approach. Thakur received complaints that some MLAs, including Lalu Prasad, Munshi Lal Rai and Jayaprakash Narayan Yadav, were allegedly making money by withdrawing their questions in the Assembly after submitting them. In order to avoid any such scope of complaints, 'Thakur convinced the Speaker to change the rules, stating that once tendered to the Assembly Secretariat, questions cannot be withdrawn. Lalu Prasad was unhappy with this and used "derogatory language" for Thakur during a Lok Dal MLA meeting in the Assembly. In response, MLA Mudrika Yadav rebuked Lalu, saying, "How can you speak like this to our leader? *Tumhara baah marod denge* (I will twist your arms).'"[16]

According to Barahiya socialist leader Shiv Kumar, Karpoori Thakur used to support Mangani Lal Mandal, the former MP and current JD(U) national vice president now, more than Lalu Prasad and Nitish Kumar. However, Nitish eventually won Karpoori's favour by 1985. While Mandal remained mainly active in the Mithila region as a representative of EBCs, Nitish outshone all of his contemporaries at the time, except for Lalu Prasad.

Author Ranjana Kumari describes Karpoori's five-pronged strategy to establish himself as a strong Opposition leader, three of which were often proved very effective. 'First, he would make general allegations against the government, particularly on matters such as law and order, inflation, and administration. Second, he would raise contentious issues to protect the interests of weaker sections, such as labourers, Dalits, and other marginalized communities, or to address their problems. Third, he would demand the establishment of industries to promote development.'[17]

1984: The Ajatshatru Loses

Senior socialist leaders had been in the doldrums before the 1984 poll campaign, mainly because of chances of the Congress riding high on a sympathy wave, following Indira Gandhi's assassination. George Fernandes, otherwise very popular in Bihar, had to shift his constituency from Muzaffarpur to Bangalore. 'It was a last-minute change, though perhaps he (George) had started to think of shifting his political base to Karnataka after his narrow victory in the fiercely contested 1980 election at Muzaffarpur. Karpoori Thakur who was electorally influential among the backward castes was now in a separate camp. He did not want George any more to stand from a Bihar constituency. The relationship between them had never been smooth. In the immediate aftermath of the Janata government collapse, they became more estranged. Karpoori Thakur had never aspired for national leadership; his heart and soul was in Bihar politics. Despite his avowed approval of OBC reservation politics, George concluded that Bihar would not stand by him in the long run.'[18]

Though many stalwarts, including Karpoori, lost the 1984 polls, there was more to Karpoori's loss from Samastipur than meets the eye.

In the midst of Dalsinghsarai's bustling market stands a palatial house, Keota Garh. Its proud resident, Vijaywant Choudhary, is a third-generation politician, who has witnessed the rise and fall of Karpoori Thakur from close quarters. A man who has played a role in the making and unmaking of Karpoori Thakur.

Vijaywant Choudhary says: 'Karpoori Thakur had an association with my grandfather Ramashray Prasad Choudhary, an ex-legislator, my father Yashwant Choudhary, also a former MLA, and me. However, Karpoori Thakur didn't approve of us supporting some Yadav leaders. Though my father supported Karpoori's reservation policy, he chose to back Ramsunder Das, who succeeded Karpoori as CM. Our family had refused to be a blind supporter of Karpoori.'[19]

He adds, 'After Karpoori decided to contest from Samastipur, a deft planning by Janata Party in collaboration with the Communist Party of India and Samata Party of Gajendra Prasad

Himanshu was made to counter Karpoori, who had formed the Dalit Mazdoor Kisan Party (DMKP).'[20]

The Samata Party had fielded Vaidyanath Mehta, an OBC Kushwaha, which created confusion among the dominant Kushwaha voters of Samastipur. As a result, Kushwaha votes were either passive or divided between Congress's Ramdev Rai, Karpoori Thakur and Vaidyanath Mehta. 'Although Mehta lost his deposit, he was successful in dividing Kushwaha votes between Karpoori and Rai. Yadav voters rallied in Rai's favour, thus marking a clear shift of Yadavs slowly turning their back on Karpoori—that too on his home turf of Samastipur. The 1984 poll marked the cut-off period of the assertion of Yadav politics at Karpoori's expense.'[21]

Karpoori, who used to claim before the elections that there was no Janata Party without him and Satyendra Narayan Sinha (who had joined Congress), now blamed the same Janata Party for his defeat.

An article published by *Dinman* also proved prophetic: 'The kind of political games he has been playing since the beginning till now, his popularity is decreasing. Just as Charan Singh has been popular as the leader despite his arbitrary and dictatorial tendencies, Karpoori Thakur has been weakening the Opposition by breaking the party for his own interests. Nevertheless, he is counted among the main leaders of the Opposition party. During the contradiction of DMKP, some people have also called Karpoori Thakur as a leader sympathetic to the Congress. The leadership of Ram Lakhan Singh Yadav will deduct the votes of the Yadavs of Samastipur. Karpoori Thakur will be overshadowed by the popularity of Congress' Ramdev Rai, who is the state education minister.'[22]

Ramdev Rai, who became a giant-killer by defeating Karpoori Thakur in the 1984 Lok Sabha polls, later admitted that he never felt good about defeating him. 'In fact, I was also his admirer like several others. Once in the Assembly, when I had lost my cool and had flashed my hands towards the Speaker's chair, Karpoori defended me. He said that I was a young man from Begusarai, where people are traditionally aggressive. He convinced the Speaker not to take action against me, saying that if a young MLA like Ramdev did not exhibit raw power, would an old legislator like Karpoori do so?'[23]

Perhaps, raw power was visibly overshadowing the Karpoori's way of politics. Francine R. Frankel and M.S.A. Rao write, 'The political odyssey of Karpoori Thakur after the 1980 elections until his death in 1988 illustrated the emergence of two contradictory potentialities in the consolidation of larger political identities within the framework of the division between the Backward classes and Forward castes. Overall, the larger caste categories, Forward and Backward, were strengthened as the basic units of political identity. At the same time, within the Backward classes, divisions emerged along class lines which simultaneously created an attrition in backward strength and opened up the portent of a broader coalition of the poor.'[24]

But despite the 1984 drubbing, Karpoori did not give up. He was now thinking of bouncing back in the 1985 Assembly elections. On 13 December 1984, Karpoori Thakur, the leader of the DMKP, said in his message through Akashvani, 'The Dalit Mazdoor Kisan Party has emerged as a shining star in the sky of Indian politics, even though the legal name is still Lok Dal. The DMKP has been formed by merging several parties to fulfill the wishes of the people. . . . The foundation stone of our constitution is federalism.'[25]

1985 Assembly Polls: The Last Hurrah

Despite facing challenges from within the socialist fold, Karpoori Thakur maintained a dominant presence as the leader of the Opposition. He was unrivalled in terms of mass appeal, presentation of facts and oratory skills, both inside and outside the Assembly. The socialist party lacked a leader who could match his popularity and influence.

Following their overwhelming success in the Lok Sabha elections, the over-enthusiastic leadership of Congress (I) made the decision to hold elections for the Legislative Assemblies in the March of 1985.

Karpoori Thakur, who had been upset with Samastipur for the 1984 loss, decided to move away from Samastipur to Sonbarsa in Sitamarhi. Popular local leader Anwarul Haque, denied a ticket by the Congress, had been contesting as an Independent against Karpoori.

Asha Rani (now deceased), Karpoori Thakur's daughter-in-law and the wife of Ramnath Thakur, recalled an instance when both Karpoori Thakur and Ramnath Thakur had been away in Sitamarhi for poll campaigning for over a month. Asha Rani had been living with her three daughters at their Patna residence. Rani said: 'At around 2 a.m., I heard a knock on my door. I did not open the door but asked who was at the door. The voice from outside said there was a courier. I wondered how a courier could be delivered at such an odd hour. I told him to place the letter at the door. As panic gripped me, I awakened my three daughters. I said in a firm voice that I would awaken my husband. I took his shoes and tapped them on the floor as if he had started walking. The ploy worked and the stranger left my house. When my father-in-law returned a month later, he explained that it could have been a ploy to terrorize us.'[26]

Bihar Energy Minister Bijendra Prasad Yadav said that the individual appeal of Karpoori as the leader remained intact despite the political muddle. Yadav recalled an incident from the 1985 Assembly poll campaign during which Karpoori Thakur had ventured into a core Yadav belt to seek votes for his candidate, despite most party leaders advising against it. 'While campaigning for Vinayak Prasad Yadav, Karpoori was warned not to visit a Yadav-dominated village as it could lead to his defeat. However, Karpoori refused to back down and insisted on visiting the village, saying, "I know you are angry with Vinayak, but won't you vote for me? Please take an oath in the name of Mother Kosi and promise me that you will vote for us."'[27]

Karpoori Thakur won his ninth consecutive election by defeating independent candidate Anwarul Haque by a margin of 24,947 votes. This election again reinstated his position as the most important leader from the Opposition camp despite Yadav leaders slowly trying to challenge his authority as the leading socialist leader. Shaad Anwar, grandson of Anwarul Haque, said: 'Among the stories I have grown up listening to is one incident from the 1985 polls when Karpoori Thakur's car got stuck on a bad road in an area where my grandfather was very popular. People gathered around Karpoori Thakur and said he should shout, "Anwarul Haque, zindabad", once, so that they could push his car out of the patch of bad road. Karpoori Thakur only smiled. It was good enough for the local residents to help the great leader.'[28]

In the state Assembly elections, Lok Dal (following the merger with DMKP before the elections) emerged as the second-largest party, securing forty-six seats in the House of 324 members behind the Congress tally of 196. Vindeshwari Dubey became the CM.

Falling out with Charan Singh

Karpoori Thakur resumed his position as the leader of the Opposition and began to reassert his role as a prominent leader in Bihar. Despite being aware of the increasing influence of Yadav legislators in the party, he continued to find ways to moderate their assertion to ensure every voice is heard.

Leading journalist and writer Pradeep Shrivastava writes: 'During the Legislative Assembly's election of the Deputy Speaker, the Opposition party had to name a candidate, and manipulations began to unfold. The party decided that it would be appropriate to name a Yadav or a Dalit candidate for the position. Despite 22 out of the 46 Lok Dal MLAs being Yadavs, both the leaders of the party legislature (Karpoori) and the state party president (Ramjivan Singh) were non-Yadavs. Hence, most leaders agreed that it would be fitting to appoint a Yadav as the deputy speaker.'[29]

Shrivastava wrote that some Yadav leaders of the State Lok Dal had spoken to Charan Singh over the phone about the matter of electing a Deputy Speaker in the Legislative Assembly. Charan Singh called Ram Vilas Paswan, who was the party general secretary, to 12 Tughlaq Road in Delhi and asked him to go to Patna and talk to Karpoori Thakur.

The astute Karpoori understood what Charan Singh wanted and told Paswan that since there were twenty two Yadav MLAs in the party, they had made up their minds to elect a Yadav as the deputy speaker. Paswan said Charan Singh had also wanted the same.

Paswan returned to Delhi and went straight to Charan Singh's house from the airport. He complained to Charan Singh that he had misunderstood Karpoori, for Karpoori had also made up his mind to make a Yadav MLA the deputy speaker. Charan Singh was relaxed now.

But the very next morning the news appeared in a newspaper with a Patna date line that Karpoori Thakur had submitted the name of Shivnandan Paswan to the government a week ago for the post of deputy speaker. 'Charan Singh called Paswan as soon as he read the news. Paswan, who had also read the news, was surprised and regretful for being proved a liar in front of Charan Singh because of Karpoori Thakur. When Paswan met Charan Singh, Singh asked Paswan, "You had said that Karpoori was talking about making a Yadav a deputy speaker?" Paswan immediately said that this is what Karpoori had told him . . . Charan Singh said in a self-deprecating tone, "This is to defy the leadership . . . "'[30]

Paswan immediately spoke to Karpoori Thakur on the phone. Karpoori Thakur did not deny the news and started clarifying on the phone, which agitated Charan Singh, who had now taken the phone from Paswan. An agitated Singh told Karpoori: 'If I were in your hands, someday you would sell me in the middle of the market.' After hanging up the phone, he turned to Paswan and vented his anger, saying, 'You see! What a deceitful man! I am announcing the decision to remove him from the post of Legislature Party leader. A person who can defy the leadership cannot be a leader. Now, you have to decide. Do you want to live with me or with Karpoori?'[31]

'This incident marked the beginning of Paswan's resentment towards Karpoori Thakur's leadership. Paswan was deeply hurt by Karpoori's double-dealing and immediately expressed his support for Charan Singh. It was during this conversation that Charan Singh revealed to Paswan that there was a plan to make him (Paswan) a minister in the Morarji government back in

1977. Charan Singh had proposed Paswan's name along with Raj Narain, George, and others, but Karpoori Thakur had opposed the idea of including Paswan as a minister at the last minute.'[32]

'Charan Singh had decided to hold a meeting of the Legislature Party (Bihar) to elect its new leader, knowing that with 22 Yadav legislators, Karpoori Thakur was going to lose his position as the legislature party leader and consequently, leader of the Opposition. This decision created an uproar in the Lok Dal.'[33]However, a few days before the scheduled meeting, Karpoori Thakur suffered a heart attack and was admitted to a hospital in Darbhanga. Charan Singh postponed the meeting. Karpoori Thakur stayed in the hospital for about ten days. With time, Charan Singh's resentment ended, and Karpoori Thakur survived the heart attack and saved his position as the Leader of the Opposition.

A few days later, on 29 November 1985, Charan Singh became ill and was paralysed. Singh died in May 1987.

The issue of ticket distribution in the Rajya Sabha and Legislative Council elections created a rift between Karpoori Thakur and many national leaders, including Ajit Singh, Ram Vilas Paswan, Budhipriya Maurya and Rajendra Singh. He gave ticket distribution rights to the state committee instead of the central committee, a move that was strongly opposed. However, after persuading Mulayam Singh Yadav of Uttar Pradesh and Choudhary Devi Lal of Haryana, Thakur had their support. This resulted in the right of ticket distribution in Bihar going into the hands of Karpoori Thakur. 'When Thakur preferred to nominate Ram Awadhesh Singh to the Rajya Sabha over Ram Vilas Paswan in 1986, it led to a showdown between Karpoori and Paswan.'[34]

But Paswan also fondly recalled his first meeting with Karpoori Thakur in 1969. 'Karpoori Thakur had visited my newly allotted MLA flat after my first Assembly win from Alauli in 1969. I had become a giant-killer by defeating the Congress stalwart Misri Sada. At that time, I had not seen our leader Karpoori Thakur. I told him that Paswan was away. But when he introduced himself, I revealed my identity and profusely apologised to him. He took me in his warm embrace. However after 1980, Karpoori Thakur often came off as an insecure leader who would resort to political gimmicks.'[35]

Veteran socialist leader Gajendra Prasad Himanshu echoed Paswan's feelings. 'As I came from Samastipur, he always remained very cautious about promoting me, may be because I was also one of the Yadav leaders. Yet, his supreme qualities as a leader outweigh such little things.'[36]

Karpoori and Bindeshwari Dubey

Karpoori Thakur, who often came off as a sharp critic of Congress CMs Jagannath Mishra and Chandrashekhar Singh, actually shared a good bond with Bindeshwari Dubey. Karpoori was often accused of not targeting Dubey enough in the Assembly.

Ram Vilas Paswan openly criticized his party leader, Karpoori Thakur, for remaining silent on the Kansara scandal in which large-scale black marketing of edible oil was alleged to have taken place. Paswan accused the party of becoming a hanger-on of the Dubey government and said that Thakur was the only obstacle in toppling the government. 'According to Paswan, Thakur did not want the government to fall because he would not benefit from it. Paswan also suggested that Thakur was afraid of losing his status as the leader of the opposition party, which also came with the facilities of a ministerial post.'[37]

But this was just one version of the Karpoori–Dubey-bonhomie story. There were occasions when Karpoori had taken on Dubey too. Bihar Energy Minister Bijendra Prasad Yadav recalled: 'Once CM Bindeshwari Dubey got MLA Prabhunath Singh arrested during the Assembly session. Enraged at this, Karpoori went straight to CM Dubey's chamber in the Assembly and said, "Are you a dictator and here to rule permanently?" Stunned, Dubey did not say anything but Prabhunath Singh was released within hours.'[38]

Finally, Karpoori Thakur explained his position, first in response to Ram Vilas Paswan questioning his leadership: '. . . My contribution was not any less than that of anyone else. From July 1979 to October 1984, there was more disintegration (of the socialists) and less consolidation. Along with many veteran leaders, I was also involved in that process. . . . It is also untrue to say that Yadav MLAs are neglected. Yadav MLAs and workers have adequate representation at every level of the party organization and in the Legislature Party as well. It is also false to say that Yadav MLAs are mobilizing under the leadership of Ram Vilas Paswan. Only two out of 19 Yadav MLAs are with Mr. Paswan.'[39]

Karpoori Thakur also added that he had never spared Bindeshwari Dubey whenever the Opposition needed to criticize the government. '. . . I have repeatedly said in no uncertain terms that whoever the Chief Minister of the Congress (I) may be, there will be neither development, nor welfare, nor upliftment of Bihar.'[40]

In Favour of 'Arming' Dalits

Karpoori Thakur was a strong advocate of arming Dalits, especially in response to the Naxalbari movement and the killings of Dalits by landlords. 'He was acutely aware that the Congress government was giving arms licences to landlords which led to series of mass killings in Bihar. He was not able to pass a government order which would have allowed for the arming of Dalits.'[41]

Anil Chamaria says, 'He had almost fought with CM Bindeshwari Dubey to get licences for the poor, arguing that the less privileged were more under threat than the affluent ones. He had countered the argument that giving arms licenses to the poor would increase violence.'[42]

Here is Karpoori Thakur's landmark speech on the matter in the Assembly in 1985, in which he stated, 'If the ballot fails, the bullet will prevail':

I have been in public life for a long time, and as everyone knows, I have never resorted to violence. Throughout my public life, I have never even touched a bomb, pistol, revolver, or gun. I was a soldier in the freedom struggle and later became a socialist, actively participating in the movement. On this day, we remember Mahatma Gandhi, who taught the people of India the lesson of non-violence and bravery. He believed that the path of non-violence is the best way, and that bravery is essential. He also said that cowardice is the worst thing and that violence is better than cowardice. Mahatma Gandhi praised the late Lok Nayak Jayaprakash Narayan for his bravery despite opposing his views. He believed that violence is a million times better than cowardice and impotence. During elections, when people with bombs, pistols and revolvers try to capture booths, the weaker sections tend to run away in fear. This is cowardice. Only a few people resist, but they are the exception. We must be brave and stand up to those who try to intimidate us.

I have clearly stated in my speech to the workers and to the public that instead of resorting to violence, we should fight with organized power - non-violent power, rather than using bombs, pistols, revolvers, or guns. We should strive to thwart the plans of the robbers by raising awareness among the public and organizing manpower. If we are unable to do so, we should not simply run away, but instead stand our ground and not let our votes be stolen. I reiterate this point and emphasize that I do not shy away from it. I am committed to working with truth and honesty. I do not want any segment of the country's population, especially the poor and weak, to be deprived of their rights or have their rights stolen. Every citizen has the legal right to self-defence in India, as stated in the Criminal Act. If someone tries to harm us or snatch our belongings, every citizen has the right to use violence to defend themselves. If a thief enters our home, we have the right to defend ourselves and our property, and the government of Delhi and Bihar even reward citizens for killing such thieves. This is our right of self-defence, and it is a legal right. When hundreds or thousands of people go to the polling booths to exercise their collective right to vote, neither their individual rights nor their collective rights should be violated. If someone tries to rob the voters or capture the booths for nefarious purposes, the voters have the right to use weapons to drive them away. I am not advocating breaking the law, but if the government thinks that I am engaged in illegal activities, they can take me to court and prosecute me. I will admit in court that I have made these statements. I have never incited violence, neither in the past, nor today, nor will I do so in the future. However, the law has granted adult franchise to the citizens of this country, and we have the right to protect our rights, our lives, and our property. If we need to resort to violence for self-defense, then we should do so. I have urged the government to understand this and have helped by making this statement. Do we want democracy to be subverted illegally in this country?

The Arms Act in our country should be repealed. This is not needed. This Arms Act is absolutely hollow. . . . Begusarai district has maximum number of illegal weapons. There are illegal weapons all over Bihar. Those who are gentlemen, they do not have weapons and they are surrounded by calamity. They live like a poor tongue between thirty-two teeth. . . . Those who are criminals, chaotic elements, they have weapons. So how will the gentleman live? Administration is useless and impotent. No one's life and property can be protected by the administration. . . . so how will the citizens survive - those who follow the law and the Constitution and those who are 'law-abiding? That's why I have said that the Arms Act should be repealed. Those who have money will buy weapons and after buying weapons, they will get it registered, the way radio is registered.

Today, the situation in the country is tumultuous and chaotic elements are prevailing. The administration seems to be non-existent in the state. Therefore, citizens should be legally allowed to possess arms for their own safety. When the ballot system fails, violence takes over. We have fought hard for adult franchise, and now it is being threatened. This is a dangerous situation. Political parties that uphold democratic values should work together to address this issue. Otherwise, democracy will not survive and the country will plunge into an era of bloodshed.'[43]

An Argumentative Indian

Karpoori was always willing to argue and engage one in conversation. But he would never harbour any ill will against anyone.

Former *Jansatta* reporter, Ali Anwar, who later served twice as JD (U) Rajya Sabha MP, recalled several such instances. 'When once I asked him why socialist leaders are behaving differently, while Mulayam Singh Yadav had been against the BJP, Karpoori Thakur was not opposing BJP, he got angry and said that he would not allow journalists to spoil his Press conference. But after the Press conference, he approached me gracefully and said, "You have done your job and I have done mine. No hard feelings," [44]said Anwar.

Karpoori Thakur was always known to quickly reach spots of violence, sometimes beating journalists to the scene. In the case of a massacre in Arwal, Anwar had assumed that Karpoori Thakur would have reached the spot before him. But he found Thakur on his way to the spot when he had been returning. Anwar recounted that beating Thakur in reaching a spot gave him a sense of victory, but it was the only time he was able to do so.

Here is another instance of Karpoori's wit and repartee. Karpoori, often criticized for being a glutton, explained to journalists once: '*Aap log petbharu hai aur mai petjaru hoon. Main petbhar khata hoon kyonki mujhhe pata nahi dusra khana kab milega* (Your stomachs are full, while mine is empty. I eat until I am full because I am not sure about my next meal).'[45]

Caste Catches up with the Social Engineer

Karpoori Thakur was invited to Haryana by Devi Lal to work on his political campaign for the 1987 Assembly polls. At the peak of the dominance of Jats in Haryana politics, Karpoori Thakur mooted the idea of Devi Lal reaching out to other sections of society. He ensured that people from lower castes also got a fair number of tickets. It worked well and Devi Lal won and became CM. In a sense, Karpoori Thakur had replicated the Bihar model in Haryana to good effect.

Karpoori was beating all efforts to confine him in a cage of caste, but caste had somehow begun to catch up with the Jannayak. A senior journalist of Karpoori's time, Harivansh Narayan Singh, who is now the Rajya Sabha deputy chairperson, recalled how Karpoori Thakur was relegated to the position of an EBC leader after 1983. Karpoori's discomfort at the site of the Dalelchak-Bhagora massacre in 1986 highlights the clear shift in the caste dynamics of Bihar politics. 'As a reporter for a magazine, I had traveled by train from Kolkata to reach Gaya and then traveled to the massacre-hit twin village of Dalelchak-Bhagora in Aurangabad. It was 6 a.m. but I was greatly surprised to see that Karpoori Thakur had already arrived there. He was standing quietly in a corner while the families of the victims were cursing the establishment. I could sense his unease.'[46]

A senior photojournalist of Patna, Deepak Kumar, completes the story: 'When the crowd started pushing Karpoori Thakur, I sensed that he could face humiliation. Our eyes met, and he sat on the pillion of my scooter. I took him to the Aurangabad main road, from where he got into his vehicle and left for Patna. I had never seen Karpoori Thakur in such a vulnerable situation before.'[47]

But Kapildeo Singh had always defended his friend on being called casteist or a caste leader. Singh had said during a poll campaign: 'People say Karpoori is a casteist. How can he be casteist? What is the population of *Nai* in Bihar? Even if he wants, he cannot be casteist. I can be casteist because my caste (Bhumihar) has a good number. And are we fools to stick to Karpoori? He is not casteist but truist who supports only the right and righteous thing.'[48]

1987: Removed as Leader of the Opposition

On 11 August 1987, the then Assembly Speaker Shiv Chandra Jha issued a letter to remove Karpoori Thakur from the post of leader of the Opposition, alleging that he had failed to comply with the requirement of applying for recognition of the Lok Dal in the House. The Speaker had ruled that since DMKP had merged into Lok Dal again, it had to be duly registered in the Assembly.

But Karpoori Thakur had argued that the Assembly form had a footnote, which mentioned that members elected before 1 March 1985 did not have to fill the form. He pointed out that all members of the Legislative Assembly were elected just before March, so the form was not applicable to them.

'While being removed as the Leader of the Opposition, he had cautioned Assembly Speaker Shiv Chandra Jha against setting a "wrong precedent". He said that the chair is not permanent and if the Speaker exceeds his power, it would finish his party one day. Karpoori Thakur's words proved prophetic as Congress vanished from the political landscape of Bihar. Shiv Chandra Jha was from Bhagalpur and ironically it was the 1989 Bhagalpur riots that put the last nail in Congress's coffin in Bihar.'[49]

In protest against the speaker's decision, Karpoori Thakur paraded thirty-three out of forty-six MLAs of Lok Dal in front of the governor. After these efforts failed, he moved to Patna High Court, but his petition was not accepted. Then he filed a petition in the Supreme Court. When the budget session of Vidhan Sabha started on 8 January 1988, Karpoori Thakur, along with thirty-four MLAs, again paraded in front of the governor. The speaker informed them that the president of Lok Dal (B) Upendra Nath Verma had written a letter on 1 January 1988, demanding separate seating arrangements for the seventeen MLAs of Lok Dal (A).

'Speaker Shiv Chandra Jha, often seen as the villain in the episode and also a pawn in the Congress ploy to demoralize Karpoori, had given his version of the story: "Karpooriji's party had its own internal problems. They wanted its diagnosis through the House. He won the 1985 Assembly polls as a DMKP nominee but became the leader of a party called Lok Dal. The party was divided into two parts, and Karpoori was keeping the MLAs together by showing fear of anti-defection law. This fact is recorded in his correspondence from the House. The party in front of me was divided. Some MLAs were joining the Ajit Singh group. To clarify the situation, I performed my legal duty under the anti-defection law. Karpoori kept avoiding the reality. This was his weakness. I removed him from the post by fulfilling my constitutional responsibility as the Speaker of the House. I was a constitutional hero, not the villain of his death."'[50]

'The legal arguments and counter-arguments aside, Karpoori's unceremonious removal as Leader of the Opposition in 1987 heavily dented his morale. An upset Karpoori had remarked after the incident that "he would not have been treated in such a manner if he was born a Yadav".'[51]

Senior JD (U) minister Vijay Kumar Choudhary, who was one of the MLAs present in the House when Karpoori Thakur was being removed as the leader of the Opposition, said: 'We knew that something grossly wrong in the House was happening. I felt like opposing it, but I was a Congress MLA, and Speaker Jha was also a Congressman.'[52]

Pitaunjhia Files

Back in Pitaunjhia, Gokul Thakur continued to reside at Karpoori's paternal house, leading a contented life. He also continued with his traditional profession of being a barber. Karpoori would visit Pitaunjhia once or twice a year, during which time the modest home would be bustling with commoners who came to catch a glimpse of their village's famous son. However, Gokul would always conceal his sense of pride behind his monk-like appearance.

Gokul Thakur had agreed to live in Patna only when he started falling ill. After a brief hospitalization at Patna, he died in his late nineties on 16 February 1987.

12

The Salty Solution and the Death Mystery

When Lalu Rushes to 'Lap Up' Karpoori's Succession

'It was sometime in 1987 that former minister, ex-MP and veteran socialist leader Ramjivan Singh was having lunch with Karpoori Thakur at his Patna residence. As Singh saw a ring on Thakur's finger, he asked: "What is this? I have not seen you wearing a ring before." The former CM said that during his recent Muzaffarpur trip someone suggested that he should wear it. Singh replied: "Agar bandhna hi hai to man ko bandhiye, tan ko baandhne se kuchh nahi hota (Tether the mind if you have to, for tethering the body is meaningless)". Soon after finishing his lunch, Karpoori Thakur threw away his ring.'[1]

* * *

Karpoori had never relied on astrology or even temples in pursuit of his political or personal goals but the unexpected and controversial decision of his removal as Opposition leader shook him to the core. Although Thakur remained active in the Assembly, making his usual interventions, he felt suffocated by the effort of being confined to the image of a backward leader or sometimes an EBC leader. However, when it came to taking up the cause of the poor, he raised his voice with his usual conviction.

He roared one last time in the Assembly in January 1988 when he spoke during an adjournment attention notice:

> The Inspector of Mohanpur police station in Deoghar district caught Hema Lal Singh and Dineshwar Raut and held them in custody without providing food for 27 hours. Raut's legs were tied, and sticks were inserted into his rectum like he was an animal. He fell ill for a month, and his treatment cost thousands of rupees. To this day, no action has been taken against the perpetrators. Mr. Speaker, can a police officer continue to commit such atrocities? If they engage in oppressive behaviour, how can justice be served? The police station is responsible for upholding the law, not breaking it. If a police officer continues to oppress people, how can democracy survive and the citizens live in peace?[2]

On the evening of 16 February 1988, Ganga Prasad, a journalist from *Navbharat Times* in Patna, called up the former CM Karpoori Thakur for a casual conversation. However, the casual conversation soon became an intense debate on the assertion of Ganga Prasad that robust social movements should take place before a socialist government is formed. Karpoori disagreed, claiming that socialists needed more time in the government to do more for the poor. 'He emphasized the importance of the political empowerment of people rather than relying on sporadic social movements.'[3]

17 February 1988

Karpoori Thakur woke up at his usual time of 4.30 a.m. even though he had slept late. After finishing his morning routine, he took his usual stroll along Deshratna Marg. It was still chilly as spring was yet to arrive, so he took precautionary measures and properly muffled his face.

Karpoori Thakur enjoyed the tranquillity of the green area as he walked leisurely, taking in the surroundings. Despite the lack of springtime bloom, he found beauty in the stillness of the air. He lost himself in the moment, finding solace in the symphony of nature that surrounded him.

He returned to his residence at 1, Deshratna Marg where a large number of visitors from humble peasants to representatives of people were waiting. On his arrival, he was surrounded by them. He gave them an audience and collected representations from them. As he felt uneasiness, he asked for a glass of tepid water and continued his daily routine of meeting every visitor at his residence. Despite his discomfort, Karpoori Thakur did not feel the need to see a doctor despite having complained of an upset stomach the previous night.

He had plans to visit his friend and former minister Kapildeo Singh over breakfast at the latter's Kankerbagh residence to discuss future strategies for the fledgling Lok Dal. On the same day, he was scheduled to visit Samastipur where party workers had planned to weigh him in coins as a gesture of respect.

At approximately 9.30 a.m., Karpoori Thakur grabbed his towel and headed towards the bathroom, but quickly returned, clutching his chest in acute pain. 'He was immediately laid down on the bed but he soon lost consciousness. His sons, Ramnath and Birendra, quickly called for assistance from some of his close associates, and he was rushed to Patna Medical College and Hospital (PMCH). Among the first politicians to arrive was Thakur's trusted aide, Dhanik Lal Mandal, who later became the Bihar Assembly Speaker and Haryana Governor.'[4]

Ramnath Thakur recalled that former minister Satyendra Narayan Sinha and Lalu Prasad had also accompanied them to take Karpoori Thakur to PMCH. 'Devi Lal had provided Lok Dal a *Nyay Rath* (a bus) for carrying out a yatra from Pusa to Shahpur Patouri in Samastipur. Instead of wasting time in looking for an ambulance, we all put the unconscious Thakurji in the bus. But by the time we reached the hospital, doctors declared him brought dead,' says Ramnath Thakur.

Kapildeo Singh, who had been expecting Karpoori Thakur for breakfast, received a call from Dhanik Lal Mandal, urging him to quickly visit PMCH. 'Mandal's voice was filled with deep panic. Kapildeo Singh and his son, Dr. Arjun Singh, hurried to the hospital, where they saw Karpoori Thakur lying on a stretcher in the Emergency ward.'[5] Thakur had died of a massive cardiac arrest. He had a history of hypertension and had also suffered a mild heart attack in 1985.

Dr Arjun Singh recalled: 'When my father and I reached PMCH, I saw Dhanik Lal Mandal sitting on piles of stone chips outside the cardiac ward. He was sobbing while waiting for others to reach the hospital. It was around 10.30 a.m. There was not much of a crowd then at the hospital.'[6]

At Pusa Road in Samastipur, Binod Paliwal and over 5000 supporters were waiting with flowers and a weighing machine adorned with flowers to receive Karpoori with cheers but what they received was the terrible news through AIR (All India Radio). They rushed to Patna with the same flowers to pay their last tributes. The news of Karpoori Thakur's death quickly spread like wildfire across the nation. Within a matter of hours, thousands of Thakur's supporters made their way to Patna, using any available means of transport. It seemed as though all roads in Bihar were leading to the state capital.

Bihar's newly appointed Chief Minister Bhagwat Jha Azad, who had taken over the reins of the state just four days ago, faced his first major challenge in controlling law and order in Patna and regulating the traffic amidst the sea of humanity converging upon the city. Despite the chaos, Thakur's supporters remained united in their grief, paying their respects to their beloved leader in a disciplined manner.

Amidst the grief and sorrow, the family members and party leaders of Karpoori Thakur brought his body to his official residence at 1, Deshratna Marg. Chief Minister Bhagwat Jha Azad was among the leaders who reached Karpoori Thakur's residence.

The atmosphere was heavy with mourning, and tears flowed freely as people grappled with the loss of their beloved leader. Mangani Lal Mandal, one of Thakur's closest aides, was seen crying bitterly, while Thakur's sons, Ramnath and Birendra, tried their best to console others and control their own emotions. Despite his position of power, even CM Azad was unable to hold back his tears as he helped others take Thakur's body to the lawns for the final preparations before the cremation.

Lalu sat near the body of Thakur and began crying inconsolably. Despite their love–hate relationship, Lalu had a filial affection for Thakur, which he 'exhibited by cradling Thakur's head in his lap'. Ramnath, however, played down Lalu Prasad's claims of having put his father's head in his lap. 'It was more of a political expression. Lalu Prasad would have meant that he had been by my father's side in his final moments.'[7] Thakur had promoted Lalu after the JP Movement, but he disapproved of Lalu's flippant ways of rising in politics. Nevertheless, Thakur often shed his bitterness for the young and flamboyant Yadav leader from Gopalganj. Many present at 1, Deshratna Marg doubted Lalu's emotions over Karpoori Thakur's death, but the solemnity of the occasion prevented anyone from stopping him.

At around 12 p.m. (18 February), an open lorry of Bihar Police adorned with layers of marigold garlands was parked outside Thakur's residence.

The body was accompanied by Lok Dal (B) president Hemwati Nandan Bahuguna, Janata Party leader Syed Shahabuddin, Lok Dal (B) leaders, Mulayam Singh Yadav and Lalu Prasad Yadav, Ram Awadhesh Singh, Vinayak Prasad Yadav, Thakur's sons Ramnath and Birendra Thakur, son-in-law Dr R.C. Sinha, and other family members, who walked alongside the truck. A large number of people present at the time burst into tears as soon as the body was placed in the vehicle. Along with BJP President L.K. Advani, others, such as socialist leaders Chandra Shekhar, Devi Lal, Ajit Singh, George Fernandes and Congress's Satyendra Narayan Singh, were also in attendance. The mournful atmosphere was filled with loud cries and sobs.

While it is usually family members who accompany the body, Karpoori Thakur had his own definition of family, which included every one he ever met. He maintained no difference between his biological and political families. Besides his supporters who managed to climb the truck, Ramnath, Birendra and other leaders remained on the vehicle alongside the mortal remains. Lalu Prasad pushed several senior leaders aside, to make way for the lorry and stand by the body, next to Ramnath and Birendra. This created the first visual of Lalu as the next leader after Karpoori.

When the truck started moving for the final departure, all barriers of emotions broke loose and everyone's face was filled with flowing tears. The sobbing and wailing sound soon subdued under the slogans 'Karpoori Thakur *Amar rahe, Jannayak zindabad*' chanted by thousands. The funeral procession from Thakur's residence to Bansghat on the banks of the Ganga drew a spontaneous crowd from all walks of life. Some were wearing tattered clothes, and others were barefoot as they bid their last farewell to Thakur. Karpoori's foot soldiers walked behind the truck carrying his mortal remains. Even though policemen and family members removed marigold garlands from the truck, more flowers and garlands continued to pile up.

The funeral procession went along Bailey Road to reach the Gandhi Sangrahalay near the historic Gandhi Maidan. Every inch of space along the route was packed with people, and only their heads could be seen. Despite the efforts of the police, the crowd was uncontrollable, and many chose to walk behind the lorry carrying Thakur's body.

H.N. Bahuguna's described: 'The scene I witnessed after Karpooriji's death left a profound impact on me. As I walked amidst his funeral procession, I saw thousands of mourners crying uncontrollably. However, amidst the sea of mourners, there was one woman who stood out—she was as silent as death itself. Her face was pale, and her eyes were dry, yet her sorrow was palpable. On the other hand, a child sitting on a man's shoulders was bowing to Karpoori's body with folded hands. I was amazed as he kept his hands folded throughout the funeral procession, a testament to the respect he held for the departed soul. Meanwhile, everyone else was crying and shouting slogans, paying their last respects to a man who was not just an individual, but a movement.'[8]

Senior journalist Ganga Prasad, who covered Thakur's funeral procession, recounted the leader's connect with people. 'An old woman, who was stopped by Patna Superintendent of Police from going near Thakur's funeral procession, almost hit out at the SP, saying "*tumhe kya hai, hamara beta mara hai* (How does Thakur's death matter to you? It is our son who is dead)."[9] The SP was moved by her words and allowed her to go,' recalled Prasad.

The scene at the Bansghat of the Ganga in Patna brought back memories of October 1979, when Lok Nayak Jayaprakash Narayan was cremated and people from all sections of society, including the government, were present in large numbers. As the procession made its way from the late Thakur's house on Deshratna Marg to Bansghat, more and more people from the capital and beyond gathered to have a final glimpse of their beloved Karpoori. The funeral procession ended at around 5 p.m. at Bansghat. The dead body was kept for the last *darshan* of the leaders at 5:05 p.m. and the fire was lit at around 5.15 p.m. by his eldest son Ramnath Thakur. The mortal remains of Karpoori were subsumed by the golden flames. But death was not so proud that day. It was the end of an era.

Karpoori had left in his Deshratna Marg residence '11 pairs of dhotis and round neck kurtas for his two sons and a daughter. They are now the property of the museum and an inspiration for humanity.'[10]

The Mystery behind the Death

Karpoori's death left behind an unresolved mystery. An ardent Karpoori Thakur follower and MLA Raghuvansh Prasad Singh wrote to PM Rajiv Gandhi on 22 February 1988, demanding a high-level inquiry into Thakur's death.

'*We are all saddened by the sudden death of Bihar's mass leader Karpoori Thakur. You will be sad too. The sudden death of Thakur has stirred the Dalit, oppressed people of Bihar. Many kinds of doubts have started cropping in the hearts and minds of the people. This has been confirmed by the reputed newspapers of Bihar and the country. People are taking the sudden death of Thakur as part of a bigger conspiracy.*

Thakur's yoga practitioner Atulanand has been missing since his death. So far, no effort has been made by the government to nab Atulanand and to prove our doubts unfounded. Rather, doubts are getting stronger. In such a situation, when the whole of Bihar is agitated by the death of Karpoori Thakur, people have started considering his death as a part of murder and a bigger conspiracy.

In such a situation, it becomes the duty of the government to get the doubts cleared by conducting a high level inquiry. A newspaper has clearly written that a meeting of the top officers of the Bihar government was held and the intelligence department was activated. At the same time, many big leaders were successful in convincing his family members that there was no conspiracy behind his death.

It may be recalled that the Government of India had conducted a sociological study in Bihar two years ago that what would happen to the political situation of Bihar in the absence of Karpoori Thakur? Where will Karpooriji's 'public base' go? This sociological study has also now come under the purview of people's doubts. Karpoori Thakur dies soon after swearing-in of new CM in Bihar.

It is creating different types of doubts in the minds of lakhs and crores of people. It is certain that the governments of the states are changing, keeping the elections in mind. Efforts are on to show the tarnished image of Congress and its government clearly. The prospects of mid-term elections are being exposed. The election that will be held now will be without Karpooriji in Bihar. In such a situation, people have started linking the sociological study done two years ago with the death of Karpooriji. This mass leader of Bihar was forcibly removed from the post of leader of the Opposition party in the assembly even after being removed for more than six months, the dispute of which was to be decided by the Supreme Court in March '88. The sudden death of mass leader Karpoori Thakur is a public question before the people of Bihar and the entire country. Now we can't hold it. The only way to clear the doubts of the public is to set up a high level inquiry committee and publish its report in three months and put it before the public. In the interest of the people and the government of the country, the announcement of the inquiry committee has become the minimum demand. The more the delay in the formation of the inquiry committee, the more people's doubts will turn stronger. I hope and trust that you will take this action as soon as possible . . .'[11]

No inquiry was ordered by the then CM Bhagwat Jha Azad, who was also marked a copy of the letter addressed to PM Rajiv Gandhi. The matter later became more of an electoral tool and kept coming up at regular intervals. Former Chief Minister Ramsunder Das had demanded in a press conference at Hajipur (district headquarters of Vaishali) on 25 March 1994 that a high level enquiry should be conducted into the cause of death of the late Karpoori Thakur at the earliest, 'so that the conspiracy behind his death could be exposed.' But then CM Lalu Prasad preferred all such issues to be kept at rest.

In his letter to PM Gandhi, Raghuvansh Prasad Singh had been referring to 'a confidential letter' that Karpoori Thakur had written on 11 September 1984 to K.K. Srivastava, the then chief secretary of the Government of Bihar. 'He had written that he had come to know through Ram Lakhan Singh Yadav (a senior Congress leader and former minister) and Kapildeo Singh (also former minister and ex-colleague of Karpoori Thakur) that some people had a secret meeting at the residence of a leader in Patna. There has been a decision to eliminate him (Karpoori Thakur).'[12]

Who Was Swami Atulanand?

This question still rankles and remains partly unanswered. Swami Atulanand, then a forty-five-year-old ambitious Ayurveda practitioner from Saharsa, was introduced by a politician to Karpoori Thakur, who would easily take health advice from anyone. Dr Birendra Thakur recalled: 'My father knew Atulanand since 1985. We were not convinced about the salty water treatment.'[13]

Atulanand's role came under the scanner when he shaved off his long hair and absconded soon after Karpoori Thakur's death. 'After all, he was the person who had been offering Thakur Ayurveda treatment since 16 February till his death on the morning of 17 February.'[14]

Karpoori Thakur's family confirmed that on 16 February 1988, Swami Atulanand made Karpoori Thakur drink and vomit 13 litres of salty water on an empty stomach. Even though Karpoori Thakur was an old patient of hypertension and had suffered a mild heart attack in 1985, Atulanand had convinced Thakur to drink and vomit rock-salt lukewarm water as part of some Sankhya yogic treatment. Thakur had overlooked the advice of Dr C.P. Thakur, who had been his personal doctor since 1976. 'Karpoori Thakur had discussed the saltwater treatment with me. I had strictly advised him against it as salt-induced blood pressure often does not subside and could result in cardiac arrest. I do not know the circumstances under which Thakur took that treatment, which could have been primarily responsible for his death. One had the right to know the credentials of Atulanand and why he was never searched and questioned? Who knows if Thakur's death was part of some political conspiracy?'[15]

Ramnath Thakur says, 'Swami Atulanand used to visit us earlier. It is true that he fled after my father's death. But it is too late to conduct any enquiry.'[16]

Karpoori Thakur's younger daughter-in-law Kanaklata recalled: 'For a month before his death, he had been drinking tepid salty water and vomiting it as part of a treatment.'[17]

Besides Raghuvansh Prasad Singh, another socialist leader and later MLA Mudrika Singh Yadav demanded an investigation into Thakur's death in 2000. Yadav had said: 'The death of Karpoori Thakur could still be investigated. After all, people have a right to know the truth.'[18]

Surendra Kishore, senior journalist and former personal assistant of Karpoori Thakur, says: 'I don't know what the truth is. But his death should have been investigated.'[19]

Shambook, a monthly Hindi magazine, pointed towards conspiracy by upper castes in an article titled, 'Identify your family enemies': 'Karpoori Thakur of the barber caste had become the Chief Minister of Bihar twice. This caused discomfort to the upper castes. . . . The conspiracy started from Delhi. The money was deposited there. A fake sanyasi came. He got entry into Karpoori's residence. By flattering, the Ayurveda practitioner won Thakur's confidence. Karpoori had not been keeping well— his blood pressure used to be high. He was made a victim on the pretext of natural cure and hydrotherapy. Thick salt solution was given. Salt is a poison for those with high blood pressure. Karpoori lost his life. Karpoori's son and son-in-law, both doctors, should have questioned the sanyasi. Karpoori fell into the trap of a Brahmin. Then there was no investigation or search for the truth. If a Brahmin leader is killed, like Indira Gandhi, Rajiv Gandhi, Lalit Narayan Mishra, then the work of heavy investigation will go on for years—crores of rupees will be spent by the government.

But if a backward or Dalit leader is killed, nothing will be done—whether the person killed is Dr Ambedkar, Dr Lohia, Jagdev Prasad or Karpoori—because the life of every backward (Shudra) is similar to those of eagles and crows according to Manusmriti.'[20] (Roughly translated from Hindi)

Lalu 'Laps Up' Karpoori's Succession

A second-time MLA, Lalu entered politics as an MP from Saran in 1977, riding the popularity wave of the JP Movement. However, he was not among the favourites of Karpoori Thakur. Despite this, Lalu Prasad, who was known for his political sagacity behind his non-serious facade and rustic humour, saw an opportunity to declare himself as the heir apparent of Karpoori's legacy. After all, he was the most promising Yadav leader from the younger generation and had fancied his chances of becoming the successor of Karpoori Thakur ahead of the senior Yadav trio of Vinayak Yadav, Anoop Lal Yadav and Gajendra Prasad Himanshu.

Lalu Prasad succeeded in 'lapping up' the political succession of Karpoori Thakur by becoming the leader of the Opposition in 1989. Lalu said: 'Karpoori Thakur died mainly because of torture by his political opponents. Shiv Chandra Jha was then the speaker of the Bihar assembly and Karpoori Thakur was the leader of the Opposition in the House. Thakur was so tortured those days that he used to frequently rush to my quarters at Bihar veterinary college to narrate his woes. He was tortured both inside and outside the Assembly by political opponents.'[21]

Recalling his long association with the socialist leader, Lalu said Karpoori became the CM for the second time in 1977 but his political opponents didn't allow him to run the government for the full term. 'They instigated a big communal riot in Jamshedpur, then a part of undivided Bihar, to ensure the fall of the Karpoori-led government. Everyone in Bihar knows who instigated the communal riots in Jamshedpur and for what purpose.'[22]

Then, Lalu went on to make big claims: 'Karpoori Ji breathed his last in my lap while being rushed to the Indira Gandhi Institute of Cardiology (IGIC) at PMCH for treatment. While taking his body for cremation at the Bans Ghat, we had raised slogan like, *Thakur Tere Armano Ko Dilli Tak Pahunchayenge* (Thakur, we will take the causes raised by you up to New Delhi).'[23]

Lalu Prasad, then an MLA paying tribute to Thakur in June 1988 in the Assembly said: 'Karpoori Thakur, the voice of the weak, was born in an ordinary household, but rose to great heights. Despite being trapped in the caste system, he achieved a high position, largely due to his belief in the primacy of karma. He had no affiliation with any particular group or fraternity, yet everyone felt that Karpoori belonged to them. It's rare to find a leader whose death brings people from every corner to pay their respects, just as it was with Karpoori Thakur. Poor people from every village in Bihar, blind and disabled people, as well as those who did not receive social or economic justice, came to Karpooriji with their questions and concerns. They wonder who will look after them now that Thakur ji is no longer with us. After the great messiah of the poor passed away, a void has been created not only in our state but throughout the country. I doubt that any party will produce a leader of his stature in the foreseeable future. I witnessed poor women and mothers from every village paying their respects to the great leader, along with their children.'[24]

Tributes

Nitish Kumar, who had become a first-time MLA from Harnaut (Nalanda), had spoken in the Bihar Assembly in June 1988: 'On the fourth day after taking oath as the Chief Minister of Bihar, the state and the country lost a great son, freedom fighter and patriot. He was a man who empathized with the sorrows and pains of the common people and opposed all forms of atrocities committed against them. His death was a great loss to the people of Bihar, especially the oppressed. Karpoori Thakur's passing still weighs heavily on the minds of the people, as was evident from his last intervention in the Assembly regarding the Deoghar incident. The first instalment of Bhagwat Jha Azad's Cabinet has been presented to the public, but will there be any reduction in police brutality and high-handedness, even if we forget about the change in their behaviour? This is the most pressing question in the minds of 90 per cent of the people of Bihar. One thing has become clear after Karpoori's death—the Opposition's ability to control and contain the ruling party's unruly conduct is significantly reduced. With no one to rein the ruling party's unparliamentary conduct, the Opposition will not have free voice to raise concerns against them.'[25]

George Fernandes wrote: 'From the moment I arrived in Patna on the morning of 18 February 1988, until my departure the next night, one thought kept floating in my heart. The farewell given by the people would have brought you (Karpoori) great joy . . .'[26]

Then the Bihar CM Bhagwat Jha Azad said in the Assembly: 'The land of *Videh* will forever remember the name of Karpoori Thakur among the great men who will be remembered for years and centuries to come. Karpoori Thakur was a revered leader not just in Bihar, but beyond its borders and even before India gained independence. Karpoori ji was an extraordinary person, who stood out from the ordinary and brought pride to Bihar. The people in the slums of Bihar were proud that one of their own had emerged to become a warrior for the welfare and happiness of the masses, giving new life to the country. Today, not just this village or this state, but socialism and the entire nation are silent, stunned and grieving after losing one of its beloved sons.'[27]

President R. Venkataraman said that 'Mr. Thakur was a dedicated patriot and our partner in the freedom movement. His death is a "national loss".' Vice President Dr Shankar Dayal Sharma said that Thakur spent his entire life working for the poor and downtrodden people. Lok Sabha Speaker Dr Balram Jakhar said that the death of Thakur was a great shock to his friends and the entire country. His contribution to the freedom struggle and public life will always be remembered. Prime Minister Rajiv Gandhi said, 'Karpoori Thakur was a staunch freedom fighter who devoted his life to uplift the downtrodden classes and remove social disparities. In his death, the country and Bihar have lost a prominent statesman . . .'[28]

Kapildeo Singh, Thakur's friend for years and his alter ego, wrote in his diary: 'Karpoori Ji is no more. Today for the first time I feel alone. There were two bodies. But our life was one. He was a partner in the struggle. We have been together for a long time. We shared so much sorrow and happiness together and faced the troubles in such a way that we did not even utter a sigh. We were walking together only for the establishment of an egalitarian society. He went ahead of me. Here too, he won. My words are drowned in tears . . .'[29]

Aryavarta, a local Hindi newspaper, wrote under the title, 'Karpoori is gone, who is the leader now?': 'Who will break the pervasive mournful silence? The Opposition gropes for light in the dark. Such great men are rare.'[30]

Socialist leader Shivanand Tiwari wrote: 'When Karpooriji was there, there used to be a feeling in every corner of Bihar that wherever injustice or oppression happened, he is such a person, whose door will be open to the poor.'[31]

Famous writer Robin Shaw Pushp writes: "I think it is easy to become great, but to become such that everyone feels that he is a man of his family, is very difficult.'[32]

13

The Family Man

Ramnath's Regrets

'*Indira Gandhi ka vanshwad vanshwad aur mera vanshwad vanshwad nahi. Aaplog aesa kijiye Ramnath ko hi chunav ladwa lijiye, main nahi ladunga phir* (If the dynastic rule of Indira Gandhi is heavily criticized, why shouldn't I be criticized if I promote my son? You may allow my son Ramnath to contest polls but take it from me that I am not going to contest then).'[1]

Former Bihar minister and ex-MP Ramjivan Singh recalls this instance from the run-up to the 1985 Assembly elections when Lok Dal's senior leaders had almost decided to give a ticket to Ramnath Thakur, the eldest son of former CM Karpoori Thakur. When Karpoori learnt about it, he lambasted his party colleagues. As a result, nobody ever discussed Ramnath after this episode. Ramnath's ambition to join politics crashed yet again, much to his frustration and dismay.

* * *

A two-storey house in Karpoori Gram on the Tajpur–Samastipur Road has been a famous address for some years now. It is the house of Karpoori Thakur's eldest son and JD (U) Rajya Sabha MP Ramnath Thakur. He built this pukka house in early 2000.

On a pleasant morning after the successful conclusion of the pre-birth anniversary function of Jannayak Karpoori Thakur, Ramnath Thakur sits in a wooden chair. A small table is placed before him. A radio set is broadcasting *pradeshik samachar* (news from the state). He listens attentively to the news even as he welcomes fellow villagers to his verandah, facing a green patch where radish and potato grow.

They discuss arrangements for Karpoori Thakur's 99th birth anniversary function on 24 January 2023. As in the past, CM Nitish Kumar has agreed to attend the function.

As he converses with fellow villagers, Ramnath makes a call to veteran JD (U) leader and former MP Mangani Lal Mandal to cross-check some facts about how Karpoori Thakur had taken on the Congress government for having returned Central funds because of its inability to use them. As Ramnath Thakur has to attend a condolence meeting in a neighbouring village, he drafts a brief note on the subject and puts it in the pocket of his kurta.

After a while, he asks for his breakfast—plain roti with two green leafy vegetables. He also asks his aide to uproot fresh radish from his garden to add to his meal. '*Bas koshish karte hain ki dharti se jude rahe* (I try my best to remain connected to the earth)', says Ramnath, in his soft voice.

In many ways, Ramnath tries hard to emulate his father's routine and mannerisms. He is earthy and accessible like his father. He does not carry an air of being a two-time MP and a former minister in the Bihar government. He too wears cotton kurtas and dhotis.

But the similarity ends here.

Ramnath has always been his father's son, more so after his death. The embargo on Ramnath joining politics ended with the death of Karpoori Thakur.

In fact, Ramnath had been living and breathing politics since 1970. He preferred to drop out of the most coveted Science College, Patna, and remain with his father to grasp politics by observing and doing, instead of reading books.

Ramnath Thakur was an old hand at politics. His first participation in any political movement took place on 1 May 1968, when he had been pursuing his ten plus two course from Patna Science College. Ramnath recalled: 'I had visited Samastipur. As several SSP leaders had been taking part in *"Jamin hadpo andolan* (movement to wrest land from landlords)", I also took part in it and was arrested and held in Darbhanga jail for two months. My father and senior socialist leader Ramanand Tiwari were among some prominent leaders jailed for taking part in the movement at different places in Bihar.'[2]

While Karpoori Thakur allowed his son to take up social causes, he was clear about not promoting his son in politics. 'Ramnath, in his early days, would often rebel against his father for not giving him a good life. Thakur would also ask his wife to spend most of her time in the village as he would be travelling out of Patna very frequently.'[3]

Ramnath Thakur said it was difficult for him to stay away from politics as he had been in the midst of it. 'I also landed in jail eleven times when I participated in political protests . . . My father would often tell me that politics is a bed of thorns and there is little scope for politics of ideology.'[4]

Ramnath Thakur also recalled how his father was a hard taskmaster: 'During the monsoon of 1987 when an embankment was breached, he made me walk for five kilometres to identify the areas most affected by the floods.'[5]

Ramnath might well be trying to be politically correct and not reveal the inside stories of his father's politics. 'It is true that I was privy to my father's sundry conversations with the top leaders of his time. But why should I reveal them now? They might hurt some people,'[6] says Ramnath.

Ramnath Thakur became an MLC only after the death of his father; he was re-nominated to the Upper House of the Bihar Legislature by Lok Dal in 1994. In the 2000 Assembly polls, he contested successfully from Samastipur as a JD (U) candidate. He won the February and November Assembly polls in 2005 on a JD (U) ticket. Nitish Kumar made Ramnath Thakur the land and revenue minister during his first term.

The Regrets of Ramnath

Having spent thirty five years in active politics, Ramnath Thakur, the second-time Rajya Sabha MP, regrets having joined politics. It could be a political confession. But he has his reasons for having taken to politics besides being the eldest son of Karpoori Thakur. 'I do regret having joined politics because my father had never wanted me to join it. I will not offer any justification now. But it is through politics alone that I have been trying my best to fulfil my father's unfinished task for Samastipur at least,'[7] says the JD (U) MP. Ramnath keeps shuttling between his paternal village and New Delhi. When Parliament is not in session, one can easily spot him in Karpoori Gram and adjoining villages.

Karpoori Thakur's thatched house was finally replaced with a pukka house in early 2000 by his son Ramnath Thakur. The house was converted into Smriti Bhavan and is now under the care of the state government. Ramnath's own house is some distance away from Smriti Bhavan.

In retrospect, Ramnath Thakur regrets having removed the thatched house, which was a symbol for the probity and honesty of Karpoori Thakur, who believed that a public representative must not spend any money on himself. It might look too idealistic and impractical in current-day politics when even a first-term *mukhiya* (village head) first builds a good house to exhibit his power.

Ramnath says: 'I should not have demolished the thatched house in which my father was born and raised and from where he made a name for himself in politics. I should have taken some lessons from the great Hindi writer Fanishwar Nath Renu's sons, who retained the writer's mud house study room at Aurahi–Hingna village in Araria district, Bihar.'[8]

Ramnath's politics has been naturally centred on the rich legacy of his father's politics, more so with the growing importance of Karpoori Thakur in today's politics. Both Lalu Prasad and Nitish Kumar have thrived all these years by using Karpoori as their primary reference, but both have different styles of functioning.

Ramnath Thakur joined as a minister of state in the Lalu government in 1990 but was not selected to be a part of the next Lalu government. In contrast, Ramnath joined as a cabinet minister of Land Revenue in the Nitish Cabinet in 2005. In the 2010 polls when the Nitish Kumar-led NDA made a record of sorts by winning 206 of 243 Assembly seats, the JD (U) candidate from Samastipur, Ramnath Thakur, lost by over 1800 votes, to his own and his party's embarrassment. Ramnath had to lie low for close to four years after losing his home turf. Just before the 2014 Lok Sabha elections, Nitish Kumar sprang a surprise by deciding to nominate Ramnath Thakur to the Rajya Sabha. An overwhelmed Ramnath told the Patna media then: 'I am speechless at Nitish Kumar's gesture. I may be the biological son of Karpoori Thakur but Nitish Kumar is the "*manas putra* (son of the mind)" of Karpoori Thakur.' Nitish re-nominated Ramnath to the Upper House in 2020.

Ramnath Thakur, however, understands his political limitations. He speaks on selected matters in Parliament or outside it to ensure that he does not invite any unnecessary media attention. He, however, loves to intervene on his favourite subject: reservations. Speaking on the Constitution (23rd Amendment Bill, 2017), and the National Commission for Backward Classes (Repeal) Bill, 2017, on 31 July 2017, in the Rajya Sabha, Ramnath Thakur said in Hindi: '. . . Our party demands that the creamy layer should be removed and reservation should be further expanded. Bringing this bill could have brought a lot of satisfaction to the souls of Rammanohar Lohia, Vivekananda and Kabir . . . I would like to refer to Jannayak Karpoori Thakur's decision to give 26 per cent reservation on 10 November 1978 . . . the Mandal Commission had not counted the poor among the backwards and who could properly avail government benefits. I would request for replication of what is called the Karpoori Thakur formula in Bihar . . .'[9]

Ramnath has not expanded his political constituency beyond Samastipur. He openly concedes: '*Maine apne pita ki bahut seva ki aur mujhe uska phal mila. Aaj main jo kuchh hoon, unke karan hi hoon* (I served my father with the utmost devotion and whatever I am today is only because of him).'[10]

Karpoori Gram villagers, however, owed the village's growth and development to three persons—Karpoori Thakur, Nitish Kumar and Ramnath Thakur. Arvind Singh, an elderly villager, says: 'Karpoori Thakur got the village a high school, a railway station and a library; Nitish Kumar got us good roads and electricity and Ramnath got us a degree college and a community hall. Ramnath also played a key role in getting the village a police station in January 2023 with the state government's help.'[11]

The Mover and Shaker at Home

Ramnath Thakur's wife Asha Rani played a pivotal role in taking care of domestic affairs during Karpoori Thakur's career. Rani would host and attend to the dozens of people visiting Karpoori daily. Karpoori Thakur's wife Phuleshwari Devi would stay mostly at Pitaunjhia. At Patna, Karpoori Thakur depended on his son Ramnath and daughter-in-law Asha Rani.

Ramnath recalls his wedding with Asha Rani: 'The wedding party had gone to Samastipur. My father had borrowed an Ambassador car, from Congress MLA Nathuni Ram.'[12]

Asha Rani (who died on 23 March 2020) had said in an August 2019 interview: 'When I got married to Ramnath Thakur on 17 May 1973 and came to his Pitaunjhia village, it was a culture shock for me, a town girl. There was no toilet at home. As womenfolk from even upper caste Rajput families would go to the fields for defecation, it was normal for families of other castes to do the same without any complaint.'[13]

Revealing why Karpoori Thakur did not convert his thatched house into a pukka one despite becoming an MLA in 1952, Rani said: 'When anyone asked my father-in-law why he had not re-built his house, he would reply that people would not feel connected with him if the house was converted into a concrete one.'[14]

Rani, the kitchen queen of the Thakurs household, said that Karpoori Thakur loved to eat *nenua* (sweet gourd) and *baingan* (brinjal). He also liked *parwal ka chokha* (mashed and roasted pointed gourd). He also loved to eat fish prepared with mustard curry and fried fish with roti. 'When he returned late at night, he would eat *sattu* (roasted gram flour) and sleep.'[15]

Karpoori also loved to eat *khichdi*. When his friend, former minister Kapildeo Singh, went to meet him on 15 February 1988, three days before his death, he had offered him khichdi to eat.

Rani also revealed how Sudha Srivastava, a minister in Karpoori Thakur's cabinet, would often go to Karpoori's house and also cook at times with her.

The leading politicians who would visit Karpoori Thakur included Bhagwat Jha Azad, Hemvati Nandan Bahuguna, Mulayam Singh Yadav, George Fernandes, Ram Vilas Paswan, Madhu Limaye and Anoop Lal Yadav. Charan Singh, Deve Gowda and V.P. Singh had also visited Karpoori's residence. Abdul Bari Siddiqui and Mangani Lal Mandal were among the closest young leaders. Karpoori Thakur had great fondness for Devendra Prasad Yadav, who had vacated his Phulparas seat for Karpoori Thakur after the 1977 polls.

Rani recalled a letter from Sharad Pawar (former Union minister) in which he had credited Karpoori Thakur for making Pawar join politics. She also recalled a hilarious instance from her father's experience. 'As my father had to often entertain Karpoori Thakur's guests, he was once served a show-cause notice. But my father said he had the option of resigning from his job but no option of quitting his samadhi.'[16]

Phuleshwari Devi would talk to her daughters-in-law in the local Maithili dialect. She would at times ask Karpoori Thakur to buy at least a *katha* (1901 square feet) of land to build a house. When Phuleshwari was brought from Pitaunjhia to Patna, she did not like it initially. She devoted most of her time to attending to her granddaughters, Namita, Sneha and Amrita. She slowly developed a taste for sipping tea while at Patna.

Phuleshwari Devi was taken ill suddenly during her visit to Pitaunjhia in July 1984 to complete the post-wedding rituals of her younger son, Birendra K. Thakur, with Kanaklata Thakur. They got married on 8 July 1984. An ailing Phuleshwari Devi was brought to Patna. Karpoori Thakur had been travelling then. But when he learnt about his wife's illness, he deferred his travel plans to be by her side. Phuleshwari Devi developed respiratory complications and died on 18 July 1984.

Karpoori Thakur was against hosting the ritual feast after his wife's death. He reasoned that they should save money to open a girls' school in the village. However, Ramnath acceded to the demand of his village elders and completed all the rituals, including the feast, which was attended by thousands. Gokul Phuleshwari Karpoori Degree College was opened in the village in later years. Karpoori Thakur's father Gokul Thakur, who had lived in his paternal village all his life, died three years later in 1987.

Benches Ahead of Chairs

Dr Birendra K. Thakur has been living quite unnoticed at his official residence, opposite Bihar Museum in Patna, for years now. His ground floor residence at Officers' Flat along Bailey Road bears two nameplates, his own and that of his son, Dr Abhinav Vikas, a doctor at IGIC at PMCH. The same flat is now allotted to Dr Abhinav Vikas in his capacity as a government doctor. The house has been officially transferred from the father to the son. Dr Birendra K. Thakur is happy to retain the house that is filled with memories relating to his entire service career. He has aged gracefully in the house, in which his son and daughter, both practising doctors, grew up and shaped their career.

Abhinav, who was only three when his grandfather died, says: 'As a doctor, I have been trying to help the poor and those coming from far-off villages to PMCH for treatment. My grandfather worked for the disadvantaged all his life. I have heard stories of his struggle, benevolence and success. We try to keep his legacy alive by trying to do what he would have loved us to do.'[17]

Birendra, who has grappled with health complications all his life, suffered a heart attack in January 2022. He has had his heart valve replaced thrice so far. Unlike his elder brother, he has not built a house in Karpoori Gram.

Dr Birendra has been honest about admitting that he owes his family's success to being the son of Karpoori Thakur. 'Right from Hemvati Nandan Bahuguna to Devi Lal to Mulayam Singh Yadav to Satyendra Narayan Sinha, all helped me financially from time to time because they knew that my father had not saved any money for us.'[18]

His son, Abhinav, studied at Santosh Medical College, Ghaziabad. Former UP CM Mulayam Singh Yadav paid part of his college fees. Abhinav's wife, Kumari Madhu, is an NIT (National Institute of Technology) engineer. Dr Birendra K. Thakur's daughter, Jagriti, is a dentist. She is married to Mrityunjay Madhav, an Indian Forest Service officer, posted in Shimla.

Kanaklata Thakur, wife of Dr Birendra K. Thakur, gives a rare insight and peep into the 'socialist' public meetings at her father-in-law's residence in the late 1980s. 'It took me some time to understand why my father-in-law would keep rows of benches in front of his chair and arrange chairs at the back of the meeting hall. Later, he revealed that it was a deliberate move so that even well-off and influential people would have no option but to sit on the benches to be able to interact with Karpoori Thakur. The poor people coming from far-off villages would get a chance to sit on chairs. This was his unique way of giving people a sense of empowerment, even if it was symbolic.'[19]

Kanaklata Thakur recalls her wedding and what Karpoori Thakur asked for as 'dowry'. 'When my father, Ramlagan Thakur, a Madhepura-based excise inspector, approached the former CM with my marriage proposal in 1984, he readily accepted the proposal, saying it should be a court wedding. My father was also told to ensure that all political workers in Madhepura should be offered food whenever there was a political function in the district. This was his dowry demand, which my father accepted with grace and gratitude and kept his word until the death of my father-in-law.'[20]

Karpoori was always eager to shower love on his sons, daughters-in-law, granddaughters and grandsons. Kanaklata recalled two instances of Karpoori Thakur's love and care for his family. When she came to 1, Deshratna Marg for the first time, Karpoori took her and his elder daughter-in-law Asha Rani shopping and asked them to purchase the best Benarasi saris. His two sons, Ramnath and Birendra, were left wondering at the 'largesse' shown by their father towards his daughters-in-law.

Sometime in 1985 when Kanaklata and her newborn son Abhinav were running a fever for several days, Karpoori Thakur came to her room and gave stern instructions to his associates to get them medical treatment immediately.

Although Karpoori Thakur was an avid reader of newspapers, he considered owning a TV set as a luxury. However, his younger son, Birendra, had somehow managed to get a black and white TV set in his room. Once, veteran socialist leader George Fernandes came to meet Karpoori Thakur at short notice. As his entire house was in disarray, he took Fernandes to Birendra's room. 'Seeing the TV set, Fernandes said, "Karpoori and TV?" Half-embarrassed and half-dismayed, Karpoori replied, *"Arre George, mera nahi, bachche logon ka hai* (George, it is not mine but belongs to my children)."'[21]

Karpoori Thakur, who frequently travelled, would sometimes try to share his learnings at home. In 1986, after returning from Haryana, he called his family members and told them about how women there were involved in agriculture, from milking cows to pasting dung cakes. Although his daughters-in-law refused to try their hands at milking cows, they did try pasting dung cakes in the backyard of their home.

Karpoori Thakur rarely allowed his family members to use his official car; the car keys were usually kept by his daughters-in-law with strict instructions not to hand out the keys for personal use.

Renu, the youngest child of Karpoori Thakur, had settled down as a housewife after her wedding. Her husband, Dr R.C. Sharma, a physician, is based in Patna.

Surendra Kishore, senior journalist and former personal assistant of Karpoori Thakur, recalled: 'Amidst the myriad tales of Karpoori's honesty is an instance when, as CM, he hired a private taxi from Ranchi—for a discussion related to the wedding arrangements of his daughter Renu with Dr Sharma of Devaltar, Ranchi. He had used his official vehicle to attend an official function but had refused to use the government vehicle for personal purposes.'[22]

Renu's wedding at a very private function in Pitaunjhia on 20 May 1971 is often referred to as an example of frugality. Arjun Singh, son of former minister Kapildeo Singh, says: 'My father was among a chosen few politicians who had attended Renu's wedding as Karpoori Thakur had not invited any politician despite being the serving CM. My father had told me how he had taken care of the wedding shopping and some ornament purchases for Renu without letting Karpoori Thakur know about it.'[23]

"Karpoori Thakur, in a rare instance of setting an example of austerity in public life, did not invite any politician except some close friends at the function. He had instructed the state chief secretary not to allow any minister to take state planes for Darbhanga and Saharsa airports, from where his paternal village could be reached fast.'[24]

Karpoori's colleague Kapildeo Singh wrote: 'In a simple and soulful atmosphere, we got engaged in entertaining the *baraatis* (wedding party). We are family members. Our duty was to receive guests. The scene of a daughter's farewell is very moving and most of us find it very painful. Only the one who is the father of a daughter can experience this.'[25]

Renu, has two sons—Manoj, who works in a private company, and Madhukar, who is a doctor. Renu died on 17 April 2015. Her husband, in his mid-70s now, practises at S.K. Nagar in Patna.

The Doting Grandpa

Karpoori Thakur shared a special bond with his three granddaughters—Namita, Sneha and Amrita (daughters of Ramnath Thakur and Asha Rani). Namita, who married Ranjit Kumar, an Indian Revenue Service officer, in 1995, has many memories of her grandfather.

'My grandfather made time for us out of his busy schedule. I have a vivid memory of him taking me, Sneha and Amrita to Vidhan Sabha for a walk whenever he had time,'[26] says Namita.

Sneha added that her grandfather would treat them to pantua (black rosgulla) at the Vidhan Sabha canteen.

Namita recalled how she and her sisters had once accompanied two friends to the Durga puja fair and later to an evening movie show. 'As we had not bothered to inform our parents, there was chaos at home. When we reached home, my grandfather looked very upset, but he did not scold us. He only advised us not to accompany strangers and avoid going out in the evening by ourselves. This lesson has stayed with me as it speaks of his care and concern for girl children,'[27] says Namita.

Namita recalled how Karpoori Thakur kept politics away from his home. 'He would discuss politics only with my father. He would discuss home and kitchen with my mother and my grandmother, when she was in Patna. He also made sure visitors did not meet us,'[28] says Namita, who lives in Mumbai.

Karpoori Thakur, says Namita, was God-fearing but never believed in rituals and would often disagree with his over-religious wife. Karpoori Thakur did not want his family members from Pitaunjhia to stay at Patna, except when someone was ailing and needed medical care. He seldom allowed anyone to overstay at Patna without any valid reason. Namita also revealed that they would avoid visiting the Pitaunjhia house because it had no toilets until the mid-1990s.

Namita added: 'Spending time at home in the company of my grandfather taught that me that there is no such thing as caste. People from all castes and religions would converge at our home and we never wanted to know their surnames. In fact, I hate surnames. I have not given surnames to my children.'[29] Asked if she wanted to join politics at some stage, Namita says: 'I am not interested in politics at present. I cannot predict the future. But one thing is sure—my grandfather hated dynastic politics so all our family members remain away from the limelight even though we regularly entertain a large number of visitors and guests, besides helping my father. My grandfather has left us a big legacy to nurture. My father took to politics because of circumstances prevailing at that time. As a son of a popular political leader, he had an obligation to be with him.'[30]

Namita recalled how it was very difficult for her and her two sisters to focus on studies in a crowded Patna house and how often they had to forego studies to take care of visitors. Yet, all three sisters studied well. Namita is a law graduate, Sneha has a doctorate and the youngest sister Amrita is a graduate. Sneha teaches at an Inter (10+2) college at Karpoori Gram. Amrita has a government job at Samastipur. Sneha is married to Tarun Jariwal, a Rajasthan native working as an HR Head in an MNC at Mumbai. Sneha shuttles between Mumbai and Karpoori Gram.

Sneha revealed that she wanted to write the Thakur surname but her parents added 'Kumari' as a surname for all three sisters. 'But I got Kumari removed during my Class 10 registration but forgot to add Thakur. I liked the Thakur surname for no particular reason. Perhaps, I liked the idea of bearing the surname of my famous grandfather. But it is too late to add a surname now.'[31]

Among sundry memories she recalls her habit of handing over to her grandmother, who had very little money, the 10 paise she received from her grandfather. 'As my grandfather hardly had any time, he would often take us to the house of his personal assistant, Lakshmi Sahu. While my grandfather would dispose of pending files, we would eat, play and sleep,'[32] recalled Sneha.

Namita's husband, Ranjit Kumar, currently posted in Mumbai as commissioner, Customs, recalled how getting a marriage proposal from the family of Karpoori Thakur was a special feeling. 'When I was doing research in IIT Delhi in 1995 after completing my BTech at IIT Kanpur, Ramnath Thakur, then an MLC, had visited my hostel. I could sense that he had come with an alliance. I qualified for IRS in 1995. I met Namita briefly in 1995. She was very nervous at the thought of leaving her parental home and we had a brief talk. My family and I were highly excited about the alliance. After all, I was going to get married to the granddaughter of one of the most influential CMs of his time, Karpoori Thakur.'[33]

On 26 November 1995, the wedding party left for Patna from Ranjit's hometown of Barh, a sub-division town of Patna. There was so much excitement and pride involved in the marriage that many influential people in the town, even though uninvited, tried to join the wedding party with their licensed guns. The more the number of licensed guns in a wedding party, the greater the purported prestige for the bridegroom's side. However, after much persuasion every one left their guns at home and joined the *baraat* (wedding party) with flowers.

Ranjit recalled: 'I was heading to the wedding venue in a car adorned with flowers, accompanied by the baraatis. However, there were thousands of people everywhere, making it impossible for my car to get anywhere close to the bride. So, I got out and somehow managed to make my way to the stage for the garland ceremony. After the wedding, I could sense what it takes to make someone a leader. People would stream in and out of the house most of the time. Though there were many rooms, all used to be full. A room was given to us when we visited but some people would come to our room as well to use the toilet at times. I could now imagine how Namita and her two sisters pursued education in such an atmosphere. I also realized that a Karpoori Thakur was not made in a day and how the entire family had to make sacrifices to enable one person to serve the masses. I saw how Namita and her sisters had to touch the feet of almost all elders visiting them. They were not allowed to show their irritation at the overdose of hospitality. When you are the son or granddaughter of Jannayak Karpoori Thakur, you are also compared with the great Karpoori Thakur from a young age. But then, it also becomes a very good training ground for children of politicians as it is very natural for them to adapt to the challenges of politics. It is not surprising that they get trained as politicians. No book of political science can teach what they learn naturally there.'[34]

Peers and juniors in politics were also treated as family by Karpoori Thakur. Former Bihar deputy CM Sushil Kumar Modi recalled Karpoori's warmth, saying,'I invited him to my wedding, and he was very happy to know about my interfaith marriage. He said he was scheduled to attend a public meeting in Mokama but still turned up at our wedding. Despite his dishevelled hair and crumpled kurta, he was not at all worried about his looks, which was a signature Karpoori Thakur trait.'[35]

1, Deshratna Marg

Barely 200 metres away from the Old Secretariat at Patna is 1, Deshratna Marg—the last official residence of Karpoori Thakur. It was converted into the Karpoori Thakur Memorial Museum on 8 May 1990 by the then CM Lalu Prasad. The two-storey bungalow, with six rooms and two halls, was constructed during the colonial period. A bust of Karpoori Thakur has been installed on the lawn. Gallery assistant Neetu Tiwari, a Deoria (UP) resident, says that the Jannayak needs to be explored further and that the museum could be enriched further with more of Thakur's belongings and a digitization of some rare documents, including papers of Vidhan Sabha proceedings, newspaper clips from his time and some rare books from his personal collections.

The room adjacent to the staircase on the ground floor brings back memories of Thakur's final moments. Once he started ailing, he shifted from his first-floor room to one on the ground floor. He was made to lie down in this room after he suffered cardiac arrest. The room still contains his single bed and a weathered sofa set. The single chair of the sofa set, in which he used to sit mostly to relax, creaks with the slightest touch. No one dares to sit in it, largely out of respect for him. The big table placed in front of the chair used to be full of books and registers during his lifetime. The table is empty now.

The hall on the first floor has been converted into a library, with books on Hindi literature, religion, the caste system, socialism and Urdu poetry. Several of them are well-worn; their fragile sepia pages need digitization. Some of the books include Dr Mahavir Prasad's *Hindi Krishna Kavya Mein Murli Prasang*, Govind Mishra's *Hujur Durbar*, Maithlisharan Gupt's *Bharat Bharati*, Walter Liefer's book on Indo-German relationships, Harivansh Rai Bachchan's *Dashdwar Se Sopan Tak*, Kubernath Rai's *Nishad Bansuri*, Firaq Gorakhouri's *Bajm-e-Jindagi: Rang-e-Shayari*, Vishnu Prabhakar's *Awara Masiha*, Jagjivan Ram's *Bharat me Jativad aur Harijan Samasya*, G.S. Ghurye's *Caste and Race in India* and S.M. Joshi's *Socialist's Quest of the Right Path*. His collection of books on Hindi literature stands out in the library.

The ground floor of the museum houses some rare photographs, giving a glimpse into his life's journey. In one photograph of the 1969 floods, he is seen with supporters and commoners in knee-deep water. He is seen with Chandra Shekhar and V.P. Singh in separate frames before they became PMs. A set of pictures from his last journey shows the man and statesman he was. A sea of humanity can be seen behind his funeral procession. Lalu Prasad is seen standing next to Thakur's body. Senior BJP leader L.K. Advani can be seen consoling Thakur's sons, Ramnath and Birendra, in another frame.

A collection of his personal belongings—a light grey coat, a black and white muffler, a brown woollen cap and some round-necked coarse khadi kurtas tell the story of his simplicity and austerity. Three pairs of his glasses and some specimens of his handwriting can take one to those times.

An HMT Rajat Automatic twenty-one jewels watch that he used to wear is also on display at the museum. The dial is stuck at 1.53.

But Karpoori's legacy keeps ticking.

14

The Trail of Camphor

Karpoori Thakur and the Three Chief Ministers

'Camphor resin is a white crystalline substance made from the bark of the camphor tree—Cinnamomum camphora . . . *Camphor resin stimulates the body's nervous system and offers a cooling sensation that is both numbing and soothing.'*[1] Camphor is called *kapoor* in Hindi.

* * *

Karpoori Thakur, the camphor of Indian politics, has left behind a long trail. His ideology of cohesion and equality is soothing and the resin of his ideas is evergreen and sprawling.

Versus the Three CMs

Comparisons are good and bad. They throw up different shades of grey, which some may call white and others black. Karpoori, in comparison with his predecessor Dr Sri Krishna Singh and two successors—Lalu Prasad and Nitish Kumar, is always a great study to understand context and perspective and find a correlation between the past, present and future.

Dr Sri Krishna Singh served as the premier of Bihar (from July 1937 to October 1939 and from March 1946 to August 1947), before assuming the position of chief minister (from August 1947 to January 1961 until his demise). Singh's stable tenure of over sixteen years before and after Independence ushered in a transformative era for Bihar. Often hailed as the architect of modern Bihar, he spearheaded numerous industrial, agricultural, infrastructural and educational initiatives that propelled the state forward. Within political constraints, where land is not merely a form of property but a symbol of social status, Singh brought in a landmark zamindari abolition law. He believed in the trickle-down theory (the theory that the benefit of economic development by the riches would percolate down to the poor, e.g., industry set up by an industrialist would automatically generate employment), prevalent at that time, for the development of the masses.

Karpoori Thakur, however, did not rely on the trickle-down theory but always advocated a people-centric policy during his terms as deputy CM and CM. He exemplified a brand of politics that was inherently pro-people and pro-poor, founded on an egalitarian model. His political ideology heralded a significant shift in social power dynamics, transitioning from the dominance of upper castes under Congress rule to the empowerment of OBCs and SCs during the socialist regime. His successful fight against the primacy of the elite in education, governance and politics only strengthened democracy. He also recognized government service as a means of participation in governance besides socio-economic upliftment with the open distribution of appointment letters to about 6700 engineers being a case in point.

Lalu Prasad and Nitish Kumar, in their respective tenures, tried to carry forward Karpoori Thakur's legacy of unwavering commitment to empowering the masses.

Harivansh Narayan Singh eloquently puts the comparison: 'Dr Sri Krishna Singh, the maker of modern Bihar, took the state far ahead of other states. Lalu Prasad gave voice to the poor. Nitish Kumar combined both—he took forward good works of Dr Sri Krishna Singh and also worked for OBC/EBC/Dalit empowerment. Giving 50 per cent reservation in the panchayat to women and 20 per cent to EBCs is one of his lasting legacies.'[2]

However, Lalu Prasad took a somewhat different and, to some extent, divisive approach compared to Karpoori Thakur's inclusive and non-confrontational politics. Karpoori Thakur worked all his life to bridge and blur the fault lines of caste while Lalu Prasad capitalized on the fault lines by creating a distinct binary between upper castes and backward classes. During his tenure, Bihar experienced a series of caste massacres between 1990 and 2003. However, Lalu Prasad's connection with the 'garib-gurua' (poor and downtrodden) consolidated his position as the most prominent voice of the subaltern during his time.

Lalu Prasad's political journey began with the 'Mandalisation of politics, followed by the secularization of politics, and finally culminating in the Yadavisation of politics—in that sequential order.'[3] However, it was during the stage of Yadavization, post-1995, that Lalu Prasad's politics stumbled and deviated from its socialist goals.

This is where he differed from Karpoori Thakur. While Karpoori Thakur's politics aimed at assimilation, Lalu Prasad's politics accentuated the caste binary.

Lalu Prasad, who had prospered at the expense of Congress's pro-upper-caste politics, found a significant political constituency in the divide between forward and backward classes and continued to exploit it throughout his career. However, Lalu never undermined the political, social and economic influence of upper castes and kept their power centres in good humour.

Later, Lalu Prasad sought to cultivate a Muslim–Yadav combination, which held some influence until 2005. But by 2009, when RJD's fortunes had reversed, three out of four Lok Sabha MPs from the party were upper-caste Rajputs.

Fast forward to 2023, the RJD has now shifted its focus towards 'A to Z' politics, emphasizing social assimilation. As the politics of the caste binary gradually gives way to the politics of reservation and populism, each political party aims to attract votes from a wide array of social groups.

Nitish Kumar drew inspiration from Dr Singh's vision for development and placed a strong emphasis on fostering progress and growth. He skillfully incorporated Thakur's principles of social engineering, recognizing the importance of unity and inclusivity in governance. In a departure from Lalu Prasad's approach, Nitish Kumar extended his efforts to provide tangible welfare benefits to the underprivileged, instilling a sense of pride and empowerment among those who had previously been neglected. By expanding infrastructure and connectivity, such as constructing roads and bringing schools and electricity to villages, and by implementing initiatives like distributing school uniforms and bicycles to students, Kumar aimed to combine the tenets of development politics with an underlying message of reaching out to the impoverished and marginalized individuals.

But one aspect that sets Nitish Kumar apart from his predecessors is his tendency to deviate from a consistent ideology and engage in a more contextualized form of politics, often oscillating between saffron (referring to BJP) and green (referring to RJD). In contrast, Dr Sri Krishna Singh maintained unwavering loyalty to the Congress party. Karpoori Thakur remained firmly rooted in socialist principles, despite his brief collaboration with the Bharatiya Jana Sangh. Lalu Prasad has consistently maintained a strong anti-BJP stance throughout his political career.

Dr Sri Krishna Singh, despite facing minimal political opposition during the monolithic reign of the Congress party, demonstrated his mettle by making several bold choices that brought industries to Bihar. While some may criticize him for concentrating thirteen industrial units in Begusarai, which is predominantly populated by his fellow upper-caste Bhumihars, it is undeniable that the state owes much of its progress to the transformative initiatives realized during Singh's tenure. While the current administration, under Nitish Kumar, often attributes the lack of industrial growth to land acquisition challenges, Singh's accomplishments stand as a testament to the contrary, as he successfully spearheaded Bihar's industrial, educational and agricultural transformation.

Karpoori Thakur, too, showcased his prowess as a remarkable decision-maker. He made significant strides by removing English as a mandatory subject in Class 10 and pioneering the landmark decision to introduce a 26 per cent quota in 1978, even at the cost of losing his government.

Lalu Prasad, with his unwavering resolve, demonstrated his ability to make tough decisions. The arrest of BJP leader L.K. Advani and stopping the BJP leader's *rath yatra* (chariot ride) in 1990 showcased Lalu's steely determination. Lalu Prasad remained committed to his ideology of secularism, even in the face of numerous court cases and his subsequent conviction in the fodder scam cases. Nitish Kumar took landmark administrative decisions, such as the pioneering 50 per cent reservation for women in panchayats and the transformative revamp of the state's infrastructure, encompassing roads, bridges, schools and hospitals. However, Nitish Kumar's legacy, although commendable, bears the weight of two missed historic opportunities. Madan Mohan Jha, then principal secretary of Education, yielded a comprehensive report on the Common School System (CSS), coupled with a substantial budget allocation of Rs 5000 crore to implement the recommendations of the Muchkund Dubey Commission's report on CSS. But the CM succumbed to pressure exerted by the education lobby, comprising various influential political stakeholders, ultimately failing to execute the envisioned reforms. Moreover, the recommendations presented by the D. Bandopadhyay Commission on land reforms were left unfulfilled due to the political cost they demanded.

'Lalu Prasad and Nitish Kumar would not have implemented Mungeri Lal Commission's report. After all, Lalu Prasad did nothing for land reforms unlike Karpoori, who had got land to the tillers at the Charpokhri movement of Arrah. Karpoori Thakur's government might have fallen because of the reservation call but his quota formula became the basis of the Mandal Commission and later of EWS and women's reservation.'[4]

Noted social scientist, Shaibal Gupta, had once poignantly remarked that 'while bridges and roads may crumble and fade from memory, it is the empowerment of society that etches a lasting legacy.'[5]Even though he refrained from directly alluding to any specific chief minister, his words resonated profoundly. Given Nitish Kumar's extensive tenure, there were lofty expectations, yet he missed the opportunity to catapult Bihar towards industrial growth, transcending the mere creation of commendable infrastructure.

Finally, what makes Karpoori distinct from Lalu Prasad is that he nurtured and created an array of second- and third-rung leaders such as Anoop Lal Yadav, Vinayak Prasad Yadav, Gajendra Prasad Himanshu, Shivnandan Paswan, Mangani Lal Mandal, Ram Vilas Paswan, Lalu Prasad, Nitish Kumar and Abdul Bari Siddiqui. In comparison, Lalu Prasad and Ram Vilas Paswan handed over their leadership only to their sons and Nitish Kumar has failed to create second-rung leaders. The two socialists, Lalu and Nitish, also failed to pass on leadership to other castes (barring the exception of stop-gap CM Jitan Ram Manjhi).

Dr Sri Krishna Singh: The Foundation Man of Bihar

Dr Sri Krishna Singh, both in his capacity as the premier of Bihar before Independence and as the state's first CM, merits commendation for his exceptional accomplishments in both roles.

He established medical colleges in Patna, Gaya and Darbhanga that revolutionized healthcare access for the people of Bihar. Simultaneously, the construction of several pivotal dams, including Tenughat, Kharagpur, Tilaiyadhar, Panchet, Badua and Mayurakshi, showcased his commitment to bolstering the state's infrastructure. Dr Singh also spearheaded the construction of essential barrages across the Kosi and Gandak rivers, enhancing water management and irrigation capabilities. The creation of prestigious research institutes such as the K.P. Jaiswal Research Institute, Anugrah Narayan Social Studies Research Institute, Arabic–Persian Research Institute and Tribal Research Institute underscored his dedication to advancing knowledge and scholarship.

Recognizing the importance of economic development, Singh established industrial estates in Patna, Bihar Sharif, Darbhanga and Ranchi. Simultaneously, he promoted cottage industries, loom weaving and pottery enterprises, invigorating the economy of undivided Bihar. His support for the Khadi Board and the establishment of over two dozen sugar mills, predominantly situated in Champaran, played a pivotal role in fostering local entrepreneurship and employment opportunities.

Infrastructure development witnessed significant milestones during Dr Sri Krishna Singh's tenure, with the construction of the illustrious Mokama Bridge over the Ganga and the establishment of an industrial centre in Barauni, Begusarai. Under his tenure, the Sindri fertilizer factory, Patratu Thermal Power Plant, Sabour Agriculture College, Rajendra Agricultural Colleges in Pusa and Ranchi, Engineering College in Sindri, and Veterinary College in Patna and universities in Ranchi, Bhagalpur and Darbhanga came up. The expansion of Patna Medical College, the establishment of engineering colleges in Muzaffarpur and the opening of polytechnics in multiple locations further strengthened the state's educational framework. The initiation of the Regional Engineering College in Jamshedpur and the establishment of the Bokaro and Hatia heavy factories contributed significantly to the industrial landscape of the region.

Veteran socialist leader and former minister Gajendra Prasad Himanshu says: 'Had there been no Sri Krishna Singh, we would not have been able to study. He created many institutions and established a series of industrial units. In comparison, Lalu and Nitish could not give Bihar even biscuit factories.'[6]

Raghav Sharan Sharma writes, 'A historic milestone was achieved on September 7, 1953, when the doors of the Deoghar temple were opened to the scheduled caste community, signifying a significant stride towards social inclusivity and equality.'[7]

Dr Singh became the first chief minister in India to establish a dedicated social welfare department for tribals and Harijans in 1948. Displaying his commitment to promoting social justice, he appointed highly qualified individuals from the scheduled castes as district welfare officers, fostering representation and empowerment.

In an assessment of public administration in states, renowned American expert Paul Appleby acknowledged Bihar as one of the best administered states, recognizing the commendable governance practices and achievements under Dr Singh's leadership.

On 27 February 1948, a significant step was taken as the Devanagari script was adopted for Hindi, further solidifying its status. Subsequently, the passage of the Official Language Act in 1950 reinforced this decision. Dr Singh played a pivotal role in these developments, contributing to the linguistic and cultural integrity of the nation.

His profound knowledge and eloquence on the subject made him a prominent speaker on foreign policy matters in Congress meetings, with his influence second only to that of Pandit Jawaharlal Nehru. Nehru himself held great admiration for Dr Singh, while renowned historian P.C. Rai Chowdhary regarded him as a veritable repository of knowledge, comparable to the esteemed figure of Tilak. Dr Singh possessed a commanding voice that had the power to inspire even the most timid of souls and rally them to action. He was widely acknowledged as one of the nation's most compelling orators, with P.C. Rai Chowdhary placing him on a par with the esteemed Surendranath Banerjee. Dr Singh's profound love for literature and learning was exemplified by his personal collection of over 46,000 books, a testament to his intellectual curiosity and passion for knowledge.

Another remarkable accomplishment of Dr Singh's tenure was the implementation of the Panchayat Act in 1947, which empowered local self-governance, and the introduction of the Zamindari Abolition Act in 1950, a transformative step towards land reforms. Despite facing accusations of not wholeheartedly supporting the farmers' movement led by Swami Sahajanand Saraswati and even being accused of attempting to weaken it through the formation of a parallel Congress organization, it was ultimately due to Dr Singh's efforts that the long-awaited zamindari abolition law became a reality. The Money Lender Act was also passed, providing relief to people burdened by exploitative moneylenders.

During his tenure from 1946 to 1952, Dr Singh exhibited exceptional leadership in 'maintaining law and order by effectively controlling riots that had erupted in places like Jehanabad, Kako, Ghosi, Kharagpur and Tarapur in response to the tragic East Bengal massacre. His unwavering commitment to secularism was evident throughout his tenure.'[8] In fact, on 28 March 1947, Mahatma Gandhi also instilled confidence in Bihar's Muslims, stating, 'Muslims have nothing to fear in Bihar because there is Sri Krishna in the cabinet who is fully alert to protect them.'[9] Dr Singh formed significant committees during this period, such as the Education Reorganization Committee under Professor K.T. Shah and the Hindustani Education Committee, which included illustrious members like Rajendra Prasad, Sachchidanand Sinha, Tarachand and Maulana Azad, with the aim of advancing educational reforms.

Even during his earlier tenure as the premier from 1937 to 1939, Dr Singh demonstrated exemplary integrity in public life by significantly reducing ministers' salaries from Rs 5000 per month to Rs 500 per month. He also displayed his commitment to the principles of cabinet governance by refusing to comply with a circular issued by chief secretary Brett, which directed district

officers and commissioners to disobey orders issued directly by
ministers. Dr Singh firmly argued that such an action could be
seen as an insult to the cabinet and stood his ground.

Dr Sri Krishna Singh led by example when it came to living
a life of austerity. When he died, he left behind four envelopes
carrying a cumulative amount of Rs 24,500. Senior journalist
Surendra Kishore provides the break-up: 'The first envelope for
the Bihar Pradesh Congress Committee had Rs 20,000 cash,
the second envelope for the daughter of former minister Ujjair
Hussain Munimi had Rs 3,000, the third envelope with Rs 1,000
was for the youngest daughter of former minister Mahesh Prasad
Singh and the fourth envelope for his "faithful servant" had Rs
500 cash.'[10]

Lalu Prasad: The Mandal Messiah and His Conviction

'. . . Perhaps, no Indian politician "vernacularized" politics in the
manner and with the same effect as Lalu. Karpoori Thakur did it
to some effect. Outside Bihar, Mulayam Singh Yadav did it in UP
politics. But Lalu took the CM's chair to the middle of villages
and well inside Dalits dingy huts.'[11]

Lalu Prasad acquired his political acumen under the guidance
of Karpoori Thakur. However, it was the Janata Dal government,
led by V.P. Singh in 1989, that significantly facilitated his
emergence in the political arena. The realization of Rammanohar
Lohia's anti-Congress ideology was fully materialized in 1990,
when Janata Dal formed the government in Bihar under Lalu
Prasad, relegating the Congress party to a distant second position.

The occurrence of the Bhagalpur riots in 1989 and Lalu's
obstruction of L.K. Advani's rath yatra effectively redirected
Muslim votes away from the Congress and towards Lalu Prasad.

This unprecedented turn of events differentiated Lalu's fortunes from those of Karpoori Thakur, who had also endeavoured to appeal to the Muslim electorate but had not experienced the same level of success as Lalu.

The implementation of the Mandal Commission's report and the subsequent reservation for backward classes triggered not only profound social changes but also political upheaval. The numerical majority of the backward classes started aligning themselves with Janata Dal, thereby reshaping the political landscape. With the added support from minority communities, the Janata Dal became an appealing choice for a significant portion of this influential majority group, swayed by the Mandal initiative. This development caused considerable concern within the Bharatiya Janata Party (BJP), as it heavily relied on Hindu votes to maintain its political clout and numerical significance. Any fragmentation of its voter base posed a significant threat to the right-wing party. Consequently, the BJP, in consultation with the Rashtriya Swayamsevak Sangh (RSS), devised a strategic response to counter the impact of the Mandal Commission. They orchestrated a Ram Rath Yatra, originating from Somnath in Gujarat and culminating in Ayodhya, Uttar Pradesh, to mobilize support for the construction of a Ram temple at the disputed site in Ayodhya.

'On 23 October, 1990, Chief Minister Lalu Prasad stopped the Advani Rath but himself rode the secular chariot, which was propelled by Mandal wheels to forge a MY (Muslim–Yadav) combination that remained unassailable till the Nitish Kumar-powered NDA dispelled the Lalu magic in the October 2005 election,'[12]

Lalu had no qualms about expressing his disdain for the BJP and said that the saffron party 'used religion to consolidate its political position; its Yatra had nothing to do with religious belief. BJP leaders exploit God; *inhe bhagwan se koi matlab nahin hai* (They have no concern with God). I ask them and the RSS, "Who are you to lecture us on Lord Ram?" Ram is an integral part of our civilization, but the RSS–BJP has made political capital out of it. "*Ram naam satya hai* (name of Ram is the only truth)" is what is chanted on a Hindu's last journey. The RSS–BJP combine has done more damage to the Hindu faith than anybody else.'[13]

Following the 1991 Lok Sabha polls, during which the Janata Dal secured an impressive victory, winning forty-eight out of fifty-four seats in undivided Bihar, Lalu Prasad Yadav emerged as a dominant and influential leader. However, his growing success seemed to have an adverse effect on his mindset. Lalu's political approach shifted towards emphasizing the concepts of Mandalization and secularization, which became his primary weapons. Unfortunately, this shift led to the neglect of developmental initiatives, with the focus being redirected towards identity-based politics.

By the end of 1990, Lalu Prasad changed his stance from governance to caste consolidation. His initial attempts to focus on governance had not paid off. 'The bureaucracy was not supporting him. The upper caste and elite were not ready to accept him as CM. He was referred to as "Lalua" in private conversations, even in offices during lunch break gossips. He was running a minority government that was on BJP support. He had been desperate to evolve a style of his own.'[14]

Former Bihar DGP D.N. Gautam says: 'The drift had started in September–October. For the initial six months, ideas of consolidation through governance or any other means had been in amorphous form. But he had now started enjoying the adulation of a large chunk of OBCs, EBCs and Dalits. Upper castes did not accept him and showed respect only to his authority. But he hardly bothered about his first choice of governance. The amorphous idea had started taking shape. He started enjoying raw power and was confident of a majority rallying behind him.'[15]

Lalu Prasad used his growing success to consolidate his core constituency of OBCs and Muslims by targeting upper castes to promote his narrative of undoing historical injustices and giving control over resources to their constituencies while losing focus on governance. Unfortunately, this shift led to neglect of developmental initiatives, with the focus being redirected towards identity-based politics.

Lalu Prasad Yadav had a distinctive approach to social empowerment. During his public meetings, he would often summon government officials and emphasize that these officers were mere servants while the people were the true masters. This unconventional practice was a stark departure from the previous awe-inspiring perception people held towards block development officers. As a result, district magistrates were readily available at the chief minister's disposal to address various public grievances. Lalu Prasad also employed symbolic gestures, such as publicly bathing underprivileged children using water tankers, in order to create a visual representation of social empowerment in the minds of the people. These actions put the government officers in a challenging position, as they had to adjust to new dynamics.

Moreover, Lalu Prasad's protocols were relatively relaxed compared to those of other chief ministers. He did not strictly adhere to hierarchical procedures, such as contacting the chief secretary or the director general of police, before reaching out to their subordinates. In fact, Lalu Prasad would occasionally directly contact station house officers, causing embarrassment to the superintendent of police. Throughout his first term from 1990 to

1995, Bihar witnessed a significant period of social transformation, during which the Other Backward Classes (OBCs) and Extremely Backward Classes (EBCs) began asserting themselves.

Lalu Prasad said: 'My understanding was very clear. I had seen that whenever the Domkhana (settlement of Doms, a caste at the bottom of the caste pyramid) people in the Gardanibagh area organized their wedding parties on the streets, policemen beat them up and chased them away for "creating commotion and blocking the traffic". They would even rough up the bride and the bridegroom. The police's insulting behaviour was evident even during the auspicious occasions of the underprivileged. Slum-dwellers had no place to organise their wedding parties. Now, the Patna Club had become accessible to them.'[16]

On the governance front, Abhishek Ranjan and Santosh Dubey write, 'Under the aegis of the Indira Awas Yojana, the government built 60,000 pucca houses for the poor in 600 blocks across the state in two years. As a result, by 1996, 3,00,000 habitable houses were built for the poor by the Rural Development Department. The government simultaneously focused on the urban poor. It raised the daily minimum wage for agricultural labourers from INR 16.50 to INR 21.50—the second-highest in the country. The state also waived the tax and cess levied on extracting toddy, providing a big relief to the then over five lakh strong and impoverished toddy tapping community in Bihar. The government also worked towards liberating education from the caste and class bias and ensured access to free education to children of underprivileged classes. Lalu Prasad established Charvaha Vidyalayas for children of cattle grazers who could study and pursue cattle grazing simultaneously.'[17]

The authors write: 'Once conceptualized as his dream school, these schools are now non-functional due to the absence of regular teacher visitations. While the government was often blamed for its lack of expenditure in the education sector, the overall low state budget also proved an impediment in this regard. Nevertheless, the government performed poorly under the Sarva Shiksha Abhiyan (SSA) enacted in 2001 and was not able to fully utilize the financial support in the initial years. However, the Lalu government devised an institutional arrangement for community participation in the management of elementary schools through Vidyalay Shiksha Samiti (VSS) and the Gram Panchayat. Unfortunately, the VSS was dysfunctional after a few years of working as education was outside the purview of the Gram Panchayat.'[18]

The second tenure of the Rashtriya Janata Dal (RJD), shared between Lalu Prasad and his wife Rabri Devi as chief ministers, marked a phase of complete Yadavization of politics in Bihar. During this time, Yadavs enjoyed a significant advantage in obtaining government contracts, which bolstered Lalu's belief that the combined support of the 18 per cent Muslim and 15 per cent Yadav population could serve as the foundation of his mass base. The term, 'MY' (Muslim–Yadav), became a well-known term during this period. With Nitish Kumar charting his own course and the state politics becoming tripolar, the division of votes ensured that the RJD remained in power until 2005. Following the 2000 elections, it aligned with the Congress party to form the government.

The most prominent manifestation of this assertion was the rise of the OBC Yadav community as a dominant social force. As a response, Yadavs were promptly offered seats of authority in police stations and government offices, a departure from previous practices.

However, the years between 1997 and 2003 were marred by a series of caste massacres, which tarnished Lalu Prasad's image as a champion of the Mandal ideology. Manoj Chaurasia writes, 'Massacres were not uncommon in central Bihar in the latter part of the 1990s, even when the state did not witness any major communal riots. As many as 16 massacres and caste riots took place between March 1997 and June 2000. The common villagers would literally pass their nights performing *ratjaga* (night keeping). Chaos prevailed and governance suffered in parts of Bihar. The Ranvir Sena—a private army of the upper caste Bhumihar landlords would target the Dalits during the dead of night and perform the "dance of death", spilling blood and then escaping without being nabbed or challenged by the proverbial "long arms of the law".'[19]

The entanglement of Lalu Prasad in the Rs 950 crore fodder scam case, followed by his conviction in five cases, further deteriorated his governance. Yet, his popularity did not wane. Even now, despite facing numerous court cases and undergoing a kidney transplant, Lalu Prasad remains defiant against the Bharatiya Janata Party (BJP), viewing the recent cases against him, such as the IRCTC and land-for-jobs cases, as political vendetta and a witch-hunt orchestrated by the BJP.

While Lalu Prasad's slogan of social justice and secularism may have lost some of its impact, his son, former Deputy Chief Minister Tejashwi Prasad Yadav, has attempted to reframe it by emphasizing the concept of economic justice.

Lalu Prasad Yadav's journey from a small village called Phulwaria in Gopalganj is a compelling case study in Indian politics, offering valuable insights into the empowerment of Other Backward Classes (OBCs) and Extremely Backward Classes (EBCs). His rise to prominence highlights the use of reservation as a tool for political empowerment rather than solely focusing on economic empowerment. Owing to his rustic demeanour and seemingly frivolous mannerisms, many may have dismissed him as a temporary figure, providing comic relief in politics. However, his enduring legacy lies in his groundbreaking efforts to challenge and dismantle the caste hierarchy, striving for social equality like never before.

Lalu Prasad's brand of aggressive socialism set him apart from other politicians. While he may have been seen as divisive, he was unequivocally assertive about the rights of OBCs and EBCs. He instilled a sense of pride among those who had been marginalized and disadvantaged, fostering the belief that they were not to be underestimated or pushed aside.

Lalu Prasad's impact transcends mere political terms. His legacy resonates with the empowerment of marginalized communities, his determination to break through barriers and his relentless pursuit of social parity. He may have been unconventional in his approach, but his contributions towards challenging caste-based inequalities and championing the rights of the disadvantaged will always be remembered.

Lalu Prasad, often termed flippant, gets profound and says in his autobiography: 'I do not think of death. I think of the manner in which I travel on the path of my life.'[20] He probably imbibed Karpoori Thakur's slogan of '*jeena hai to marna sikho* (If you have to live with dignity, get rid of the fear of death)'.

Nitish Kumar: The Development Man and His Political Somersaults

Santosh Singh writes, 'The national media was beholden to Nitish Kumar for two reasons and in two phases. Nitish attracted attention with a shift from sad stories of massacres and kidnappings to one of repair, damage-control and construction stories. Nitish invited mention because he was trying to write the turnaround story of a state that had been declared a lost case by many. The media that had swooned on stories of Lalu's buffoonery also wanted to get serious. Nitish Kumar attracted big editors to travel to Bihar and read those writings on the wall and decipher them.'[21]

N.K. Singh writes: 'Nitish saw himself as a champion gladiator in Bihar politics. He had outplayed everyone in the arena. He had made JD(U) the number one party. He had doubled its vote base from 3.2 million to 6.5 million in ten years, beginning in 2000. He had endeared himself to large sections of the poor and women. He had earned the appreciation of Muslims by restraining Hindu extremists from pursuing their vicious and violent agenda in Bihar and by expanding state patronage to the lower castes of Muslims despite being in alliance with the BJP. However, most Muslims had expressed their appreciation only in words thus far, not in votes. Now that he had dissociated himself from the BJP, he expected them to do so in a big way.'[22]

Sunita Lal and Shaibal Gupta write, 'Almost every activity in the state is viewed in terms of a caste or communal divide; vote politics overshadows sensible economics. This needs a thaw and, at least for the next five years, a shift of focus from politics to economics. The de-politicization includes civil service reforms, including improvement in the quality of the public delivery system, security of tenure, merit-based placements and reviving the confidence of field organizations, particularly in roads and irrigation which can significantly improve both the efficiency and quality of projects.'[23]

The Nitish Kumar government has not only reconsolidated state institutions, but in many cases these institutions are emerging stronger than they were before the politics of caste empowerment erupted in the 1990s. This is because the networks of patronage that had long placed state institutions under the control of the upper caste landed elite have been progressively weakened by three decades of lower caste politics.

Nitish Kumar recalled: 'I was inaugurating an aid camp for scheduled caste disabled children in a rural belt near Patna. It may have been sometime in 2008 or 2009. I was on the stage distributing certificates and I saw this little girl approaching me on crutches, and the thought struck me like a flash: what has disability got to do with caste, age or economic status, disability is disability, it strikes all equally cruelly. That is when we decided to extend assistance across all sections. Bureaucrats murmured dissent. The eligibility circle was far too wide. Where would the money come from? Tersely they were told they would have to find the ways,'[24] recalled Nitish.

In a Princeton University case study, Professor Juliette John highlighted that mismanagement of financial resources, obsolete methods of data entry and reporting, a low-skilled workforce, insufficient transparency and scarce accountability hindered service delivery in Bihar. Abhishek Ranjan and Santosh Dubey write, 'To combat these challenges, Nitish Kumar launched a series of reforms to streamline operations, boost revenues, and improve the government's responsiveness to citizens' needs. It focused on three areas: land registration, finance and freedom of information. The objective was for the government to be efficient, responsive, transparent and cost-effective. The strategic targeting of public spending on development programmes and fiscal strengthening is driving Bihar's strong development performance.'[25]

But before Nitish Kumar went on to achieve all this and more, it was Karpoori Thakur, who had offered him a job as an engineer in his struggling days of politics. More than once, Karpoori offered Nitish help in getting some job as an engineer. 'You can do the job temporarily, just to tide over the present economic difficulties, until you get a break in legislative politics,' Karpoori told him. Nitish said he wanted to do nothing but politics and was ready to go through difficulties until he achieved his objective.

Bihar CM Nitish Kumar is never tired of mentioning him. Nitish lays his heart bare on Karpoori Thakur's birth anniversary every year. This is what the Bihar CM said on 24 January 2023 at Bapu Sabhagar, Patna:

Jannayak Karpoori Thakur worked for the upliftment of every class and development of every area. In the year 1978, he implemented reservation for backward and most backward classes. His government was running with the support of many parties. Only after two years, some people here and there evicted him from power, but the reservation was not removed. He did all the works of development in the interest of the people, also worked to save people from floods. . . . (After Karpoori's death) we took a pledge that we will make his dream come true. Jannayak worked for the upliftment of the most backward, backward, scheduled caste/tribe, Hindu, Muslim, upper caste. He had no differences with anyone. He never worked against anyone. When we got a chance to work, following his path, [we] started working for the upliftment of all religions and communities. For the first time in the country, we gave 50 per cent reservation to women in the year 2006, in which provision was made for reservation of 20 per cent for most backward, 16 percent for Scheduled Castes and 1 percent for Scheduled Tribes. Women were also given 50 per cent reservation in the municipal elections in Bihar in the year 2007. . . We have done many things for the education and advancement of children belonging to poor families, started dress scheme and cycle scheme for girls which was not there anywhere

in the country. People coming from abroad saw this work and
appreciated it a lot.[26]

Nitish Kumar will surely go down in history as one of the best
chief ministers in the country but his political flip-flops—leaving
NDA in June 2013 and then rejoining it in July 2017 and then
again quitting in August 2022, make his alliance a subject of
scrutiny. Nitish returned to NDA on 28 January 2024. He
might call it the contextualization of politics; he is often accused
of political opportunism. But what still stands out for him is
that he remained a socialist at the core and never allowed saffron
to dominate his green shades. His achievement is that he always
reined in fundamentalist and communal elements. Nitish is still
the last man standing against the BJP. Bihar still remains the
final frontier for the BJP. On 28 January, 2024, Nitish Kumar
returned to NDA. But Nitish Kumar continues to remain the
most dominant factor for the state politics. He stays relevant till
the next Assembly elections because of being the common factor
between RJD and BJP.

Karpoori: The Camphor That Does Not Evaporate

Karpoori Thakur's lifespan can be divided into three phases. From
his birth in 1924 to 1967 was the first phase when he participated
in the Indian national movement for Independence, and the
students and peasants' movement, and articulated the common
interests of the underprivileged as a prominent socialist. In the
second phase—from 1967–1980, he was identified as the leader
of the backward classes and emerged as the Jannayak. In the third
phase—from 1980 till his death in 1988, once again he struggled
for new political support.

After the death of Lohia in October 1967, Karpoori emerged as the tallest socialist leader who mobilized the youth leadership of the backward classes in Bihar. Karpoori Thakur's popular politics, on the streets, to mobilize the common people during the 1960s and the 1970s is a relatively lesser known aspect of his career, particularly to today's youth. He, along with Ramanand Tiwari, Bhola Prasad Singh and Kapildeo Singh, dominated socialist politics in the state.

The lasting legacy of Karpoori Thakur is his desire to take society forward. Harivansh Narayan Singh writes, 'He also taught fellow politicians to think beyond promoting family and engaging in self-aggrandizement. He was a torch-bearer in the still darkness.'[27]

While making a public speech in 1986, Karpoori Thakur praised B.R. Ambedkar and subtly criticised Gandhism. He was talking of backward classes, not castes. Congress talked about the socialist pattern of society and Communists talked about socialist society under government care but Karpoori rooted for democratic socialism. 'This is why whenever he got an opportunity to govern; he took people-friendly decisions, not populist as some would say. Right from the waiver of school fees to waiving rent on unirrigated land, he thought of the poor. Through reservation, he wanted to ensure that its benefits are not limited to a handful of castes but most of the backward class. His idea was an egalitarian society.'[28]

Karpoori would not miss the solemnization of any inter-caste marriage. His efforts for the poor and low caste people mounted enough pressure on the subsequent Congress government (1971– 77) to institute the Mungeri Lal Commission.

Former Congress MLC and nephew of Mungeri Lal, Lalbabu Lal, says: 'I often wonder why Congress is not taking the credit for instituting the commission under the Congress-supported Bhola Paswan Shastri government in 1971. But it is true that when the report was submitted to Congress's Jagannath Mishra government in 1976, he did not find ways to implement its recommendations. It was left to Karpoori Thakur to do so and he became a national hero."[29]

Dr Santosh Kumar writes, 'He created a stir in the social life of Bihar. An enthusiasm was created (among common people). People who live a life of comfort in palaces can never understand the importance of Karpoori Thakur.'[30]

Veteran socialist leader and former Bihar Minister Gajendra Prasad Himanshu says: 'Karpoori's honesty is unmatched in Bihar politics. His very name was his capital. He was a mass leader in the true sense. Karpoori might well be a barber by birth but I hardly know any Brahmin who can match his intellect.'[31]

Author Narendra Pathak says: 'I see two main reasons for Karpoori Thakur being akin to Dr Lohia. First, Lohia was probably never a Marxist, not at all after 1940. He gradually developed an independent ideology of his own. After 1948, he clearly called himself a disciple of Gandhi and later "Kujat Gandhiwadi". The second reason is probably more important. Like Lohia, Karpoori Thakur had faith in Satyagraha and was highly influenced by Dr Lohia's definition of "Kujat Gandhian". Karpoori Thakur meant Satyagraha and Gandhism for social transformation.'[32]

BJP has also started co-opting Karpoori Thakur. PM Narendra Modi openly praised Thakur on 16 July 2022 at a function in Patna, naming only two former CMs, Dr Sri Krishna Singh and Karpoori Thakur, and calling incumbent CM Nitish Kumar 'a valuable ally'. Somehow, the PM saw potential in Nitish to get into that big league but he did not say so for Nitish was opposing him.

BJP Rajya Sabha MP and former Bihar deputy CM Sushil Kumar Modi says that Karpoori had only risen in stature as one of the most prominent EBC icons. 'We first brought the idea of celebrating the anniversary of Karpoori Thakur in 1990–2000. When we discussed this with our leader Kailashpati Mishra, he got angry and asked: "Who is Karpoori? Don't you have icons in your own party?" We kept quiet for a while but pushed the idea under the tenure of Nand Kishore Yadav as BJP state president. In subsequent years, we started organizing Karpoori anniversary on a bigger scale and even Karpoori fortnight across Bihar. Our ABVP training had shown how the Dalit movement had changed the politics of Maharashtra. These days, Karpoori Thakur is celebrated more than B.R. Ambedkar in Bihar as all parties are trying to appease EBCs. Karpoori Thakur's lasting legacy is reservation, the idea of quota within quota that has now made him a national icon. The best part of his reservation idea was its cohesiveness. While he separated quota for EBC and OBC, he also thought of women and the poor among upper castes,'[33] said Sushil Kumar Modi.

When Nitish Kumar had been part of NDA, he had brought up the idea of celebrating Karpoori Jayanti together. 'We were very happy. But soon, we knew the main reason behind it. As we had booked S.K. Memorial Hall (in Patna) two months in advance and he found no better place for JD (U), he had brought up the idea of a joint celebration. The very next year, JD (U) booked SKM Hall three months in advance. That is why one calls Nitish a wily politician,'[34] says Modi.

Social Justice: From Class to Caste, Constituency to Consumer

Shivanand Tiwari, former MP and RJD national vice president, has been a bridge between the political journey of Karpoori

Thakur and that of his two scions, Lalu Prasad and Nitish Kumar. Tiwari (80) has been in active politics since 1965 when he had accompanied his father Ramanand Tiwari and Karpoori Thakur to a dharna at Patna's Gandhi Maidan against the K.B. Sahay government. Tiwari was among those injured in the police lathicharge.

He says, 'Most often people associate Karpoori Thakur only with quota-within-quota. But it was just one facet of Karpoori Thakur, who was a cumulative product of the socialist, farmers' and freedom movements. He transcended his caste and religion while taking up the farmers' cause during the Bakasht and bataidari agitations. He emerged as a consensus leader because of his hard work, eloquence and wide acceptability.'[35]

Tiwari says: 'I vividly remember Dr Lohia's speech at Patna's Gandhi Maidan in 1967 in which he had taken a vow to defeat the Congress and had said that the Socialists had to do something extraordinary within three months of formation of its government to prove that they were different from the Congress.'[36] He adds that the Sanyukt Vidhayak Dal (SVD government), led by Mahamaya Prasad Sinha and his deputy Karpoori Thakur, had become very popular because of its effective handling of the food crisis. 'And when the government fell in January 1968, people had vented their ire by pelting stones at those they believed were responsible for the fall of the government . . .'[37]

Tiwari also cited the example of Lakhan Lal Kapoor, the only Hindu candidate to have won from the Muslim-dominated Kishanganj Lok Sabha seat (in 1967) since Independence till date. It was all because of his outreach to maximum voters irrespective of their castes, says Tiwari.

The veteran socialist leader said that social justice had now been relegated to freebies and caste parties with the sole objective of winning power. 'It was very heartening to see Congress leader Rahul Gandhi spend two hours in the field with farmers. One may dismiss it as optics but politicians have largely moved away from farmers and common people.'[38]

The *Pasmanda* (those who are left behind) movement, led by former Rajya Sabha MP Ali Anwar, also drew inspiration from Karpoori Thakur's landmark quota decision. 'Since the late 1990s, I have been impressing upon those in power that the poor among Muslims also need a special push in the form of quotas. I am happy now that even PM Narendra Modi has started using the term, Pasmanda. But we are still waiting for something concrete to be done.'[39] Prominent Dalit scholar and author Kancha Ilaiah Shepherd writes: 'Caste and feudalism delayed the advancement of Pasmanda Muslims, just as Brahmanism and feudalism did among the non-Muslim shudras, dalits and adivasis. Thus the curse of caste continued to penetrate deeper and deeper into the Muslim community as several caste communities, along with their occupational backgrounds, converted into Islam particularly during the Mughal period. Even after conversion, education and equal opportunities eluded most of them.'[40]

Prem Kumar Mani, a socialist thinker and writer, who has worked with Ram Vilas Paswan, Lalu Prasad and Nitish Kumar, has also tracked Karpoori Thakur's contribution from close quarters.

Mani says: 'Social justice has now entered the phase of liberal consumerism, gift culture or instant populism in search of a shortcut to power. The journey that had begun with the formation of caste associations in the 1890s traversed its path through caste associations, parties taking up the cause of farmers to reservations to caste rallies and caste organizations to caste parties now.'[41] The very idea of social empowerment slowly gave way to instant populism, with caste affiliations working more as a topping of the government doles and promises. It is true that India is a welfare state and it is taxpayers' money that is distributed among people in the name of quick doles. Yet, voters are largely being treated as consumers in a give-and-take relationship.

When the Socialist Party decided to merge with Archarya J.B. Kriplani's Krishak Majdoor Praja Party to become Praja Socialist Party in 1952, it erred in agreeing to Kriplani's condition of shedding the class war and taking up the non-violent approach. In doing so, socialists shed their core principle of 'class struggle'. By the time Sanyukt Socialist Party was formed in 1965, there were hardly any land movements and class consciousness had given way to caste consciousness. This trend only got crystallized in 1977 when socialists formed the Bharatiya Lok Dal under Charan Singh, who had formed AJGAR, a caste conglomeration of Ahir (Yadav), Jat, Gujjar and Rajput castes.

In the post-Mandal phase when reservation was introduced in the central government and Lalu Prasad took over as CM, socialists' politics was openly woven around caste and the social combination with inclusion of Muslims as a key constituency. While Lalu's social justice was bereft of development, Nitish Kumar re-christened it with a new slogan 'development with justice' in 2005.

Mani says: 'While Karpoori Thakur took initiatives such as removing mandatory English from Class 10 board examination and waiver of rent on unirrigated land up to 6.5 acres besides landmark quota within quota, Nitish also took the key decision of giving 50 per cent quota to women in the three-tier Panchayati Raj. These decisions are great examples of social justice but today's doles and gift culture are direct allurements, shorn of any tinge of socialism. The mushrooming of caste parties in the last two decades has further shown how political parties are taking caste and reservations as an easy route to power.'[42]

One of India's foremost public intellectuals, Pratap Bhanu Mehta, argues: 'Caste still structures opportunity and power in Indian society, and has to be reckoned with on any journey to a just society. But this social justice agenda, in response to Hindutva, is a deeply poisoned chalice. It will do almost nothing to address the real issues that arise from caste inequalities. It will again sell snake oil in the name of social justice. Its moral logic shares more with the majoritarianism it seeks to combat. And it is politically prudent. Even if it brings short-term gains, its long-term political logic will be self defeating. India needs strong affirmative action programmes, particularly for Dalits, and some deeply marginalised sections of OBCs. But post Mandal, the logic of social justice discourse has rarely focused on the ethical issues of discrimination, the agenda of creating economic growth that is inclusive, or of creating a state and public institutions that deliver the material basis for dislodging the inequalities of caste.'[43]

RJD Rajya Sabha MP and Delhi University Professor Manoj Kumar K. Jha and Jawaharlal Nehru University professor Ghazala Jamil offered a counter: 'Let us remember that caste-based oppression creates material conditions. This materiality of caste inequality is produced not just in economic and socio-cultural norms but also through political and socio-cultural terms and through political, especially electoral–political, machinations . . .'[44]

Manish Kumar, assistant professor (economics), JP University, Chhapra, argues: 'India's early socialists were largely concerned with building a better society by using the developmental power of the state. However, as politics deepened and became more competitive, social justice underwent a transformation, limiting its catchment area to justice for caste. The proliferation of caste-based organisations and the rise of caste leaders is a painful reality of Indian politics today. The erosion in the meaning and purpose of social justice has not stopped here. The higher growth rates and globalisation of the economy since the 1990s has generated humongous revenue for the government, emboldening the politics of giveaways. The commercialization of politics has reduced the voter from a civic participant to a consumer ready to negotiate his vote for doles.'[45]

There has also been a lot of hue and cry over the Justice G. Rohini Commission report on the sub-categorization of OBCs. Senior journalist and author Shyamlal Yadav says: 'Reservation within reservation or sub-categorization of Other Backwards Classes (OBCs) is based on a general perception that Yadav, Koeris, Kumis, Banias and some other OBCs have captured most of the seats reserved for OBCs. This question is prompted primarily by the political assertion and certain empowerment of Yadavs and Kurmis in prime states like UP and Bihar in the last three decades. Ironically, those who advocate the idea of sub-categorization, do not support the caste census. But sub-categorization, as a principle, should be supported as government benefits should reach all. But the government should first reveal the caste-wise number of people and also their respective numbers in various government services and admissions in the premier institutions.'[46]

Our final thoughts are on democracy and development.

Leading political scientist Ashutosh Varshney says: 'India's recent democratic decline is not because elections are not free. India remains electorally vigorous. The decline concerns the liberal dimensions of democracy. It is rooted in an ideology, which seeks Hindu primacy above all. It is not very different from the idea of White supremacy in American history, especially in Jim Crow American South, 1880–1965. Liberal democracy, while it might not have flourished in the North, was dead in the American South in those eight decades. Democrats worldwide hope that India's turn towards Hindu supremacy does not last as long.'[47]

Prof. Varshney made the above observations while delivering the Third Manoj Srivastava Memorial Lecture in Patna in 2023. Srivastava, a 1980-batch Bihar cadre IAS officer, who lost his life during the Covid pandemic in 2020, was known for his pro-poor and pro-people approach as a civil servant during his entire career. He had an easy option of going on a Central deputation but chose to stay back in his home state. Srivastava somehow exemplified the socialist and democratic shift in Bihar bureaucracy that Karpoori Thakur's style of functioning as deputy CM and CM had impacted. Thakur, who had faced resistance from babus as deputy CM in 1967 in democratizing the use of the lift at the state secretariat, saw a marked change in the attitude of bureaucracy when he got Yashwant Sinha as his principal secretary, who would happily work with CM Karpoori till the late hours in the secretariat to match the commitment of the 'people's CM' in 1977–79. It was a sheer coincidence that there had been a month-long protest in Arrah in 1988 when Srivastava had been transferred within a year of his posting as the Bhojpur district magistrate for taking a host of pro-people initiatives such as holding a regular janata durbar, and moving around areas seldom visited by his predecessors to listen to people's problems. It had happened just a few months after the former CM Karpoori Thakur died but Karpoori was very much represented as his party, Lok Dal, had been at the forefront of the protest in Arrah. A senior Congress leader and then Union minister K.K. Tiwari, belonging to Arrah, had held it against Srivastava for showing extra zeal in implementing sundry welfare schemes and also for speaking truth to power. The protests included over 50,000 ordinary residents, who squatted on railway lines, carried out multiple processions, closed down shops and educational institutions, and threatened the then CM Bhagwat Jha Azad to make Arrah 'a Rangoon (in terms of lawlessness)'. Noted poet Nilay Upadhyay recalled the extraordinary events: 'The people of Bhojpur had given its Collector Srivastava "*nagrikta* (citizenship)" of the district.'[48]

Srivastava was one of the officers who believed it to be his duty not just to formulate policies but also to have a regular interface with those whom these policies and programmes were meant for. In later years, Srivastava won praise from PM Dr Manmohan Singh. But it was not sufficient reason for him to leave Bihar and the people he served until his retirement in 2016.

The adulation of the people of Bihar towards any officer, regardless of caste, politics and ideology, who selflessly brings about development with justice, is a testament to people's demand for growth with justice. Caste is a reality not only in Bihar but throughout India and among Indians around the world. The challenge lies in preventing caste from hindering progress and impeding the dispensation of justice. There is no doubt that Bihar is on a growth trajectory. However, it is also true that it lags behind its peer states, necessitating a higher growth rate and innovative solutions to meet the aspirations of its people.

As a student of public policy, my one-line prescription would be to focus on an education-centric urbanization approach and a reduction in state control over businesses. Managing an economy can be likened to driving a multi-horse chariot. If you tighten the reins too much, it slows down. A skilled charioteer would keep the reins under control, using them only for direction rather than unnecessarily slowing down. Thus, the government can streamline its state control processes without requiring additional investments. This would provide a much-needed boost to local enterprises and encourage young people to explore business opportunities, as government jobs alone cannot meet the demand for millions of jobs. Establishing high-quality schools and colleges and facilitating towns to develop around them, with their own small and medium enterprises through policy intervention and infrastructure development, would enable each town to grow organically. Any attempt to bring about prosperity overnight through a big bang approach, such as attracting large industries or massive investments, is likely to backfire. Bihar needs to embrace the philosophy of kaizen, which Nitish Kumar has done to some extent, even if not within its formal framework. Now, the time is ripe to propel it onto a higher growth trajectory by abandoning the 'jugaad' approach and adopting a well-thought-out, evidence based technology-enabled policy approach.

Democracy will not come
Today, this year
Nor ever
Through compromises and fear
I have as much right
As the other fellow has
To stand
On my two feet
And own the land . . .

—Langston Hughes, *Democracy*

Acknowledgements

EDITORS AT INDIAN EXPRESS: Raj Kamal Jha, Unni Rajen Shanker, Rakesh Sinha, P.V. Iyer, Shalini Langer, Uma Vishnu, Rahul Sabharwal and Shahid Pervez.

PUBLISHERS AND EDITORS: Penguin Random House India, Milee Ashwarya, Premanka Goswami and Saba Nehal.

ACADEMICIANS AND MEDIA PERSONS: Pratap Bhanu Mehta, Jeffrey Witsoe, Ashutosh Varshney, Surendra Kishore, Arun Kamal, D.N. Gautam, Manisha Priyam, Ravish Kumar, Rajdeep Sardesai, Kamlesh K. Singh, Chinki Sinha, Saurabh Dwivedi, Ajit Anjum, Ashutosh, Naresh Kumar Vikal and Harinandan Sah.

POLITICIANS: Lalu Prasad, Nitish Kumar, the late Ram Vilas Paswan, Sushil Kumar Modi, Shivanand Tiwari, K.C. Tyagi, Jagdanand Singh, Prem Kumar Mani, Dr C.P. Thakur, Umesh

Prasad Singh, Dr Sanjay Paswan, Neeraj Kumar, Ali Anwar, Sudhakar Singh and Prof. Subodh K. Mehta.

KARPOORI THAKUR'S FAMILY: Ramnath Thakur, Dr Birendra K. Thakur, the late Asha Rani, Kanaklata Thakur, Namita, Ranjit Kumar, Sneha and Amrita.

FRIENDS: Dr Arjun Singh, Kumar Shakti Shekhar, Brajmohan Singh, Ranjeet Nirguni, Swayam Prakash, Vivek Rai, Praveen Mishra, Guru Prakash Paswan, Abhinav Das, Abhijeet Srivastava, Ashutosh K. Thakur, Atul K. Thakur, Supriy Ranjan, Saagar Srivastava and Deepak Tenguriya.

FAMILY: Chitra, Gaurav, Shaswat, Shivangi, Vikram (Vicky), Ranjeev Singh and Meenakshi Singh.

SPECIAL MENTION: Deepak Kumar, the housekeeper, for his selfless service at odd hours during the writing of the book.

Notes

Why Karpoori Thakur?

1. *RJD Samachar* (Ranchi: Doranda Press, January–February 2022 issue).
2. Narendra Modi, 'I am delighted . . .', X, 23 January 2024, available at https://twitter.com/narendramodi/status/1749806381497270300?lang=en.
3. Jagpal Singh, 'Karpoori Thakur: A Socialist Leader in the Hindi Belly', *EPW*, 19 January 2015, Vol. 1, No. 3.
4. Jeffrey Witsoe, *Democracy Against Developement* (Chicago: University of Chicago Press, 2018).
5. Francine R. Frankel and M.S.A. Rao, *Dominance of State Power in Modern India:Decline of a Social Order* (Oxford University Press, 1989–90).
6. Bihar CM Nitish Kumar speech at a Patna function, 2 September 2005.
7. Prof. Keshav Rao Jadhav, ed., *Dr Rammanohar Lohia, Gandhi, Marx and Socialism* (Hyderabad: Lohia Vigyan Samiti, originally published in 1977, republished in www.indiatoday.com in 2019).

8.   Interview with former DGP, D.N. Gautam, 10 August 2022.

9.   Naresh Kumar Vikal and Harinandan Sah, *Saptkranti Ke Samvahak Jannayak Karpoori Thakur Smriti Granth* (New Delhi: Prabhat Prakashan, 2019).

10.   Mohammed Sajjad, 'Karpoori Thakur and the Power of Street Politics', 23 January 2019, Rediff.com https://m.rediff.com/amp/news/column/karpoori-thakur-and-the-power-of-street-politics/20190123.htm.

11.   Rajiv Malhotra and Vijaya Vishwanathan, *Snakes in the Ganga: Breaking India 2.0* (OCCAM, 2022).

12.   Ibid.

13.   United Nations (2016). Report of the Special Rapporteur on Minority Issues. Retrieved from https://documents-dds-ny.un.org/doc/UNDOC/GEN/G16/013/73/PDF/G1601373.pdf?OpenElement.

14.   'India caste: How a centuries-old hierarchy has persisted in the US', BBC News, 9 June 2023. Retrieved from https://www.bbc.com/news/world-asia-india-65819688.

15.   Social Realities of Indian Americans: Results from 2020 Indian American Attitudes Survey. Carnegie Endowment for International Peace. 9 June 2021. Retrieved from https://carnegieendowment.org/2021/06/09/social-realities-of-indian-americans-results-from-2020-indian-american-attitudes-survey-pub-84667; 'The U.S. isn't safe from the trauma of caste bias', 8 March 2019. Retrieved from https://theworld.org/stories/2019-03-08/us-isn-tsafe-trauma-caste-bias.

16.   'India caste: How a centuries-old hierarchy has persisted in the US'. BBC News, 9 June 2023. Retrieved from https://www.bbc.com/news/world-asia-india-65819688.

17.   Interview with Ramnath Thakur, Rajya Sabha member and elder son of Karpoori Thakur, Karpoori Gram, Samastipur, 23 January 2023.

18.   Interview with Hemant, senior journalist (Patna: *Pradeep* and *Hindustan*, 13 July 2022).

19.   'Why Socialism? Congress Socialist Party', Jayaprakash Narayan (1 January 1936).

20. Manish Kumar Jha, *Contentious Politics and Popular Movements: Enigma of Karpoori Thakur* (https://mail.google.com/mail/u/0/#inbox/KtbxLzGStvfCsTNQCtKmngHWgDhpZChgbV?projector=1&messagePartId=0.1).

21. Paul R. Brass, as quoted by Omprakash Mahato, 'Jannayak Karpoori Thakur and Quintessence of His Politics', Countercurrents.org, 24 January 2023, https://countercurrents.org/2023/01/jananayak karpoori-thakur-and-quintessence-of-his-politics/.

22. Santosh Singh, *JP to BJP: Bihar After Lalu and Nitish* (New Delhi: Vitasta Sage Select, 2021).

23. Christophe Jaffrelot, *India's Silent Revolution: The Rise of the Lower Castes in North India*(New York: Columbia University Press, 2003).

Chapter 1: Petrograd to Pitaunjhia

1. 'This Day in History: 1917— February Revolution Begins, Leading to the End of Czarist Rule in Russia,' History.com, https://www.history.com/this-day-in-history/february-revolution-begins.

2. Lilian Osborne, '9 Fascinating Facts about the Russian Revolution,' 28 June 2020, HistoryColored, https://historycolored.com/articles/5020/9-fascinating-facts-about-the-russian-revolution/.

3. Interview with Pushya Mitra, author of the book, *Jab Neel Ka Dag Mita,* Patna, 10 August 2022.

4. Dr Santosh Kumar, *Samajwad Ke Vikas Me Bihari Nayakon Ki Bhumika* (Patna: Janaki Prakashan, 2019).

5. S.A. Dange, *Gandhi Vs. Lenin* (Liberty Literature, 1921).

6. Interview with Om Prakash Singh, erstwhile Durbar resident of Pitaunjhia (now Karpoori Gram), Samastipur, 23 January 2023.

7. Ibid.

8. Arvind Singh, an elderly villager from Karpoori Gram, 23 January 2023.

9. Ibid.

10. Interview with Ramnath Thakur, JD (U) Rajya Sabha MP and Karpoori Thakur's elder son, Karpoori Gram, Samastipur, 22 January 2023.

11. Interview with Ashutosh Bhushan Narayan Singh, teacher, Middle School, Karpoori Gram, 23 January 2023.

12. Interview with Shambu Nath Jha, teacher, Karpoori Gram, Samastipur, 22 January 2023.

13. Interview with Arvind Singh, an elderly villager from Karpoori Gram, 23 January 2023.

14. Ibid.

15. Interview with Jagdanand Singh, former MP and RJD state president, Patna, 20 December 2022.

Chapter 2: Saraswati, Triveni and the Freedom Struggle

1. Vishnudev Rajak, *Karpoori Thakur Ka Rajnitik Darshan* (Patna: Janaki Prakashan, 2012).

2. Ibid.

3. Jeffrey Witsoe, *Democracy Against Development: Lower-Caste Politics and Political Modernity in Postcolonial India* (Chicago: University of Chicago Press, 2013).

4. Sho Kuwajima, *Peasants and Peasant Leaders in Contemporary History: A Case of Bihar in India* (New Delhi: L.G.Publishers Distributors, 2017).

5. Walter Hauser and Kailash Chandra Jha, trans., *My Life Struggle* (translation of *Mera Jeevan Sangharsh* by Swami Sahajanand Saraswati) (Delhi: Manohar Publishers and Distributors, 2018).

6. Ashwani Kumar, *The Community Warriors: State, Peasants and Caste Armies in Bihar* (London: Anthem Press, 2008).

7. Arvind N. Das, *Republic of Bihar* (Penguin Books, 1992).

8. Jeffrey Witsoe, *Democracy Against Development: Lower-Caste Politics and Political Modernity in Postcolonial India* (Chicago: University of Chicago Press, 2013).

9. Walter Hauser and Kailash Chandra Jha, trans., *My Life Struggle* (translation of *Mera Jeevan Sangharsh* by Swami Sahajanand Saraswati) (Delhi: Manohar Publishers and Distributors, 2018).

10. Francine R. Frankel and M.S.A. Rao, *Dominance of State Power in India: Decline of a Social Order* (Oxford University Press, 1989–90).

11. Jeffrey Witsoe, *Democracy Against Development: Lower-Caste Politics and Political Modernity in Postcolonial India* (Chicago: University of Chicago Press, 2013).

12. Ibid.

13. Ibid.

14. Arvind N. Das, *Republic of Bihar* (Penguin Books, 1992).

15. Ibid.

16. Ibid. See also Ashwani Kumar, *The Community Warriors: State, Peasants and Caste Armies in Bihar* (London: Anthem Press, 2008).

17. Ashwani Kumar, *The Community Warriors: State, Peasants and Caste Armies in Bihar* (London: Anthem Press, 2008).

18. Om Prakash Deepak, *Dinman*, 1972.

19. Walter Hauser and Kailash Chandra Jha, ed., *Culture, Vernacular Politics and the Peasants: India, 1889–1950* (An edited translation of Swami Sahajanand Saraswati's *Mera Jeevan Sangharsh*)(Delhi: Manohar Publishers and Distributors, 2015).

20. Fanishwarnath Renu, *Naye Savere Ki Aasha, Janvani* (Varanasi: January 1950 edition).

21. Interview with Dr Satyajeet Kumar Singh, Shri Sitaram Ashram Trust secretary, 8 August 2023, over the phone.

22. Ibid.

23. Interview with Kailash Chandra Jha, 9 August 2023, on WhatsApp.

24. Interview with Anish Ankur, cultural activist and trustee of Shri Sitaram Ashram, Bihta, 8 August 2023, over the phone.

25. Prasanna Kumar Choudhary and Shrikant, *Bihar Mein Samajik Parivartan Ke Kucch Aayam* (Patna: Vani Prakashan, 2002).

26. Ibid.

27. Neha Ranjan, *Adhunik Bihar Mein Jatiya Sangharsh* (Patna and Delhi: Janaki Prakashan, 2015).

28. Prasanna Kumar Choudhary and Shrikant, *Bihar Mein Samajik Parivartan Ke Kuchh Aayam* (Patna: Vani Prakashan, 2002).

29. Neha Ranjan, *Aadhunik Bihar Mein Jatiya Sangharsh* (Patna and Delhi: Janaki Prakashan, 2015).

30. Ashwani Kumar, *Community Warriors: State, Pesants and Caste Armies in Bihar* (London: Anthem Press, 2008).

31. Kingsley Davis, *Human Society* (Berkeley: University of California andMacmillan Company, 1949).
32. Narendra Pathak, *Karpoori Thakur Aur Samajwad* (New Delhi: Medha Books, 2016).
33. Neha Ranjan, *Adhunik Bihar Mein Jatiya Sangharsh* (Patna and Delhi: Janaki Prakashan, 2015).
34. William R. Pinch, *Peasants and Monks in British India* (Berkeley: University of California Press, 1996).
35. Jeffrey Witsoe, *Democracy Against Development: Lower-Caste Politics and Political Modernity in Postcolonial India* (Chicago: University of Chicago Press, 2013).
36. Ibid.
37. Sachchidanand Sinha, *Jati Vyavastha: Mithak, Vastvikta Aur Chunoutiya* (Delhi: Rajkamal Prakashan, 2009).
38. M.N. Srinivas, *India: Social Structure* (New Delhi: Hindustan Publishing Corporation (India), 1980).
39. S.R. Nene, *Dr Rammanohar Lohia Remembered: His Philosophy, Scholarship and Vision* (Delhi: Rupa Publications, 2011).
40. Indumati Kelkar, *Rammanohar Lohia* (New Delhi: National Book Trust—NBT India, 2014).
41. Neha Ranjan, *Adhunik Bihar Mein Jatiya Sangharsh* (Patna and Delhi: Janaki Prakashan, 2015).
42. Naresh Kumar Vikal and Harinandan Sah, *Saptkranti Ke Samvahak Jannayak Karpoori Thakur Smriti Granth* (New Delhi: Prabhat Prakashan, 2019).
43. Interview with Ramnath Thakur, JD (U) MP, Samastipur, 22 January 2023.
44. Ibid.
45. Interview with Shivanand Tiwari, former MP, 10 August 2022, over the phone.
46. Interview with Hemant, senior journalist, Patna,13 December 2022.
47. Jeffrey Witsoe, *Democracy Against Development: Lower-Caste Politics and Political Modernity in Postcolonial India*, (Chicago: University of Chicago Press, 2013).

Chapter 3: Krishna Talkies

1. Nagarjun *Harijan Gatha*, (http://kavitakosh.org/kk/%E0%A4%B9%
    E0%A4%B0%E0%A4%BF%E0%A4%%E0%A4%A8_%E0%
    A4%97%E0%A4%).

2. Santosh Singh, *JP To BJP*: *Bihar After Lalu and Nitish* (Vitasta Sage
    Select, 2021).

3. Naresh Kumar Vikal and Harinandan Sah, *Saptkranti Ke Samvahak
    Jannayak Karpoori Thakur Smriti Granth* (New Delhi: Prabhat
    Prakashan, 2019).

4. Ibid.

5. Raghuvir Sahay, *Dinman*, 1989.

6. Dr Santosh Kumar, *Samajwad Ke Vikas Mein Bihari Nayakon Ki
    Bhoomika* (New Delhi: Janaki Prakashan, 2019).

7. Ibid.

8. Ibid.

9. Professor Pralayankar Bhattacharyya, *Uttar Bihar*, 3 October 1977
    issue.

10. Interview with Muneshwar Singh, villager from Pitaunjhia,
    Samastipur, 23 January 2023.

11. Interview with Ramnath Thakur, elder son of Karpoori Thakur and
    JD (U) Rajya Sabha MP, Samastipur, 22 January 2023.

12. Vishnudev Rajak, *Karpoori Thakur Ka Rajnitik Darshan* (Patna:
    Janaki Prakashan, 2012).

13. Naresh Kumar Vikal and Harinandan Sah, *Saptkranti Ke Samvahak
    Jannayak Karpoori Thakur Smriti Granth* (New Delhi: Prabhat
    Prakashan, 2019).

14. Vishnudev Rajak, *Karpoori Thakur Ka Rajnitik Darshan* (Patna:
    Janaki Prakashan, 2012).

15. Narendra Pathak, *Karpoori Aur Samajwad* (Delhi: Medha Books,
    2016).

16. Ibid.

17. Neha Ranjan, *Adhunik Bihar Mein Jatiya Sangharsh*, (Patna and
    Delhi: Janaki Prakashan, 2015).

18. Ibid.

19.   Interview with Dr Birendra K. Thakur, Patna, 20 February 2023.

20.   Interview with Ramnath Thakur, elder son of Karpoori Thakur and JD (U) Rajya Sabha MP, Samastipur, 23 January 2023.

Chapter 4: The Tajpur Tower

1.   *Karpoori Thakur Ka Sansdiya Jeevan*, Pustakalaya Evam Shodh Sandarbh Shakha, Bihar Vidhan Sabha Sachivalaya (Patna: Messrs Screena, 2003).

2.   Naresh Kumar Vikal and Harinandan Sah, *Saptkranti Ke Samvahak Jannayak Karpoori Thakur Smriti Granth* (New Delhi: Prabhat Prakashan, 2019).

3.   Ibid.

4.   *Karpoori Ka Sansdiya Jeevan*, Part-I, Pustakalaya aur Shodh Sandarbha Shakha, Bihar Vidhan Sabha Sachivalaya (Patna: Messrs Screena, 2003).

5.   Ibid.

6.   Ibid.

7.   Ibid.

8.   Ibid.

9.   Ibid.

10.   Ibid.

11.   Ibid.

12.   Ibid.

13.   Ibid.

14.   Ibid.

15.   Narendra Pathak, *Karpoori Thakur Aur Samajvad* (New Delhi: Medha Books, 2016).

16.   Ibid.

17.   Prof. Keshav Rao Jadhav, editor, (Hyderabad: Lohia Vigyan Samiti, originally published in 1977, republished in www.indiatoday.com in 2019).

18.   Ibid.

19.   Ibid.

20.   Ibid.

21.   Ibid.

22. Interview withUmesh Prasad Singh, Socialist leader and close aide of Dr Rammanohar Lohia (Patna, 10 August 2022).

23. *Karpoori Ka Sansdiya Jeevan*, Pustakalaya aur Shodh Sandarbha Shakha, Bihar Vidhan Sabha Sachivalaya (Patna: Messrs Screena, 2003).

24. Ibid.

25. Ibid.

26. Ibid.

27. Interview with Bijendra Prasad Yadav, Bihar minister, Patna, 4 October 2022.

28. Manish Kumar Jha, *Contentious Politics and Popular Movements: Enigma of Karpoori Thakur* (https://mail.google.com/mail/u/0/#inbox/KtbxLzGStvfCsTNQCtKmngHWgDhpZChgbV? projector=1&messagePartId=0.1).

29. *Karpoori Ka Sansdiya Jeevan*, Pustakalaya aur Shodh Sandarbha Shakha, Bihar Vidhan Sabha Sachivalaya (Patna: Messrs Screena, 2003).

30. Interview with Ramlal Mahato, former principal, LKVD College, Patauri, Karpoori Gram, Samastipur,22 January 2023.

31. Shashi Tharoor, *Nehru: The Invention of India* (New York: Arcade Publishing, 2003).

32. L.P. Shahi, *Freedom and Beyond* (Muzaffarpur: Shrikrishna Shiksha Pratisthan, 2008).

33. Interview with Ramlal Mahato, former principal, LKVD, College, Patauri, Karpoori Gram, Samastipur, 22 January 2023.

34. Interview with Dr Birendra K. Thakur, Patna, 20 February 2023.

35. Ibid.

36. Ibid.

37. Interview with Ramnath Thakur, Karpoori Thakur's elder son and JD (U) Rajya Sabha MP, Karpoori Gram, Samastipur, 23 January 2023.

Chapter 5: SP to SSP

1. Gorakh Pandey,*Samajwad* (a poem) https://www.hindwi.org/geet/samajawad-gorakh-pandey-geet.

2. Prof. Keshav Rao Jadhav, ed., (Hyderabad: Lohia Vigyan Samiti), Originally published in 1977, republished in www.indiatoday.com in 2019.

3. Ibid.

4. Vishnudev Rajak, *Karpoori Thakur Ka Rajnitik Darshan* (Patna: Janaki Prakashan, 2012).

5. Ibid.

6. Interview with Umesh Prasad Singh, Socialist leader and close aide of Dr Rammanohar Lohia, Patna, 10 September 2022.

7. Dr Santosh Kumar, *Samajwad ke Vikas Me Bihari Nayakon Ki Bhumika* (Patna: Janaki Prakashan), 2019.

8. Interview with Surendra Kishore, Patna, senior journalist, 10 January 2022.

9. Ravindra Bharti, *Kapildeo Samagra*, Kapildeo Singh Samajwadi Foundation, Patna, 2007.

10. Interview with Shivanand Tiwari, former MP, Patna, 10 February 2022.

11. Dr Dilip Kumar, *Samajik Badlaw Aur Bihar* (Patna: Janaki Prakashan, 2015).

12. Prasanna Kumar Choudhary and Shrikant, *Bihar Mein Samajik Parivartan Ke Kucch Aayam*, (Patna: Vani Prakashan).

13. Interview with Prem Kumar Mani, Socialist leader and litterateur, 10 March 2022.

14. Francine R. Frankel and M.S.A. Rao, *Dominance of State Power in India: Decline of a Social Order* (Oxford University Press, 1989–90).

15. Dr Santosh Kumar, *Samajwad ke Vikas Me Bihari Nayakon Ki Bhumika* (Patna: Janaki Prakashan, 2019).

16. Interview with Shivanand Tiwari, Patna, 15 March 2022.

17. Ravindra Bharti, *Kapildeo Samagra*, Kapildeo Singh Samajwadi Foundation, Patna, 2007.

18. *Karpoori Thakur Ka Sansdiya Jeevan*, Pustakalaya Evam Shodh Sandarbh Shakha, Bihar Vidhan Sabha Sachivalaya, Patna, 2003.

19. Ibid.

20. Francine R. Frankel and M.S.A. Rao, *Dominance of State Power in India: Decline of a Social Order* (Oxford University Press, 1989–90).

21. Jeffrey Witsoe, *Democracy Against Development: Lower-Caste Politics and Political Modernity in Postcolonial India* (Chicago: University of Chicago Press, 2013).

22. Interview with Ramnath Thakur, Rajya Sabha MP, Karpoori Gram, Samastipur, 23 January 2023.

Chapter 6: 1967: Socialists' Tryst with Power

1. Interview with Umesh Prasad Singh, Socialist leader and close aide of Dr Rammanohar Lohia, Patna, 10 March 2022.

2. Nakamizo Kazuya, *Violence and Democracy: The Collapse of One-Party Dominant Rule in India* (Kyoto: University Press and Balwyn North Victoria: Trans Pacific Press, 2020).

3. Interview with Shivanand Tiwari, former MP, Patna, 2 January 2023.

4. Sho Kuwajima, *Peasants and Peasant Leaders in Contemporary History: A Case of Bihar in India* (New Delhi: LG Publishers Distributors, 2017).

5. Interview with Ramnath Thakur, JD (U) MP, Samastipur, 23 January 2023.

6. Radhanandan Jha, Bihar Vidhan Mandal, *Udbhav Aur Vikas*, Sharda Prakashan.

7. Ibid.

8. Vishnudev Rajak, *Karpoori Thakur Ka Rajnitik Darshan* (Patna: Janaki Prakashan, 2012).

9. Santosh Singh, *JP To BJP: Bihar After Lalu and Nitish* (Vitasta Sage Select, 2021).

10. Interview with Prem Kumar Mani, Socialist leader and former MLC, Patna, 20 January 2023.

11. Vishnudev Rajak, *Karpoori Thakur Ka Rajnitik Darshan* (Patna: Janaki Prakashan, 2012).

12. Interview with Gajendra Prasad Himanshu, former minister and socialist leader, Patna, 25 March 2023.

13. Interview with Prem Kumar Mani, Socialist leader, Patna, 10 May 2022.

14. Interview with Umesh Prasad Singh, Socialist leader and Dr Rammanohar Lohia's aide, 29 March 2023.

15. Ibid.
16. Interview with Dr Arjun Singh, son of former minister Kapildeo Singh, 10 August 2022.
17. Madhu Limaye, 'Main Kahta Rah gaya ki RSS ke saath hamara taalmel nahi baithta' (https://mediavigil.com/op-ed/document/coalition-with-rss-was-a-mistake-madhu-limaye/).
18. Naresh Kumar Vikal and Harinandan Sah, Saptkranti Ke Samvahak Jannayak Karpoori Thakur Smriti Granth (New Delhi: Prabhat Prakashan, 2019).
19. Ibid.
20. Speech of V.S. Dubey, former Bihar chief secretary, at the Centenary function of Kapildeo Singh, Babu Jagjivan Ram Shodh Sanasthan, Patna, 22 December 2022.
21. Ibid.
22. Manish Kumar Jha, Contentious Politics and Popular Movements: Enigma of Karpoori Thakur (https://mail.google.com/mail/u/0/#inbox/KtbxLzGStvfCsTNQCtKmngHWgDhpZChgbV?projector=1&messagePartId=0).
23. Narendra Pathak, Karpoori Thakur Aur Samajvad (New Delhi: Medha Books, 2016).
24. Interview with Ramnath Thakur, Samastipur, 22 January 2023.
25. Aryavarta, 25 December 1970.
26. S.K. Jain, Caste and Politics in India (New Delhi: Commonwealth Publishers, 1989).
27. L.P. Shahi, Bante Bihar Ka Sakshi (Patna: Sri Krishna Siksha Sansthan, 2008).
28. Narendra Pathak, Karpoori Thakur Aur Samajvad (New Delhi: Medha Books, 2016).
29. L.P. Shahi, Bante Bihar Ka Sakshi (Patna: Shrikrishna Siksha Sansthan, 2008).
30. Bihar Vidhan Sabha Mein Bindeshwari Prasad Mandal Ke Sambhashan, Bihar Rajya Abhilekhagar Nideshalaya, Cabinet Secretariat Department (Patna: Impression Publication, 2020).
31. Ibid.

32. Interview with Nikhil Mandal, JD (U) leader and B.P. Mandal's grandson, 2 August 2023.

33. L.P. Shahi, *Bante Bihar Ka Sakshi* (Patna: Sri Krishna Siksha Sansthan, 2008).

34. Francine R. Frankel and M.S.A. Rao, *Dominance of State Power in India: Decline of a Social Order* (Oxford University Press, 1989–90).

35. Jeffrey Witsoe, *Democracy Against Development: Lower-Caste Politics and Political Modernity in Postcolonial India* (Chicago: University of Chicago Press, 2013).

36. Interview with Ramnath Thakur, Patna, 10 August 2022.

37. Rambriksh Singh, Karpoori Gram villager, Samastipur, 3 October 2022.

Chapter 7: No English, Please

1. Prof. Keshav Rao Jadhav, ed., *Dr Rammanohar Lohia, Gandhi, Marx and Socialism* (Hyderabad: Lohia Vigyan Samiti, originally published in 1977, republished in www.indiatoday.com in 2019).

2. Interview with Surendra Kishore (then Surendra Akela), senior journalist and former personal assistant of Karpoori Thakur, Patna, 9 January 2023.

3. Jeffrey Witsoe, *Democracy Against Development: Lower-Caste Politics and Political Modernity in Postcolonial India* (Chicago: University of Chicago Press, 2013).

4. Naresh Kumar Vikal and Harinandan Sah,*Saptkranti Ke Samvahak Jannayak Karpoori Thakur Smriti Granth* (New Delhi: Prabhat Prakashan, 2019).

5. Prasanna Kumar Choudhary and Shrikant, *Bihar Mein Samajik Parivartan Ke Kucch Aayam* (Patna: Vani Prakashan, 2002).

6. Narendra Pathak, *Karpoori Thakur Aur Samajvad* (New Delhi: Medha Books, 2016).

7. Ibid.

8. Interview with Jagdanand Singh, RJD state president and former MP, Patna, 20 December 2022.

9.   Prem Kumar Mani, *Sach Yahi Nahi Hai* (New Delhi: Pustak Bhavan, 2012).

10.   Rajeev Ranjan Dwivedi, spokesperson, BSEB, Patna, 8 January 2023.

11.   Interview with Ramnath Thakur, JD (U) Rajya Sabha and Karpoori Thakur's elder son, 10 August 2022, over the phone.

12.   Interview with Bijendra Prasad Yadav, Bihar energy minister, Patna, 4 October 2022.

13.   Interview with Muneshwar Singh, villager, Karpoori Gram, Samastipur, 23 January 2023.

14.   Amarjeet Sinha, *An India for Everyone: A Path to Inclusive Development* (New Delhi: HarperCollins Publishers India, 2013).

15.   Naresh Kumar Vikal and Harinandan Sah, *Saptkranti Ke Samvahak Jannayak Karpoori Thakur Smriti Granth* (New Delhi: Prabhat Prakashan, 2019).

16.   Ibid.

17.   Mohammed Sajjad, 'Karpoori Thakur and the Power of Street Politics', https://m.rediff.com/amp/news/column/karpoori-thakur-and-the-power-of-street-politics/20190123.htm).

18.   Interview with Ramjivan Singh, Socialist leader and former MP, Begusarai, 12 July 2021.

19.   Naresh Kumar Vikal and Harinandan Sah, *Saptkranti Ke Samvahak Jannayak Karpoori Thakur Smriti Granth* (New Delhi: Prabhat Prakashan, 2019).

20.   Ibid.

21.   Ibid.

22.   Ibid.

23.   Interview with Ramnath Thakur, Rajya Sabha MP, 10 August 2022, over the phone.

24.   Interview with Manisha Priyam, professor, Department of Education Policy, National Institute for Educational Planning and Administration, New Delhi, 23 June 2023, through email.

25.   PM Narendra Modi's speech at Akhil Bhartiya Shiksha Samagam at Bharat Mandapam, New Delhi, 29 July 2023 (https://indianexpress.com/article/india/education-in-mother-tongue-initiating-new-form-of-justice-pm-modi-on-nep-anniversary-8866615/).

Chapter 8: Yes, Chief Minister

1. Shrikant, *Chitthiyon Ki Rajniti* (New Delhi: Vani Prakashan, 2012).
2. Interview with Surendra Kishore, senior journalist and former personal assistant of Karpoori Thakur, Patna, 11 August 2022.
3. Manish Kumar Jha, *Contentious Politics and Popular Movements: Enigma of Karpoori Thakur* (https://mail.google.com/mail/u/0/# inbox/KtbxLzGStvfCsTNQCtKmngHWgDhpZChgbV? projector=1&messagePartId=0.1).
4. Interview with Shivanand Tiwari, former MP, Patna, 12 September 2022.
5. Interview with Ramnath Thakur, JD (U) MP, Samastipur, 22 January 2023.
6. Neha Ranjan, *Adhunik Bihar Mein Jatiya Sangharsh* (Patna and New Delhi: Janaki Prakashan, 2015).
7. Mohammed Sajjad, 'Karpoori Thakur and the Power of Street Politics', https://m.rediff.com/amp/news/column/karpoori-thakur-and-the-power-of-street-politics/20190123.htm).
8. Radhanandan Jha, *Bihar Vidhanmandal: Udbhav Aur Vikas* (Patna: Sharda Prakashan).
9. Interview with Umesh Prasad Singh, a close aide of Dr Rammanohar Lohia, Patna, 12 April 2022.
10. Interview with Ramnath Thakur, JD (U) MP, Samastipur, 23 January 2023.
11. *Karpoori Thakur Ka Sansdiya Jeevan*, Pustakalaya Evam Shodh Sandarbh Shakha, Bihar Vidhan Sabha Sachivalaya, Patna, 2003.
12. Ibid.
13. Ibid.
14. *Aryavarta*, 25 December 1970.
15. *Karpoori Thakur Ka Sansdiya Jeevan*, Pustakalaya Evam Shodh Sandarbh Shakha, Bihar Vidhan Sabha Sachivalaya, Patna, 2003.
16. Interview with Shiv Kumar, close Karpoori aide, Patna, 7 January 2023.
17. Interview with, Socialist leader Umesh Prasad Singh, Patna, 10 October 2022.

18. Interview with Muneshwar Singh, villager, Karpoori Gram, Samastipur, 22 January 2023.

19. Interview with Bijendra Prasad Yadav, Bihar minister, Patna, 4 October 2022.

20. Santosh Singh, *JP to BJP: Bihar After Lalu and Nitish* (Vitasta Sage Select, 2021).

21. Interview with Anisur Rahman, former associate professor, LKVD College, Tajpur, Samastipur, 22 January 2023.

22. https://samtamarg.in/2023/08/26/that-conversation-between-karpoori-ji-and-his-son/.

23. Interview with Surendra Kishore, senior journalist and former personal assistant of Karpoori Thakur, Patna, 17 January 2023.

24. Santosh Singh, *Ruled or Misruled: The Story and Destiny of Bihar* (New Delhi: Bloomsbury, 2015).

25. Ibid.

26. Interview with A.N. Pandey, founder principal, Karpoori Phuleshwari Degree College, Karpoori Gram, Samastipur, 22 January 2022.

27. Santosh Singh, *Ruled or Misruled: The Story and Destiny of Bihar* (New Delhi: Bloomsbury, 2015).

28. Narendra Pathak, *Karpoori Aur Samajwad* (Delhi: Megha Books, 2016).

Chapter 9: Let's Go to JP

1. Letter of Karpoori Thakur to Jayaprakash Narayan, Naresh Kumar Vikal and Harinandan Sah, *Saptkranti Ke Samvahak Jannayak Karpoori Thakur Smriti Granth* (New Delhi: Prabhat Prakashan, 2019).

2. Vishnudev Rajak, *Karpoori Thakur Ka Rajnitik Darshan* (Patna: Janaki Prakashan, 2012).

3. Ibid.

4. Naresh Kumar Vikal and Harinandan Sah, *Saptkranti Ke Samvahak Jannayak Karpoori Thakur Smriti Granth* (New Delhi: Prabhat Prakashan, 2019).

5. Interview with Sushil Kumar Modi, Rajya Sabha MP and former Bihar deputy CM, Patna, 11 March 2022.

6. Interview with Ramnath Thakur, JD (U) Rajya Sabha MP, 21 May 2023.

7. Pupul Jayakar, *Indira Gandhi:a Biography* (New Delhi: Penguin Books India Limited, 1995).

8. Ibid.

9. Ibid.

10. Ibid.

11. Bimal Prasad and Sujata Prasad, *Dream of a Revolution: A Biography of Jayaprakash Narayan* (New Delhi: Penguin Random House India, 2021).

12. Ibid.

13. Interview with Ramnath Thakur, JD (U) MP, Samastipur, 23 January 2023.

14. Interview with Surendra Kishore, senior journalist, Patna, 17 January 2023.

15. Interview with Harivansh Narayan Singh, Rajya Sabha deputy chairman, Patna, 2 December 2022.

16. Interview with Shiv Kumar, Socialist leader and a close aide of Karpoori Thakur, Patna, 7 January 2023.

17. Interview with Ramnath Thakur, JD (U) MP, Samastipur, 22 January 2023.

18. Interview with Bijendra Prasad Yadav, Bihar energy minister, Patna, 4 October 2022.

19. Interview with Ramnath Thakur, JD (U) MP, Samastipur, 22 January 2023.

20. Ibid.

21. Ibid.

22. Ibid.

23. Interview with Noor Ahmad, a close Karpoori aide, 10 October 2022.

24. Ibid.

25. Interview with K.C. Tyagi, former MP, Delhi, 21 February 2023.

26. Naresh Kumar Vikal and Harinandan Sah, *Saptkranti Ke Samvahak Jannayak Karpoori Thakur Smriti Granth* (New Delhi: Prabhat Prakashan, 2019).

27. Ibid.

28. Ibid.

29. Ibid.
30. Interview with Muneshwar Singh, Karpoori Gram villager, 23 January 2023.
31. Ibid.
32. Naresh Kumar Vikal and Harinandan Sah, *Saptkranti Ke Samvahak Jannayak Karpoori Thakur Smriti Granth* (New Delhi: Prabhat Prakashan, 2019).
33. Ibid.
34. Interview with K.C. Tyagi, former MP, 10 January 2023, over the phone.
35. Vishnudev Rajak, *Karpoori Thakur Ka Rajnitik Darshan* (Patna: Janaki Prakashan, 2012).
36. Naresh Kumar Vikal and Harinandan Sah, *Saptkranti Ke Samvahak Jannayak Karpoori Thakur Smriti Granth* (New Delhi: Prabhat Prakashan, 2019).
37. Narendra Pathak, *Karpoori Thakur Aur Samajvad* (New Delhi: Medha Books, 2016).
38. Interview with Ramnath Thakur, JD (U) MP, Samastipur, 23 January 2023.
39. Shashidhar Khan, *Naxal Andolan Ke Pachas Saal, Raasta Kidhar?* (Kanpur: Aman Prakashan, 2021).
40. Ibid.
41. Interview with Shiv Kumar, Socialist leader and a close aide of Karpoori Thakur, Patna, 7 January 2023.
42. Vishnudev Rajak, *Karpoori Thakur Ka Rajnitik Darshan* (Patna: Janaki Prakashan, 2012).
43. Interview with Dr Birendra K. Thakur, Patna, 20 February 2023.
44. Ibid.
45. Ibid.
46. Ibid.

Chapter 10: Pioneering Quota Politics

1. Interview with Karpoori Thakur, 9 October 1982, Dr Narendra Pathak, *Karpoori Aur Samajwad* (New Delhi: Medha Books, 2016).

2. Shantanu Gupta, *Bharatiya Janata Party, Past, Present and Future: Story of the World's Largest Political Party* (Delhi: Rupa Publications, 2020).

3. Coomi Kapoor, *The Emergency, A Personal History* (Gurgaon: Penguin Random House India, 2015).

4. Harivansh and Ravi Dutt Bajpai, *Chandra Shekhar:The Last Icon of Ideological Politics* (Delhi: Rupa Publications, 2019).

5. Ashwani Kumar, *The Community Warriors: State, Peasants and Caste Armies in Bihar* (London, Anthem Press, 2008).

6. Harry W. Blair, 'Rising Kulaks and Backward Classes in Bihar: Social Change in the Late 1970s', *Economic and Political Weekly*, Vol. 15, No. 2, 12 January 1980, p. 67.

7. Francine R. Frankel and M.S.A. Rao, *Dominance of State Power in India: Decline of a Social Order* (Oxford: Oxford University Press, 1989–90).

8. Lalit Kumar, *Shrimakon Ke Hitaishi Neta Itihas Purush Basavan Singh*, (Patna: Bihar Hindi Granth Akademi, 2000).

9. Arun Sinha, 'Janata Elects a Leader', *Economic and Political Weekly*, Vol. 12, No. 26,25 June 1977), p. 1001.

10. Interview with Ram Lakhan Singh Yadav, 10 October 1979. He was interviewed by Narendra Pathak.

11. Interview with Nikhil Kumar, former MP and ex-governor and son of former CM Satyendra Narayan Sinha, Patna, 26 July 2022.

12. L.P. Shahi, *Bante Bihar ka Sakshi*, (Patna: Shrikrishna Shiksha Pratisthana).

13. Nakamizo Kazuya, *Violence and Democracy: The Collapse of One-Party Dominant Rule in India* (Kyoto: University Press, and Balwyn North Victoria: Trans Pacific Press, 2020.

14. Mohammed Sajjad, 'Karpoori Thakur and the Power of Street Politics' https://m.rediff.com/amp/news/column/karpoori-thakur-and-the-power-of-street-politics/20190123.htm.

15. Francine R. Frankel and M.S.A. Rao, *Dominance of State Power in India: Decline of a Social Order* (Oxford: Oxford University Press, 1989–90).

16. Narendra Pathak, *Karpoori Aur Samajwad* (New Delhi: Medha Books, 2016).

17. D.N. Gautam, *Agneepath Se Nyaypath* (New Delhi: Prabhat Prakashan, 2022).

18. Interview with Umesh Prasad Singh, a close aide of Dr Rammamnohar Lohia, Patna, 25 January 2022.

19. Ravindra Bharti, *RJD Samachar* (Ranchi: Doranda Press, January–February 2022).

20. *RJD Samachar* (Ranchi: Doranda Press, January–February 2022).

21. Interview with Sushil Kumar Modi, BJP Rajya Sabha MP, Patna, 11 March 2022.

22. Naresh Kumar Vikal and Harinandan Sah, *Saptkranti Ke Samvahak Jannayak Karpoori Thakur Smriti Granth* (New Delhi: Prabhat Prakashan, 2019).

23. Interview with Dr Jagannath Mishra, former Bihar CM, Patna, 10 August 2015.

24. *Karpoori Thakur Ka Sansdiya Jeevan*, Pustakalaya Evam Shodh Sandarbh Shakha, Bihar Vidhan Sabha Sachivalaya, Patna, 2003.

25. Interview with Jabir Hussain, former minister, *Saptkranti Ke Samvahak Jannayak Karpoori Thakur Smriti Granth* (New Delhi: Prabhat Prakashan, 2019).

26. Ibid.

27. A note written by Karpoori Thakur in June 1977, Rajya Sabha MP Ramnath Thakur, 21 October 2022.

28. Interview with Shiv Kumar, Barbigha Socialist leader, Patna, 7 January 2023.

29. Yashwant Sinha, *Relentless:An Autobiography* (New Delhi: Bloomsbury India, 2019).

30. Interview with Shiv Kumar, a socialist leader from Barbigha and a close aide of Karpoori Thakur, Patna, 7 January 2023.

31. Yashwant Sinha, *Relentless: An Autobiography* (New Delhi: Bloomsbury India, 2019).

32. Mohammed Sajjad, 'Karpoori Thakur and the Power of Street Politics' https://m.rediff.com/amp/news/column/karpoori-thakur-and-the-power-of-street-politics/20190123.htm.

33. Interview with D.N. Gautam, former Bihar DGP, Patna, 10 December 2022.

34. Interview with Dr Arjun Singh, son of former minister Kapildeo Singh, Patna, 11 October 2022.

35. *Karpoori Thakur Ka Sansdiya Jeevan*, Pustakalaya Evam Shodh Sandarbh Shakha, Bihar Vidhan Sabha Sachivalaya, Patna, 2003.

36. Interview with Shivanand Tiwari, former Rajya Sabha MP, Patna, 2 January 2023.

37. Dhirubhai Seth, *Satta Aur Samaj*, Lok-Tilak Granthmala (New Delhi: Vani Prakashan, 2009).

38. Yashwant Sinha, *Relentless:An Autobiography* (New Delhi: Bloomsbury India, 2019).

39. Aastha Singh, 'Karpoori Thakur, the other Bihar CM who banned alcohol', The Print, 24 January 2019, https://theprint.in/theprint-profile/karpoori-thakur-the-other-bihar-cm-who-banned-alcohol/182593/.

40. *Karpoori Thakur Ka Sansdiya Jeevan*, Pustakalaya Evam Shodh Sandarbh Shakha, Bihar Vidhan Sabha Sachivalaya, Patna, 2003.

41. Ibid.

42. Seema Chisti, 'One Diwali, Bihar Got a Novel Reservation Policy. Can India Think Beyond Mandal?'https://www.thequint.com/voices/opinion/how-mandal-commission-data-reflects-indias-backwardness-in-identifying-caste#read-more.

43. Neerja Chowdhury, *How Prime Ministers Decide* (New Delhi: Aleph Book Company, 2023).

44. Letter No. 11/1-501/78756-11, Bihar Government Personnel and Administrative Reforms Department Resolution, 10 November 1978.

45. Letter No. 1-501/78- 755-10 in No. 11, Bihar Government Personnel and Administrative Reforms Department Resolution, 10 November 1978.

46. Letter No. 11/Pr.01-501/78--757-. Bihar Government Personnel and Administrative Reforms Department of Resolution, 10 November 1978.

47. Christophe Jaffrelot, *India's Silent Revolution: The Rise of the Lower Castes in North India* (New York: Columbia University Press, 2003).

48. Ibid.

49. Ibid.

50. Mohammed Sajjad, 'Karpoori Thakur and the Power of Street Politics' https://m.rediff.com/amp/news/column/karpoori-thakur-and-the-power-of-street-politics/20190123.htm.

51. Narendra Pathak, *Karpoori Thakur Aur Samajvad* (New Delhi: Medha Books, 2016).

52. Ibid.

53. Ibid.

54. Jagpal Singh, 'Karpoori Thakur: A Socialist Leader in the Hindi Belt', *Economic and Political Weekly*, Vol. 50, No. 3 (17 January 2015), pp. 54–60. https://www.jstor.org/stable/24481124).

55. Manish Kumar Jha, 'Contentious Politics and Popular Movements: Enigma of Karpoori Thakur' (https://mail.google.com/mail/u/0/#inbox/KtbxLzGStvfCsTNQCtKmngHWgDhpZChgbV?projector=1&messagePartId=0.1).

56. Narendra Pathak, *Karpoori Thakur Aur Samajvad* (New Delhi: Medha Books, 2016).

57. Ashwani Kumar, *The Community Warriors: State, Peasants and Caste Armies in Bihar* (London: Anthem Press, 2008).

58. Francine R. Frankel and M.S.A. Rao, *Dominance of State Power in India: Decline of a Social Order* (Oxford: Oxford University Press, 1989–90).

59. Jagpal Singh, 'Karpoori Thakur: A Socialist Leader in the Hindi Belt', *Economic and Political Weekly*, Vol. 50, No. 3 (17 January 2015), pp. 54–60. https://www.jstor.org/stable/24481124.

60. Interview with Sushil Kumar Modi, Rajya Sabha MP and former Bihar deputy CM, 11 March 2022.

61. Interview with Ramnath Thakur, JD (U) Rajya Sabha MP and Karpoori Thakur's elder son, 10 December 2022, over the phone.

62. Ravindra Bharti, *Kapildeo Samagra*, Kapildeo Singh Samajwadi Foundation, Patna, 2007.

63. *Dinman*, Narendra Pathak, *Karpoori Thakur Aur Samajvad* (New Delhi: Medha Books, 2016).

64. *Karpoori Thakur Ka Sansdiya Jeevan*, Pustakalaya Evam Shodh Sandarbh Shakha, Bihar Vidhan Sabha Sachivalaya, Patna, 2003.

65. Interview with Anil Chamaria, senior journalist, on Zoom, 4 October 2022.

66. Interview with Harivansh Narayan Singh, Rajya Sabha deputy chairperson and senior journalist, Patna, 2 December 2022.

67. December 1978 issue of *India Today (Hindi)*.

68. Interview with Jagdanand Singh, RJD state president and former MP, Patna, 20 December 2022.

69. Interview with Mantosh Kumar, 2 November 2023.

70. *Indra Sawhney Etc. vs Union Of India And Others, Etc* . . . on 16 November 1992 (AIR 1993 SC 477, 1992 Supp 2 SCR 454).

71. Ibid.

72. U.S. Department of Justice, *Fisher vs. University of Texas at Austin et al.*, 23 June 2016,Retrieved from https://www.justice.gov/d9/fisher_v._university_of_texas_no._14-981_issued_06-23-16.pdf.

73. Library of Congress, *Metro Broadcasting, Inc. v. Federal Communications Commission*,(1990), Retrieved from https://www.loc.gov/item/usrep497547.

74. Library of Congress, *Fullilove v. Philip M. Klutznick*, (1980), Retrieved from https://tile.loc.gov/storage-services/service/ll/usrep/usrep448/usrep448448/usrep448448.pdf.

75. Interview with Ramnath Thakur, Rajya Sabha MP and elder son of Karpoori Thakur, Karpoori Gram, Samastipur, 22–23 January 2023.

76. Farzand Ahmed, 'Resentment in 'upper' castes over Bihar govt's move to reserve jobs for backward castes', *India Today*, 15 April 1978, https://www.indiatoday.in/magazine/states/story/19780415-resentment-in-upper-castes-over-bihar-govts-move-to-reserve-jobs-for-backward-castes-822914-2014-12-22.

77. Ibid.

78. Ibid.

79. Ibid.

80. *Karpoori Thakur Ka Sansdiya Jeevan*, Pustakalaya Evam Shodh Sandarbh Shakha, Bihar Vidhan Sabha Sachivalaya, Patna, 2003.

81. Yashwant Sinha, *Relentless: An Autobiography* (New Delhi: Bloomsbury India, 2019).

82. *Karpoori Thakur Ka Sansdiya Jeevan*, Pustakalaya Evam Shodh Sandarbh Shakha, Bihar Vidhan Sabha Sachivalaya, Patna, 2003.

83. Ibid.

84. Ibid.

85. Yashwant Sinha, *Relentless: An Autobiography* (New Delhi: Bloomsbury India, 2019).

86. *Karpoori Thakur Ka Sansdiya Jeevan*, Pustakalaya Evam Shodh Sandarbh Shakha, Bihar Vidhan Sabha Sachivalaya, Patna, 2003.

87. Ibid.

88. Interview with Jagdanand Singh, RJD state president and former MP, Patna, 20 December 2022.

89. Santosh Singh, 'Forgotten by All Belchhi Struggles to Remember Indira', *Indian Express*, \https://indianexpress.com/article/news-archive/web/forgotten-by-all-belchhi-struggles-to-remember-indira/; Manish Kumar Jha, 'Contentious Politics and Popular Movements: Enigma of Karpoori Thakur' (https://mail.google.com/mail/u/0/#inbox/KtbxLzGStvfCsTNQCtKmn gHWgDhpZChgbV?projector=1&messagePartId=0.1).

90. Santosh Singh, 'A lasting signature on Bihar's most violent years', *Indian Express*, 4 June 2012, http://archive.indianexpress.com/news/a-lasting-signature-on-bihar-s-most-violent-years/957421/0).

91. Rajendra Sharma, *Karpoori Ji Ka Jeevan Sangram*, 1979, *Saptkranti Ke Samvahak Jannayak Karpoori Thakur Smriti Granth* (New Delhi: Prabhat Prakashan, 2019).

92. Interview with Ramnath Thakur, Samastipur, 23 January 2023.

93. Yashwant Sinha, *Relentless: An Autobiography* (New Delhi: Bloomsbury India, 2019).

94. Interview with Prem Kumar Mani, 1 February 2024.

95. Yashwant Sinha, *Relentless: An Autobiography* (New Delhi: Bloomsbury India, 2019).

96. Interview with Prem Kumar Mani, author and socialist leader, 10 October 2022.

97. Interview with Manisha Priyam, professor, Department of Education Policy, National Institute for Educational Planning and Administration, New Delhi, 23 June 2023, over the phone and through email.

98. Neerja Chowdhury, *How Prime Ministers Decide* (New Delhi: Aleph Book Company, 2023).

99. Ravindra Bharti, *Kapildeo Samagra*, Kapildeo Singh Samajwadi Foundation, Patna, 2007.

100. Ibid.

101. Ibid.

102. Ibid.

103. Ibid.

104. Jagpal Singh, 'Karpoori Thakur: A Socialist Leader in the Hindi Belt,' *Economic and Political Weekly*, Vol 50, No. 3, 17 January 2015.

105. Christophe Jaffrelot, *India's Silent Revolution: The Rise of the Lower Castes in North India* (New York: Columbia University Press, 2003).

Chapter 11: Caste Catches Up

1. Interview with Vijaywant Choudhary, leader, Dalsinghsarai, Samastipur, 6 May 2022.

2. Interview with Harivansh Narayan Singh, Rajya Sabha deputy chairperson, Patna, 2 December 2022.

3. Interview with Shiv Kumar, a close Karpoori Thakur aide and Barbigha leader, Patna, 7 January 2023.

4. Interview with Gajendra Prasad Himanshu, socialist leader and former minister, Patna, 25 March 2023.

5. Christophe Jaffrelot, *India's Silent Revolution: The Rise of Lower Castes in North India* (New York: Columbia University Press, 2003).

6. Interview with Sushil Kumar Modi, BJP Rajya Sabha MP and former Bihar deputy CM, Patna, 11 March 2022.

7. Interview with Durga Prasad Sah, former MLA, Samastipur, 6 May 2022.

8. Ibid.

9. Ibid.

10. Interview with Prem Kumar Mani, socialist leader and littérateur, Patna, 14 January 2022.

11. *Karpoori Thakur Ka Sansdiya Jeevan*, Pustakalaya Evam Shodh Sandarbh Shakha, Bihar Vidhan Sabha Sachivalaya, Patna, 2003.

12. Interview with K.C. Tyagi, former MP, 14 February 2023, over the phone.

13. Interview with Durga Prasad Sah, former MLA, Samastipur, 6 May 2022.

14. Ibid.

15. *Karpoori Thakur Ka Sansdiya Jeevan*, Pustakalaya Evam Shodh Sandarbh Shakha, Bihar Vidhan Sabha Sachivalaya, Patna, 2003.

16. Interview with Shiv Kumar, a close Karpoori Thakur aide and Barbigha leader, Patna, 7 January 2023.

17. Ranjana Kumari, *Karpoori Thakur: Neta Virodhi Dal Ke Rup Mein Sanasdiya Bhoomika* (Patna: Rajkamal Prakashan, 2003).

18. Rahul Ramagundam, *The Life and Times of George Fernandes* (Gurgaon: Penguin Random House India, 2022).

19. Interview with Vijaywant Choudhary, a close Karpoori Thakur aide, Dalsinghsarai, Samastipur, 6 May 2023.

20. Ibid.

21. Ibid.

22. Nijat Ali Dehlvi, *Dinman*, 16–21 December 1984.

23. Interview with Ramnath Thakur, Samastipur, 23 January 2023. Thakur had interviewed Rai.

24. Francine R. Frankel and M.S.A. Rao, *Dominance of State Power in India: Decline of a Social Order* (Oxford: Oxford University Press, 1989–90).

25. Akashwani, 13 December 1984.

26. Interview with Asha Rani, daughter-in-law of Karpoori Thakur and wife of JD (U) MP Ramnath Thakur, Delhi, 19 August 2019.

27. Interview with Bijendra Yadav, Bihar energy minister, Patna, 4 October 2022.

28. Interview with Shaad Anwar, grandson of Anwarul Haque, Patna, 28 May 2023.

29. Pradeep Shrivastava, *Ramvilas Paswan: Sankalp, Sahas Aur Sangharsh* (Gurgaon: Penguin Random House India, 2020).

30. Ibid.

31. Ibid.

32. Ibid.

33. Ibid.

34. Interview with Ram Vilas Paswan, 5 June 2021, over the phone.

35. Ibid.

36. Interview with Gajendra Prasad Himanshu, veteran socialist leader and former minister, Patna, 25 March 2023.

37. Pradeep Shrivastava, *Ramvilas Paswan: Sankalp, Sahas Aur Sangharsh*, (Gurgaon: Penguin Random House India, 2020).

38. Interview with Bijendra Prasad Yadav, Bihar energy minister, Patna, 4 October 2022.

39. Naresh Kumar Vikal and Harinandan Sah, *Saptkranti Ke Samvahak Jannayak Karpoori Thakur Smriti Granth* (New Delhi: Prabhat Prakashan, 2019).

40. Ibid.

41. Mithilesh Kumar, 'Making of a Populist Government: A Study of Karpoori Thakur's Regime'https://mail.google.com/mail/u/0/#inbox/KtbxLzGStvfCsTNQCtKmngHWgDhpZChgbV?projector=1&messagePartId=0.1).

42. Interview with Anil Chamaria, senior journalist, 4 October 2022.

43. Excerpt from a speech by Karpoori Thakur as Leader of the Opposition in the Bihar Legislative Assembly, 1985, Shrikant, *Bihar Me Chunav: Jati, Booth loot Aur Himsa* (Delhi: Vani Prakashan, 2002).

44. Interview with Ali Anwar, former Rajya Sabha MP, Patna, 13 March 2022.

45. Ibid.

46. Interview with Harivansh Narayan Singh, senior journalist and Rajya Sabha deputy chairperson, Patna, 2 December 2022.

47. Interview with Deepak Kumar, senior photojournalist, Patna, 19 January 2020.

48. Interview with Dr Arjun Singh, son of former minister Kapildeo Singh, Patna, 10 August 2022.

49. Interview with Jagdanand Singh, former MP and RJD state president, Patna, 20 December 2023.

50. Naresh Kumar Vikal and Harinandan Sah, *Saptkranti Ke Samvahak Jannayak Karpoori Thakur Smriti Granth* (New Delhi: Prabhat Prakashan, 2019).

51. Interview with Ramnath Thakur, JD (U) MP, Samastipur, 22 January 2023.

52. Interview with Durga Prasad Sah, former MLA, Samastipur, 6 May
     2022. Sah had quoted Choudhary.

Chapter 12: The Salty Solution and the Death Mystery

1.   Interview with Ramjivan Singh, former minister and ex-MP,
     Manjhual, Begusarai, 10 March 2020.
2.   Last speech during call attention notice in Bihar Vidhan Sabha,
     Saptkranti Ke Samvahak Jannayak Karpoori Thakur Smriti Granth
     (New Delhi: Prabhat Prakashan, 2019).
3.   Interview with Ganga Prasad, senior journalist, 18 March 2023, over
     the phone.
4.   Interview with Dr Birendra K. Thakur, Patna, 20 February 2023.
5.   Interview with Dr Arjun Singh, son of former minister Kapildeo
     Singh, Patna, 19 March 2023.
6.   Ibid.
7.   Interview with Ramnath Thakur, JD (U) MP, 21 May 2023, over
     the phone.
8.   Socialist leader and former UP CM Hemvati Nandan Bahuguna,
     Saptkranti Ke Samvahak Jannayak Karpoori Thakur Smriti Granth
     (New Delhi: Prabhat Prakashan, 2019).
9.   Interview with Ganga Prasad, senior journalist, 18 March 2023, over
     the phone.
10. Interview with Muneshwar Singh, a close aide of Karpoori Thakur,
     Samastipur, 23 January 2023.
11. MLA Raghuvansh Prasad Singh's letter to PM Rajiv Gandhi,
     Saptkranti Ke Samvahak Jannayak Karpoori Thakur Smriti Granth
     (New Delhi: Prabhat Prakashan, 2019).
12. Naresh Kumar Vikal and Harinandan Sah, *Saptkranti Ke Samvahak
     Jannayak Karpoori Thakur Smriti Granth* (New Delhi: Prabhat
     Prakashan, 2019).
13. Interview with Dr Birendra K. Thakur, younger son of Karpoori
     Thakur, Patna, 20 February 2023.
14. Kumar Amrendra, *Karpoori Thakur: Jan se Nayak Tak* (Patna: Jagriti
     Sahitya Prakashan, 2016).

15. Interview with Dr C.P. Thakur, former Union minister and personal doctor of Karpoori Thakur, Patna, 3 May 2023.

16. Interview with Ramnath Thakur, JD (U) MP, 21 May 2023, over the phone.

17. Interview with Kanaklata Thakur, younger daughter-in-law of Karpoori Thakur, Patna, 20 February 2023.

18. Naresh Kumar Vikal and Harinandan Sah, *Saptkranti Ke Samvahak Jannayak Karpoori Thakur Smriti Granth* (New Delhi: Prabhat Prakashan, 2019).

19. Interview with Surendra Kishore, senior journalist and former personal assistant of Karpoori Thakur, 10 March 2023, over the phone.

20. Krishna Kumar Verma, *Shambook*, Issue 14, 15 August 1999.

21. Lalu Prasad, RJD national president, at the RJD function to commemorate the socialist leader on his 92nd birth anniversary.

22. Ibid.

23. Madan Kumar, 'Karpoori died premature because of torture by political opponents, says Lalu', *Times of India*, 24 January 2016, https://timesofindia.indiatimes.com/india/karpoori-died-premature-because-of-torture-by-political-opponents-says-lalu/articleshow/50709256.cms?from=mdr.

24. *Karpoori Thakur Ka Sansdiya Jeevan*, Pustakalaya Evam Shodh Sandarbh Shakha, Bihar Vidhan Sabha Sachivalaya, Patna, 2003.

25. Nitish Kumar, MLA, *Saptkranti Ke Samvahak Jannayak Karpoori Thakur Smriti Granth* (New Delhi: Prabhat Prakashan, 2019).

26. George Fernandes, *Saptkranti Ke Samvahak Jannayak Karpoori Thakur Smriti Granth* (New Delhi: Prabhat Prakashan, 2019).

27. CM Bhagwat Jha Azad, Bihar Legislative Assembly, *Karpoori Thakur Ka Sansdiya Jeevan*, Pustakalaya Evam Shodh Sandarbh Shakha, Bihar Vidhan Sabha Sachivalaya, Patna, 2003.

28. Naresh Kumar Vikal and Harinandan Sah, *Saptkranti Ke Samvahak Jannayak Karpoori Thakur Smriti Granth* (New Delhi: Prabhat Prakashan, 2019).

29. Ravindra Bharti, *Kapildeo Singh Samagra*, Kapildeo Singh Samajwadi Foundation, Patna, 2007.

30. *Aryavarta, Saptkranti Ke Samvahak Jannayak Karpoori Thakur Smriti Granth* (New Delhi: Prabhat Prakashan, 2019).

31. Former MP Shivanand Tiwari, *Saptkranti Ke Samvahak Jannayak Karpoori Thakur Smriti Granth* (New Delhi: Prabhat Prakashan, 2019).

32. Litterateur Robin Shaw Pushp, *Saptkranti Ke Samvahak Jannayak Karpoori Thakur Smriti Granth* (New Delhi: Prabhat Prakashan, 2019).

Chapter 13: The Family Man

1.   Interview with Ramjivan Singh, former Bihar minister and ex-MP, Manjhaul, Begusarai, 2020.

2.   Interview with Ramnath Thakur, JD (U) MP, Karpoori Gram, Samastipur, 23 January 2023.

3.   Santosh Singh, *JP to BJP: Bihar After Lalu and Nitish* (New Delhi: Vitasta Sage Select, 2021).

4.   Interview with Ramnath Thakur, JD (U) MP, Karpoori Gram, Samastipur, 23 January 2023.

5.   Ibid.

6.   Ibid.

7.   Ibid.

8.   Ibid.

9.   Sansad TV, available at https://youtu.be/gwITiWYqQT0).

10. Interview with Ramnath Thakur, 10 March 2022, over the phone.

11. Interview with Arvind Singh, villager, Karpoori Gram, Samastipur, 23 January 2023.

12. Interview with Ramnath Thakur, JD (U) MP, Karpoori Gram, Samastipur, 23 January 2023.

13. Interview with Asha Rani, wife of Ramnath Thakur, New Delhi, 17 August 2019.

14. Ibid.

15. Ibid.

16. Ibid.

17. Interview with Dr Abhinav Vikas, grandson of Karpoori Thakur, Patna, 10 July 2023.

18. Interview with Dr Birendra K. Thakur, younger son of Karpoori Thakur, Patna, 20 February 2023.

19. Ibid.

20. Interview with Kanaklata Thakur, wife of Dr Birendra K. Thakur, Patna, 20 February 2023.

21. Ibid.

22. Ibid.

23. Interview with Surendra Kishore, senior journalist and former personal assistant of Karpoori Thakur, 10 March 2022, over the phone.

24. *Ek Activist ki Notebook*, *Kapildeo Samagra*, Kapildeo Singh Samajwadi Foundation, Patna, 2007.

25. Interview with Dr Arjun Singh, son of former minister Kapildeo Singh, Patna, 15 March 2022.

26. Interview with Namita Kumari, granddaughter of Karpoori Thakur, 28 June 2023, through WhatsApp audio call.

27. Ibid.

28. Ibid.

29. Ibid.

30. Ibid.

31. Interview with Sneha, granddaughter of Karpoori Thakur, 2 July 2023, over the phone.

32. Ibid.

33. Interview with Ranjit Kumar, husband of Namita Kumari and IRS officer, Patna, 26 February 2023.

34. Ibid.

35. Interview with Sushil Kumar Modi, former Rajya Sabha MP, 11 March 2022.

Chapter 14: The Trail of Camphor

1. Chanelle Adams, 'The Trail of The Camphor', Adi Magazine, Fall 2022, https://adimagazine.com/articles/trail-camphor/.

2. Interview with Harivansh Narayan Singh, Patna, 2 December 2022.

3.   Santosh Singh, *Ruled or Misruled: The Story and Destiny of Bihar*, (New Delhi: Bloomsbury India, 2015).

4.   Interview with Prem Kumar Mani, Socialist leader and litterateur, Patna, 13 December 2022.

5.   Interview with Shaibal Gupta, social scientist, Patna, 10 January 2015.

6.   Interview with Gajendra Prasad Himanshu, socialist leader and former minister, Patna 25 March 2023.

7.   Raghav Sharan Sharma, *Yugpurush Dr Sri Krishna Singh: Prabal Rashtravadi* (New Delhi: Pustak Pratisthan, 2017).

8.   Ibid.

9.   Ibid.

10. Interview with Surendra Kishore, senior journalist, 19 July 2023, over the phone.

11. Santosh Singh, *Ruled or Misruled:The Story and Destiny of Bihar* (New Delhi: Bloomsbury, 2015).

12. Ibid.

13. Lalu Prasad Yadav and Nalin Verma, *Gopalganj to Raisina: My Political Journey* (Delhi: Rupa Publications, 2019).

14. Santosh Singh, *Ruled or Misruled: The Story and Destiny of Bihar* (New Delhi: Bloomsbury, 2015).

15. Ibid.

16. Lalu Prasad Yadavand Nalin Verma, *Gopalganj to Raisina: My Political Journey* (Delhi: Rupa Publications, 2019).

17. Abhishek Ranjan and Santosh Dubey, *Show or Substance* (Chennai: Notion Press, 2020).

18. Ibid.

19. Manoj Chaurasia, *Rabri Devi: Lalu's Masterstroke* (New Delhi: Vitasta Publishing, 2008).

20. Lalu Prasad Yadav and Nalin Verma, *Gopalganj to Raisina: My Political Journey* (Delhi: Rupa Publications, 2019).

21. Santosh Singh, *Ruled or Misruled: The Story and Destiny of Bihar* (New Delhi: Bloomsbury, 2015).

22. N.K. Singh, *The Politics of Change: A Ringside View* (New Delhi: Penguin Books India, 2007).

23. Sunita Lal and Shaibal Gupta, *Resurrection of the State: A Saga of Bihar* (NewDelhi: Manak Publications, 2013).

24. Sankarshan Thakur, *Single Man: Life and Times of Nitish Kumar of Bihar* (Gurgaon, HarperCollins Publishers India, 2014).

25. Abhishek Ranjan and Santosh Dubey, *Show or Substance* (Chennai, Notion Press, 2020).

26. Chief Minister's Office (Public Relations Cell), Press release Number-cm-81 24/01/2023, Patna, 24 January 2023.

27. Interview with Harivansh Narayan Singh, Patna, 2 December 2022.

28. Interview with Prem Kumar Mani, socialist leader and litterateur, Patna,14 December 2022.

29. Interview with Lalbabu Lal, former Congress MLC and nephew of Mungeri Lal,10 February 2023.

30. Dr Santosh Kumar, *Samajwad Ke Vikas Mein Bihari Nayakon Ki Bhoomika* (New Delhi: Janaki Prakashan, 2019).

31. Interview with Gajendra Prasad Himanshu,socialist leader and former minister, Patna, 25 March 2023.

32. Narendra Pathak, *Karpoori Thakur Aur Samajwad* (New Delhi: Medha Books, 2016).

33. Interview with Sushil Kumar Modi, BJP Rajya Sabha MP, Patna, 11 March 2022.

34. Ibid.

35. Interview with Shivanand Tiwari, former MP and RJD national vice president, 23 July 2023, over the phone.

36. Ibid.

37. Ibid.

38. Ibid.

39. Interview with Ali Anwar, former Rajya Sabha MP, Patna, 10 May 2023.

40. Ali Anwar, *Masawat Ki Jung: The Battle for Equality* (New Delhi: Forward Press, 2023).

41. Interview with Prem Kumar Mani, social thinker and former MLC, 23 July 2023, over the phone.

42. Ibid.

43. Pratap Bhanu Mehta, 'Pratap Bhanu Mehta writes: The mirage of social justice', *Indian Express*, 23 April 2023, https://indianexpress.com/article/opinion/columns/pratap-bhanu-mehta-opposition-social-justice-8569145/.

44. Manoj Kumar Jha and Ghazala Jamil, 'Manoj Kumar Jha and Ghazala Jamil write: Why Pratap Bhanu Mehta is wrong about social justice politics and caste census', *Indian Express*, 29 April 2023, https://indianexpress.com/article/opinion/columns/pratap-bhanu-mehta-social-justice-politics-caste-census-8581223/.

45. Interview with Manish Kumar, assistant professor of Economics, Yadunandan College, Dighwara, Saran, JP University, Chhapra, 7 August 2023.

46. Interview with Shyamlal Yadav, senior journalist and author, 20 August 2023, over the phone.

47. Ashutosh Varshney, Brown University, Third Manoj Srivastava Memorial Lecture, Patna, 18 August 2023.

48. Nilay Upadhyay, noted Hindi poet, Second Manoj Srivastava Memorial Lecture, Patna, 13 August 2022.

Further Reading

Abhishek Ranjan and Santosh Dubey, *Show or Substance* (Chennai: Notion Press, 2020).

Ali Anwar, *Masawat Ki Jung: The Battle for Equality* (New Delhi: Forward Press, 2023).

Amarjeet Sinha, *An India for Everyone: A Path to Inclusive Development* (New Delhi: HarperCollins Publishers India, 2013).

Anant Shukla, *Bihar Mein Rajnitik Hinsa: Kaaran–Nivaran* (Patna: Janaki Prakashan, 2014).

Arun Sinha, *Batlle for Bihar:Nitish Kumar and the Theatre of Power* (Gurgaon: Penguin Random House India, 2020).

Arvind N. Das, *Republic of Bihar* (New Delhi: Penguin Books India, 1992).

Ashwani Kumar, *The Community Warriors: State, Peasants and Caste Armies in Bihar* (London: Anthem Press, 2008).

Bimal Prasad and Sujata Prasad, *The Dream of Revolution: A Biography of Jayaprakash Narayan* (Gurgaon: Penguin Random House India, 2021).

Christophe Jaffrelot, *India's Silent Revolution: The Rise of the Lower Castes in North India*, (New York: Columbia University Press, 2003).

Coomi Kapoor,*The Emergency:A Personal History* (Gurgaon: Penguin Random House India, 2015).

D.N. Gautam, *Agneepath Se Nyaypath* (New Delhi: Prabhat Prakashan, 2022).

Dhirubhai Seth, *Satta Aur Samaj*, Lok-Tilak Granthmala (New Delhi: Vani Prakashan, 2009).

Dr Dilip Kumar, *Samajik Badlaw Aur Bihar* (Patna: Janaki Prakashan, 2015).

Dr Santosh Kumar, *Samajwad Ke Vikas Mein Bihari Nayakon Ki Bhoomika* (New Delhi: Janaki Prakashan, 2019).

Fanishwarnath Renu, *Naye Savere Ki Aasha: Janvani* (Varanasi, January 1950 edition).

Francine R. Frankeland M.S.A. Rao, *Dominance of State Power in India: Decline of a Social Order* (Oxford University Press, 1989–90).

Hari Kishore Singh, *A History of The Praja Socialist Party (1935–1959)* (Lucknow: Narendra Prakashan, 1959).

Harivansh andRavi Dutt Bajpei,*Chandra Shekhar: The Last Icon of Ideological Politics* (Delhi: Rupa Publications, 2019).

Hemant, *Biharnama*, Bihar Vidhan Parishad.

Hemant, *Biharnama*, Bihar Vidhan Parishad Sachivalaya, Prabhat Prakashan, 2011–12.

Indumati Kelkar, *Rammanohar Lohia* (New Delhi: NBT India, 2014).

Jagannath Mishra, *Bihar Badhkar Rahega*, Lalit Narayan Mishra Vyapar Prabhandhan Sansthan, Muzaffarpur, 2018.

Jeffrey Witsoe, *Democracy Against Development: Lower-Caste Politics and Political Modernity in Postcolonial India* (Chicago: University of Chicago Press, 2013).

Karpoori Thakur Ka Sansdiya Jeevan, Pustakalaya Evam Sodh Sandarbh Sakha, Bihar Vidhan Sabha Sachivalaya, Patna, 2003.

Kingsley Davis, *Human Society* (Berkeley: University of California, and Macmillan Company, 1949).

Kisan Patnaik, *Badlaw Ki Kasauti* (Kolkata: Sutradhar Prakashan, 2019).

Kumar Amrendra, *Karpoori* Thakur: Jan se Nayak Tak (Patna: Jagriti Sahitya Prakashan, 2016).

L.P. Shahi, *Bante Bihar Ka Sakshi* (Patna: Shree Krishna Siksha Pratisthan, 2008).

L.P. Shahi, *Freedom and Beyond* (Muzaffarpur: Shrikrishna Shiksha Pratisthan, 2008) .

Lalit Kumar, *Shramiko Ke Hitaishi Neta Itihas Purush Basavan Singh* Bihar Hindi Granth Akademi, Patna, 2000.

Lalu Prasad Yadav and Nalin Verma, *Gopalganj to Raisina: My Political Journey* (Delhi: Rupa Publications, 2019).

M.N. Srinivas, *India: Social Structure* (Delhi: Hindustan Publishing Corporation (India), 1980).

Manoj Chaurasia, *Rabri Devi: Lalu's Masterstroke* (New Delhi: Vitasta Publishing, 2008).

N.K. Singh, *The Politics of Change: A Ringside View* (New Delhi: Penguin Books India, 2007).

Nakamizo Kazuya, *Violence and Democracy: The Collapse of One-Party Dominant Rule in India* (Kyoto: Kyoto University Press, and Balwyn North Victoria, TransPacific Press, 2020).

Narendra Pathak, *Karpoori Thakur Aur Samajvad* (New Delhi: Medha Books, 2016).

Naresh Kumar Vikal and Harinandan Sah, *Saptkranti Ke Samvahak Jannayak Karpoori Thakur Smriti Granth* (New Delhi: Prabhat Prakashan, 2019).

Neerja Chowdhury, *How Prime Ministers Decide* (New Delhi: Aleph Book Company, 2023).

Neha Ranjan, *Adhunik Bihar Mein Jatiya Sangharsh* (Patna and New Delhi: Janaki Prakashan, 2015).

Parishad Sakshya: Jannayak Karpoori Thakur Smaran, Bihar Vidhan Parishad, February 2014, .

Paul R. Brass, *Politics of India Since Independence* (Cambridge University Press, 1994).

Pradeep Srivastava, *Ramvilas Paswan:Sangharsh, Sahas and Sankalp* (Gurgaon: Penguin Random House India, 2021).

Pradeep Srivastava, *Ramvilas Paswan:Sankalp, Sahas Aur Sangharsh* (Gurgaon: Penguin Random House India, 2020).

Prasanna Kumar Choudharyand Shrikant, *Bihar Mein Samajik Parivartan Ke Kucch Aayam*, (Patna: Vani Prakashan, 2002).

Prem Kumar Mani, *Sach Yahi Nahi Hai* (New Delhi: Pustak Bhavan, 2012).

Prof. Keshav Rao Jadhav, Lohia Vigyan Samiti, Hyderabad, originally published in 1977, republished in www.indiatoday.com in 2019.

Pupul Jayakar, *Indira Gandhi: A Biography* (New Delhi: Penguin Books India, 1995).

Radhanandan Jha, *Bihar Vidhanmandal: Udbhav Aur Vikas* (Patna: Sharda Prakashan).

Raghav Sharan Sharma, *Yugpurush Dr Shrikrishna Singh:Prabal Rashtravadi* (New Delhi: Pustak Pratisthan, 2017).

Rajiv Malhotraand Vijaya Vishwanathan, *Snakes in the Ganga: Breaking India 2.0*, Occam (An imprint of BlueOne Ink), NOIDA (UP,2022).

Ramchandra Guha, *India After Gandhi: A History of the World's Largest Democracy* (London: Picador India, 2017).

Ranjana Kumari, *Karpoori Thakur: Neta Virodhi Dal Ke Rup Mein Sansdiya Bhoomika*, Rajkamal Prakshan, Patna, 2003.

Ravindra Bharti, *Kapildeo Samagra* Kapildeo Singh Samajwadi Foundation, Patna, 2007.

Ravindra Bharti, *Kapildeo Singh Samagra* (Patna: Kapildeo Singh Samajwadi Foundation, 2007).

S.A. Dange, *Gandhi Vs Lenin* (Liberty Literature, 1921).

S.K. Jain, *Caste and Politics in Bihar* (New Delhi: Commonwealth Publishers, 1989).

S.R. Nene,*Rammanohar Lohia Remembered: His Philosophy, Scholarship and Vision* (Delhi: Rupa Publications, 2011).

Sachchidanand Sinha, *Jati Vyavastha: Mithak, Vastvikta Aur Chunautiya* (Delhi: Rajkamal Prakashan, 2009).

Sanjeev Kumar, *Jatigat Janganana, Sab Hain Raaji, Phir Kyon Bayanbaji* (Patna and Madhubani: HTH Publication, 2022).

Sankarshan Thakur, *Single Man: Life andTimes of Nitish Kumar of Bihar* (Gurgaon: HarperCollins Publishers India, 2014).

Santosh Singh, *JP To BJP: Bihar after Lalu and Nitish* (New Delhi: Vitasta Sage Select, 2021).

Santosh Singh, *Ruled or Misruled: The Story and Destiny of Bihar* (New Delhi: Bloomsbury, 2015).

Shantanu Gupta, *Bharatiya Janata Party, Past, Present and Future: Story of the World's Largest Political Party* (Delhi: Rupa Publications, 2020).

Shashi Tharoor, *Nehru: The Invention of India* (New York: Arcade Publishing, 2003).

Sho Kuwajima, *Peasants and Peasant Leaders in Contemporary History: A Case of Bihar in India* (New Delhi: LG Publishers Distributors, 2017).

Shrikant, *Bihar Mein Chunav:Jaati, Booth Loot Aur Himsa*, Vani Prakashan, New Delhi, 2005.

Shrikant, *Bihar: Chitthiyon Ki Rajniti* (New Delhi: Vani Prakashan, 2012).

Sunita Lall and Shaibal Gupta, *Resurrection of the State: A Saga of Bihar* (New Delhi: Manak Publications, 2013).

Sushil Kumar Modi, *Bich Samar Mein* (New Delhi: Prabhat Prakashan, 2015).

Vishnudev Rajak, *Karpoori Thakur Ka Rajnitik Darshan* (Patna: Janaki Prakashan, 2012).

Walter Hauser and Kailash Chandra Jha, ed., *Culture, Vernacular Politics and the Peasants: India, 1889–1950* (An edited translation of Swami Sahajanand Saraswati's *Mera Jeevan Sangharsh*) (Delhi: Manohar Publishers and Distributors, 2015).

Walter Hauserand Kailash Chandra Jha, *My Life Struggle* (A Translation of Swami Sahajanand Saraswati's *Mera Jeevan Sangharsh*) (Delhi: Manohar Publishers and Distributors, 2016).

William R. Pinch, *Peasants and Monks in British India* (Berkeley: University of California Press, 1996).

Yashwant Sinha, *Relentless: An Autobiography* (New Delhi: Bloomsbury India, 2019).

Scan QR code to access the
Penguin Random House India website